T0893971

Advanced Design and Implementation of Virtual Machines

Advanced Design and Implementation of Virtual Machines

Xiao-Feng Li

CRC Press
Taylor & Francis Group
Boca Raton   London   New York

CRC Press is an imprint of the
Taylor & Francis Group, an **Informa** business

CRC Press
Taylor & Francis Group
6000 Broken Sound Parkway NW, Suite 300
Boca Raton, FL 33487-2742

© 2017 by Taylor & Francis Group, LLC
CRC Press is an imprint of Taylor & Francis Group, an Informa business

No claim to original U.S. Government works

Printed on acid-free paper
Version Date: 20160714

International Standard Book Number-13: 978-1-4665-8260-6 (Hardback)

Library of Congress Cataloging-in-Publication Data

Names: Li, Xiao-Feng, 1971- author. Title: Advanced design and implementation of virtual machine / Xiao-Feng Li. Description: Boca Raton, FL : CRC Press, Taylor & Francis Group, 2017. | Includes bibliographical references. Identifiers: LCCN 2016028064| ISBN 9781466582606 (hardback) | ISBN 9781315386690 (Web PDF) | ISBN 9781315386683 (ePub) | ISBN 9781315386676 (Mobipocket/ Kindle) Subjects: LCSH: Virtual computer systems. Classification: LCC QA76.9.V5 L525 2017 | DDC 005.3/4--dc23 LC record available at https://lccn.loc.gov/2016028064

**Visit the Taylor & Francis Web site at
http://www.taylorandfrancis.com**

**and the CRC Press Web site at
http://www.crcpress.com**

Printed and bound in the United States of America by
Edwards Brothers Malloy on sustainably sourced paper

Contents

SECTION V **Optimizations of Thread Interactions**

Foreword

A COMPUTING SYSTEM HAS TRADITIONALLY been built on a hardware platform supporting an operating system on which application programs run in the form of machine
instructions executed by the hardware. As programming languages evolve, programmers
have come to appreciate the benefits that dynamic or managed languages can bring in
improving programming productivity. By also offering greater security and software portability, virtual machine has grown to become the preferred environment on which software
programs execute nowadays. Today's state of the art in virtual machine design represents
the results of research and development activities undertaken in the past few decades.
Those works by and large aimed to improve the implementation of virtual machine with
respect to both functionalities and performance. Nowadays, production quality virtual
machines are sophisticated and often represent huge implementation efforts accumulated
over time. It has become a challenge even for experienced software engineers to understand how a virtual machine performs its work.

I have known Xiao-Feng Li for more than 15 years, since his post at Intel Corporation
where he led the development of various compilers and managed runtime systems on Intel
platforms. Xiao-Feng was the key contributor to the JVM in the Apache Harmony project.
He has also done extensive studies and research work in the design of virtual machines
related to Perl, Ruby, JavaScript, and Android. Xiao-Feng's experience in the engineering and production of VM has allowed him to gain substantial insights into the different
areas of VM design, which in turn uniquely positioned him to address the full range of
VM-related topics of this book.

Being both a researcher and an engineer, Xiao-Feng has written this book from the
unique perspective of a system architect. He emphasizes practical engineering considerations, bringing attention to the interactions among various components, how they work
together, and the impact this has on the design of the interface layers. Such details are
often not discussed in other books addressing virtual machine. This book also provides
detailed figures and code snippets to make the presented ideas easy to understand. This
book has become my excellent technical reference on many advanced topics in VM design
and implementation. I highly recommend this book to system software developers, especially to those working on managed runtime systems, as it will provide clear answers to
many of their questions as they explore the various topics.

By consummating this treatise on VM, Xiao-Feng has made a significant contribution to the design and engineering of virtual machines.

Fred Chow
Chief Scientist
Futurewei Technologies, Inc

Preface

THIS IS A BOOK on the design and implementation of virtual machines (VMs) for programming languages such as Java and JavaScript.

Virtual machine, also known as managed runtime system, managed execution environment, and more generally, sandboxing, and the like, has been invented for decades and has been constantly attracting the interests and attention from software researchers and developers due to the important properties that a VM brings to the software, such as safety, productivity, and portability. VMs have become omnipresent in today's computing systems, from the nodes in IoT (Internet of things), to mobile phones, personal computers, and cloud platforms.

Many of my friends in software-related jobs are curious to learn about the inside of a VM. They frequently ask me questions regarding the VMs they use in their daily work. I found that many of the questions were about common technologies used in a VM, while my friends had difficulties to access the information from existing books and other documents, because those are either mainly focused on the specifications and principles, or are too academic and available in research papers. When my friend Ruijun He, the editor of Taylor & Francis Group, came to me for a book on the topic, I agreed that it would be a good idea to write a book specifically tailored to software developers who have interests in exploring how a VM really "works."

I have been invited to give lectures on VMs at universities and companies; the lecture notes gradually accumulated into a sequence that appeared as a book. I thought it could be easy to assemble them into a book, but the actual process turned out to be a challenge when I was trying to shape the materials systematically and coherently with both insightful theory support and practical code snippets.

I tried my best to make the book different from the existing literature on similar topics by organizing the contents from the viewpoint of a VM architect who tries to design a VM with a holistic approach. This book tries to organize contents into a consistent framework so that the topics discussed advance step by step, and one algorithm discussed naturally leads to the next. Moreover, this book puts efforts on the parts that are critical to a VM design that are not usually discussed in other documents such as runtime helpers, stack unwinding, and native interface. The algorithms are illustrated in figures and implemented in code snippets, so as to make the abstract concepts tangible and programmable to a system software developer.

The contents of this book were largely finished by the end of 2014. I have been witnessing since then the new VM developments in the industry. However, I did not try to cover various VM implementations, but focused more on the most important technologies that are common to different VMs. I am more than willing to enhance or adjust the contents based on the readers' feedback. Comments on this book are welcome and can be sent to the publisher or to the author at li@xiaofeng.info.

Xiao-Feng Li

About This Book

A LONG WITH THE INCREASINGLY important runtime engines pervasive in our daily-life computing, there is a strong demand from the software community for an extensive presentation on the design and implementation of modern virtual machines, including the Java virtual machine (JVM), JavaScript engine, and Android execution engine. The community expects to see not only formal algorithm descriptions, but also pragmatic code snippets; it also hopes to understand not only research topics, but also engineering solutions. This book tries to meet the demands by providing a unique description that combines high-level design features and low-level implementations, and it combines advanced topics and commercial solutions.

This book takes a holistic approach to the design of VM architecture, with contents organized into a consistent framework, introducing topics and algorithms in an easily understood step by step process. It focuses on the critical aspects of VM design, which are often overlooked in other works, such as runtime helpers, stack unwinding and native interface. The algorithms are fully illustrated in figures and implemented in easy to digest code snippets, making the abstract concepts tangible and programmable for system software developers.

Author

Xiao-Feng Li has been working with Intel for 15 years, with extensive technical experience in parallel computing, operating system, compiler, and runtime technologies. He was the major contributor to the JVM of Apache Harmony and the creator of a microkernel VM that later became Intel Micro Runtime. He built and led a software lab on runtime technologies at Intel and published 20 academic papers in the related areas. Xiao-Feng holds a PhD degree in computer science. In his spare time, Xiao-Feng enjoys investigating the technologies of human–computer interactions.

I

Basics of Virtual Machines

CHAPTER 1

Introduction of the Virtual Machine

I N THIS CHAPTER, WE introduce the concept of the virtual machine. Virtual machines have been developed for decades in various forms. They became known to normal developers in 1995 when Sun Microsystem published the Java programming language and the associated Java virtual machine (JVM).

1.1 TYPES OF VIRTUAL MACHINES

Virtual machine is a computing system. The ultimate goal of a computing system is to execute programmed logics. The logics can be expressed at a very low level with all the details of an actual computer, or at a very high level with scripting or markup language. From this perspective, virtual machines can be broadly categorized into four types according to the level of abstraction and scope of emulation.

Type 1. **Full instruction set architecture (ISA) virtual machine** provides a full computer system's ISA emulation or virtualization. Guest operating system and applications can run on the top of the virtual machine as on an actual computer (e.g., VirtualBox, QEMU, and XEN).

Type 2. **Application Binary Interface (ABI) virtual machine** provides a guest process ABI emulation. Applications against that ABI can run in the process side by side with other processes of native ABI applications (e.g., Intel's IA-32 Execution Layer on Itanium, Transmeta's Code Morphing for X86 emulation, and Apple's Rosetta translation layer for PowerPC emulation).

Type 3. **Virtual ISA virtual machine** provides a runtime engine so that applications coded in the virtual ISA can execute on it. Virtual ISA usually defines a high level and limited scope of ISA semantics, so it does not require the virtual machine to emulate a full computer system (e.g., Sun Microsystem's JVM, Microsoft's Common Language Runtime, and Parrot Foundation's Parrot virtual machine).

Type 4. **Language virtual machine** provides a runtime engine that executes programs expressed in a guest language. The programs are usually presented to the virtual machine in source form of the guest language, without being fully compiled into machine code beforehand. The runtime engine needs to interpret or translate the program and also fulfill certain functionalities that are abstracted by the language such as memory management (e.g., the runtime engines for Basic, Lisp, Tcl, and Ruby).

The boundaries between virtual machine types are not clear-cut. There are many virtual machine designs crossing the boundaries. For example, a language virtual machine can also employ the technique of a virtual ISA virtual machine by compiling the program into a kind of virtual ISA and then executing the code on a virtual machine of that virtual ISA. Still it is meaningful to categorize the virtual machine types so as to facilitate community communications.

The first two types of virtual machines are of ISA or ABI emulation. Their goal is to run existing guest operating systems or guest applications that are developed for ISA or ABI other than the host native one. Sometimes, they are also called emulators.

The other two types of virtual machines are of language runtime engines whose goal is to execute the logics programmed in the form of virtual ISA or guest language. In some context, virtual ISA is considered a special kind of language; apart from that, there is no essential difference between the two types of language runtime engines.

The topic of this book is the language runtime engines. The key phrase "virtual machine" in the following chapters refers only to language runtime engine unless otherwise stated, and "runtime engine" can be used interchangeably as "virtual machine." "Runtime engine" is so called because the services provided by the virtual machine are mostly only available at runtime. As a comparison, in the traditional setting of "compiler + operating system," applications are compiled statically by a compiler before its distribution. For the same reason, some people use "runtime system" to refer to the services available at runtime that enables a software to execute.

1.2 WHY VIRTUAL MACHINE?

Virtual machines are indispensable to modern programming. They help (computer) security, (programming) productivity, and (application) portability.

Virtual machines are necessary for safe languages. *Safe language* is a very broad term here and mainly refers to the language that has properties of memory safety, operation safety, and control safety. With a safe language, it is easier to catch program bugs or execution errors early and safely.

1. Memory safety ensures that a certain type of data in the memory always follow the restrictions of that type. For example, a variable of pointer type never holds an illegal pointer; an array never has elements out of bound.

2. Operation safety ensures that the operations on a certain type of data always follow the restrictions of that type. For example, a variable of pointer type does not allow arbitrary arithmetic operations on it.

3. Control safety ensures that the flow of code execution never reach any point that either gets stuck or goes wild, for example, jump to a malicious code segment. Control safety can be considered a special kind of operation safety.

Almost all modern languages such as Java, C#, Java bytecode, Microsoft Intermediate Language, and JavaScript are safe languages, although their individual safety extents can be different.

To support a safe language, a virtual machine is necessary because the safe language itself cannot fulfill all the safety requirements. For example, the program should not directly allocate a piece of memory that has no type associated; it needs the assistance of a virtual machine to provide the typed memory for it, such as a certain type of object.

Virtual machine provides "management" on the code and data of the safe language. Therefore, the code and data sometimes are called "managed code" and "managed data." In turn, the virtual machine is sometimes also called "managed runtime," "managed system," or "managed execution environment."

Since it is harder for a program written in a safe language to be attacked by a malicious code, virtual machine is sometimes employed in security sandboxing. One example is the Google Chrome NaCl technique.

Since a safe language can catch program bugs or execution errors early and safely at the compile-time or runtime, it largely improves developer's productivity.

Virtual machine helps portability in the sense that the virtual ISA or guest language is not tied to any specific native ISA or ABI definition. Applications in virtual ISA or guest language can run on any systems that have the virtual machine deployed. Another perspective of portability is that many applications written in other programming languages choose to compile to the virtual ISA or guest language rather than the machine native code directly because then they can benefit from the virtual machine's various properties such as portability, performance, and security.

Virtual machine can be designed to support unsafe languages too, but that is only an extension rather than the original design purpose. An unsafe language is used to facilitate the safe language to access low-level resources or to reuse legacy code written in the unsafe language.

1.3 VIRTUAL MACHINE EXAMPLES

A virtual machine, as the runtime engine of the guest language, can be categorized according to the implementation of its execution engine. An execution engine is the component that expresses the applications' operational semantics. The two basic execution engines are interpretation and compilation.

With interpretation, there is usually no machine code generated from the application code. The application code is parsed by an interpreter into certain form of internal representation that can express the program's semantics, based on the syntax specification of the guest language, and then the execution engine manipulates the program's states (i.e., executes the code) by following the operational semantics of the internal representation.

With compilation, the application code is also parsed syntactically, but is then translated into the machine code according to the operational semantics. Later the machine code is executed by the host machine through which application states are manipulated.

There is no strict boundary between the two types of virtual machines. It is quite common for the interpreter-based virtual machine to compile the application code in one guest language into the code of another guest language and then interpret it. The code of another guest language is usually called "intermediate representation" (IR) in the compiler community. It is also common for a virtual machine to execute a piece of the application code with interpretation and then do the next piece with compilation.

A virtual machine can be implemented in software or hardware or both combined. Some hardware is designed to directly execute the virtual ISA instructions, which is no longer a virtual machine since the virtual ISA is no longer virtual. Conventionally, it is still called virtual machine but implemented in hardware.

Since almost all modern programming languages rely on a virtual machine, it is no surprise that a user probably cannot live without one virtual machine or two. The following are some of the examples.

1.3.1 JavaScript Engine

The most commonly used virtual machine can be the one for JavaScript in web browsers. For example, Google Chrome has V8 JavaScript engine; Mozilla Firefox has SpiderMonkey; Apple Safari has JavaScriptCore; and Microsoft Internet Explorer has Chakra. Each of them has been developed independently and adopted different techniques to accelerate JavaScript code execution.

SpiderMonkey is the name of the world's first JavaScript engine. Firefox has evolved it from a purely interpretation-based virtual machine into a compiler-based engine through projects such as TraceMonkey, JägerMonkey, and IonMonkey. The current version of SpiderMonkey as of year 2015 translates the JavaScript code into its IR in the form of bytecode and then invokes IonMonkey to compile the bytecode into the machine code. Internally, IonMonkey, as a traditional static compiler, builds up a control flow graph (CFG) with a static single assignment (SSA) representation so as to make advanced optimizations possible.

1.3.2 Perl Engine

Another kind of widely used virtual machines are for traditional scripting languages such as Unix shell, Windows PowerShell, Perl, Python, and Ruby. They are called scripting languages because they are commonly used in an interactive way of "type and run," and with a fast development turnaround. Interactive execution means the program executes one line of code then waits for the programmer's input to execute the next line of code. Scripting languages are also commonly used to batch or automate the execution of a sequence of tasks.

To support the batch execution of tasks, scripting languages have to be at a higher level in language design than the languages used to program the batched tasks. They are usually categorized as "high level" or even "very high level" languages in the programming language community, implying they are safe languages and easy to program domain-specific tasks. As we have described, a safe language requires a virtual machine to provide the safety requirements and low-level supports. The interactive mode support then usually suggests the virtual machine to have an interpretation-based execution engine.

Perl was one of the most popular scripting languages in the late 1990s for its widespread usage in the web common gateway interface programming. A Perl virtual machine is an interpreter. It has two stages: The first stage translates the Perl program into a sequence of operation codes (called op code or bytecode) and then the second stage traverses the op code sequence one by one to execute them. For every op code, a corresponding function (called pp code) is called that implements its semantics. Between the two stages, some optimizations are conducted to shorten the op code sequence or to specialize the sequence with a faster substitute.

The Perl language now splits into two variants, Perl 5 and Perl 6, due to incompatibility between the diverged language specifications, although the majority of features are still shared. Perl 5 is a natural continuation of the traditional Perl, whereas Perl 6 is actually a new design from the scratch. There are a couple of Perl 6 implementations available today, whereas none of them are 100% complete. Rakudo Perl as well as ParrotVM is one of them. Rakudo translates a Perl program into a kind of bytecod defined by ParrotVM and then ParrotVM executes the bytecode sequence. The actual design is more complicated due to the bootstrapping issue, since Perl 6 community tries to develop the compiler (Rakudo) with (a subset of) Perl 6 itself.

1.3.3 Android Java VM

Google Android is an operating system for smart devices. The primary programming language for the Android application is a variant of Java. The Java program is compiled to the JVM bytecode and then translated to another form of bytecode called dex. The Android application is then distributed with the dex code packaged, together with other forms of codes and resources.

When a smart device executes an Android application, it needs a virtual machine to execute the dex code. Before the Kitkat version of Android release, the virtual machine was called Dalvik, which has both an interpreter and a just-in-time compiler. (The interpreter actually includes a portable one and a fast one.) Dalvik starts dex code execution with an interpreter and keeps a counter to record the execution times of the same piece of the dex code. When it believes a piece of the dex code is hot enough, Dalvik invokes the compiler to compile that piece of the code into the machine code, then the next time it can directly execute the machine code for better performance.

Starting from version Kitkat, Android introduced a new virtual machine called ART (Android Runtime). What ART does is to compile the dex code of an application to the machine code when it is installed on the device, rather than when the application is executed as Dalvik does. The compiled code is cached in persistent storage. This approach is called ahead-of-time (AOT) compilation. When the application is executed, the ART runtime engine directly invokes the precompiled code without interpreting or just-in-time compiling; hence it achieves a faster application startup. ART trades longer installation time for a faster application launch time. It is reasonable because an application is only installed once but usually executed many times, and the installation time is expected to be long due to downloading through network, whereas the launch time is in the critical path of a user's interaction with the device.

1.3.4 Apache Harmony

Apache Harmony was an open source Java implementation by Apache Software Foundation with contributors from the community. It includes a JVM implementation named Dynamic Runtime Layer Virtual Machine (DRLVM), more than 97% completeness of Java SE 6 class libraries, a set of tools and documentations.

Google Android adopted a subset of Apache Harmony implementation for its Java core libraries, which is now installed in more than a billion of devices. Apache Harmony project itself was discontinued in year 2011. The code base is still available at the Apache's website. In 2015, Google Android started to shift its libraries from Apache Harmony to OpenJDK.

It requires huge efforts to implement a complete Java platform, especially the abundant class libraries, whereas it is relatively easy to implement a JVM. To the knowledge of the author, there are dozens of claimed JVM implementations, whereas there have been only three independent Java class library implementations: OpenJDK, GNU Classpath, and Apache Harmony. To date, OpenJDK library implementation is probably the only actively maintained Java library.

Although the code bases can be completely different for different implementations of JVM, the technologies used can be similar between them because of the active communications in the community, including academia and industry.

CHAPTER 2

Inside of a Virtual Machine

A FULL LANGUAGE IMPLEMENTATION USUALLY includes no less than three major parts: the virtual machine, the language libraries, and the tool set.

Unless the language is of a very low level and is primitive such as assembly language for a specific processor, a common language implementation usually includes the core libraries of the language as part of the virtual machine. Sometimes the virtual machine has to hard-code certain logics that only work with the associated libraries. For example, a Java virtual machine (JVM) cannot live without the library package of java.lang, because some of the core data structures such as Java object and Java class rely on the definitions in packages java.lang.Object, java.lang.Class, and so on.

To enable program development with a language, a tool set for the language is usually needed that works with the virtual machine to support debugging, profiling, packaging, and so on.

The libraries and tool set have very different design considerations and require different expertise from virtual machine design. This book does not cover these two parts, but only discusses the virtual machine.

2.1 CORE COMPONENTS OF VIRTUAL MACHINE

Virtual machine implementations for the same language can vary dramatically in every aspect. But all of them must follow and support the same language specification; therefore, a set of core components are usually mandatory for every implementation.

Based on the common nature of virtual machines, an implementation has to have components that load the application code into memory and resolve the symbols to internal addresses (loader and dynamic linker), perform the operations of the program (execution engine), manage the computing resource including memory (memory manager) and processors (thread scheduler), and provide a way to access external resources that are not directly accessible to the language (language extension or native interface).

2.1.1 Loader and Dynamic Linker

What loader does is to load the application package into memory, parse the package into data structures, and potentially load additional resources needed by the application.

The data structures in memory have semantic meanings such as code and data. Sometimes reflection data or metadata are produced at load time that help the virtual machine to understand the application.

Dynamic linker tries to resolve all the referenced symbols into accessible memory addresses. It may trigger the loader to load more data and code if those are referenced as symbols but not already loaded.

Loader and dynamic linker are sometimes inseparable and implemented in single component. In some systems they are together solely called loader, while in some others called dynamic linker.

Note virtual machine usually does not include linker. Linker is conventionally used to refer to the component that links multiple object files generated by a compiler into a single integral application package. It is a compile-time component, whereas dynamic linker is a runtime component used when the application is going to be executed. With that clarified, in the following text of the book, the term linker usually just means dynamic linker.

For security purpose, loader may also check the data and code integrity of the loaded application. In some virtual machine designs, this checking operation may be deferred to the execution engine.

2.1.2 Execution Engine

Once the application is loaded and linked, it is ready to be executed through the execution engine. Execution engine is the component that performs the operations specified by the program code and is the core component of a virtual machine. This is obvious, since the existence of an application is, if not all, for execution.

As we have discussed, execution engine can be implemented in interpreter or compiler or a flexible hybrid of both and is a major factor to classify a virtual machine implementation. We will discuss more about it later in Chapter 4, Design of Execution Engine.

2.1.3 Memory Manager

Virtual machine usually has a component called memory manager to manage its data (and the memory containing the data). The data needed by a virtual machine can be roughly partitioned into two categories according to whether the data are visible to the application.

- Virtual machine data: Virtual machine needs memory to load the application code and hold supporting data. The data in this category are invisible to the application while necessary for the application's execution.

- Application data: An application needs storage for its static data and dynamic data. The data in this category are visible to the application. Application dynamic data are stored in the application's heap.

Memory manager usually manages only the application data, leaving the virtual machine data to internal management or underlying system. In actual implementations of virtual machines, memory managers are designed to manage mainly the application dynamic data, that is, the memory of application heap. This is a tradeoff between the design complexity and benefits, since application heap data are the most vibrant and dynamic part in all the data of a virtual machine execution instance, and focusing on heap data can largely solve most of the memory issues in a virtual machine. The management of the rest of the data can largely refer to the underlying system.

Depending on the design, memory manager may choose to delegate the management task to the underlying system, for example, by invoking `malloc()` and `free()` functions. No matter in which case, the memory manager component is always necessary and desirable for a virtual machine.

- Necessary: As we have mentioned, safe languages do not allow the application to manipulate the memory directly. None of the data accessed by the application code can be a piece of raw memory, like that allocated through `malloc()`. They have to be associated with certain metadata or management information to indicate the data type, size, the operations allowed, and so on. Metadata are language specific, and the underlying system cannot provide the data. A memory manager is necessary as a middle layer between what the application can see and what the underlying system can provide.

- Desirable: Application in safe language usually does not explicitly release the memory allocated for its data. The application may give hint on the data's life time but relies on the virtual machine to dispose. Although the underlying system may provide certain level of memory reclamation support, it is desirable for the virtual machine to directly manage the application data (and the associated memory), because only virtual machine accurately knows the application's data type and life cycles. If memory manager does not help recycle the no-longer useful data, the virtual machine may still run correctly, but the footprint and performance may suffer.

A traditional memory manager in an operating system is focused on memory allocation and relies on the application to reclaim the memory explicitly or waits for the application to exit thus reclaim the whole process memory. As a contrast, the memory manager in a virtual machine is focused on the memory reclamation. To reclaim memory efficiently, the memory manager has to deal with memory allocation as well. Since the memory reclamation is done automatically by the memory manager for applications, the community usually calls it "automatic memory manager" or more often "garbage collector."

2.1.4 Thread Scheduler

Multithreading allows the system to have multiple control flows, which is needed when the system does not want to operate everything in a single sequence. Multithreading sometimes is referred to as "threading" for simplicity without causing any confusion.

Some languages have built-in threading feature. Some others do not. But almost all the virtual machines for nontrivial languages have threading support in one way or another, even if the language itself does not have the built-in support, because threading is a straightforward way to provide multitasking, parallelization, and event coordination. Threading is not the only way for multitasking, but it is the most popular way on Von Neumann computer. As in other systems, the virtual machine component that implements threading is called thread scheduler, since its main role is to schedule tasks execution.

Garbage collector helps the execution engine to use the RAM resource, whereas thread scheduler helps to use the processor resource. With current Von Neumann model of computer architecture, these two always stay together.

2.1.5 Language Extension

Safe language or high-level language has to depend on the virtual machine to access low-level resources due to the safety requirements. There are two complementary ways to provide this kind of capabilities:

1. **Runtime services**

   Memory manager is an example that bridges the application to low-level memory resource. Program code only needs to declare a new class or create a new object with a well-encapsulated application programming interface (API), knowing nothing about memory, either virtual or physical. Then runtime services of the virtual machine implement all the support transparently to the application. Other runtime service examples include profiling, debugging, exception/signal handling, and interoperability.

   Sometimes, the runtime services can be implemented through client/service architecture. The service provider does not necessarily stay in the same process as the application, or not even in the same machine.

   Runtime services can be provided to the application in various forms, such as APIs, runtime objects, and environment variables. For example, JavaScript uses document object model objects extensively to access webpage contents that are not directly accessible to JavaScript.

2. **Language extension**

   Runtime services may not be flexible enough and usually limited to specific features that are defined by the language specification and its execution model. Language extension, as a contrast, can provide the language with extra capabilities beyond current language specification and execution model. It is sometimes called "foreign function interface" (FFI) in programming language community.

   Depending on the design, a language can access the code written in other language (i.e., the foreign language) in many different ways. For example, in some languages, code of the foreign language can be embedded or inlined in the host language; or in some other languages, the foreign language code can only be invoked through a well-wrapped function interface, or an object, a class, a module, and so on.

C language is probably the most used foreign language due to its low-level nature, used as the major programming language for operating systems and system libraries, controlling all the system resources.

The C extension in Java is called Java Native Interface that allows implementing Java methods in C language. PhoneGap extends JavaScript to access all native resources in a smartphone environment. Actually, JavaScript itself can be considered as a foreign language to HTML, the markup language.

Note language extension here is different from the normal libraries that add features to the language. Normal libraries cannot provide any feature beyond what the language proper can provide. In other words, normal libraries just put together the commonly used programs to avoid duplicate development. Language extension is a capability to extend the language specification. The confusion sometimes comes from the fact that many language extensions are provided in the form of libraries. The extended features are wrapped in normal libraries and hidden from the developers. For example, in Java language, file-related operations and system calls are wrapped in Java standard library such as Java.io.File.

2.1.6 Traditional Model versus Virtual Machine Model

Looking from the perspective of traditional computing, virtual machine actually shares almost the same components but organized in a different way. For example, to support C language on a target X86 machine, one needs a compiler such as GNU GCC to translate the source code into X86 machine code and then a linker to package the result into an executable file. When the executable is executed, a loader is needed to load the file into memory and then a dynamic linker resolves all the referenced symbols to memory addresses. Finally, the runtime services prepare the runtime stack and execution context and then transfer program control to main() function as the entry point to execute the application. In a real system that has multiple tasks and multiple users, operating system is needed to coordinate the usage of system resource, especially the memory and processors. Besides the runtime services, operating system also provides a form of language extensions, that is, system calls, to give the language full access to native resources. Figure 2.1 shows the traditional model of language support.

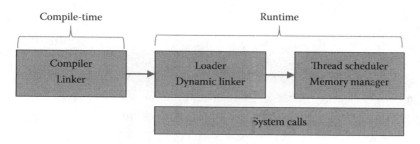

FIGURE 2.1   Traditional model of language support.

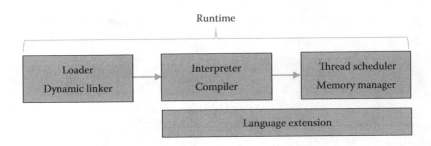

FIGURE 2.2   Virtual machine model of language support.

Basically, the traditional model decouples a language's support into two stages: the compile-time stage centered on a compiler and the runtime stage around an operating system. The factor to make the decoupling possible is the use of the compiler, which is not part of the execution engine in traditional model. The decoupling is impossible if an interpreter is used.

As a comparison, virtual machine puts all the components together and does everything at runtime. If one wants to have an operating system that can directly run C# program in source code, then what the system ends up with is a C# language virtual machine, that is, a machine that can virtually execute C# language directly. So essentially the difference between the two models is where the program code is processed. If it is only at runtime, the system is a virtual machine. That is why virtual machine is also called runtime engine or runtime system. Figure 2.2 shows the virtual machine model of language support.

The difference between the two models is not always clear-cut. A virtual machine may partially preprocess or compile the application code ahead of time to reduce runtime overhead. Here are a few installation-time processing examples: Android Dalvik preprocesses the application dexcode at installation time with a program called dexopt that makes the code sequence more succinct. Android Runtime compiles the application dexcode to machine code with dex2oat. Microsoft .NET has a tool named NGEN.exe (native image generator) that compiles Common Intermediate Language (CIL) bytecode into machine code.

2.2 VIRTUAL ISA

A language virtual machine can implement an actual language or a virtual language. Virtual language here means that it is not directly used by anyone in programming; instead, it is only automatically generated through tools. In other words, virtual language is usually used as the compilation target of other languages.

Some languages are born to be compilation target languages while some others are invented as programming source languages but often used as virtual languages. For example, JavaScript has been used as compilation target of many other languages due to its popularity and universality across Internet. Once the programs in a specific language can always be translated to JavaScript code, that language can automatically be supported by all the platforms that have browsers or server side JavaScript engines.

However, virtual languages are born to be compilation target languages. Although some developers may be able to directly program in them, virtual languages are more used for intermediate representation purpose. Hence, virtual languages are mostly not human readable, such as Java bytecode, LLVM bitcode, and ParrotVM bytecode. "Human unreadable" here means "too different from human languages and relatively not human programmable." Assembly language, though was invented as a programming language, falls into this virtual language category due to its primitive form.

Virtual instruction set architecture (ISA) is a kind of virtual language that defines the instruction set and execution model of a virtual machine. The instruction set can be similar to that of actual machine ISA. That is why it is called virtual ISA and why the implementation is called virtual machine. One of the mostly known virtual ISA probably is JVM.

2.2.1 Java Virtual Machine

JVM specification is not only a set of virtual instructions, but also all the architectural models of an abstract computing machine, including the execution model, memory model, threading model, and security mode. These are indispensable for a compatible implementation of JVM.

The JVM instruction's opcodes are encoded into one byte, thus called bytecode. Opcode is the data that specifies the operation to perform by the instruction. Some JVM instructions include additional bytes following the opcode to specify the parameters, called operands. There is a special bytecode "wide" used as an instruction prefix to allow its following opcode to operate on wider-length parameters.

A byte can encode 256 numbers, of which 198 are currently used, 51 are unused, and 3 are reserved for JVM implementation's runtime services and should never appear in application code. One of the reserved bytecode is 0xca for JVMs "breakpoint" support. In the following text, we use "Java bytecode," "JVM instruction," and "JVM language" interchangeably.

Note Java bytecode has no inherent or mandatory relation with Java programming language. It is called Java bytecode only because it was originally designed to be the compilation target language of Java language; therefore, they share some concepts and vocabulary. As an analog, we can consider Java bytecode as X86 assembly language, JVM as Intel X86 processor, and Java language as C language. We know that X86 assembly language has technically little to do with C language. The relation is illustrated in Figure 2.3 below.

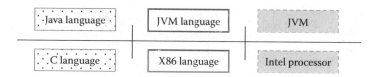

FIGURE 2.3 Java language versus JVM language.

Java bytecode is not necessarily compiled from Java source file. Many other languages can be compiled into Java bytecode, thus run in JVM, as long as the compiled result follows JVM specification. Another way of running other languages in JVM is to develop their virtual machines (such as an interpreter) in Java language. In other words, their virtual machines are actually Java applications. Then the applications in other languages can run in their virtual machines, which in turn as Java applications run in a JVM, which again as an executable run in an actual machine.

For those who are really curious, a JVM can also be developed in Java language, although it is not very convenient, because Java language is a safe language that makes some low-level operations difficult. Some tricks to work around the language limitation are usually necessary.

Java application is distributed in the form of Java class files. A Java class file contains the definition of a single class or interface. Like other binary file format such as executable and linkable format, Java class file includes mainly bytecode sequence and symbol table that contains the symbols referenced by the bytecode sequence.

Below is the data structure of a Java class file expressed in C-like syntax:

```
ClassFile {
  u4 magic;                             //0xCAFEBABE
  u2 minor_version;                     //class file minor version
  u2 major_version;                     //class file major version
  u2 constant_pool_count;               //count of entries in next item
  cp_info constant_pool[constant_pool_count-1];    //constants
  u2 access_flags;                      //class assess flags
  u2 this_class;                        //index of this class to const pool
  u2 super_class;                       //index of super class to const pool
  u2 interfaces_count;                  //number of interfaces implemented
  u2 interfaces[interfaces_count];      //indices of interfaces
  u2 fields_count;                      //number of fields in the class
  field_info fields[fields_count];      //fields descriptions
  u2 methods_count;                     //number of methods in the class
  method_info methods[methods_count];   //methods descriptions
  u2 attributes_count;                  //number of attributes of the class
  attribute_info attributes[attributes_count];  //attributes
}
```

One of the most interesting items is the code_attribute in every method_info. The data structure of code_attribute is given below.

```
Code_attribute {
  u2 attribute_name_index;   //code_attribute always has name "code"
  u4 attribute_length;       //length of following items
  u2 max_stack;              //maximum stack depth during execution
  u2 max_locals;             //maximum number of local variables
```

```
u4 code_length;              //length of bytecode sequence
u1 code[code_length];        //bytecode sequence of the method
u2 exception_table_length;   //number of exceptions
{  u2 start_pc;              //start of an exception active range
   u2 end_pc;               //end of an exception active range
   u2 handler_pc;           //start of exception handler
   u2 catch_type;           //index of exception class
} exception_table[exception_table_length]; //table of all exceptions
u2 attributes_count;         //number of attributes of the method
 attribute_info attributes[attributes_count]; //attributes
}
```

Here is an example bytecode sequence compiled from a simple Java for-loop.
Java source code is given first:

```
public static void main(String args[]){
        int j=1;
        for (int i=0; i<10; i++){
                j*=2;
        }
        return;
}
```

Then is the compiled bytecode sequence with opcode mnemonics and semantics in comments. Note the bytecode sequence is not necessarily generated by compiling the Java source code above. It can be generated by compiling source code in other languages or even directly programed, as assembly code.

```
// Method descriptor ([Ljava/lang/String;)V
// max stack: 2, max locals: 3
// Local variables:
//     args: index: 0 type: java.lang String[]
//        j: index: 1 type: int
//        i: index: 2 type: int

04        // 0: iconst_1  ; push constant value 1 on stack
3c        // 1: istore_1  ; pop stack top and store to variable 1 (j)
03        // 2: iconst_0  ; push constant value 0 on stack
3d        // 3: istore_2  ; pop stack top and store to variable 2 (i)
a7 00 0a  // 4: goto +10  ; jump to bytecode at position 14 (=4+10)
1b        // 7: iload_1   ; push local variable 1 (j) to stack
05        // 8: iconst_2  ; push contant 2 on stack
68        // 9: imul    ; pop top two items multiply, push result to stack
3c        // 10: istore_1 ; pop stack top and store to variable 1 (j)
```

```
84 02 01 // 11: iinc 2 1          ; increment variable 2 (i) by 1
1c        // 14: iload_2           ; push local variable 2 (i) to stack
10 0a     // 15: bipush 10         ; push value 10 to stack
a1 ff f6 // 17: if_icmplt -10      ; pop top two items,
          //                       ;conditionally jump to position 7
                                      (=17-10)
b1        // 20: return ; return
```

JVM has two possible meanings based on the context. One is to refer to the abstract computing machine defined in JVM specification by Sun Microsystem (now Oracle) and the other is a virtual machine implementation of JVM specification. Sometimes, we use JVM with all capital initials to refer to the abstract model and use JVM to the implementation. There is single JVM specification (regardless the version numbers), whereas there are many different JVM implementations. JVM specification was released independent of the Java language specification. But starting from Java Standard Edition (SE) 7, both JVM specification and Java language specification are published in tandem under the same Java SE version.

When an application is provided to a JVM, the JVM's class loader loads and parses the initial class file and puts the items into corresponding data structures in memory. Then JVM resolves all the symbolic references into direct references as memory addresses. After the class is initialized (i.e., its initializer is invoked), JVM calls the `main()` method of the initial class to execute the application.

A Java platform (e.g., Java SE 8) is a collection of specifications for Java language, JVM, Java Class Library, and tools. A Java implementation (e.g., OpenJDK 8) is a full implementation of a Java platform. Java platform has different editions (or profiles) called Standard Edition (Java SE), Enterprise Edition (Java EE), etc. They all share the same specifications of Java language and JVM but define different libraries and may have different implementations.

2.2.2 JVM versus CLR

Microsoft, after struggling with Java for a few years, designed C# safe language, and more broadly the .NET framework. .NET framework is an implementation of Common Language Infrastructure (CLI) specification. Like Java platform, CLI includes multiple components such as the virtual machine specification called Virtual Execution System (VES) and class libraries specification called CLI Standard Libraries. Common Language Runtime (CLR) virtual machine is the .NET implementation of VES.

Java as a term is much overloaded. CLI tries to separate the names of specification from those of implementation, although it may add some other confusions.

A very high-level comparison of the terminologies between Java and CLI is given in Table 2.1.

TABLE 2.1   Concepts Comparison between CLI Platform and Java Platform

Platform Concepts	Common Language Infrastructure	Java Platform
Virtual machine	Virtual execution system	Java Virtual Machine
Virtual machine language	Common intermediate language	Java bytecode
Distribution package	Assembly	JAR (Java class file)
Library	Standard libraries	Java class library
Major high level language	C#	Java
Language extension	Platform invocation service	Java Native Interface
A Platform implementation	Microsoft .NET framework	Oracle OpenJDK
A VM implementation	Common language runtime	Hotspot

There are two notable "distinguishing" features between CLI and Java.

1. Since it was invented, CLI has been trying to provide cross-language interoperability between the languages that follow CLI's language specification. The known CLI-compliant languages include C#, C++/CLI, VB.NET, IronPython, and IronRuby. Although language interoperability is not Java's design goal, Java has it achieved automatically when the language can be compiled into Java class file. JVM-compliant languages include Java, Groovy, Scala, Jython, and JRuby. Due to the similarity, Java and C# can actually be implemented in each other's system.

2. Since Microsoft has abundant legacy native libraries especially Win32 API services that would be troublesome to rewrite in C#, CLI provides Platform Invocation Services (P/Invoke) for the safe code to access unsafe native code. It allows the developers to simply import and declare the target native function in C# code, and the compiler and runtime will do all the rest for the developers. In contrast, Java Native Interface is much more cumbersome to wrap the native function with manual data transformation code. However, it is not difficult for Java to provide P/Invoke kind of support. Java Native Access is an effort for this purpose.

Here is an example CIL bytecode sequence compiled from a simple C# for-loop.

C# source code is given first:

```
static void test( ){
    int i = 0;
    while(i < 10){
        i++;
    }
}
```

Then is the compiled CIL bytecode sequence (only showing the opcode mnemonics) and semantics in comments. Same as Java bytecode, the CIL bytecode sequence is not necessarily generated by compiling the C# source code above. It can be generated by compiling source code in other languages or even directly programmed, as assembly code. It is easy to find the similarity between CIL and Java bytecode.

```
.method private hidebysig static void test() cil managed
{
    .maxstack  2
    .locals init ([0] int32 i,
                  [1] bool CS$4$0000)
    IL_0000:  nop                //no operation, for debugging only
    IL_0001:  ldc.i4.0           //load constant 0 on stack
    IL_0002:  stloc.0            //pop stack, store to local var at
                                     index 0 (i)
    IL_0003:  br.s    IL_000b    //jump to IL_000b
    IL_0005:  nop                //no op
    IL_0006:  ldloc.0            //load local var i to stack
    IL_0007:  ldc.i4.1           //load constant 1 to stack
    IL_0008:  add                //pop stack top two entries, add, push
                                     result to stack
    IL_0009:  stloc.0            //pop stack, store to local var i
    IL_000a:  nop                //no op
    IL_000b:  ldloc.0            //load local var i 0 to stack
    IL_000c:  ldc.i4.10          //load constant 10 to stack
    IL_000d:  clt                //pop stack top two, compare (<),
                                     push result to stack
    IL_000f:  stloc.1            //pop stack top, store to local var
                                     at index 1
    IL_0010:  ldloc.1            //load local var at index 1 to stack
    IL_0011:  brtrue.s IL_0005   //pop stack top,
                                 //if it is true, branch to IL_0005
    IL_0013:  ret                //return
}
```

It is not the purpose of this book to discuss or compare any specific VM specification. The idea here is to sketch a brief profile of Virtual ISA that is adequate for the readers to understand the contents of following chapters.

CHAPTER 3

Data Structures in a Virtual Machine

THERE ARE A COUPLE of core data structures for a Java virtual machine (JVM) implementation, such as object, class, and virtual function table.

3.1 OBJECT AND CLASS

JVM language (i.e., the bytecode instruction set) has two kinds of data types: primitive types and reference types. A variable of primitive types holds a direct value, such as a number, a Boolean, or a return address. Primitive types sometimes are also referred to as value types in some other languages. A variable of reference types holds a pointer to an object. Every object is an instance of a reference type such as a class or an array. In the rest of the book, we use term "class" to include both classes, array and interface, unless stated otherwise. Note there is no instance of any interface, but instance whose class implements an interface. The relation is shown in Figure 3.1.

A class defines two parts of data: instance data and class data. Instance data is owned by every object individually, while class data is shared by all the instances of same class. Every class is also internally represented as an object.

There are two special classes in Java: Object and Class. Both are packaged under java.lang in Java application programming interface. Class Object is the super class of all classes, and class Class is the type of all classes. They are part of the system classes that must be supported by JVM to fully express the semantics. For example, a reference variable ovar holds a pointer to an instance of class Bar. Class Bar itself is an instance of Class, which in turn is an instance of itself. Class Bar is a subclass of class Object, which in turn is a subclass of itself.

Array is a special kind of class that is created by the virtual machine (VM), rather than loaded from a class file. As other class, an array class is also an instance of class Class and a subclass of class Object.

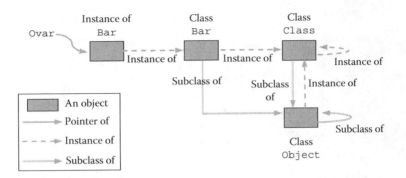

FIGURE 3.1 Relation between object, `Object`, and `Class`.

3.2 OBJECT REPRESENTATION

A class basically defines two kinds of information. One is the instance data, including the object fields and virtual methods and the other is the class data, including the static fields and static methods.

To represent an object, a piece of memory is allocated to hold the instance data defined by its class and all super classes. Actually, only object fields need to allocate memory for every instance because virtual methods are shared by all the instances of a class. Only one copy of virtual methods representation is needed, as long as the object has a way to access its virtual methods. In other words, a pointer (or pointer chain) to the virtual methods data structure should be associated with the object.

This is not enough to represent an object. An object also needs a way to access its class data, for example, to check which class it belongs to. It can be achieved by simply putting the class data together with the virtual methods, so that one can always reach the other one. Based on this discussion, a simple object layout in memory includes two parts: object header and object fields. Object header encodes a pointer to class data, which includes or points to the virtual methods data structure, as shown in Figure 3.2a.

Although there are many different implementations, the most common design is for the object to have a pointer pointing to a virtual method pointer table (called "vtable"). Vtable includes the function pointers to the virtual methods so that the virtual method invocation can be executed with only a few instructions. This design is based on an observation that the most frequent memory accesses in a VM are two kinds of operations. One is object

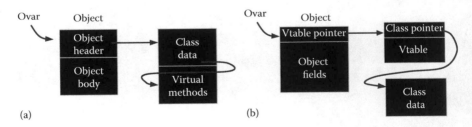

FIGURE 3.2 Object representation with metadata in its header and fields in its body. (a) Class pointer in object header, (b) Vtable pointer in object header.

fields access, and the other is virtual method invocation. Putting them together helps the performance. Other information about the methods such as the names and signatures can be put into class data. Vtable is unique to a class; therefore, sometimes vtable pointer can be used as the identifier of a class as shown in Figure 3.2b.

The class data has all kinds of description information about its fields, methods, implemented interfaces, etc. Especially, since every class is an instance of class Class, class data includes the instance data of class Class.

3.3 METHOD DESCRIPTION

A method need a data structure in the VM to describe its information. Code below gives the method information in a typical JVM implementation.

```
typedef struct Method{
    char *name;                    //method name
    char *descriptor;              //method descriptor
    Class *owner_class;            //class that owns this method
    unsigned char *byte_code;      //byte code sequence
    Handler *handlers;             //exception handlers
    LineNum *linenums;             //line number table
    LocalVar *localvars;           //local variables
    Exception *exceptions;         //exceptions that may throw

    uint16 modifier;               //method access modifier
    uint16 max_stack;              //max stack depth
    uint16 max_locals;             //max number of local vars

    uint16 vtable_offset;          //offset in vtable
    JIT_STATUS state;              //JIT compilation status
    unsigned char *jitted_code;    //compiled code

    struct {
        unsigned is_init       : 1;
        unsigned is_clinit     : 1;
        unsigned is_finalize   : 1;
        unsigned is_overridden : 1;
        unsigned is_nop        : 1;
    } flags;             //properties of the methods

} Method;
```

The data structure includes all the information about a method to compile, debug, profile, and link the method at runtime, including the information for exception handling and garbage collection. Depending on the VM implementation, the data structure may not have the jitted_code field, which is used for just-in-time compilation. The is_nop flag is for optimization purpose and indicates the method has empty body.

II

Design of Virtual Machines

CHAPTER 4

Design of Execution Engine

E XECUTION ENGINE IS THE component that performs the actual operations of the application code. Since the ultimate purpose of application is to execute, execution engine is usually considered the core component of a virtual machine (VM), and the rest components are supportive to the execution engine. Sometimes, the design of the execution engine largely dictates the design of a VM. The two basic execution mechanisms are interpretation and compilation.

4.1 INTERPRETER

It is straightforward to design an interpreter. Once the application code is loaded into memory and parsed into semantic data structures, VM can fetch the code sequence one by one and performs defined operations. The pseudocode for a simple interpreter is as follows.

```
interpret(method)
{
    while( code remains in sequence ){
        read the next code from the sequence;
        if (the code needs more data){
            read more data from the sequence;
        }
        perform actions specified by the code;
    }
}
```

This interpreter should work for many languages. The core in this algorithm is the big loop (called dispatching loop) over the code sequence, which fetches, decodes, and executes every code. The real complexity is hidden in the step of "perform actions defined by the code." For example when the code is to create a new instance of a class, the interpreter calls into garbage collector to allocate a piece of memory, zero the memory content, initialize the object header (e.g., installing a vtable pointer of the class), and then return the object pointer.

When the code is to invoke a virtual method, the interpreter needs to find out the method address, prepare a stack frame, push the arguments, call the method by recursively interpreting it, and return the result. The invocation of a target method may incur the loading and parsing of the method code if it is not in memory or initialized yet. In other words, all the supportive functionalities of the VM are mobilized and busy working around the interpreter.

The interpreter logic will become less straightforward when the execution flow is intercepted by an exception. Exception leads the control flow into the exception handler that may be out of current method. We will discuss exception handling later in Chapter 11.

4.1.1 Super Instruction

Interpretation usually is slow. One reason among others is its big dispatching loop design that involves branches for every interpreted code. Branches can incur branch miss prediction and instruction cache miss, both of which are expensive. The dispatching also involves lots of memory accesses to read and decode every code. It is easy to think of an acceleration technique that combines two or more codes into one in a preprocessing pass. Then the interpreter can fetch and execute more than one code at a time thus reduce the number of dispatches. The combined code is sometimes called super instruction, quick instruction, or virtual instruction.

For example, the code to add a constant to a local variable in Java bytecode usually needs four bytecodes:

```
//var_1 = var_2 + 2;
1:   iload_1   ; push variable 1 on stack
2:   iconst_2  ; push constant 2 on stack
3:   iadd      ; add the stack top two items
4:   istore_1  ; pop stack and store to variable 1
```

If this is a common pattern in a method, we can combine them into one quick instruction with an unused bytecode. Then the interpreter only needs to interpret single bytecode that gives same result as the four.

Since there are only limited number of unused bytecodes, super instructions have limited applicability. An idea is to define different super instructions for different workloads by profiling the workloads and finding out the most efficient bytecode combinations.

4.1.2 Selective Inlining

One another acceleration technique is to compile the execution logic of a bytecode into binary machine code ahead of time in a VM implementation. When that bytecode is dispatched, the interpreter directly transfers its control to the machine code maintained by the VM. Furthermore, the machine codes of multiple bytecodes can be concatenated together so as to eliminate their dispatches. This technique is a workaround of dynamic super-instruction generation and sometimes is called "selective inlining."

Since the binary machine code has to be generated statically for each bytecode as part of the VM implementation, the VM developer has to make sure the generated binary code is universal enough for all potential execution contexts. Stitching code is still needed some-times when two pieces of binary codes cannot directly connect. As a result, the quality of the concatenated code is not high. Just-in-time (JIT) compilation can solve this problem.

4.2 JIT COMPILATION

JIT compilation compiles a piece of application code at runtime into binary machine code, then allows the VM to execute the generated code directly rather than interpret the original piece of application code. It is like treating the entire piece of application code as a single super instruction.

The first question to JIT is how to select the piece of application code to compile. It is natural to consider a method as a compilation unit because of its well-defined semantic boundary. That is why almost all the typical JITs are method based.

4.2.1 Method-Based JIT

Since method is a fundamental language construct, the design of method-based JIT fits into the VM architecture very well. The key data structure is vtable. When JIT is used in a VM, the vtable of a class is installed with function pointers to the virtual methods. For example, to call `ovar.foo()`, the function pointer can be found from `ovar` through its vtable. Vtable data structure is shown in Figure 4.1.

During the class initialization when the methods are not yet compiled, the function pointer to a virtual method actually points to a trampoline that invokes the compiler to compile the virtual method. When the virtual method is called for the first time, the compiler is thus invoked. The compiler compiles the virtual method and installs the compiled binary code address (i.e., the function pointer to the compiled method) into the vtable slot, replacing the original pointer to the trampoline and then transfers the control to the binary code to finish the first-time invocation. Starting from next time, any invocation on the method will directly go to the compiled code through the vtable. The trampoline code

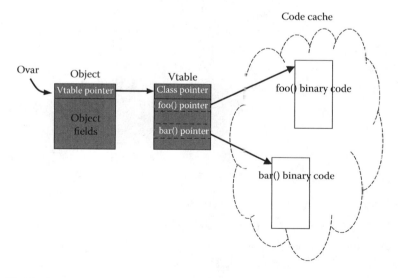

FIGURE 4.1 Vtable data structure.

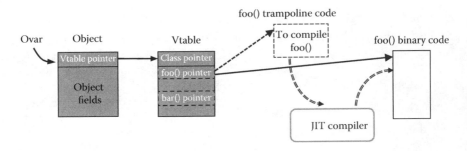

FIGURE 4.2   Trampoline and JIT compilation.

can be released if no one needs it, or be kept for later use again, in case the compiled code is released to save the memory consumed by the code cache. Illustration of trampoline code is given in Figure 4.2.

In this way, the virtual method invocation can be very fast in a few machine instructions. For example, to call ovar.foo(), the steps can be expressed in following pseudocode.

```
vtable = *ovar; .    // Get vtable pointer from ovar pointer
foo_funcptr = *(vtable + foo_offset); //get pointer to foo()
(*foo_funcptr)();    //invoke foo()
```

If it is a VM for X86 processor, the instructions to invoke an virtual method of an object are like the following, assuming eax register holds ovar, the first slot of an object (offset 0) is the vtable pointer, method foo's function pointer is at offset 16 of vtable.

```
movl (%eax), %eax        //eax now has vtable pointer
movl 16(%eax), %eax      //eax now has foo's func_ptr
call %eax                //invoke foo()
```

Before a method call, all the arguments should have been prepared by the caller (the method that makes the call), so we do not need to prepare them here again. When the last call instruction is executed, X86 processor automatically pushes the return address of the call on the stack, which points to the instruction after the call instruction.

When the method is not compiled, the invocation actually goes to the trampoline as shown below, assuming method foo()'s description data structure is at 0x7001234, JIT compiler's entrance is at address 0x7005678.

```
pushl $0x7001234    //address of foo()'s description
call $0x7005678     //address of jit_compile(method)
jmp %eax            //eax holds the compiled code entry address
```

The trampoline code first pushes the address of method data structure of virtual method foo(). The runtime stack now has an extra item besides the original state of calling foo(), that is, the arguments and return address. The extra item is then consumed by the call to VM's function jit _ compile() and then the stack returns to the state of calling foo(). To clean up the argument by the callee (the function that is called), jit_compile() has to be defined to use STDCALL calling convention. Function jit_compile() has following prototype.

```
void* STDCALL jit_compile(Method* method)
```

The function attribute STDCALL should be defined as the VM development environment requires. For example, with GCC, it can be defined like the following, and STDCALL may have to be put in the end of the function prototype.

```
#define STDCALL __attribute__((stdcall))
```

According to X86 calling convention, the return value of the function call is kept in register eax. Here, it holds the entry point address of the compiled binary code. Although the address is supposed to be used as a call target, a jmp instruction suffices because the return address has been pushed on the stack by the call instruction already. Next time when fco() is invoked, the call instruction will directly go to the binary code, skipping the trampoline, because the vtable slot has been updated by the compiler to point to the binary code.

When multiple threads want to call the same method and trigger the JIT compilation of the method, VM needs to ensure the mutual exclusion of the compilation on same method. Following is a reduced version of jit_compile() implementation in Apache Harmony.

```
void* STDCALL jit_a_method(Method* kmethod)
{
    uint8* funcptr= NULL;

    /* ensure the class owning this method initialized*/
    class_initialize( kmethod->owner_class );

    /* exclusive compilation */
    spin_lock( kmethod );

    /* if compiled already, return */
    if( kmethod->state == JIT_STATUS_Compiled ){
        spin_unlock( kmethod );
        return kmethod->jitted_code;
    }

    /* now this thread owns the compilation */
    kmethod->state = JIT_STATUS_Compiling;

    if( ! kmethod->is_native_method ){
        funcptr = compile( kmethod );
    } else{  /* a wrapper from jitted code to native */
        funcptr = generate_java_to_native_stub( kmethod );
    }
    /* update the vtable slot with the new funcptr,
```

```
         replacing the original pointer to trampoline  */
      method_update_vtable( kmethod, funcptr );

      /* the method is compiled */
      kmethod->state = JIT_STATUS_Compiled;
      spin_unlock( kmethod );

      return funcptr;
}
```

The compile() function in the code above fulfills the actual compilation that translates the application code into machine code.

Note in the trampoline code above, we have largely simplified the code sequence to be a direct call into jit_method(). In reality, compiling a method may throw exception, or enter Java code execution and trigger garbage collection (GC), so the procedure from Java code execution to JIT compiler (written in native code) needs full Java-to-native transition. Bookkeeping is needed to make sure all the information be well prepared before entering the native code and be cleaned up after returning from the native code. We leave this discussion to Chapter 7.

4.2.2 Trace-Based JIT

In recent years, trace-based JIT has attracted lots of attentions. Trace is a snippet of code path executed at runtime. Trace-based JIT only compiles the code in the specific path and leaves alone any other code paths that branch off the specific path.

The main motivation of using trace as the compilation unit is to avoid compiling the cold code so as to reduce the compilation overhead, in both time and space. Method-based JIT compiles the whole method including both hot and cold code, even if some code may never be executed. Trace-based JIT profiles the code execution at runtime and only compiles the hot code path, which is called "trace."

Trace-based JIT has to conduct following tasks.

1. Identify and form the trace

2. Compile the trace and cache the binary code

3. Manage the trace adaptively

Since it is the hot execution path, a trace has to be identified at runtime through profiling. A common way of profiling is to instrument a counter at the potential entrance of a trace. The counter is incremented every time when the code following the entrance is executed. When the counter reaches a threshold, the executed code is considered hot.

Depending on the design, there are normally three kinds of places to instrument a counter: a method prolog, a loop header, and a basic block.

Method-based profiling is usually used in method-based JIT, that is, when the method is hot enough, the VM can choose to compile it (if it was only interpreted) or to recompile it with more advanced optimizations (if it has been compiled). Method-based profiling is straightforward to implement because method entrance is always known to the execution engine. But method-based profiling is not enough to identify all the hot codes. Sometimes, the application spends most of its time in hot loop(s) of a method, while the method itself is invoked only a few times, such as the main() method of a Java application. Even if method-based profiling identifies hot methods, the code in the methods may not all be hot.

Loop usually is considered mostly important for the performance optimization of an application, because a time-consuming application usually spends its execution time in loops. Many advanced compilation optimizations have been developed specifically for loop, such as loop invariant hoisting, parallelization, and vectorization. Therefore, it is natural to try loop-based profiling to identify hot code. A loop construct can be identified at compile-time by analyzing the code control-flow structure, or at runtime by profiling the back edges.

Compile-time loop identification requires the VM to build up the control-flow graph of the application code and then traverse the graph in depth-first order. The edge that points to a node that has already been visited is called back edge, which is the indicator of a potential loop structure. Compile-time loop identification may not be suitable for trace-based JIT if the execution engine does not build control flow graph. Another issue is that compile-time analysis may only be able to find iterative loop but hardly find recursive loop.

Runtime loop identification can be easier. A loop can be identified whenever the control flow goes back to the already-executed code, which is then considered the loop header, where a counter can be instrumented. This approach can only be implemented in an interpreter, because it needs to monitor the execution of every branch operation, which includes normal jump, branch, switch, call, return, and exception-throwing. TraceMonkey of Mozilla Firefox uses this approach.

Dalvik VM in Google Android profiles hot code at basic-block level. It instruments a counter in every maximal basic block. Here, basic block is a compiler term referring to the piece of code that has single entry point and single exit point. Maximal basic block refers to the basic block that cannot be bigger, that is, including more instructions makes it no longer a basic block.

Once a piece of hot code is identified, a trace can be formed by recording the operations in its next time execution (i.e., tracing execution) from the entrance, which is the start point of the trace. This process sometimes is called "tracing." For loop-based tracing, the trace end point is where the control goes back to the start point. For basic-block-based tracing, the end point is the exit point of the basic block. In both approaches, the length of a trace is limited to avoid the execution strays away from the expected path. Tracing process may give up due to some unsupported conditions, such as exception-throwing or entering runtime services.

Loop-based trace may have some intermediate points where the control branches off the hot path. Tracing process only records the actual taken branches at those points during the tracing execution. But in the following rounds of executions, the control may take other branches rather than the ones recorded in the trace. The VM should ensure correct execution in this situation. In other words, the execution should be able to leave the trace at intermediate points.

When recording the trace, the VM also records the conditions that must be met to keep the trace valid. When the trace is compiled, condition-checking code is inserted into the generated code to ensure the conditions be met to follow the trace; otherwise, control flow aborts the trace execution and transfers gracefully to the off-trace path according to the new conditions. The condition-checking code is called "guard" or "side exit." For example, with the following loop,

```
for (i = 0; i < n; ++i)
      j += i;
```

The trace pseudocode may look like below,

```
start_trace (int i, int j):
      ++i;
      temp = j + i;
      guard( temp not overflow );
      j = temp;
      guard( i < n );
      goto start_trace (int i, int j);
```

In dynamic typing languages like JavaScript, the variable type can be dynamically changed. The "same" operator such as "+" can have different operations at runtime when the variables' types change. The trace only records the types in the tracing execution and can become invalid if the types change in later execution. So the trace also needs to guard the specialized types. On the other hand, specialized types enable the trace to apply many compiler optimizations. For example, if the variables in a trace are all small integers, compiler can easily optimize the code with advanced register allocation technique. Otherwise, memory allocation is necessary to accommodate large integers. Actually, one of major motivations of TraceMonkey is based on the observation that the types in most programs do not change frequently, and the specialized types of the trace can cover most of the runtime possibilities.

Side exiting from a trace incurs high overhead. When side exiting becomes frequent, the whole purpose of trace can be compromised. A solution to frequent side exiting is to expand the tracing scope dynamically.

For loop-based tracing, when a guard fails at runtime, the VM checks its position in the trace. If it is at the trace start point, a new trace is recorded. For dynamic-typed language, the new trace is usually same piece of hot code as original trace, but with a new set of specialized types. If the guard fails in the middle of a trace, the VM recognizes a branch in the trace and starts to profile its hotness. When the branch becomes hot enough, a new trace will start from it. A "trace tree" is then formed together with the original trace. The number of traces for branches should be well controlled to avoid "trace explosion."

For basic-block-based tracing, the traces of basic blocks can be "chained" so as to avoid involving runtime services or the interpreter. That is, when a trace is known to exit to another trace, the control can transfer to the next trace directly. A guard can be inserted to ensure the chaining be valid. Chained traces can also form a trace tree or trace graph.

Loop-based tracing has an advantage that it can inline methods automatically, as long as the methods are in the execution path of the loop trace. Basic-block-based tracing does not usually cross the method boundary, unless the method is extremely simple that can be inlined ad hoc. Neither of them can handle recursive method tracing. Although loop-based tracing can identify the repetitive execution of a recursion, to form the trace for the recursion is challenging. Except tail recursion, a normal recursion has two disjoint phases of repetitive execution: one is the "downward iterations" that keeps pushing new method frames on the stack, and the other is the "upward iterations" that pops the frames off the stack. The two phases do not know each other, so the second phase has to know how to pop the frames and feeds the return value to the caller frame. This is very ad hoc and difficult to get right. Even this situation works out, indirect recursion is still an untouched problem where a method calls itself through calling other methods.

A question to trace-based JIT is how the VM knows a trace is compiled. This question is solved in method-based JIT by using vtable that links to either the jitted code or the trampoline when it is not compiled. Trace-based JIT does not have vtable, because trace does not have well-defined unit as method does. Trace-based JIT needs a way to maintain the traces and their status. A straightforward solution is to use a dynamic table that can insert the information of a newly identified trace. Dalvik VM uses hash table that maps the trace start address to the hash index, which sometimes leads to hash conflict hence inaccurate trace status. For example, Dalvik VM stores the profiling counter in the hash entry that will be reset when a new trace is mapped into the same entry. As a result, a cold trace may override the information of a hot trace, thus counteracts the design purpose of trace-based JIT.

To the best knowledge of the author, there is no method-based tracing in trace-based JIT. It is not impossible but not very useful. If a method has a hot loop while the method itself is invoked only a few times, method-based tracing may have no way to discover the hot loop and then compile it. If the method is hot because it is invoked in a hot loop, only compiling the method alone without other part of the loop body may not help the loop's performance. Method-based tracing may be useful for a dynamic language where the method behavior is mainly determined by the argument types. But in this case, JIT method-based compilation with type specialization can be a better solution.

As of year 2015, all the best-known VMs have ceased to use trace-based JITs, mostly due to inferior performance or incredible design complexity for superior performance. Compared to method-based JIT, the benefit of saving compilation time is either unsubstantial or not critical in many cases. The performance benefit due to runtime type specialization and data instantiation is not specific to tracing, but can also be achieved with type inference or other JIT analysis. Ultimately, trace is not a right level of semantic unit for compiler to fully perform its potential.

4.2.3 Region-Based JIT

Region-based JIT can be regarded as a hybrid of method-based JIT and trace-based JIT. The compilation unit can be a basic-block or bigger unit, but it does not necessarily depend on tracing. Region-based JIT is like as a method-based JIT in a smaller granularity, while it can also leverage the runtime information for type specialization and data instantiation.

For static typing languages like Java, region-based JIT can be useful in highly memory-constrained platform by avoiding compiling the whole method. It is also useful when the method is too big in size and takes too long time to compile. The method can be partitioned into regions and only select regions are compiled. To some extent, the region-based compilation can be regarded as a combination of "outlining" and method-based compilation. Outlining is a compilation technique. It moves a piece of code out of the original method and wrapped it as a new method. The original code is replaced by a method call to invoke the newly formed method. The new method is compiled as in a method-based JIT.

For dynamic typing languages, region-based JIT can apply type specialization while avoiding trace explosion. It is based on the fact that basic block does not involve control flow. Compilation at the basic-block level does not have to deal with all the branches, which reduces the chance of exponential increase of the potentially compiled paths. Still guards are needed for type specialization and data instantiation.

Facebook's HipHop virtual machine (HHVM) for PHP language implements region-based JIT. It does not employ profiling or tracing but compiles the basic block first time it meets, with the runtime types available to the compiler for type specialization. HHVM calls the specialized code for a region "a tracelet." Guards are generated at the entry of the compiled region to ensure the input variables have the expected types at runtime; otherwise, the compiler is triggered again to generate a new piece of type-specialized code for newly encountered input types. It chains the compiled pieces of the same region with different type specializations as a linked list to match the runtime actual input types, and a right match triggers the trace execution. In the end of the list is a trampoline to trigger a new trace compilation when no matched trace is found in the list. HHVM calls the traces of the region "parallel tracelets." Parallel tracelets virtually extend the guard code to be a sequence of conditional branches to trigger either a matched tracelet execution or a nonmatched tracelet compilation.

Dalvik VM's trace-based JIT can be considered to be a region-based JIT to some extent.

4.3 RELATION BETWEEN INTERPRETER AND JIT COMPILER

Although interpreter is usually slower than a JIT, it is still widely used in various VM implementations. Interpreter has some benefits such as lower memory footprint and faster application startup time. But those are nonessential. Among other reasons, the major one to use interpreter is its simplicity. When a new language or a new feature of an existing language is introduced, it is much faster to implement in an interpreter than in a JIT compiler. With interpreter, the logic of the new language feature is programed directly by the developer in the VM implementation language such as C. In other words, the developer has only two dependences:

1. Familiarity with the VM implementation language

2. Understanding of the new language feature, including its syntax and semantics

As a contrast, to implement the new language feature with a JIT compiler, the developer has additional dependences:

1. Familiarity with the target machine Application Binary Interface (ABI) specification

2. Skills in runtime technology to map the new language feature to target machine ABI

3. Skills to develop the compiler to generate the expected target machine code

Consequently, interpreter can help the developers to focus on the new language feature, accelerates the development, and enables fast community adoption.

Another important reason for using interpreter is that some language features are very hard or not worth to implement in a compiler, considering the return on investment, such as,

- Function `eval()` to evaluate a program in the form of a string, which involves the reentrance of the VM

- Statement `throw()` to throw an exception, which needs to unwind the runtime stack hence involves reflection of the VM status

- Operator `new()` to create a new object, which requires support from the memory manager, and may trigger a GC

Even in the most complete compilation-based VM, these features are usually implemented on top of runtime services of the VM, which needs control switch between the jitted code and the VM code. VM code and jitted code usually have different execution contexts, such as different stack frame arrangements for their respective convenience. For example, in jitted code, the stack frames are arranged to enable direct method invocation and return, so it uses the hardware native frame-pointer and instruction pointer (also called program counter), that is, `bp` and `ip` registers in X86 architecture. In VM code, the program counter is usually stored in a global variable and points to the current bytecode position that is under execution. The VM may also allocate specific memory area to store the method stack frames. Control switch between the jitted code and the VM code may require the saving and restoration of the execution context. Since interpreter does not have jitted code, nor requires the execution context for jitted code, it is an integral part of the VM. It is straightforward to implement those language features based on runtime services in an interpreter.

Although interpreter is not designed for performance, it does not prevent an interpreter from using compilation for better performance. There are usually two orthogonal ways to introduce a JIT compiler to an interpreter. One is to switch the execution engine between interpretation and compilation back and forth, where JIT is applied to the hot code. The other way is to compile the application code into intermediate representation (IR) such as bytecode and then interpret the IR code. The benefit of this approach comes from the well-formatted IR code, which enables the interpreter's fast dispatching. This approach is commonly used in today's interpreter-based VMs. Since it does not generate machine code, the syntax and semantics of IR can be defined with flexibility to encode all the language features while still keeping the interpreter's portability across different hardware architectures.

4.4 AHEAD-OF-TIME COMPILATION

Although compilation helps performance, JIT works only at runtime, which inevitably adds runtime overhead to the application execution. Ahead-of-time (AOT) compilation tries to reduce the runtime overhead as much as possible by compiling the application code before it is executed.

All the traditional compilers conduct AOT compilation at application development time. But for applications in safe languages that normally run in VMs, AOT compilation is seldom carried out at development time, because that may more or less lose the original benefits of safe language programming. The prebuilt binary code, if without extra security measures, can hardly guarantee the safety and has no way to run across multiple instruction set architectures (ISAs) natively with a single copy.

The AOT compilation is usually conducted after the application's distribution or deployment. For example, OdinMonkey is an AOT compiler for asm.js language developed by Mozilla Firefox, as part of SpiderMonkey internal implementation. OdinMonkey compiles the application in asm.js language when the application is loaded in the browser before the application starts to execute. Since the application is not compiled before it is loaded into the browser, it keeps the same benefits as JavaScript in safety and portability, which is essential for web applications.

Asm.js is a subset of JavaScript so application in it can still be JIT-compiled with IonMonkey, a method-based JIT implementation in SpiderMonkey. The difference is that asm.js has no runtime features such as dynamic typing, exception-throwing, and GC, which virtually makes asm.js no longer a dynamic language, but similar to C language that can be compiled ahead of time. As a matter of fact, asm.js code is usually automatically generated from C/C++ programs. LLVM clang compiles C/C++ code into LLVM bitcode, which in turn can be translated by Emscripten into asm.js code. So asm.js acts more like an intermediate language for the deployment of web applications developed in C/C++.

Google Chrome's PNaCl (portable native client) technology does not use asm.js as the intermediate language of web applications; instead, it compiles C/C++ web application code into LLVM bitcode and directly distributes the web application in bitcode, which in turn is AOT-compiled when loaded into Chrome.

As a comparison, Google Chrome's NaCl and Microsoft Windows' ActiveX technologies compile the web application code into native machine binary code at development time. A natural consequence is that a web application has to be compiled into multiple copies for different ISAs. Since they do not employ safe language for application distribution, these technologies have to provide other security measures such as sandboxing in Chrome for NaCl code, or digital signing the ActiveX code in Windows.

Besides the benefits of portability and safety, there is a deeper reason why AOT compilation is usually not conducted at development time. That is, the dynamic features of safe language may make it very challenging, if not impossible at all, to fully compile an application with AOT compilation. The dynamic features, such as reflection, eval() function, dynamic class loading, dynamic typing, and GC, make some application information only available at runtime while that information is needed for complete AOT compilation.

For instance, safe language usually does not specify the physical layout of an object, which is subject to the discretion of GC at runtime. When AOT compiler compiles the expression related to object field or property access, it does not even know if the object data is consecutive or discrete in memory. There is no way for it to generate native instructions for object data access unless the object layout information is available, or through reflection support that is much slower. JIT compiler has no such problem because it can get all the information from VM and GC at runtime when it generates instructions.

Dynamic class loading also makes AOT difficult. If a class is not loaded during AOT compilation time, there is no way to compile its methods. Dynamic typing is similar. It allows the variable's type dynamically vary at runtime. If the AOT compiler cannot infer the variable type, there is no easy way to generate efficient code for the variable's operations.

For these problems, AOT compiler usually generates code to link with some runtime libraries so as to defer them to runtime. An extreme solution is to compile the entire runtime system together with the application code, which virtually bundles the VM into the application package for distribution. This is a typical approach today to distribute HTML5 applications. It does not actually compile the application ahead of time.

To ease AOT compilation, it is common to conduct the compilation in pseudo-runtime state, that is, setting up the runtime state as much as possible while avoiding actual code execution. For example, an AOT compiler may load all the needed classes and gets the object layout information from the target VM. Or the AOT compilation can be conducted after the VM starts and before any code is executed. The VM can shut down when the compilation is finished, if the VM launch purpose is to assist AOT compilation. In pseudo-runtime AOT compilation, the application execution result should not be committed to the system.

Yet another AOT solution is to only compile the code that is possible to be compiled, leaving the not-compiled part to runtime.

Firefox OdinMonkey can do AOT compilation for asm.js code because asm.js virtually removes all the dynamic features of JavaScript. Android application's intermediate language dexcode keeps certain dynamic features of Java bytecode, Android Runtime (ART) has to conducts AOT compilation on dexcode in pseudo-runtime state. To identify the right classes to compile, ART needs to load the needed classes and hence executes the class initializers with a built-in interpreter during AOT compilation. In other words, the AOT compiler involves almost a full VM.

Since some AOT compilers need to execute the application code, it is interesting to discuss the real boundary between JIT and AOT compilations. They have following differences:

1. AOT compilation is usually conducted without actually executing the application or committing the execution result. In other words, the application is not at "runtime" state. AOT may execute some code of the application, but the reason for the execution is a compromise to make AOT compilation possible, rather than to get the execution result for which the application is developed.

2. AOT compilation does not surely know whether the methods it compiles will or not be executed in an actual run of the application, because it does not have the all

runtime information on the control flow. AOT may have some heuristics or profiling information that can help the method selection. As a comparison, JIT only compiles the methods that are surely to be executed.

3. AOT compilation and application execution are two strictly separated phases. These two phases are not interleaved and can be separated in both time and space. In other words, when needed, the AOT phase can save the compiled result in one place, and later the execution phase can use the result in another place and does not need to compile again. The AOT compilation can be conducted at application development time, deployment time, installation time, launch time, and so on, depending on the design of the VM, the language, and the application.

The major motivation for AOT compilation is to save the runtime overhead incurred by JIT in time and space while still keeping the performance benefit over interpreter. But AOT may not be able to implement all the optimizations available to JIT, because of the nonruntime nature. For instance, type specialization for dynamic language requires the compiler know the runtime types of the variables, which is not usually possible in AOT. Another example is on runtime safety enforcement. Java VM (JVM) requires to ensure the access to an array element to be always within the array bound, so an array bound checking is enforced before any array element access. If the compiler knows that the access is always within the array bound, it may eliminate the redundant bound checking. The element index and array length are usually much easier to obtain at JIT time than at AOT time.

However, AOT compilation can enable some heavy-weighted optimizations that are usually not used in JIT, due to the excessive runtime overhead for the optimizations. Long compilation time in JIT may cause user-perceivable stuttering in the application's execution, so sometimes it has to balance between compilation time and execution time. AOT may not need this tradeoff; hence, AOT can apply optimizations like interprocedural optimizations and whole-application escape analysis that are usually not fully touched in JIT.

Although all the traditional static compilation can be regarded as AOT compilation, they are not usually called this way. AOT compilation—when it is explicitly stated—is usually considered a special form of JIT as a kind of dynamic compilation, rather than a kind of static compilation.

4.5 COMPILE-TIME VERSUS RUNTIME

Compile-time refers to the time when a compiler is compiling. Runtime refers to the time when an application is running. Traditionally, these two phases are decoupled, while in JIT-based VM they are overlapping, because JIT compiles at runtime. A better definition of the terms should correlate the subject and object of the phases.

Assuming program P written in language L is compiled to machine code C, compile-time refers to the time when program P is compiled from L to C, and runtime refers to the time when program P is executed in the form of C.

In a VM, there are two different runtimes. One is the time when program P is executed, that is, program runtime, or application runtime, or simply runtime. The other is the time when the compiled code C is executed, that is, compiled-code runtime. When VM is launched to run program P, it enters application runtime state, but it does not necessarily run any compiled code C yet. When the application code is compiled from L to C, it is at compile-time. Both code compile-time and code runtime happen during the application runtime. Figure 4.3 below illustrates the relation.

The distinction between compile-time and runtime is important to VM developers, because it tells what are available, what can happen and at what time. For example, in JVM, when an object `ovar` has been created, and its method `foo()` is first time invoked, the JIT will be triggered to compile method `foo()`. In method `foo()`, there is an object field access to `ovar.data` as the code below.

```
int local = ovar.data;
```

The corresponding bytecode seen by JIT can be the following.

```
getfield 2   // load field #2 "data" from object
istore_4     // store the value to local variable
```

When JIT generates native machine code, the object is already created, and the address, say 0x00abcd00, can be got by JIT when it compiles the bytecode. But JIT should not generate the code for "`getfield 2`" like below,

```
// Assuming "data" field is at object offset 0x10
// from the object start address, i.e., at 0x00abcd10,
// since 0x00abcd10 = 0x00abcd00 + 0x10

movl 0x00abcd10, %eax   //copy "data" content to eax. Wrong!
movl %eax, $16(%esp)    //copy eax value to local stack
```

The code sequence is incorrect to access `ovar.data` directly at 0x00abcd10. The reasons are the followings.

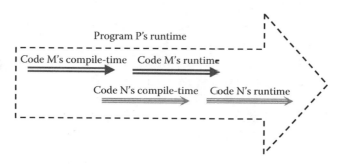

FIGURE 4.3   The relation between compile-time and runtime in a VM.

1. Although object `ovar`'s address is `0x00abcd00` at the compile-time of the byte-code, its address can be different at runtime of the compiled code, because the object can be moved by garbage collector.

2. Although method `foo()` is compiled due to its invocation upon object `ovar`, `ovar` is only an instance of a class, say `kclass`, that may have other instances created. Method `foo()` can be invoked upon those other instances.

Actually, although object `ovar` is the one that triggers `foo()` compilation, it may not even be the first object that invokes the compiled code of `foo()`. In a multithreaded application, another thread may invoke `foo()` right after the compiled code address is installed in the vtable of `kclass`, before the thread that triggers the compilation starts to run `foo()`'s compiled code. So the right code sequence generated should be as follows.

```
// Assuming ovar is stored at stack offset 0x20
// from stack top (saved in register esp).

movl $0x20(%esp), %eax        //copy "ovar" to eax
movl $0x10(%eax), %eax        //copy "ovar.data" to eax
movl %eax, $16(%esp)          //copy eax value to local stack
```

Another example is to invoke the virtual method of an object `ovar`, such as,

```
ovar.foo();
```

The corresponding bytecode sequence can be the following.

```
aload_0              //load ovar to stack
invokevirtual #16 //invoke ovar.foo()
```

At compile-time, JIT knows the current object `ovar`'s class `kclass`' vtable address (say `0x00001000`). At the known offset (say `0x10`) of the vtable, JIT can find `foo()`'s entry point (say `0x00002000`). But JIT cannot generate instruction to directly call the entry point like below, even if the compiled code never moves.

```
call 0x00002000    //invoke kclass' foo() method
```

The reason is, at runtime, the actual object pointed by `ovar` may be an instance of a sub-class of `kclass`, say `sclass`, and `sclass` may override `kclass`' method `foo()`. That means, the method `foo()` known to JIT at compile-time may not be the `foo()` that is actually invoked at runtime. So the right code generated should try to identify the right method from object `ovar`'s vtable, as the following code shows.

```
movl $0x20(%esp), %eax        //copy "ovar" to eax
movl (%eax), %eax             //load vtable pointer to eax
```

```
movl $0x10(%eax), %eax   //load foo()'s entry point
call %eax                //call ovar.foo )
```

Some application runtime information can be used at method compile-time. For example, as we already have seen, the offset of a method in vtable is available at compile-time in JVM. JIT does not need to generate instructions to retrieve the offset every time calling the method, as below.

```
pushl $16                //push method index
pushl $0x20(%esp)        //push "ovar" to stack
call get_vtable_offset   //foo()'s offset in eax
movl $0x20(%esp), %ebx   //copy "ovar" to ebx
movl (%ebx), %ebx        //load vtable pointer to ebx
addl %ebx, %eax          //eax now holds foo()'s entry
call %eax                //call ovar.foo()
```

Since the offset of a method in vtable is fixed in JVM once the class is loaded throughout the application's runtime, it can be used by JIT in method compile-time without any problem at method runtime.

Note the information available at compile-time or runtime is different from language to language. In some dynamic languages, the object properties (or fields) can be added or deleted at runtime, so normally it is impossible to identify fixed positions for the properties in compile-time. For instance, in JavaScript, it is common to use a hash table to map the property names to the values. In this situation, the access function to the property has to be called at runtime to retrieve the value.

The boundary between compile-time and runtime is not as clear as the figure shows. The subtlety is that the two stages are usually interleaved. For example, to compile a method (when this method is under compiling), the compiler may have to execute another method (e.g., class initializer) before it can finish this method compilation.

On the other hand, when the compiled code of a method is executed, it may invoke another method, hence trigger the JIT compilation of that method. So it is very common to see that method A's compilation triggers method B's execution, which in turns triggers method C's compilation, and when again triggers method D's compilation, and so on. Consequently, the runtime stack of the VM can be interleaved by compilation frames and execution frames.

In a pure interpreter-based VM, we can say it has no compile-time, hence no distinction between program runtime and compiled-code runtime. The whole lifetime of the VM is to execute the application code and is at runtime. That is one reason why VM is also called runtime system.

CHAPTER 5

Design of Garbage Collection

S AFE LANGUAGES DO NOT provide direct memory management application programming interfaces (APIs) to programmers, but delegate the task to a virtual machine
(VM). A programmer only needs to create an object whenever needed, without worrying
about where the object is allocated and how the object data is laid out. Furthermore, the
programmer does not need to monitor the lifetime of the object or release the memory
occupied by the object when it becomes useless to the program.

Garbage collector (GC) is the VM component that does all the jobs on dynamic data
management for the programmer. The name "garbage collector" is not very accurate because
GC does more than just reclaiming the useless objects (i.e., the garbage). Reclaiming always
goes together with reusing. Once the algorithm of garbage collection is designed, the way
how to reuse the recycled space for object allocation is largely decided, and vice versa. So
some developers prefer the name "automatic memory management" to "garbage collection."

The key to garbage collection is to identify the liveness of objects, that is, when an object
can be recycled.

5.1 OBJECT LIFETIME

When an object is no longer useful to the program, it is dead and can be recycled. This is
a circular definition, while it does highlight the point about when to recycle an object. The
statement "an object is useful to the program" means the object will be accessed by the
program sometime in the future.

Traditional static compiler determines the lifetime of a variable with "liveness analysis"
algorithm, so as to assist optimizations such as register allocation. It considers a variable
as alive if the variable holds a value that may be used in the future. The lifetime covers the
range from a write to the variable till the last read of the written value. Object's liveness
ultimately can be defined in a similar way that an object is considered live if its data may
be read in the future. The differences from variable liveness analysis are as follows:

1. Liveness analysis only analyzes local variable live range "within the method," if without interprocedural analysis. As a contrast, an object can be passed "across methods,"
   which is the common case and is hard to analyze with traditional liveness analysis.

2. Liveness analysis provides live information that "may" be true. If it is untrue, nothing would go wrong, but the variable is kept longer than necessary. The death information for GC "must" be true; otherwise, if a live object is reclaimed, the program may go wrong.

3. Even with interprocedural analysis, liveness analysis can hardly handle complex program logic, especially dynamic program behavior whose information is unavailable statically, such as exception-throwing and virtual method call.

Because of the reasons mentioned earlier, the applicability of traditional liveness analysis is very limited in object lifetime management. Dynamic analysis then is more feasible to find live objects, with techniques like reference counting (RC) and object tracing. Liveness analysis is still useful though. For example, it can be used in RC when compiler instruments the code, which we will see in next section. It can also be used in escape analysis to identify the method-local objects. Method-local objects live only within a method (i.e., never escape from the method); thus they can be managed as a local variable and allocated in the stack frame of the method. This situation is not what GC is mainly targeted at, and we leave it to future discussion. The common situation that GC needs to handle is when objects live across methods and even across threads.

5.2 REFERENCE COUNTING

It is very hard to exactly know when an object is no longer useful to the application, because that requires to predict the future behavior of the program. However, it is easier to know if an object is reachable to the application at a point of runtime. If the application loses its reference to the object, it has no way to access the object any more, and hence the object is surely no longer useful to the application.

An object can become useless to an application before the application loses all its references to the object. In other words, object reachability is more conservative than object usefulness, which means the objects are recycled later than they can. But it is a reasonable compromise between the recycling promptness and analysis complexity.

To identify whether the application still holds any reference to an object, it is intuitive to use RC technique. The idea is to keep track of the number of references to every object with a counter. The counter is incremented when a new reference to the object is installed in the system, such as written in memory, loaded onto stack, or stored in a register. The counter is decremented when an existing reference is overwritten with other value.

The object is unreachable when the counter reaches zero and then the object can be reclaimed. When an object S is reclaimed, all other objects referenced by S should decrement their respective reference counters. If any of the counters then become zero, the corresponding objects should be reclaimed too. The process need transitively continue till no more objects become unreachable.

In a straightforward implementation, the primitives in Table 5.1 are needed to accomplish RC operations. RC represents reference count or reference counting depending on the context.

TABLE 5.1   Primitives of Reference Counting

Opcode	Operands	Semantics
incRC	*obj1*	Increment RC of object *obj1*
decRC	*obj1*	Decrement RC of object *obj1*
testRC	*obj1*	Test if RC of object *obj1* drops to 0, and if so, recycle it and update recursively

TABLE 5.2   Additional Primitives for Reference Counting

dectestRC	*obj1*	**decRC** and then **testRC**
updSlot	*obj1, obj2*	**incRC** *obj2* and **dectestRC** *obj1*

Table 5.2 gives additional primitives that make the implementation convenient.

The primitives of RC are usually instrumented by compiler into the generated code. The compiler needs to scan a method twice for the instrumentation. In the first scanning pass, the compiler does the following when a reference is written to stack or heap. (In actual implementation, some references are kept out of stack and heap. Writing to them should also be instrumented. For example, the static fields of class may be allocated in separate memory space and may contain references. Here we use stack and heap to represent all the places where references may be written according to the VM semantics).

- Insert **incRC** for an object *obj1* every time when it has reference loaded onto the stack;

- Insert **updSlot** for an object every time when an object field containing value *obj1* is overwritten with value *obj2*.

The compiler does not instrument a reference used as a method argument or return value, because the argument is held in the caller's stack frame, and the return value will also appear in the callers' context when current method returns.

In the second scanning pass, the compiler conducts liveness analysis for the objects whose RC is incremented with **incRC** or **updSlot** and then does the following.

- Insert **dectestRC** at the end points of their live range, that is, the places right after where their references are last-time used, to decrement their RCs and recycle them if their RCs drop to zero. If the live range ends at a return statement, **decRC** is used instead of **dectestRC** because the object RC is known nonzero when its reference is returned to the caller.

In the Java VM (JVM) implementation of RC, objects may be passed between Java code and native code through Java Native Interface (JNI). The objects need to update their RC in native code as well. The following JNI-related operations need instrumentation: set a field of reference type, set a static field of reference type, object clone, and array copy. In a well-modularized implementation such as Apache Harmony, only four functions need to be modified.

The RC operations can incur high runtime overhead. Many of the operations can be eliminated as redundant. For example, the adjacent pair of **incRC** and **dectestRC** on same object can be replaced by a **testRC** to catch the possible zero RC. Since the references to same object can be from different variables alias analysis can help to tell if they point to same object hence to apply the optimization.

To implement RC algorithm, a question is where to store the reference counter for every object. The value of the counter cannot be too small to record a large count and cannot be too big to become substantial memory overhead. It can be one byte, two bytes, or even four bytes depending on the targeted application characteristics. When RC value overflows the counter storage, the VM has to give up the tracking and considers the object live forever, or use additional GC algorithm to recycle it.

The least size of the counter can be one bit. Value "1" means it is referenced once, which is true once the object is created, and its reference is installed to the system. When single reference is lost, the object is recycled. When it has one more reference, the counter is overflowed, and object lives forever. This is sometimes reasonable when the application's objects are mostly referenced once.

An immediate following question is how to update the counter in a multithreaded application. The increment and decrement operations are essentially read-modify-write. Without atomic control, two simultaneous operations on same counter by two threads may result with incorrect value. Some GC implementations choose to use atomic operations for the increment and decrement. In this design, "decrement and test" does not have to be atomic in a race-free program. Once the counter reaches zero, it cannot change.

Atomic instruction is expensive in almost all known processors. RC algorithm can choose not to use atomic RC update. The tradeoff is that, when the object is referenced by a second thread, it gives up RC tracking and becomes long live. To implement this, extra bits are needed to track the thread ID of its creating thread. When a thread tries to update the RC of an object, it always tests whether the stored thread ID is equal to its own thread ID. If they are the same, the thread continues the RC updating; otherwise, the RC is set overflowed. This design is especially useful when most of the objects are thread local.

Besides the high runtime overhead, the major drawback of RC GC is the cyclic reference problem, where objects form reference cycle. The extreme case is a self-pointing reference. In this situation, the RC of the objects in the cycle can never reach zero, even when the application cannot reach any of them. They become "floating garbage" that cannot be recycled.

Various techniques have been proposed by the community either to avoid or correct reference cycles. For example, Apple uses "weak" or "unowned" qualifier on a reference to instruct the Swift runtime system that the reference is not counted in its RC algorithm.

To instrument RC operations in the generated code increases code size. This may lead to more instruction cache misses. In systems with small memory, the code bloat may become significant enough that prevent reference-counting algorithm from being effective or applicable. Interpreter does not have this problem.

5.3 OBJECT TRACING

The root problem of RC is in its nature. It tries to track the number of references to determine the object's liveness, but only the references from the application can tell the object's reachability. When a reference to object S is installed in object T, it only means object S is referenced by object T, rather than by the application.

As we have mentioned, we use "object reachability" to approximate "object usefulness." A nonzero RC does not necessarily mean the object is reachable by the application. Only when an object is referenced by an application directly or indirectly, can it be considered reachable.

When an object is directly referenced by an application, its reference must be installed in the application's execution context, including stack frames, registers, and global variables. These places are directly accessible to the application through their names or addresses. Object references stored in these places are called "root" references.

If an object is indirectly referenced by an application, its reference is not installed in application's execution context but in other reachable object. So reachability is a transitive relation. All reachable objects can be considered live. This is conservative and may include objects that are never used by the application in future, but it does not retain more useless objects than RC, because all the reachable objects are sure to have nonzero references. RC retains all the reachable objects plus the floating garbage retained by cyclic reference.

The process to determine object reachability is called "reachability analysis." According to the definition, the process includes two phases: the first is to find the directly reachable objects ("root" objects) and the second is to find all the indirectly reachable ones.

- Phase one examines the application's execution context and identifies all the slots (in stack, registers, or global variables) that hold an object reference. These slots collectively are called "root-set," and this process is called "root-set enumeration." The references held in root-set are "root references," or simple "roots."

- Phase two starts from the root objects and traverses the object connection graph by following the references in reachable objects transitively till all the objects have been visited. This process is usually called "heap tracing" or "object tracing."

All the reachable objects are marked live, and the rest are garbage. So the phase two is also called "live-object marking." GC algorithm using reachability analysis is called "tracing GC."

Object tracing normally cannot be conducted when the application is actively running, because both the execution context and object graph are constantly changing. It is a race condition between application execution and reachability analysis. For example, after stack enumeration and before register enumeration, a reference S in register R is installed to the stack, and register R is set null. Then reference R is lost from root-set.

For this reason, when GC starts reachability analysis (root-set enumeration and heap tracing), the application's execution usually is paused. When the application is multithreaded, all the threads have to be suspended. This is called "stop-the-world." The application's execution can resume after GC finishes. GC pause time can impact the application's responsiveness. Algorithms exist to reduce the pause time, or even try to completely eliminate it. Which we will discuss later in Section IV.

The pseudocode for object-tracing phase is given below. It traverses the object connection graph from root-set in depth-first order.

```
void traverse_object_graph()
{
    mark_stack = load_root_references();

    while ( !stack_is_empty(mark_stack) ){
        Object* ovar = stack_pop( mark_stack );
        for (each object oref referenced by object ovar){
            if( obj_is_marked(oref) )
                continue;
            mark_object( oref );
            stack_push( mark_stack, oref);
        }
    }
}
```

The algorithm first loads the root-set references to a stack (`mark_stack`), then pops the top stack element for object scanning. The unmarked object references are pushed to the stack. The process continues until the stack is empty, when all the reachable objects are marked.

5.4 RC VERSUS OBJECT TRACING

The characteristics of RC and object tracing are interestingly complementary.

1. RC tries to find the objects that are no longer referenced (i.e., dead). Object tracing tries to find the objects that are reachable (i.e., live).

2. RC is conducted at runtime and is part of the application's execution. Object tracing requires to suspend the application's execution. RC has runtime overhead, whereas object tracing has pause time.

3. RC identifies a dead object in real time once the application loses its reference to the object. Objects die one after another. Object tracing identifies dead objects in batch mode. When all the reachable objects are marked, the rest are dead all at once. Before object tracing finishes, all objects are considered live.

4. RC can recycle the dead objects and reuse the memory in real time. The heap contains only live objects. Object tracing recycles the space only after a collection. When it starts the collection, the heap may be mostly occupied by dead objects. In other words, the memory utilization efficiency is lower with object tracing.

RC and object tracing can be implemented in one GC algorithm to leverage the advantages from both. A hybrid algorithm can dynamically track some objects with RC and leave others for object tracing.

Intuitively, we can use RC on the areas where references are not intensively updated. If we partition the heap into areas, it is possible that objects in one area have more intensive reference updates than another area. The most intensive reference update area is the application's execution context.

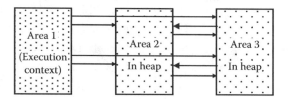

FIGURE 5.1   Areas that have references in an application.

Figure 5.1 illustrates the areas, where Area 1 is the execution context. The arrows between the areas are the references from one area to objects in another area.

Deferred reference-counting (DRC) is a hybrid algorithm that uses both RC and object tracing. DRC only tracks the reference updates in heap (i.e., Areas 2 and 3 in Figure 5.1), which can save lots of runtime overhead to track the reference updates in execution context. When the RC of an object drops to zero, it is put into a table called ZCT. When heap becomes fully occupied or ZCT is full, an object-tracing process is triggered that only identifies roots (i.e., references in Area 1). Objects in ZCT that are referenced by roots are considered live, and the rest are dead and recycled.

In another situation, if the objects in Area 3 are known to be mostly live, there is no need to spend time tracing objects in it during a collection, so as to save object-tracing time and reduce GC pause time. Since some live objects in Area 2 are reachable through the objects in Area 3, GC has to find those references from Area 3 to Area 2.

The idea is to dynamically track those references at runtime. Whenever there is a reference installed in a slot of Area 3 that points to Area 2, the slot address is recorded in a "remembered set" or simply "remember set." When the heap is fully occupied or remember set is full, a tracing GC kicks in to collect Area 2 (since Area 3 is considered all live). Now the starting references for object tracing include both the ones from root-set (in Area 1) and those from remember set (in Area 3). Object tracing is conducted only in Area 2. This idea has been applied in "regional GC" and "generational GC."

It is also possible to use RC only on certain types of objects, so as to recycle their spaces in real time. When the heap becomes full, a normal object-tracing collection is triggered. This is useful when the reference-counted objects are the major active objects that are born and die frequently. Using RC on them can recycle the memory in real time so as to delay next object-tracing collection. This idea has been used in "Cycler GC."

5.5 GC SAFE POINT

In GC community, the application threads are usually called mutators, since they mutate the heap. The threads conducting garbage collection are called collectors, since they recycle the heap. Note mutators and collectors are not necessarily separate threads. One thread can shift its role between mutator and collector.

As we have mentioned, object tracing needs to suspend the mutators for garbage collection. To enumerate root-set, collectors needs to know where the references are installed in the execution context. This information is provided by the runtime and compiler. For example, only the compiler knows which stack slots and registers hold references at certain point of the code execution. The precondition is that the compiler bookkeeps the information when it compiles the program. If the compiler does not maintain this kind of information, the collectors have to use some heuristics to conservatively guess the references from the context. For example, a value in a stack slot looking like a pointer can be regarded as a reference and then the collector validates it by checking if the pointed position in heap is indeed an object header. If it is an object, the collector regards it as live, although it is not necessarily true, because the value in the stack may be an irrelevant datum such as an integer. This kind of GC algorithm retains a superset of live objects, hence called conservative GC. If the collectors can get precise root-set, it is called precise GC.

To support precise root-set enumeration, the compiler can bookkeep related information for every instruction, in case the execution is suspended at that instruction. But it is too expensive to keep the information for every instruction, and it is also unnecessary, because only a very small ratio of instructions will have the chances to be the suspension points in actual execution. The compiler only needs to maintain the information for those points, which are called GC safe points, where it is safe to conduct root-set enumeration and garbage collection.

The ability for a compiler to support precise root-set enumeration is not universally available for all languages. Only safe languages have the ability because unsafe languages may, for instance, store a reference to an integer variable, which can confuse the compiler.

There are basically two kinds of approaches to suspend a mutator, preemptively or voluntarily. The pre-emptive approach is to suspend the mutator whenever the collector needs to have a collection. If it finds the mutator is suspended at an unsafe point, it can resume the mutator, rolling it forward to a safe point. Currently, almost no VM takes this approach.

With voluntary suspension, when the collector wants to trigger a collection, it sets a flag or fire a notification to the mutators. The mutators will suspend themselves at a safe point once they find the flag is set or receive the notification. The mutators can poll the flag at GC safe points, then the polling points are the safe points. It is the compiler's responsibility to insert the polling instructions at the safe points. VM code sometimes also needs to have some safe points which are inserted by the VM developer.

The pre-emptive and voluntary approaches sometimes are called interrupt-based and polling-based approaches respectively. The polling-based approach is commonly used today. There are a few basic principles for polling-point insertion:

1. First, polling points in program code should be close enough so that the collector does not wait too long for a mutator to suspend. When a collector sets the collection flag, the heap might be full, so some other mutators are eagerly waiting for the collector to recycle the heap to proceed. There should be no mutator that runs for a long time without polling the flag.

2. Second, polling points should be as few as possible in program code. Every polling-point execution incurs certain overhead. Too many polling-points incur high runtime overhead.

The two principles are self-confronting. The best compromise is to have only adequate polling points that are necessary and sufficient. Here are the considerations.

- Object allocation site must be a safe point. An allocation may fail if the heap is full and then should trigger a collection to reclaim memory for the allocation.

- Polling points should be inserted at the sites that long-time execution may happen. Normally, if an application runs for a long time, it must have repetitive code sequence, either with loop or through recursive call. Therefore, it is important to have polling points at loop-back site and method call site.

- The last site that should have safe point is the blocking or sleeping site, where the thread cannot make progress. The blocked (or sleeping) thread cannot respond to a collection trigger event, but it should allow the collection to happen by preparing its state before going to sleep or be blocking.

Other than the aspect of execution time control, it is helpful to think about the safe-point site selection in another way. We can consider the selection strategy with regard to the stack state.

When a mutator is suspended for GC, the stack of the mutator consists of stack frames of invoked methods, with the bottom frame for main() if it is the main thread of a Java application. Every stack frame is at a call site except the top one. The top stack frame is either at an object allocation site that triggers the GC, or at a state of long running (in a loop) or blocking (at a system call). All those sites should be safe points with stack information prepared for root enumeration.

In actual implementation, safe region is used to support the blocking (and sleeping) situation. Since a thread has no way to poll the GC flag if the flag is set when the thread is already in blocking state, safe region is needed to allow the collection to continue. Safe region refers to the section of code that the enumeration context is prepared when the thread enters the region, and there are no references mutated within the region. In other words, it is safe for root-set enumeration and object tracing at any points of the region. Safe region can be viewed as a big-extended safe point.

When the mutator resumes from blocking and before it leaves the safe region, it checks if a collection is undergoing. If the answer is yes, the mutator stays in the safe region by suspending itself as in a safe point till the collection finishes. If there is no collection undergoing when the mutator resumes from blocking, it can proceed to leave the region.

Below is the pseudocode for a collector to suspend all the mutators for root-set enumeration.

```
stop_the_world_root_set_enumeration()
{
    vm_suspend_all_threads();
    for ( each thread tvar ) {
        vm_enumerate_roots_in_thread( tvar );
    }
    vm_enumerate_root_in_globals();   //in global data
}
```

The following pseudocode is a typical implementation of a polling point.

```
void gc_polling_point()
{
    VM_Thread* self = current_thread();
    if( !self->suspend_event )
        return;

    self->at_safe_point = true;
    wait_for_resume( self->resume_event );
    self->at_safe_point = false;
}
```

The following pseudocode is a typical implementation of entry and exit of a safe region.

```
void gc_safe_region_enter()
{
    VM_Thread* self = current_thread();
    self->at_safe_point = true;
}

void gc_safe_region_exit()
{
    VM_Thread* self = current_thread();
    if( !self->suspend_event )
        return;

    wait_for_resume( tself->resume_event );
    self->at_safe_point = false;
}
```

The actual control for thread interactions between collectors and mutators can be much more complex, but the concept is the same. We will discuss the topic in depth later in Chapter 6.

5.6 COMMON TRACING GC ALGORITHMS

After object tracing marks all the live objects in the heap, the collector recycles the dead objects.

According to how to recycle the dead objects, there are basically two kinds of collection algorithms. One is to sweep the dead objects after the object-marking phase, which is called mark-sweep GC. The other is to move all the live objects to a new space and then the left space is free, which is called trace-copy GC.

5.6.1 Mark Sweep

Figure 5.2 illustrates mark-sweep collection process.

In mark-sweep GC, there are at least two passes, one for marking and the other for sweeping. A collection is triggered when the heap is full. After collection, the freed

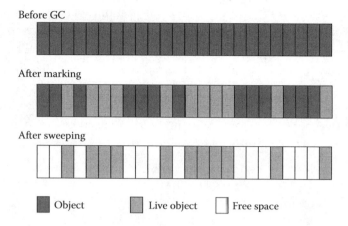

FIGURE 5.2   States of the heap in different stages of mark-sweep GC.

spaces are labeled for new object allocation. The pseudocode for mark-sweep GC is like below.

```
void mark_sweep()
{
   pass1:
    traverse_object_graph()
   pass2:
    sweep_space();
}
```

5.6.2 Trace Copy

Trace-copy GC integrates the two passes into one. It basically has two spaces, one is for allocation and the other is reserved for copying. Once it marks a live object, it moves it to the reserved space and then continues with other objects by traversing the object connection graph. Figure 5.3 below illustrates trace-copy collection process.

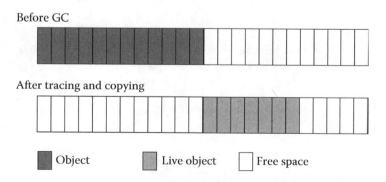

FIGURE 5.3   States of the heap in different stages of trace-copy GC.

When the collection finishes, the roles of allocation space and reserved space are switched. Mutators will then allocate new objects in the allocation space and triggers another round of collection once it is full.

Apparently, trace-copy GC has benefits of single pass, better data locality with adjacent live objects, and contiguous free space for faster object allocation. The downside is it has to reserve enough space for object copying. A conservative design reserves half heap, in case that most of the objects are live. This algorithm variation is then called semi-space GC. As a contrast, mark-sweep GC is "in-place collection," that is, it does not need extra space for collection.

In trace-copy GC, when an object is copied to the reserved space, the original copy remains in the allocation space because some other objects may still reference it. A pointer (called forwarding pointer) to the new copy is installed in the original copy, so that other objects can find the new address from the original copy. Other objects that have a reference to the original copy should update their references to point to the new copy. The pseudo-code for trace-copy GC is like below.

```
void trace_copy()
{
    stack mark_stack = load_root_set();

    while ( !stack_is_empty(mark_stack) ){
        Object** slot = stack_pop( mark_stack );
        Object* ovar = *slot;
        Object* new_ovar = null;

        if( obj_is_copied(ovar) ){
            //ovar has been copied
            new_ovar = forwarding_pointer(ovar);
            // update slot pointing to new addr
            *slot = new_ovar;
            continue;
        }
        mark_object( ovar );
        //copy ovar, install forwarding pointer in ovar
        new_ovar = copy_object( ovar );
        // update slot pointing to new addr
        *slot = new_ovar;
        for (each reference slot **pref** in **new_ovar**){
            stack_push( mark_stack, pref );
        }
    }
}
```

Note a nonobvious change in this algorithm from the one in `traverse_object_graph()`. That is, the element type of the marking stack (`mark_stack`) is not object reference (expressed in type `Object*`), but slot address that contains object reference, that is, reference slot (expressed in type `Object**`). This change is critical because the value in the slot needs to be updated if the referenced object is moved. Therefore, the first statement is `load_root_set()` instead of `load_root_references()` as used before.

5.7 VARIANTS OF COMMON TRACING GCs

There is no single GC algorithm that can perform best with all applications. Which algorithm to use depends on the target application's behavior. In this section, we discuss a few tracing GC variants by modifying the mark-sweep and trace-copy algorithms.

5.7.1 Mark-Compact

With mark-sweep GC, we can change the sweeping to be compacting, hence to leave a contiguous free space. The idea is to move all the live objects to one end of the heap, as Figure 5.4 below shows. This algorithm is called mark-compact GC.

Although mark-compact GC has the benefits of contiguous free space, the cost is the extra object movement, compared to mark-sweep GC. Therefore, it is usually not used as a standalone algorithm in a GC implementation but in combination with other collection algorithm.

5.7.2 Slide-Compact

Mark-compact algorithm can be designed in a way that the live objects maintain the same order in heap before and after the compaction. That is to move objects in linear order according to their original heap addresses. This variant is called slide-compact GC. Its cache locality is usually better than trace copy. Trace copy moves objects in the order of how the live objects are reached during the object-graph traversal, which is usually different from the original heap address order. The original heap address order usually means the object allocation order and also the object access order. Maintaining this order implies good access locality.

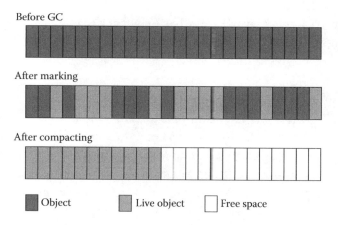

FIGURE 5.4   States of the heap in different stages of mark-compact GC.

A typical slide-compact GC has to add two additional passes in the collection process. One pass computes the new locations for all the surviving objects and the other pass updates all the references in live objects to point to the new locations of their referenced objects. It needs the extra pass because, as an in-place moving-GC, the order of objects movement is critical to correctness. Otherwise, moving a live object may overwrite another live object before the latter has been moved. The pseudocode of slide-compact GC is given below.

```
void slide_compact()
{
    pass1:
     traverse_object_graph();
    pass2:
     compute_new_locations();
    pass3:
     fix_object_references();
    pass4:
     compact_space();
}
```

Note the extra passes and the order of the passes are not mandatory for a slide-compact GC. We will discuss various optimizations on it later in Chapter 15.

5.7.3 Trace Forward

A variant of trace-copy GC does not flip the roles of allocation space and reserved space every time. Instead, it always uses one space for allocation and another space for copying. We call it trace-forward GC. This is based on the observation that some applications have only small ratio of live objects when the heap is full. It does not need to reserve half heap for copying, as shown in Figure 5.5.

In every collection, live objects are forwarded to the reserved space. The old objects that have been forwarded in past collections do not participate in the forwarding in current round of collection. After a few rounds of collections, the reserved space is not enough to hold the forwarded objects; the collection has to fallback to an in-place GC algorithm such as mark-compact.

5.7.4 Mark-Copy

A hybrid algorithm between trace-forward and mark-compact is mark-copy. It marks all the live objects without forwarding them during the marking process. Instead, the mark-copy algorithm uses a second pass to copy the marked objects (live objects) to the reserved space, so it is not an in-place collection algorithm. The benefit of mark-copy compared to mark-compact is that it can combine the passes of fixing references and moving objects because the referenced objects are not overwritten by the object movement. The new locations of forwarded objects can be found through forwarding pointers in the original copies.

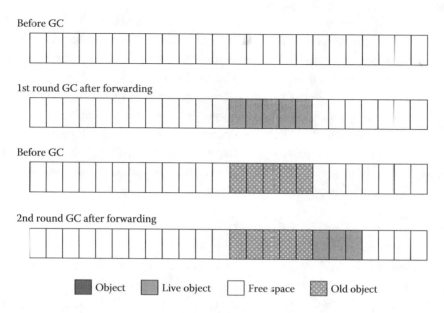

Before GC

1st round GC after forwarding

Before GC

2nd round GC after forwarding

■ Object   ▨ Live object   □ Free space   ▧ Old object

FIGURE 5.5   States of the heap in different stages of trace-forward GC.

```
void mark_copy()
{
   pass1:
    traverse_object_graph();
   pass2:
    compute_new_locations();
   pass3:
    compact_space();
}
```

In an extreme case of mark-copy collection, the reserved free space can be as small as a single page (or any other arbitrary size depending on the design). We call it the "seed page." The live objects in one or more pages can be evacuated to the seed page and then those evacuated pages are freed and can act as the reserved free pages for other used pages. This design benefits from both compaction and copying collections while reserving very small free space for copying. The feature is especially useful in concurrent collection where heap is recycled part by part. We will discuss concurrent moving collection in Chapter 17.

5.7.5 Generational Collection

In trace-forward collection, although the old objects do not participate in object forward-ing, it has to participate in object marking; otherwise, GC cannot correctly find all the live objects in the allocation space. There are two ways for the old objects to participate in object marking. One is the same as the objects in the allocation space except that the reached old objects (i.e., live) are not forwarded, as in regional GC. The other way does not trace the old objects at all but uses remember set as in generational GC.

Generational GC is designed based on the observation that the survival objects from last collection are usually live longer. The GC does not spend time tracing them again in next collection but assumes they are all live. It requires to record all the references from the old objects to new objects in remember set as part of root references.

As Figure 5.6 shows, the allocation space is now generation 1 (or called young generation, or nursery, etc.), and the forwarding space is generation 2 (or old generation, mature generation, etc.). Since GC does not trace into generation 2, all the references to generation 2 are ignored as shown in dotted arrows. Objects in generation 2 are not recycled at all. GC only needs to care about the references to generation 1, which includes the references from execution context and generation 2, shown in solid arrows.

5.7.5.1 Remember Set and Write-Barrier
In a generational collection with heap layout as shown in Figure 5.6, the references to generation 1 are kept in two sets, one is the root-set from the execution context and the other is the remember set from the generation 2. Root-set is got from enumeration in the execution context. Remember set is got, depending on the algorithm, from last time collection and from write-barrier. We call the part of remember-set got in a collection "collector remember set" and the part got with write-barrier "mutator remember set," respectively. Figure 5.7 shows all the references to generation 1.

Collector remember set holds the references that are recorded during last time collection. Some GC algorithms choose not to forward all the live objects from generation 1 to generation 2 but to keep some live objects in generation 1. When other objects are forwarded to generation 2, the references from the forwarded objects (in generation 2) to the nonforwarded objects (in generation 1) become cross-generation references and should be remembered by the collector.

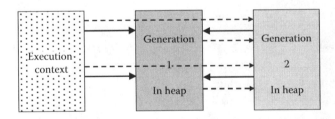

FIGURE 5.6   Generations in heap and references from/to generations.

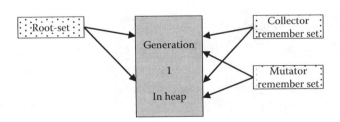

FIGURE 5.7   Root-set and remember sets.

Mutator remember set holds the references that are recorded during application execution after last collection. The application may write some cross-generation references from generation 2 to generation 1 during its execution. Those references can be caught by write-barrier, which is a callback function called whenever a reference is written to heap. Write-barrier checks if the written reference is from generation 2 to generation 1 and records it if the answer is yes. Code below is an example implementation of write-barrier. It is called when reference ovar is written into slot.

```
void write_barrier(Object** slot, Object* ovar)
{
    if ( slot is in old-generation){
        if ( ovar is in young-generation)
            mutator_remember( slot );
    }
}
```

Similar to RC instrumentation, write-barrier is inserted by the compiler for every reference write in heap. JNI code needs to follow the convention as well.

When the application executes operations of object clone or array copy, there is no need to use write-barrier for every reference write. A single write-barrier can be implemented to record all the reference writes to the object.

It is possible to use virtual memory support of the underlying operating system to implement write-barrier implicitly rather than instrumenting every reference write operation. That is, GC protects the memory pages of generation 2 and then every write to them causes a page fault. The fault handler acts as the write-barrier and will process the remembering operation.

Note write-barrier usually records the slot address (slot) rather than the reference itself (ovar). The reason is the slot can be written again soon before next collection and then the reference value is replaced by a new one. The object referenced by the old value ovar may be dead at the time of collection; hence, there is no need to remember it. Write-barrier here only tells GC that the recorded slot may hold a cross-generation reference. It is GC's responsibility to check the actual value in the slot during collection.

5.7.5.2 Cart-Table and Remember-Set Enumeration

Remember set can effectively reduce the tracing time in generation 2. A question is how to store the remember set. A straightforward solution is to allocate runtime data structure in VM, which may incur big memory overhead when there are lots of cross-generation reference writes.

An alternative solution is not to store the slot address for every reference write but to label the slot in heap to indicate that the slot may contain a cross-generation reference. Furthermore, GC can label the heap area (such as a page) where the slot locates, rather than label every slot individually. When a collection happens, GC will enumerate those labeled areas to find the slots that contain cross-generation references. This is remember-set enumeration, similar to what GC does with root-set enumeration.

The implementation of remember-set enumeration depends on the design of heap data structure. For instance, in some design, the heap is arranged in page granularity that each page has a page header to store the metadata of the page. When a reference write happens in the old generation during application execution, write-barrier can mark a bit in the header of the page where the written object stays. The bit indicates that this page has a slot that may contain cross-generation reference. When a collection happens, GC scans this page to check the objects one by one, find out the cross-generation references. This technique is called "card-table" or "card marking." The page in this example is a card. It is a special implementation of remember set, which in turn is a special form of RC.

Compared to remember set, card-table trades enumeration time for memory overhead. Since card-table only needs to know if a heap area is written, it is possible to reuse operating system (OS) support that a written page is labeled dirty in its page table entry. In this way, there is no need to implement write-barrier in VM but to read the page table's dirty bits for remember-set enumeration. Since the mutator remember set should be emptied after a collection, the page table's dirty bits should be reset as well in a collection.

Again there is no single algorithm always out-performing others. It is all decided by how well the application's behavior matches with the GC algorithm.

5.8 MOVING-GC VERSUS NONMOVING GC

Mark-sweep GC does not move the objects, thus is a nonmoving GC. Copying or compacting GCs are moving-GC. In this section, we discuss a few pros and cons of them.

5.8.1 Data Locality

With nonmoving collection, live objects are interleaved with the dead objects and free space. Accesses to live objects are scattered across the memory, leading to poor data locality.

Moving-GC can move live objects together, which solves the scattered access problem. The cost is it needs to copy objects from old locations to new locations and subsequently to fix all the stale references to point to new locations.

5.8.2 Bump-Pointer Allocation

After moving live objects away, moving-GC leaves a contiguous free space, which makes object allocation super easy and fast.

Moving-GC can use an allocation pointer that points to current free position in the free space. When it allocates an object, moving-GC simply bumps the allocation pointer with the object size. This is called "bump-pointer allocator," whose pseudocode is given below. A ceiling pointer is used to guard the border condition when the free space runs out.

```
typedef struct Allocator{
    void* free;
    void* ceiling;
} Allocator;
```

```
Object* object_alloc(int size, Allocator* allocator)
{
        int free =(int)allocator->free;
        int ceiling = (int) allocator->ceiling;

        int new_free = size + free;
        if ( new_free > ceiling)
                return null;

        allocator->free = (void*)new_free;
        return (Object*)free;
}
```

With contiguous free space, it is also easy to accommodate large object allocation.

5.8.3 Free-List and Allocation Bitmap

For nonmoving GC, bump-pointer allocation is hard to achieve. The free space can be quickly fragmented into fine-grained blocks after a collection. Nonmoving GC usually arranges the free blocks into a free list. A new allocation picks a block off the list that meets the size requirement. If the block is bigger than the object size, the remaining part after allocation can be put back to the free list. After a collection, the free list is reconstructed.

The efficiency of list traversal and manipulation is much slower than bumping a pointer. A workaround, similar to card marking for remember set, is not to use dedicated free-list data structure but to use some bits in the heap to indicate available blocks. The implementation, for example, can use the page header as a bitmap where one bit corresponds to certain unit size in the page. Bit value 1 means the unit is allocated, 0 means it is free. Some microprocessor can identify the first 1 or 0 bit position in a word with one instruction, which can be used to examine the bitmap, thus find free units in the page quickly.

5.8.4 Size-Segregated List

To make nonmoving GC's allocation faster, size-segregated list, instead of free list, is more often used. The idea is to arrange the heap into blocks, one block for objects of a specified size. The size is called the "slot size" of the block. A block only holds objects of its slot size. The slot size of block can start from a small value like 8 bytes up to a big number like 1 kB, with a fixed or variable increments. An object is allocated in a block with best-fit slot size, that is, equal to or nearest bigger than the object size. Objects with size bigger than the maximal slot size are allocated separately, but not in the blocks.

When application allocates an object of certain size, while there is no free block of best-fit slot size available, a free block is allocated from the global free space. The free block is assigned a matching slot size for the object allocation.

When a collection is triggered, there can be many blocks of certain slot sizes, and no blocks of other slot sizes. After a collection, some blocks may have no live objects remaining. These blocks can be returned to the global free space.

In the block header, there is a bitmap to indicate the status of the block space usage or object allocation, one bit (or a set of bits) for one slot. When a bit has value 1, the corresponding slot has been allocated for an object; otherwise, it is free.

5.8.5 Mark Bits and Allocation Bits

After a collection, there are only live objects in a block, whose status should be reflected in the bitmap to indicate the space usage. That is, a slot that holds a live object after a collection should have its allocation bit set before mutator's execution.

If object tracing also uses the block header bitmap to indicate the objects marking status, the bits for live objects marking after a collection can act as the bits for object allocation before application execution. Based on this observation, a natural design is to reuse the mark bits as allocation bits after a collection. In this design, there are two bits for each slot, one for allocation bit and the other for mark bit. Their roles are flipped after a collection.

The bits are used in the following way:

1. Right after a collection, the bitmap has all the bits set 0 except some allocation bits are 1, indicating those slots are taken. During the execution, more allocation bits are set 1 with more objects allocated in the block.

2. When a collection happens, the mark bits are used when GC is tracing the objects. Bit with value 1 means the corresponding slot holds a live object.

3. When object tracing finishes, all the live objects are marked in the bitmap. The slots with mark bit value 0 hold dead objects that can be recycled. GC clears the allocation bits of those slots. This effectively does the job of "sweeping."

4. After the collection finishes and before application execution resumes, GC flips the role of allocation bit and mark bit. That is, the mark bits are then used as allocation bit in following application execution. The process goes back to bullet 1.

Figure 5.8 illustrates the design in steps.

5.8.6 Thread-Local Allocation

Bump-pointer allocation is only possible when the free space is owned by single thread. If there are multiple threads, the allocation should be thread safe. The bump pointer has to be modified atomically, as the pseudocode below.

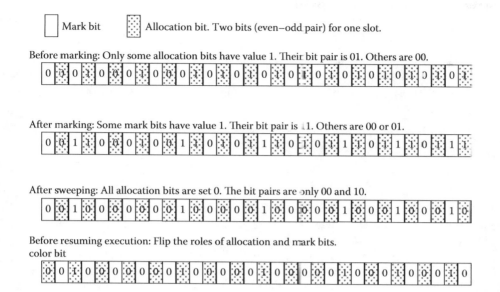

□ Mark bit   ▦ Allocation bit. Two bits (even–odd pair) for one slot.

Before marking: Only some allocation bits have value 1. Their bit pair is 01. Others are 00.

After marking: Some mark bits have value 1. Their bit pair is 11. Others are 00 or 01.

After sweeping: All allocation bits are set 0. The bit pairs are only 00 and 10.

Before resuming execution: Flip the roles of allocation and mark bits.
color bit

FIGURE 5.8   Bitmap design for block that has single slot size.

```
Object* cbject_alloc(int size, Allocator* allocator)
{
  int ceiling = (int) allocator->ceiling;
  int free, new_free;
  do{
     free = allocator->free;
     new_free = size + free;
     if ( new_free > ceiling)
        return null;

     bool ok = CompareExchange(&allocator->free, free, new_free);
  }while( !ok );

  return (Object*)free;
}
```

To use atomic instruction for every object allocation is too expensive. A typical solution is to use it only for block allocation. Every thread grabs a free block from the global free space with atomic instruction and then uses bump pointer for object allocation in the block without atomic instruction. The block is thread local for allocation.

Heap arranged in size-segregated list can also benefit from thread-local block. Every block is owned by a single thread for object allocation. Otherwise, multiple threads have to use atomic instruction to compete for a slot in a shared block.

Thread-local block cannot be too small in size. Allocation of a block from global free space requires atomic instruction. Frequent block allocations would defeat the purpose of thread-local block. However, block size cannot be too big, if there are many threads in the application. Some threads may be inactive in object allocation, hence wastes the block space with only a few objects in a block.

5.8.7 Hybrid of Moving and Nonmoving GC

Although size-segregated list supports fast allocation, it is possible that a GC cannot find a free block of best-fit slot size for a new object allocation while there are lots of free slots in other slot-sized blocks. It may introduce three kinds of memory fragmentations:

- Inner-block fragmentation. If the slot sizes of blocks are not incremented by one word, a block's slot size may be bigger than the size of objects allocated in it. Then every slot may waste one or more words space.

- Interblock fragmentation. Application's object sizes can distribute unevenly, so that some slot sizes may use many blocks, whereas some other slot sizes may have only a few objects. Even if a slot size has only one object, a block of that slot size has to be allocated. The block space is then wasted.

- Interthread fragmentation. Every thread grabs its own thread-local blocks. One thread may allocate lots of objects in certain size, whereas another thread may allocate only a few objects in same size. The block space is wasted since the blocks are not shared between threads.

The fragmentation problem becomes more serious if the block size is big. To solve the problem, moving algorithm can be introduced to a nonmoving GC.

There are usually a few hybrid approaches between moving and nonmoving GC.

For different collections: One hybrid is to use different algorithms in different collections. For example, when the space is too much fragmented after rounds of mark-sweep collections, GC can use a compacting collection to pack the blocks of same slot sizes.

The compacting collection moves the objects of same size to those blocks of same slot size that are partially full. After the compaction, for every slot size, only one block is partially full. All other blocks of same slot size are either full or free. The free blocks are returned to global free space. This can help alleviate the fragmentation problem.

For different heap spaces: Moving and nonmoving algorithm can also work together to manage different parts of the heap. For example in a generational GC, moving algorithm can be used for the young generation, while nonmoving algorithm for the mature generation.

This is reasonable. The young generation usually has high dead ratio. It means the number of its surviving objects in a collection usually is small. It is worth to move small number of objects while leaving a large free space. However, the mature generation is only for young generation's surviving objects allocation, which is much less intensive than mutator's object allocation. As a result, the fragmentation issue of the mature generation with a nonmoving GC can be tolerable.

For different objects: A moving-GC may also need the help of nonmoving algorithm, since it cannot simply support conservative GC that is needed by some languages. These languages do not have precise root-set. For example, they may store an object reference in an integer. When scanning application execution context, GC has to conservatively treat any datum that looks like a reference as reference. Since the ambiguous references can be actually integers, objects pointed by these ambiguous references should not be moved; otherwise, the integers in the slots will be incorrectly changed. A solution is to allow pinning objects in a moving-GC, so that the objects pointed by ambiguous references are pinned, that is, not moved. This is a hybrid of moving and nonmoving GC.

CHAPTER 6

Design of Threading

M OST PROGRAMMING LANGUAGES SUPPORT threading (i.e., multithreaded programming), either in language construct (such as Thread in Java) or through external
library (such as Pthreads in C). Language construct is a preferred approach because, as a
language feature, its semantics can be guaranteed for both portability and security. Some
researchers argue that threads cannot be implemented as a library without any issue.

When a language has threading construct, it is the virtual machine's (VM) responsibility to implement the support. Since a VM usually runs as a user application that does not
have access to system task scheduling, a VM implementation often relies on operating system (OS) functionality for full threading support. The application programming interfaces
(APIs) for threading in different OSes may be different, but they provide similar fundamental functionalities. The most common features are thread creation, mutex (two-way synchronization), conditional variables (one-way synchronization), and atomic operations. We use
Java VM (JVM) as an example to discuss how these common features are used to implement
Java Thread. First of all, we should answer what a thread is.

6.1 WHAT IS A THREAD

A thread is nothing but a control flow of execution. It is a concept only valid in control-flow
machine, which is the case for almost all current processors.

Control flow is the execution of a sequence of instructions. To represent a control flow,
two entities are essential: the program counter and the stack pointer. Program counter
points to the **next** instruction to execute in the sequence. Stack pointer points to the **next**
location to store temporary execution result. Program counter and stack pointer together
can uniquely identify a control flow of execution. They normally cannot be shared with
other threads; otherwise, incorrect result can be caused by either messed instruction or
messed data. All of other computing resources can be shared between threads, such as
heap, code, and processor. The reason is those resources are not necessarily sequentially
accessed. Due to the uniqueness to a thread, program counter and stack pointer together
are called thread context.

Thread context means that if a system provides threading support, it should at least provide a way to distinguish one thread context from another. The distinct thread contexts can be implemented in software, hardware, or their hybrid. If they are provided in processor hardware, the thread is called hardware thread. Different hardware threads can share same processor pipeline or use different pipelines, depending on the design. The former is called simultaneous multithreading (SMT). Hyperthreading (HT) is an implementation of SMT. A control-flow processor must provide at least one hardware thread context; otherwise, there would be no control flow.

If the processor has only one thread context, it does not support hardware multithreading. Then the multithreading can be provided by software. That is, multiple software threads can multiplex over the same hardware thread context. When a software thread is scheduled to run, its context is loaded into the hardware thread context. If it is scheduled off the processor, its context is stored somewhere else to give way to next scheduled software thread. This is called context switch.

Now that multiple software threads can share the same hardware context, it is not hard to think that a software thread context can also be multiplexed by another level of multiple software threads. Conceptually, software threads can be built with infinite levels, every higher level threads multiplex the contexts of its next level threads. It is called M : 1 mapping if multiple higher level threads multiplex one thread context in its next level.

It is possible to build 1 : 1 mapping and M : N mapping. They are just special forms of M : 1 mapping. 1 : 1 mapping is useful when the lower level threading capability is adequate to the higher level, whereas the higher level cannot directly use that capability without the mapping. For example, the lower and upper levels can be from hardware to software, from kernel to user land, from OS to VM, and so on.

M : N mapping refers to the case when multiple threads multiplex multiple contexts. For example, a multiple-core processor has multiple hardware thread contexts, one on each core; when it executes multiple software threads, each software thread can be scheduled to any of the cores. The result is M software threads running on N hardware cores.

Due to the levels of threading support, when we talk about a thread, we should specify which level it is. A thread in one level may contain multiple threads of upper level.

In reality, it is not very useful to build many levels of threads. Usually, there are no more than three levels. Level 2 shares the hardware context of level 1, and level 3 shares the software context of level 2.

In Linux design, kernel threads (software threads) multiplex hardware contexts in M : N mapping, and glibc's user threads use kernel thread contexts in 1 : 1 mapping. Some systems have M : N or M : 1 mapping between user threads and kernel threads, such as GNU Portable Threads, and Windows Fiber. But these features are either not commonly used or only used in special situations.

Note, process is an irrelevant concept in this context, although process is often confused with thread. Thread is mainly about the "control flow of an execution," whereas process is mainly about "memory space isolation." If two threads run in separated memory spaces, they are considered running in different processes. In Linux kernel, all the tasks share the kernel memory space; so there are no processes in kernel level but kernel threads. Process only exists in user land where isolated virtual memory space is established for each process. It is not completely wrong to talk about process in kernel context, but then a process actually refers to the kernel thread that is 1 : 1 mapped to a user process.

6.2 KERNEL THREAD AND USER THREAD

The second question in threading design that immediately follows the thread context one is how to switch the thread context between threads, that is, the design of thread scheduling.

If the threading is completely implemented in software, the thread scheduling is conducted in software. To avoid starving other threads by one thread long time occupying the thread context, software threading design has to guarantee there are chances to conduct the switch operation. An easy way is to leverage regular hardware interrupt. Once a thread receives a hardware interrupt (mostly timer), it traps to the interrupt handler and, within the handler, it schedules the threads by storing current thread context, and loading next thread context. When the execution resumes from the interrupt handler, it continues with the new thread execution.

Sometimes, timer is not enough. In a M : 1 mapping, all the software threads at higher level are treated as a single thread at the lower level. Therefore, they are scheduled as one thread at the lower level. That means they together share the time slice of a single thread at the lower level. If the lower level thread is scheduled off the processor, none of the higher level threads contained in it can continue execution. This is a common issue of M : 1 mapping.

As a consequence, when the current thread is sleeping (i.e., scheduled off the processor), no other threads can be scheduled to execute before a timer interrupts the sleep. The lower level scheduler only sees one sleeping thread, and it does not know there are many ready threads sharing the same thread context (and one time slice). This is undesirable because the computing resource is idle and wasted while some threads are ready to run. A straightforward solution is, if a thread is going to sleep, it invokes the scheduler voluntarily. The scheduler then can switch the context to next thread. This is called yield. It is similar to the garbage collection polling point before the application invokes a blocking system call.

When the sleeping thread yields, it only sleeps in the eyes of its level's thread scheduler. In the eyes of the lower-level thread scheduler, it may see the thread continues execution without sleeping, since it regards all the upper level threads as a single thread. Yielding for a blocking operation needs support in the blocking operation implementation. For example, the sleep operation now includes two actions: One is to schedule the thread off the context and put into sleeping status; and the other is to schedule another thread onto the context. In other words, the blocking operation at upper level is actually nonblocking at lower level.

Nonblocking operation cannot solve the wasted one time slice issue in M : 1 mapping. No matter how well the thread scheduler is designed at the upper level, it at best can only guarantee the shared one time slice is fully utilized without any waste. It cannot get more time slices than a single lower-level thread can get. Only the lowest level threading has the control of all the available time slices. That is the kernel threads in Linux OS. If a higher level threading wants to use as much resource as possible, it has to leverage the kernel threading support. This is the reason why there is usually no more than one additional level of threading above kernel threads, unless the upper level threading uses 1 : 1 mapping, which keeps the scheduling benefits of kernel threads. M : N or M : 1 mapping above the kernel thread level is not very useful with regard to resource utilization but increases design complexity.

Figure 6.1 below shows the typical threading design in current OSs.

The typical threading design has three levels. The bottom level is the hardware threading in processor. Every core has one or more thread contexts. The middle level is the kernel threads that multiplex the hardware threads. If the hardware is a single-core single-thread processor, the mapping between kernel threads and the hardware threads is M : 1. Otherwise, if the hardware has more contexts, the mapping is M : N. The mapping is implemented by the OS kernel scheduler.

The top level is the native threads that run in user land. The mapping between native threads and kernel threads are usually 1 : 1, for the reason we have described above. The mapping is implemented by glibc with a user wrapper of kernel threads. Native threads are usually considered the level of threads provided by OSs in user space, hence sometimes also called OS threads.

The threading libraries on top of native threads are usually called user-level threads or green threads, which are not very popular today, although user-level threads have their own advantages in some scenarios.

For instance, in an M : 1 mapping user-level thread design, multiple user threads never run in parallel on multiple cores because they are just single thread at kernel level or hardware level, sharing single-thread context of lower level. Then there is no need to use atomic instruction for the user threads programming. For this reason, M : 1 mapping is sometimes used as a quick and simple threading design for scripting language VMs, such as Ruby.

The other example of M : 1 mapping user-level thread design is in input or output (I/O) intensive environment. The user-level threading can provide nonblocking I/O operations to multiple ongoing tasks. These tasks are actually running in one native thread and cannot run in truly parallel on multicore processor. It is not a problem in the environment because these tasks are not CPU-intensive, but mostly waiting for I/O. The shared time slice of one native thread is good enough. This is the model used by Node.js.

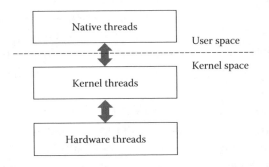

FIGURE 6.1 Typical threading design in modern operating systems.

6.3 MAPPING OF VM THREAD TO OS THREAD

To implement safe-language's thread construct, the most productive way is to use 1 : 1 mapping between its VM threads and OS threads (native threads). Other mappings usually do not add value, unless there is special language requirement for certain domain.

Java thread is defined in the same way as traditional (and classic) thread, as quoted from Java Language Specification: "Java Virtual Machine can support many threads of execution at once. These threads independently execute code that operates on values and objects residing in a shared main memory. Threads may be supported by having many hardware processors, by time slicing a single hardware processor, or by time-slicing many hardware processors." As defined in JVM specification, each JVM thread has its own pc (program counter) register and JVM stack; JVM has a heap that is shared among all JVM threads. This definition makes 1 : 1 mapping the best choice.

Following code is a typical definition of VM thread structure to support JVM thread.

```
struct VM_Thread {
    void* os_thread;        // OS thread handle
    Object* java_thread;    // JVM thread handle

    uint32 tid;             // JVM thread identifier
    volatile int status;    // JVM thread state
    int priority;           // thread priority
    bool is_daemon;         // daemon or not
    // other additional fields will be introduced later
}
```

As Java API specification says, invoking `Thread.start()` will start the thread execution from the `run()` method of the Thread instance. So we need to implement two wrappers, one for `Thread.run()` and the other one for `Thread.start()`. Following pseudocode gives a conceptual design.

`Thread.start()` starts a thread execution.

```
//when the method is called, java Thread object is argument
void thread_start(Object* jthread)
{
    //create the VM_Thread data structure
    VM_Thread* kthread = vmthread_data_init( );

    if ( !jthread || !kthread) {
        vm_throw_exception("NullPointerException");
    }

    if (kthread->status != THREAD_STATE_STARTED){
        vm_throw_exception("IllegalThreadStateException");
    }
    //connect the Java and VM threads data/objects
```

```
    bind_java_and_vm_thread(kthread, jthread);
    set_init_java_thread_priority(jthread);
    //lock here, unlock in thread_run()
    global_thread_lock();
    //create the thread execution from thread_run()
    kthread->os_thread =
        os_thread_create(thread_run, kthread);

    return;
}
```

Thread.run() is invoked in a new thread context by Thread.start().

```
unsigned STDCALL thread_run(VM_Thread* kthread )
{
    //set thread status
    kthread->status = THREAD_STATE_RUNNING;
    // the locking part is in thread_start()
    global_thread_unlock();

    //find out the method struct of Thread.run()
    vm_string* sname = string_pool_lookup("run");
    vm_string* sdesc = string_pool_lookup("()V");
    Object* jthread = kthread->java_thread;
    vm_class* thread_class = object_get_class(jthread);
    vm_method* km_thread_run =
        class_lookup_method( thread_class, jname, jdesc);

    //execute Thread.run()
    vm_execute_java_method( km_thread_run, jthread, NULL);

    //exit thread
    destroy_thread_data(kthread);
    return 0;
}
```

Below is the thread state definition used in the conceptual code above.

```
enum thread_state{
    THREAD_STATE_UNKNOWN,    // Status is unknown
    THREAD_STATE_ZOMBIE,     // Completed execution
    THREAD_STATE_RUNNING,    // Thread is active
    THREAD_STATE_SLEEPING,   // Thread is sleeping
    THREAD_STATE_MONITOR,    // Waiting on a monitor
    THREAD_STATE_WAIT,       // Waiting on an object
    THREAD_STATE_STARTED     // Started before run
}
```

In the definition of thread state, the states are mutual exclusive, which is sometimes not very efficient or comprehensive enough. For example, when the application checks if a thread is alive, the VM returns true for all states except UNKNOWN and ZOMBIE. In some other JVM design such as Apache Harmony, the thread status is defined to be bit flag that can be combined. It actually designs the thread states in multiple layers. One layer is for running states (e.g., SLEEPING, RUNNING), and the other is for executed code type (e.g., IS_NATIVE), and yet another is for the grouped states (e.g., ALIVE).

In the example code for thread structure and states, there are data related to monitor and wait, which are the fundamental threading constructs that we discuss next.

6.4 SYNCHRONIZATION CONSTRUCTS

For multiple threads to cooperate, there have to be at least two fundamental synchronization constructs. One is to support mutual exclusive access to shared data. The other is to support conditional access to shared data. The former is usually implemented with lock (i.e., mutex). The latter is needed because mutual exclusion alone cannot productively implement the conditional access. For example with the classic producer–consumer problem, the producer only enqueues an item when the shared queue is not full. Following code is obviously incorrect.

```
while( true ){
      //producer locks the queue to check
      lock( Queue );
      while( Queue is full ){
            continue;
      }
      enqueue(Queue, Item);
      unlock( Queue );
}
```

The code is incorrect because when the producer locks the queue, the consumer cannot access the queue to consume the items hence to change the queue's status. If the queue is full, the producer will spin checking the queue's status forever, hence a live lock.

The following code is incorrect either.

```
while( true ){
      //producer checks the queue without lock
      while( Queue is full ){
            continue;
      }
      lock( Queue );
      enqueue(Queue, Item);
      unlock( Queue );
}
```

The above code only puts the enqueue operation into the critical section while leaving the condition checking outside. When one producer finds the condition is true and proceeds to the critical section, another producer may conduct the same operations and enqueues an item to the last vacant entry before current producer. Then the current producer continues to enqueue an item to a full queue, which is incorrect.

To avoid the race condition, the condition checking and the enqueue operations should both be protected by the lock. The following code provides a correct solution.

```
while( true ){
        //producer locks the queue to check
        lock( Queue );
        while( Queue is full ){
                unlock( Queue );
                lock( Queue );
        }
        enqueue(Queue, Item);
        unlock( Queue );
}
```

The code above semantically is correct, but it is not efficient, because the producer locks the queue immediately after it unlocks the queue in the busy loop. A consumer may not be able to get a chance to lock the queue for item consumption. As a result, the producer may loop for a long time uselessly.

A more efficient design usually inserts a `yield()` or `sleep(n)` for n milliseconds in the busy loop, to give away the CPU slice to other threads before it tries to lock again.

```
while( true ){
        //producer locks the queue to check
        lock( Queue );
        while( Queue is full ){
                unlock( Queue );
                yield(); //or sleep(n) for a period
                lock( Queue );
        }
        enqueue(Queue, Item);
        unlock( Queue );
}
```

The design pattern is very cumbersome and not flexible to deal with various conditions. It is better if the thread can sleep and only wakes up when the condition is satisfied, something like the code below.

```
while( true ){
        //producer locks the queue to check
        lock( Queue );
        while( Queue is full ){
                unlock( Queue );
                sleep_waiting( Queue is not full );
                lock( Queue );
        }
```

```
        enqueue(Queue, Item);
        unlock( Queue );
}
```

In this way, the producer does not waste CPU cycles but works when it is necessary. JVM defines monitor to achieve both mutual exclusive and conditional access.

6.5 MONITOR

Monitor consists of mutex and conditional variable.

6.5.1 Mutual Exclusion

In JVM, every object is associated with a monitor, and a thread uses bytecode instruction *monitorenter* and *monitorexit* to lock and unlock the monitor. The lock is re-entrant in that, if a thread locks it multiple times, it needs to unlock same times to reverse the effect. Every *synchronized* block or method in Java program is wrapped by a pair of *monitorenter* and *monitorexit* at the block/method's entrance and exit points.

To assist conditional access, each object is also associated with a wait queue. A thread is added into the queue and put to sleep when it invokes wait() method on the object, and is wakened up by other thread when the latter calls notify() or notifyAll() method on the object.

Back to the classic producer–consumer problem, with monitor bytecode, the pseudo-code looks like below conceptually.

```
while( true ){
        //producer locks the queue to check
        monitorenter( Queue );
        while( Queue is full ){
                monitorexit( Queue );
                sleep_waiting( Queue );
                monitorenter( Queue );
        }
        enqueue(Queue, Item);
        monitorexit( Queue );
}
```

Using synchronized keyword, the code can be rewritten in the following way.

```
while( true ){
        //producer locks the queue to check
        synchronized( Queue ){
            while( Queue.full() ){
                monitorexit( Queue );
                sleep_waiting( Queue );
                monitorenter( Queue );
            }
            Queue.enqueue(Item);
        }
}
```

6.5.2 Conditional Variable

The key point of Java wait () operation is that the thread invoking wait () on an object should have held the lock of the object monitor. The wait () operation releases the lock and puts the caller thread into sleep atomically. Once it is wakened up from sleeping, the thread automatically locks the object monitor. Therefore, wait () on an object actually includes following three operations.

```
object.wait():
        monitorexit( object );
        sleep_waiting( object );
        monitorenter( object );
```

With wait(), the Java code to implement a producer looks like below.

```
while( true ){
        synchronized( Queue ){
            while( Queue.full() ){
                Queue.wait();
            }
            Queue.enqueue(Item);
        }
}
```

The wait queue of a Java object is not associated with the condition for which the thread is waiting. It is possible that multiple threads waiting on the same object may be waiting for different conditions. It is the thread's own responsibility to check if its waited condition becomes true or not after it wakes up.

In the producer case, when the producer returns from Queue.wait() method, it has to check if Queue is full or not. If it is still full, the thread goes to wait() again. Otherwise, it can move forward to enqueue an item. The thread does not need to worry about atomicity between the condition check and the enqueue action because the lock is held already when it returns from wait().

A thread wakes up when the object it waits for receives a notification. The notification is delivered when other thread invokes either notify() or notifyAll() on the object. An interrupt to the waiting thread can also wake it up.

6.5.3 Monitorenter

To implement monitor in JVM, the key is to maintain the threads that are sleeping for locks and for conditions. A simple solution keeps the information in thread lists. Figure 6.2 shows the thread data structure that includes the fields for monitor support.

Every thread has a list of entered monitors (locked_obj_list), an object that it is blocked for locking (blocked_lock), and an object that it is waiting for a condition (waited_condition).

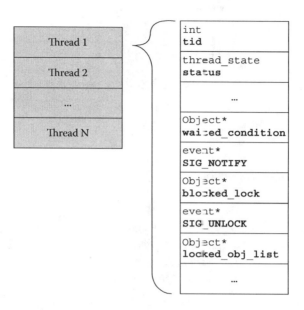

FIGURE 6.2   Data structure to implement JVM monitor.

We use a bit LOCK_BIT in the object header metadata to indicate the object is locked or not by a thread. If it is locked by a thread, it is recorded in the list of locked_obj_list of the thread. Locked_obj_list is a list of nodes of the following type.

```
struct Locked_obj{
{
    Object* jobject;    //the monitor object locked
    int recursion;      //times of recursive locking
    Locked_obj* next;   //next node in the list
}
```

The operational semantics of monitorenter are the following:

- Step 1. Check if the monitor is locked;

- Step 2. If the monitor is not locked, lock it and return;

- Step 3. If the monitor is locked, check if it is locked by self. If yes, increment the recursion number and return;

- Step 4. If the monitor is locked by other thread, wait to lock it again later.

The pseudocode for monitorenter can look like below.

```
void STDCALL vm_object_lock(Object* jmon)
{
    Locked_obj* plock = null;
    Locked_obj* head = thread_get_locked_obj_list();
```

```
// try non-blocking lock on the object;
// test&set the object LOCK_BIT.
bool result = lock_non_blocking(jmon);
if( !result ){
    //object is locked already
    //lookup current thread's locked_obj_list
    plock = lookup_in_locked_obj_list(head, jmon);
    if( plock->jobject == jmon){
        //locked by self thread, increment enter times
        plock->recursion++;
        return;
    }else{
        //locked by other thread, sleep on the monitor
        jmon = lock_blocking(jmon);
        //when it returns from sleep, it holds the lock
        //reload jmon in case moved by GC
    }
}
//Current thread holds the lock the first time
//Record the object in its locked_obj_list
plock = (Locked_obj*)vm_alloc(sizeof(Locked_obj));
plock->jobject = jmon;
plock->recursion = 0;
plock->next = head;
thread_insert_locked_obj_list(plock);

return;
}
```

The conceptual code for `lock_non_blocking()` is like below. It does not block the thread but returns success or failure from the locking operation. Note the code itself is incorrect, because the required atomic operation is not guaranteed. When multiple threads compete for locking, the result would be unexpected, for example, every thread believes it acquires the lock. We will show how to implement it correctly in atomic instruction later.

```
bool lock_non_blocking(Object* jmon)
{
    //assume the second word of an Object for lock metadata
    uint32* pheader = (uint32*)object_header_addr(jmon);
    uint32 lock_bit_mask = 1 << LOCK_BIT;
    { //the following operations should be atomic, such as
        //compare-exchange (or test-swap, or test-set)
        //we will discuss it later.
        uint32 orig_bit_val = (*pheader) & lock_bit_mask;
        *pheader |= lock_bit_mask;
    }
    return !orig_bit_val;
}
```

The reverse of lock_non_blocking() is lock_release(), which clears the LOCK_BIT of the object header, indicating the lock is free. Because only the lock owner can release the lock, it does not need to be atomic.

```
void lock_release(Object* jmon)
{
    uint32* pheader = (uint32*) object_header_addr(jmon);
    uint32 lock_bit_mask = 1 << LOCK_BIT
    *pheader &= ~lock_bit_mask;
}
```

The pseudo-code for lock_blocking() is given below.

```
Object* lock_blocking(Object* jmon)
{
    VM_Thread* self = thread_self();
    //try to hold the lock
    while( !lock_non_blocking(jmon) ){
        //cannot hold the lock, go to sleep
        //record the blocked lock
        self->blocked_lock = jmon;
        self->status = THREAD_STATE_MONITOR;
        //sleep waiting for wakeup
        wait_for_signal( self->SIG_UNLOCK, 0);
        //woken up by a thread that unlocks the monitor
        self->status = THREAD_STATE_RUNNING;
        //reload object, in case moved by GC
        jmon = self->blocked_lock;
        self->blocked_lock = null;
        //loop back competing for lock again
    }
    //finally hold the lock and then return
    return jmon;
}
```

When the lock is unavailable, the thread waits on an event self->SIG_UNLOCK. After it is wakened up from the waiting, the thread loops back to lock the monitor again. The function returns when the thread locks the monitor.

6.5.4 Monitorexit

Monitorexit is the reverse operation of monitorenter. Its operational semantics are the following:

- Step 1. Check if the lock is held by self;

- Step 2. If it is not locked by self, throw an exception for IllegalMonitorState and return;

- Step 3. If it is locked by self, check the recursion number. If the recursion number is bigger than zero, decrement it and return;

- Step 4. If recursion is zero, release the lock;

- Step 5. Check if there is any thread blocked waiting to lock the object; return if there is no waiting thread. If there is waiting thread, wake it up and return.

The pseudocode for `monitorexit` is given below.

```
void STDCALL vm_object_unlock(Object* jmon)
{
    //check if jmon is a locked object
    Locked_obj* plock = null;
    Locked_obj* head = thread_get_locked_obj_list();
    plock = lookup_in_locked_obj_list(head, jmon);

    if( !plock ) {
        //lock is not held by current thread
        vm_throw_exception("IllegalMonitorState");
    }
    //lock is held by current thread
    plock->recursion--;
    if (plock->recursion == -1) {
        //no longer holding the lock, release the lock record
        plock->jobject = null;
        delete_from_locked_obj_list(head, jmon);
        //clear the LOCK_BIT in object header
        //corresponding to lock_non_blocking()
        lock_release(jmon);
        //corresponding to lock_blocking()
        notify_blocking_threads(jmon);
    }
    return;
}
```

Only the locking thread can unlock the monitor. Therefore, the unlocking function is straightforward to implement without worrying about race condition. Once the monitor is unlocked, current unlocking thread needs to wake up the threads that are blocked waiting to lock the monitor. There is no specification about how many sleeping threads to wake up. No matter how many are wakened up, only one of them can win the lock in the competition. So it is ok to wake up one thread. The pseudocode for `notify_blocking_threads()` is like below.

```
void notify_blocking_threads(Object* jmon)
{
    VM_Thread* kthread = vm_thread_list();
    //iterate thread list to find the blocking thread
```

```
    for ( ; kthread != null; kthread = kthread->next){
        Object* blocked_lock = kthread->blocked_lock;
        if( blocked_lock == jmon ){
            //wake up the thread
            deliver_signal(kthread->SIG_UNLOCK);
            return;
        }
    }
    return;
}
```

In the monitor locking and unlocking implementation, the code uses OS support to wait for and deliver a signal. Every thread has two signals (or events) to communicate with other threads and OS kernel. In Windows system, the signals can be implemented as Event object. In Linux system, the signals can be implemented with condition variable. They should not be confused with Java methods Object.wait() and Object.notify(). One can regard them as similar constructs but at different levels.

This is not a surprise since monitor is a common fundamental thread synchronization construct. Current OSes have been designed either to support monitor directly or to support other constructs that can be used to implement monitor semantics easily. In other words, other system's synchronization constructs can also be built on top of JVM monitor, though not necessarily resulting with good performance or scalability.

6.5.5 Object.wait()

With monitor enter and exit implemented as above, object's wait() and notify() can be implemented in similar way. The only thing worth noting is that before unlocking the monitor in wait(), current thread should record the lock recursion number, so that when it reacquires the lock, the recursion number can be restored.

```
void object_wait(Object* jmon, unsigned int ms)
{
//check if jmon is a locked object
Locked_obj* plock = null;
Locked_obj* head = thread_get_locked_obj_list();
plock = lookup_in_locked_obj_list(head, jmon);

if( !plock ) {
        vm_throw_exception("IllegalMonitorState");
        return;
    }

    //record the jmon in current thread
    VM_Thread* self = thread_self();
    self->waited_condition = jmon;
    self->status= THREAD_STATE_WAIT;
```

```
        // release lock before waiting. Remember lock times
        int temp_recursion = plock->recursion;
        plock->recursion = 0;
        vm_object_unlock(jmon);

        bool signaled = wait_for_signal(self->SIG_NOTIFY, ms);
        //wake up
        self->status= THREAD_STATE_RUNNING;
        self->waited_condition = null;
        //re-acquire the lock, insert into locked_obj_list
        vm_object_lock(jmon);
        //restore the lock recursion number
        head = thread_get_locked_obj_list();
        //find the node
        plock = lookup_in_locked_obj_list(head, jmon);
        plock->recursion = temp_recursion;

        if(self->interrupted) {
            self->interrupted = false;
            vm_throw_exception("Interrupted");
        }
}
```

6.5.6 Object.notify()

The object notify() is very similar to notify_blocking_threads(jmon) except that it delivers a signal to the thread(s) that wait for SIG_NOTIFY, instead of SIG_UNLOCK.

```
void object_notify(Object* jmon)
{
//check if jmon is a locked object
Locked_obj* plock = null;
Locked_obj* head = thread_get_locked_obj_list();
plock = lookup_in_locked_obj_list(head, jmon);

if( !plock ) {
        vm_throw_exception("IllegalMonitorState");
        return;
    }

    VM_Thread* kthread = vm_thread_list();
//iterate thread list to find the blocking thread
for ( ; kthread != null; kthread = kthread->next){
    Object* waited_cond = kthread->waited_condition;
    if(waited_cond == jmon ){
```

```
    //wake up the thread
    deliver_signal(kthread->SIG_NOTIFY);
    return;
  }
}
return;
}
```

Figure 6.3 below shows the state transition graph of a thread operating a monitor. A large body of works from the industry and academia have explored the opportunities to optimize monitor implementation, such as meta-lock, thin-lock, and so on. We will discuss some of the techniques later in Chapter 18.

6.6 ATOMICS

The JVM monitor is a blocking operation. That means the thread blocks sleeping when it cannot acquire the lock. There is no way for an application (not VM) to try the lock without being blocked. Sometimes, a thread may just want to know if it can acquire the lock or if the lock has been acquired. The thread can then decide what to do next, either block, retry, or give up.

For example, in a parallel graph traversal algorithm, multiple threads try to mark the graph nodes with flag "VISITED." The initial state of the nodes is "NULL." If a node is already "VISITED," no action is needed. When a thread reaches a graph node, it basically does the following:

```
if(flag == NULL ){
    flag == VISITED;
}
```

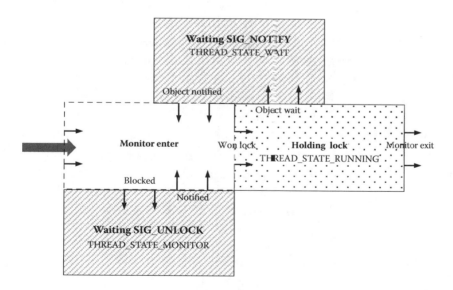

FIGURE 6.3   Thread state transition when operating on monitor.

When the node is already visited, the current thread just gives up and moves on to traverse next node in the graph. It does not want to be blocked sleeping if another thread is visiting the same node, nor does it want to sleep waiting for the flag to be NULL again, so JVM monitor in code below does not work as desired.

```
synchronized( Node ){
    if( flag == NULL ){
        flag == VISITED;
    }
}
```

In the code above, if another thread has locked the monitor of object Node, current thread cannot move on but block waiting for the monitor to be unlocked. This is redundant because current thread should move on to next node. The operations on the flag are a typical sequence of test&set on a memory value. If they can be executed atomically, it does not need to involve monitor. The following conceptual model is desirable.

```
atomic{
    if(flag == NULL ){
        flag == VISITED;
    }
}
```

For this purpose, Java introduces atomic variables that can operate atomically with a few basic operations such as test&set. We can use atomic variables to implement the graph traversal.

```
AtomicInteger flag = new AtomicInteger(NULL);
flag.compareAndSet(NULL, VISITED);
```

The efficiency of this operation depends on the implementation of the atomic variables in VM.

All the modern microprocessors have atomic instructions for simple memory operations like test&set. In X86 CPU, instruction prefix "lock" is used to ensure the atomicity of the instruction. For instance, the following inlined assembly code implements atomic compare and swap of a word in memory. It simply puts "lock" prefix in front of the nonatomic instruction "cmpxchg." This instruction compares the value in memory "address" to "comperand." If they are equal, then value "exchange" is stored in "address"; otherwise, no store happens. In both cases, the original value in memory "address" is returned.

```
inline int AtomicCompareExchange(int *address,
                                 int comperand,
                                 int exchange)
{
#ifdef __LINUX__

        __asm__ (
```

```
        "lock \tcmpxchg %1, (%2)\t\n"
        :"=eax"(comperand)
        :"edx"(exchange), "r"(address), "eax"(comperand)
        );
#else
#ifdef __WINDOWS__
        __asm {
        mov eax, comperand
        mov edx, exchange
        mov ecx, address
        lock cmpxchg [ecx], edx
        mov comperand, eax
        }
#endif
#endif
}
```

When it executes the instruction with "lock" prefix, one implementation is that the processor asserts the memory bus for mutual exclusive access to memory. The memory operations by other processor are then blocked waiting for the bus assertion to lift.

With AtomicCompareExchange, VM can implement the compareAndSet method of atomic variables in pseudocode below.

```
boolean compareAndSet(int* this, int comp, int set)
{
    int original;
    original = AtomicCompareExchange(this, comp, set)
    if( original == comp)
        return true;

    return false;
}
```

Some processors have hardware lock support for critical section of multiple instructions. This feature is usually available in the processors that support hardware multiple threads. That can be used to implement atomics too.

In a multiple-core computer that does not use bus-based memory subsystem, or in a distributed shared-memory computer system, the overhead for memory access mutual exclusion can be much higher than in a bus-based system. The implementation of atomics can be very different.

In a single core system, instruction level atomicity is usually naturally satisfied by the processor. Even if the instructions can be executed out-of-order in the pipeline, the processor must present the developers with results as if the code is executed in order of the instruction sequence. So in a uniprocessor system, the bus assertion is unnecessary. For example, we can omit the "lock" prefix in the implementation of "AtomicCompareExchange" to reduce the processor overhead.

6.7 MONITOR VERSUS ATOMICS

Atomics help to avoid blocking synchronization that is considered a shortcoming of monitor. So atomics sometimes are called nonblocking synchronization. But essentially atomics and monitor are the same, and the only difference is the lock's granularity.

6.7.1 Blocking versus Nonblocking

With monitor, the mutual exclusion is achieved through checking shared data in memory, and the waiting is achieved at OS level through thread scheduling. With atomic instruction, the mutual exclusion is achieved by the processor asserting the memory bus, and the waiting is achieved at processor level through instruction pipeline scheduling. Other memory instructions are held in a queue and cannot enter the pipeline until the bus assertion is lift. Since the bus assertion is only for a single instruction with "lock" prefix, the blocking time for other memory operations is very short, for example, bounded in a few cycles or up to hundreds of cycles.

As a comparison, the waiting time for monitor through thread scheduling is decided by the duration of the critical section guarded by the lock and the OS scheduling efficiency. There is no guarantee on its finish time. If the developer only puts short code sequence in the critical section, the waiting time can be as short as a scheduling time slice or even shorter.

For mutual exclusion, blocking always happens, just at different levels or with different granularities. Atomics can be considered as atomicity at instruction level and with instruction granularity, whereas monitor as atomicity at OS level and with time-slice granularity. When we talk about them at OS level, it is fine to claim that atomics do not block, that is, do not involve OS scheduling. If an algorithm only uses atomics, it is considered nonblocking, because the threads never block sleeping.

6.7.2 Central Control Point

No matter what granularity the atomicity is to implement mutual exclusion, the key is to find a central control point that all the participating threads have to go through. For atomic instruction, the central control point is the bus, since all memory operations in the computer have to go through it. (Here we only discuss shared memory multiprocessor (SMP), but the concept is still valid with non-SMP.) As a result, all atomic instructions are mutual exclusive to each other, no matter if they are operating on the same memory address.

For monitor synchronization, the central control point is the monitor object. As a result, a locked monitor only blocks the threads that try to lock the same object, while other threads are not impacted. If all the threads use the same monitor, then it is a global large lock.

6.7.3 Lock versus No-Lock

To decide if a lock is necessary for a critical section, we need to check if the execution instances of the critical section can interleave or run in parallel simultaneously.

The instructions from one processor are always committed in order, so from program's point of view they are not interleaved. Every instruction (as a fine-grained critical section) is considered atomic, and the "lock" prefix can be omitted. When there are multiple cores, all of them can issue memory operations to the bus at the same time. Instructions from different cores may interleave their accesses to the bus, which requires the "lock" prefix for instruction atomicity guarantee.

As a comparison, if critical sections are code regions in different threads, their executions can interleave if the threads are on same processor; or the critical sections can run in parallel if the threads are on different processors. Consequently, monitor lock cannot be omitted for the mutual exclusion here.

However, it is also possible for monitor to omit its lock in special case. For instance, if the application has only one thread, then all the locks can be eliminated.

Even multiple threads may omit locks. This is possible with user-level threading library where all the threads share same native thread context. First, parallel execution of critical section is impossible with single native thread context. Second, interleaving execution can be avoided if the code meets following two conditions:

- The threading library never preemptively schedules the threads but switches the context only when a user thread voluntarily yields its execution.

- All the user threads only yield in code regions out of critical sections.

This property has been leveraged by some systems.

6.7.4 Blocking on Top of Nonblocking

Due to the relation between monitor and atomics, monitor is mostly implemented with atomics. In other words, blocking lock is often implemented with non-blocking lock plus waiting, as shown in the conceptual code below.

```
void lock_blocking(Object* jmon)
{
retry:
    ok = lock_non_blocking(jmon);
    if( ok ) return;
    wait_on_lock(jmon);
    goto retry;
}
```

In the example above for monitor locking, the core operation is lock_non_ blocking(jmon), which uses atomic test&set to hold the lock. As we have mentioned, we use bit LOCK_BIT in the object header to indicate if the object is locked or not. So the pseudocode for lock_non_blocking(jmon) is shown below.

```
bool lock_non_blocking (Object* jmon){
{
    volatile int* pheader = jmon->header;
    int orig = 0;

#ifdef __LINUX__
        __asm__ __volatile__ (
            "lock btsl %2,%1\n\t"
            "sbbl %0,%0"
            :"=r" (orig),"=m" (*pheader)
            :"Ir" (LOCK_BIT) : "memory");
#else
#ifdef __WINDOWS__
        __asm{
            mov eax, pheader
            mov edx, LOCK_BIT
            xor ecx, ecx
            lock bts dword ptr [eax], edx
            sbb ecx, ecx
            mov orig, ecx
        }
#endif
#endif
        return (bool)!orig;
}
```

In this example code, instruction "bts" is used with "lock" prefix, which atomically swaps the specified bit of specified memory with value 1. The original bit value is saved in CF (carry flag) of the processor. CF value 1 means the lock is held by others, value 0 means that current thread locks it successfully.

The pattern is similar to that of cmpxchg instruction, but the difference is bts does not save the original value in a register. The code then has to use "sbb" instruction to convert the value in CF to a register. Instruction sbb adds its source operand and CF, and subtracts their sum from the destination operand. The subtraction result is stored in the destination operand. Since both source and destination operands are 0, if CF has 0, the result in destination operand is still 0; otherwise, if CF has 1, the result is −1 (i.e., nonzero). Since CF's value is reverse of the expected boolean result, the code returns its negated value.

Atomics cannot replace monitor because sometimes blocking is needed when the waiting duration is indefinitely long. Monitor and atomics are usually complementary in developing multithreaded applications.

6.8 COLLECTOR AND MUTATOR

When an application is running in a VM, there are usually a few kinds of threads. The primary kind is the application thread. From memory management point of view, application thread is also called mutator, since it mutates the memory. The threads for garbage collection are called collectors. Depending on the VM design, garbage collection can be conducted in the context of mutator thread(s) or in dedicated threads.

With stop-the-world GC, the mutators are suspended for garbage collection, then the collection can be done in the context of the suspended mutators. In this design, collectors and mutators are the same native threads in different phases.

It is common to use dedicated threads for garbage collection, where mutators and collectors are supported with different native threads. With stop-the-world GC, the collectors resume execution when a collection happens and sleep when the collection is done. With concurrent GC, mutators and collectors run concurrently.

In JVM, mutators are Java threads that are normally started from `Thread.start()` and need binding with Java thread object. Collectors are not Java threads. Both of them can reuse the thread entities from a thread pool so as to reduce the cost of creating new threads.

Besides mutators and collectors, just-in-time (JIT) compilation can be conducted in dedicated threads. For example, when JIT compiler is compiling a method, it finds the current method will invoke a couple of other methods that are not compiled. It can pass them to another dedicated JIT thread to compile in parallel in a multiple core system. This can potentially reduce the application's execution time by moving the method compilation out of the critical path.

In JVM, there are usually dedicated threads for finalization and weak-reference processing. JVM specification does not specify the execution timing requirement on the finalization of dead objects and on the enqueuing of unused weak reference objects. It is convenient to use dedicated threads to process them separately out of any critical path. The threads have to be Java threads because they are executing Java methods. In this regard, they should be also considered as mutators. We will discuss this topic more later in Chapter 12.

In Apache Harmony, both mutators and collectors are subclasses of allocator thread. Allocator is responsible to allocate memory from the heap. Mutators allocate objects from the heap during application execution. Collectors allocate objects from the heap when they move live objects from one place to another. Here is the simplified definition of `Allocator`.

```
struct Allocator{
    void *free;            //address for allocation start
    void *ceiling;         //allocation ceiling
    void* end;             //allocation block boundary
    Block *alloc_block;    //thread-local allocation block
    Space* alloc_space;    //global space for block allocation
    GC   *gc;              //gc algorithm
    VM_Thread *thread;     //the thread of the allocator
}
```

`Allocator` maintains a thread-local block (`alloc_block`) so that memory allocation can be done without mutual exclusion. The address of `Allocator` data structure of current thread is stored in thread-local storage (TLS) in Windows or thread-specific data (TSD) in Linux, so that every thread (mutator or collector) can quickly find its `Allocator` data for object allocation.

6.9 THREAD-LOCAL DATA

Thread-local data refer to those data owned solely by one thread. The data are only accessed by that thread. Thread local data are interesting to developers because the property of "thread-local" can be utilized in various aspects. The most obvious property is that accesses to thread-local data do not require locking for mutual exclusion. There are basically three kinds of thread-local data. They are register file, runtime stack, and thread-local heap.

As we have discussed, thread context basically consists of program counter and stack pointer. They are the registers holding data private to a thread, or uniquely identifying a thread. In reality, thread context may include all the registers, sometimes called register file.

Thread context may be multiplexed by multiple threads, but when a thread is executing, it normally cannot access the context of another thread. There are some exceptions. For instance, when a thread suspends or debugs another thread, some OS allows the thread to access the context of the suspended or debugged thread. Some processors have global registers that are shared across threads. These exceptions are known special cases that do not impact the thread-local discussion.

Runtime stack, as runtime temporary data of a thread, is thread-local too. Since stack is normally allocated in system memory, it is accessible to other threads if the stack address is passed to other threads. Like registers, the cross-thread accesses to runtime stack are well-controlled special cases that do not change the thread-local nature in normal situations.

Register file and runtime stack are OS-supported thread-local data in a way that, by default, applications can assume their thread-local nature without any extra work. That is, when a datum is put into a register or onto the stack of a thread, it is not accessible by other threads.

Thread-local heap is different from registers or stack. It is not supported by OS design, but by convention of the application. Heap by default is sharable to all threads. A heap region is local to one thread means either of the following two situations:

- In the first situation, the region is not accessible to other threads. The region can be protected by virtual memory mechanism or whatever technique to enforce the convention, or it is simply a rule complied with by all the threads. For instance, thread-local block is held by one thread for object allocation. The block is only local to a thread in the sense of object allocation. Once the object is allocated, it is accessible to all threads.

- In the second situation, the region is not designed to be thread-local, but the fact is only one thread actually accesses it. We call the data "nonescape," that is, they are confined to a single thread's territory. Once the data are accessed by other thread, it becomes "escape" from the current thread. "Escape analysis" is an important compiler technique that tries to find the "nonescape" data and hence applies optimizations on them as thread-local data.

Thread-local heap can be temporary. It can be thread-local for a period. After that period, it may be accessible to other threads, or may be handed over to be thread-local to a second thread.

Sometimes, the threads may want to access their respective thread-local heaps with same variable name (or same API). It is desirable that, when different threads access variable my_region (or API my_region()), the respective thread-local heap is returned to the caller thread. That is, different caller threads have different thread-local heaps that share same name. This feature is called "thread-local storage (TLS)" or "thread-specific data (TSD)."

The feature can be built on top of OS-supported thread-local data. For example, every thread puts the address of its thread-local heap into a same register. Then all threads can access their own thread-local heaps by accessing the same register. Although the register name is the same, the register contents are from different thread contexts. The other solution is to put the thread-local heap address into the same slot of respective runtime stack. Different threads then can retrieve the thread-local heap addresses in the stacks with same slot number.

6.9.1 Thread-Local Allocator

In Apache Harmony, every thread allocates a heap region for thread-local data. The address of this region is stored in a TLS variable that can be accessed with API vm_thread_local(). That is,

```
void*  tls_base = vm_thread_local();
```

Within the thread-local region, the address of Allocator data structure is stored in a fixed position, that is, the offset to the region start is a constant, which is saved in a global variable tls_alloc_offset. With this design, we can access the allocator with the following code sequence.

```
extern int tls_alloc_offset;
inline Allocator* thread_get_allocator()
{
        void* tls_base = vm_thread_local();
        char* tls_slot = (char*)tls_base + tls_alloc_offset;
        int* allocator = *(int*)tls_slot;
        return (Allocator*) allocator;
}
```

Then the bump-pointer allocator can be implemented as the following pseudocode.

```
//this routine does not deal with any slow path operations,
//but returns null if unsuccessful.
Object* gc_alloc_fast(unsigned size, Vtable* vt)
{
    //return if object to be allocated has finalizer
    if(type_has_finalizer(vt)) return NULL;

    //return if it is large object
    if ( size > GC_OBJ_SIZE_THRESHOLD ) return NULL;

    Object* p_obj = null;
    Allocator* allocator = thread_get_allocator();
    int free = (int)allocator->free;
    int ceiling = (int)allocator->ceiling;

    int new_free = free + size;
    if (new_free <= ceiling){
        p_obj = (Object*)free;
        allocator->free= (void*)new_free;
    }else{
        return null;
    }

    //install vtable pointer to the object header
    obj_set_vt(p_obj, vt);
    return p_obj;
}
```

This routine tries to allocate an object as fast as possible. Especially, when it cannot allocate an object, it simply returns null. There is another routine `gc_alloc()` that will deal with the slow-path cases that fail `gc_alloc_fast()`. When the compiler generates code for object allocation (such as bytecode new or `newarray` family in JVM), it generates the following pseudocode in machine code.

```
p_obj = gc_alloc_fast(size, vt);
if(p_obj == null){
    prepare_for_native_call();
    gc_alloc(size, vt);
    clean_after_native_call();
}
```

The slow path `gc_alloc()` may trigger garbage collection, so the compiler needs to maintain the stack to support root-set enumeration as a safe point. The stack preparation and cleanup may take hundreds of instructions, which is too expensive to afford for every object allocation. Routine `gc_alloc_fast()` avoids the stack maintenance overhead by never triggering garbage collection. We will discuss the slow path support later in Chapter 10.

6.10 THREAD SUSPENSION SUPPORT FOR GC

When a stop-the-world GC happens, VM needs to suspend all the mutators to avoid any race condition. Even in a concurrent GC when the mutators and collectors can run at the same time, it usually still needs to suspend the threads briefly for root-set enumeration.

6.10.1 GC Safe Point

In typical VM implementations, it is not suggested to use the suspend-and-roll-forward approach to suspend a thread at a GC safe point; instead, the mutators suspend themselves at a safe point when they detect a collection event. For every safe point, VM needs to insert the polling code. The polling code checks if there is a collection event triggered by the VM, and if yes it suspends current thread. When the collection finishes, VM sends another event to notify the mutator to resume from the safe point.

To abstract the design, the protocol between VM and threads can be implemented with two events, one to indicate a suspend request and the other one to indicate a resume request. The suspend request can be a global flag set by the VM when GC happens, or a thread-local data that specifically delivered to the thread to be suspended. The resume request can be implemented by resetting the same flag.

The interactions between VM and the target thread can be illustrated as Figure 6.4 below.

The conceptual code looks like below. We need to introduce two flags (or events) in thread data structure. The flags should be modified with "volatile" to ensure their

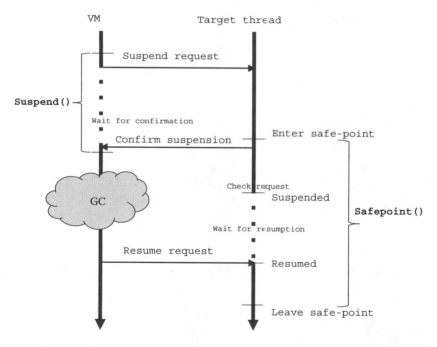

FIGURE 6.4 Interaction between threads for safe point.

accesses are always loaded from memory, and their access order follows the program order. Both values are set to FALSE when the owner thread starts.

```
struct VM_Thread{
    //other fields
    ...
    //set by VM, requesting suspension
    volatile bool to_suspend;
    //set by self, indicating GC safe status
    volatile bool gc_safe;
}


void vm_suspend_thread(VM_Thread* target)
{
    //send the suspend request
    target->to_suspend = TRUE;
    //busy waiting for target to confirm suspension
    while( !target->gc_safe ){
        //do nothing but give fother threads a check to run
        thread_yield();
    }
    //target confirmed suspension
    return;
}


void vm_resume_thread(VM_Thread* target)
{
    target->to_suspend = FALSE;
}


void vm_safepoint()
{
    self = current_thread();
    //confirm to suspend
    self->gc_safe = TRUE;

    //if there is a request, suspend self
    //until resumed by other thread
    while( self->to_suspend ){
        thread_yield();
    }

    //leave safepoint
    self->gc_safe = FALSE;
}
```

Another design of the polling code at safe point can be a write to a memory location. When GC happens, the VM write-protects the location, and only unprotects it when GC finishes. When GC happens and a mutator executes the polling code, a memory protection fault is triggered, and the OS kernel will deliver an event to the faulting thread. The application has registered the fault handler, which is then invoked to process the event. The handler notifies VM that it is blocking and then sleeps waiting for the resume event from the VM when GC finishes. This design of safe point could be more efficient because the fast path (when GC does not happen) is only one memory write, while the code above needs at least a memory read and a compare & branch for the fast path.

6.10.2 GC Safe Region

The VM may want to conduct some operations in safe point (e.g., for root-set enumeration, and for bulk biased-lock reset) The operations can be inserted in three places of safe-point code as shown in code below. The three pieces of operations should usually be safe and cannot touch any object data which is GC-unsafe and contradicting the safe-point purpose. Operations on the common path (in place 1 and 3 in code blow) should be very brief to keep the safe point light-weighted.

Some VM design may ask each mutator to report its root-set by itself, rather than enumerate all the mutators root sets by the VM. Then the root-set enumeration work can be conducted in place 2 of the safe-point code. Before it starts to enumerate, the thread checks if it already has the root-set. The situation is possible when the mutator wakes up from suspension and finds another collection round happens again before it leaves the suspension loop, that is, the self->to_suspend was set 0 and then 1 again when it was sleep.

```
void vm_safepoint()
{
    self = current_thread();
    //confirm to suspend
    self->gc_safe = TRUE;
    self->root_set = NULL;

//... GC-safe operations 1, can be no-op

    //if there is a request, suspend self
    //until resumed by other thread
    while( self->to_suspend ){
//     GC-safe operations 2, can be no-op
        if( self->root_set == NULL ){
            self->root_set = thread_enumerate_roots();
        }
        thread_yield();
    }

//... GC-safe operations 3, can be no-op
    //leave safepoint
    self->gc_safe = FALSE;
}
```

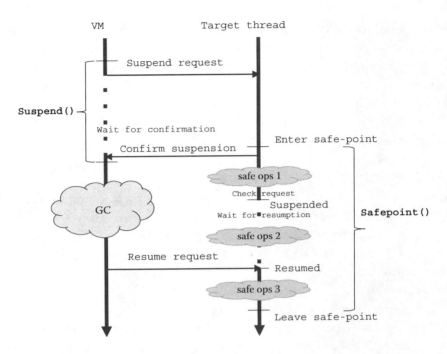

FIGURE 6.5   Thread can conduct GC-safe operations in safe-point code.

Figure 6.5 shows the places where safe operations can be put.

If we extend the GC-safe operations in place 1 above to include a big chunk of code, we can form a safe region. Safe region is another scenario that is needed for GC support. Safe region is not a point, but a region within which GC is safe. For example, a native method following Java Native Interface (JNI) APIs is usually GC-safe and then can be put into safe region, because the native code does not directly touch objects. There is no inserted safe point in the native method by JIT compiler, so the native method cannot be suspended in the middle. It is good to keep the whole JNI method body GC-safe. In this sense, we can regard the native method as a huge safe point. (This is very high-level description and not accurate. We will know why it is inaccurate later.)

To implement safe region is similar to implement safe point, it is similar to putting the native method in place 1 of the safe-point code. The only difference is that the original safe-point implementation is split into two halves now for safe region. The first half is executed at the entrance of a safe region and the second half at the exit. The interactions between VM and target thread can be illustrated in Figure 6.6.

The vm_thread_suspend() code is the same as above. The safe-region part becomes the following.

```
void thread_enter_saferegion()
{
    self = current_thread();
    //claiming we are safe to GC, no matter if
    //there is a request or not
```

```
    self->gc_safe = TRUE;
}

void thread_leave_saferegion()
{
    self = current_thread();
    //if there is request, suspend self
    while( self->to_suspend ){
        thread_yield();
    }
    //leave saferegion
    self->gc_safe = FALSE;
}

bool thread_in_saferegion()
{
    self = current_thread();
    return self->gc_safe;
}
```

Based on the discussions, safe point and safe region are almost the same thing. Safe point reflects the fact that it is the only point where a collection is allowed to happen, whereas safe region means the collection is enabled throughout the region. So the pair of thread_enter_saferegion() and thread_leave_saferegion() are sometimes also referred as **vm_enable_gc()** and **vm_disable_gc()**.

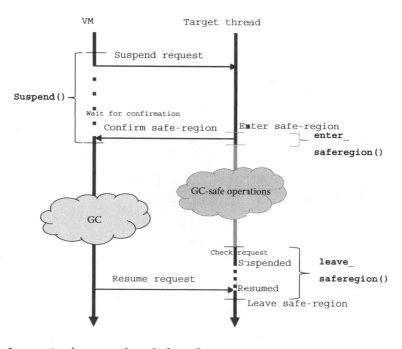

FIGURE 6.6   Interaction between threads for safe region.

As a matter of fact, the safe point can be implemented by calling the safe-region code.

```
void vm_safepoint()
{
    thread_enter_saferegion();
    thread_leave_saferegion();
}
```

When the entering and leaving operations are split into two halves, it is possible that the safe operations in between may call another native method or even Java method. In other words, the control flow may go out of the safe region. This is common in reality. The VM design should ensure that the GC-safe status is well maintained across the call chain.

- Java code is GC-unsafe and native method is GC-safe.

- When the code goes from Java method to native method, it enters safe region.

- Native code leaves safe region if the code goes from native method to Java method.

We will discuss with details later why and how this variant is kept in VM when Java and native code interacts in Chapter 9.

6.10.3 Lock-Based Safe Point

When looking closely into the implementation code of thread interactions, we can find that the idea is similar to Peterson's mutual exclusion algorithm. The semantics here are for the VM and target thread to compete for the object access (or heap mutation). The VM that wants to collect garbage tries to acquire the mutation lock. The mutator thread who normally holds the lock will release its mutation lock from time to time when it does not mutate the heap, that is, at safe points and safe regions. In other words, entering a safe region is like releasing the mutation lock, meaning the thread does not mutate the heap for the moment, while leaving the collector to acquire the lock.

In this conceptual model, the data structure for thread suspension can replace the two volatile flags with one re-entrant blocking lock (or monitor).

```
struct Thread{
    //other fields
    ...
    //lock for privilege of heap mutation
    Lock* mutable;
}

void vm_suspend_thread(VM_Thread* target)
{
    lock( target->mutable );
}
```

```
void vm_resume_thread(VM_Thread* target)
{
    unlock( target->mutable );
}

void thread_enter_saferegion()
{
    VM_Thread* self = current_thread();
    unlock( self->mutable );
}

void thread_leave_saferegion()
{
    VM_Thread* self = current_thread();
    lock( self->mutable );
}

void vm_safepoint()
{
    VM_Thread* self = current_thread();
    unlock( self->mutable );
    lock( self->mutable );
}
```

In this implementation, the algorithm reuses the lock's semantics for waiting and notification support. When a lock is released, all the waiting threads will compete for the lock. For example, in a safe point, the thread may release and acquire the lock immediately, even if VM (e.g., collector) is waiting for the lock. This is not an issue in most systems, where lock's implementation guarantees fairness, and the waiting thread should be able to acquire the lock in bounded time (e.g., at next safe point). Or a thread_yield() can be inserted between the unlocking and locking of safe point so as to ensure a waiting thread gets a chance to acquire the lock.

However, this lock-based design is unlikely to be used in real implementation, because the locking and unlocking operations can be too expensive to be useful for a safe point, not mentioned the thread_yield(). The implementation of thread_in_saferegion() can also be problematic, because usually there is no direct primitive to tell if a thread holds a lock.

6.10.4 Thread Interaction in a Collection

If GC needs to stop the world, VM can use the primitives above to suspend all the mutators one by one. A VM implementation does not necessarily use a dedicated thread to suspending mutators. Instead, the thread that suspends other mutators can be itself a mutator because a collection may be triggered when the mutator cannot allocate an object successfully due to heap is low. This mutator traps into VM code to start garbage collection.

It is possible that multiple mutators fail to allocate objects and try to trigger a collection simultaneously, especially in a parallel computer. Each of these mutators may try to suspend other mutators, hence causing mutual suspension deadlock. To avoid the deadlock, it is safe to use a global lock that only allows one mutator to suspend other mutators, as given in the code below. The idea is to allow only a central control to conduct the stop-the-world suspension. To hold the global lock also prevents the system from creating new thread that may otherwise escape from suspension.

```
void vm_suspend_all_threads()
{
    //This is essential. Potential blocking operation below
...//requires to be in safe region
    assert( thread_in_saferegion());

    //acquire the global lock, can be blocking
    global_thread_lock();

    for( each target thread ){
        vm_suspend_thread( target->mutable );
    }

}

void vm_resume_all_threads()
{

    for( each target thread){
        vm_resume_thread( target->mutable );
    }

    //release global lock
    global_thread_unlock();
}
```

When multiple mutators fail to allocate new objects and trigger GC simultaneously, they may compete for the global suspension lock. One of them wins the lock and conducts the suspension. Other competing mutators will wait on the lock. Waiting on the lock is not a problem because they are at safe point (or safe region).

The problem with the algorithm above is that, when VM releases the global lock and resumes all the mutators while they are waiting on the global lock, the wakened up mutators will compete to acquire the global block. One of them who wins the lock will start another round of mutators suspension, although they were just suspended moment ago.

In actual implementation, the acquisition and release of the global suspension lock can be put in outer caller before/after stop-the-world. Putting them outside is useful because the mutator can double check if the heap is enough to satisfy its object allocation after it acquires the global lock and before it goes to actually stop the world. This can avoid the case when multiple mutators waiting on the global lock try to stop the world one after another, because a later-winning mutator may find free space available and then quits the collection process. When a mutator finds the heap is still low after it acquires the lock, it conducts the real stop-the-world. For example,

```
void vm_trigger_gc()
{
    thread_enter_saferegion();

    if( !heap_is_low() ) return;

    global_thread_lock();
    if( !heap_is_low() ){
        global_thread_unlock();
        return;
    }

    vm_suspend_all_threads();
    vm_reclaim_heap();
    vm_resume_all_threads();

    global_thread_unlock();

    thread_leave_saferegion();

    return;
}
```

As showed in the code, the thread that triggers a collection should be in safe region because it may be blocking when it acquires global thread lock. A blocking thread should allow a collection to happen.

However, it is indeed in safe region because if the GC is triggered by an object allocation, the allocation site should be a safe point in Java code, so it is not a problem to call thread_enter_saferegion() before the thread may be blocked in the locking operation. If the allocation is from native method, it is in a safe region by itself. If the GC is triggered by system invoking GC directly, it is a call site and then a safe point as well.

III

Supports in Virtual Machine

CHAPTER 7

Native Interface

THROUGHOUT THE DISCUSSIONS ON just-in-time (JIT), garbage collection (GC), and threading, we mentioned a couple of core functionalities that need supports in a virtual machine (VM). In the following few chapters in Section III, we will discuss them with more details.

7.1 WHY NATIVE INTERFACE

Native interface is needed for high-level languages to access low-level system resource and VM services. They cannot directly access low-level resource for security, portability, and implementation reasons.

- Security reason: High-level language is not allowed to directly manipulate memory address, machine instruction, input or output (I/O) interfaces, and so on. These accesses are necessary when the program needs to deal with low-level logics or to provide high performance.

- Portability reason: High-level language is designed to be platform independent. To access platform-specific features such as file system, it has to use the native language of the platform.

- Implementation reason: Sometimes, certain libraries are only available in native languages such as media libraries that are either not ported to high-level languages or only available as legacy implementation.

To bridge the gaps, native interface is needed for the high-level language, which is implemented in its VM. The word "native" here refers to the nature that the interface provides the access to the native language of the operating system (OS) underlying the VM. Since C programming language is the native language in major OSs available today, it makes sense for Java Native Interface (JNI) to support C language access, while Java VM (JVM) does not exclude other languages from programming native methods.

Native interface design has following properties:

Native language: The native language of an OS is not necessarily C language, or even not necessarily low-level language. It all depends on the implementation. For a Java-based OS, Java can be regarded the native language of the OS. However, such an OS still needs native interface for Java to access the low-level hardware or system resource, unless the hardware is designed in a way that allows for secure programming. The ultimate question is whether the world is safe by itself that can be modeled by a computing machine. If the answer is not, then a native interface is always necessary on the boundary between safe and unsafe worlds. As a result, the native language can be lower level than C, as long as the interface convention is well defined.

Native code to managed code: Native interface is defined not only for the high-level language to access a low-level one, but also for the reverse direction, that is, the low-level language to access the high-level one. The latter is needed, because otherwise there is no way to launch the VM system from the OS, or to call back from native code to the high-level program. For example, a C-written listener application on a network socket wakes up for a socket event and invokes the event handler that is written in Java program.

Data sharing: Native interface is needed not only because of the code access between high-level and low-level languages, but also for the data sharing between them. The low-level language should be able to access the data created by the high-level language. It is also desirable for the low-level language to create data that is accessible to the high-level language.

High-level properties: Although it is designed for low-level language access, native interface is part of the high-level language design. That means, the application programming interface (API) of native interface should not break the important safety properties of the high-level language. For example, the object layout should still be opaque to native code. Same exception-throwing process should still be observed in native code.

The safety property maintenance is a feature of the program only when it is written in "native interface," because the native interface is under VM's control. Programs written in "native code" but not following "native interface" do not maintain the safety property. Native code can do anything it is designed for. It can allocate virtual memory, create native thread, and others, with the low-level language API. Those entities are then not managed by the VM but by the low-level language's implementation. For example, the directly allocated virtual memory in native code is not subject to the VM's garbage collection.

In recent years, web application is becoming popular, where the high-level programming language is HTML/Javascript. The VM for web application is called web runtime that is usually embedded in a web browser. As a result, although the term "native language" in *web browser community* refers C/C++ as in Java community, it refers to different things in *web application community*.

For example, the web application community calls Java the native language of Android, because Java is the major programming language of Android, in contrast to the web programming language HTML/Javascript. Similarly, Object-C or Swift is referred as the native language of iOS by web application community. However, to the browser developers of Chrome or Safari (not web application developers), the native language to the web runtime is still C/C++, because that is the language implementing the web runtime and providing it the low-level resource access.

In the remaining part of this chapter, we use JNI as an example to discuss the details of a common native interface implementation while the design is not limited to JNI.

7.2 TRANSITION FROM MANAGED CODE TO NATIVE CODE

The primary requirement of native interface is to allow the managed code to call native code and vice versa. Then the key is to agree on a calling convention between the two worlds. Calling convention defines the Application Binary Interface (ABI) for the program control flow to transfer into and out of a function (or method), that is, how to pass arguments and return values, how to prepare and restore the stack. Sometimes, it also needs to maintain the stack frame information to support the requirements of debugging, exception handling, and garbage collection. Once a calling convention is defined for a language on a platform, any compiler when generating code for that language on that platform should follow the convention. Code from different languages may be able to interact with each other if they follow the same calling convention.

Native code is compiled by a different compiler than the VM's JIT compiler, and the native code compiler is usually not part of the VM. In other words, the calling convention of native code is not defined by the VM. If the managed code wants to interact with the native code, it should follow the native code's calling convention. That is, JVM should know C's calling convention to support JNI.

7.2.1 Wrapper for Native Method

A common way to implement native call in JVM is to generate wrapper code to conduct the calling convention transformation between Java and native code. The wrapper code does all the necessary preparation and bookkeeping for the control flow transference, as shown in Figures 7.1 and 7.2.

When compiling the caller's Java code, the JIT compiler generates a call instruction to the wrapper code, which in turn calls into the actual native method. The wrapper follows Java calling convention to the Java caller and follows native calling convention to the native callee. It needs to do a couple of things as the bridge, especially to make the native method look like a Java method to the Java caller:

- Arguments preparation and restoration;

- Stack-unwinding support;

- Garbage collection support;

- Exception support;

- Synchronization support.

Expected control flow semantics (in source code):

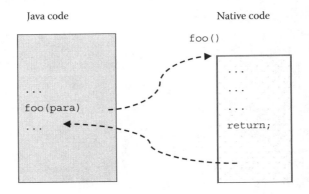

FIGURE 7.1   Expected control flow by direct calling.

Actual control flow (in assembly code):

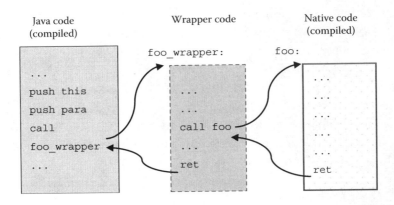

FIGURE 7.2   Wrapper code for native call.

In this chapter, we only discuss the first bullet on arguments and leave the rest to following chapters. The same logic can be implemented in compile-time generated code or interpreter runtime code.

To call a method in Java, JVM specification has defined the calling convention at bytecode level. The arguments are pushed onto the stack in order from left to right. When a method returns the callee's stack frame is cleared. As a contrast, the arguments for C language are pushed onto the stack in reverse order from right to left, and the arguments are cleared by the caller, because the callee does not always know the number of arguments pushed by the caller.

The other difference is that in JVM the first argument for an instance method invocation (bytecode `invokevirtual`) is current instance reference "`this`," which is the local variable at slot 0 in callee's stack frame. The argument "`this`" is not explicit in instance method signature definition. For static Java method invocation, JVM does not have such implicit argument. For native method invocation, JVM requires to have "`this`" reference passed as an argument for virtual native method as for Java while to have the class instance reference passed for static native method. Additionally, a JNI environment variable should be passed too, which stores a function table for all the JNI APIs, allowing the native method to access all needed JVM resources.

Following is an example to illustrate the wrapper support.

The Java method in Java code:

```
public class Add{
    public static native int native_add(int x, int y);
    public static int java_add(int x, int y);
    public static int add(int x, int y){
        return native_add(x, y);
    }
}
```

Generated bytecode for the above Java method add(x, y):

```
0: iload_0
1: iload_1
2: invokestatic #2   // Method native_add:(II)I
5: ireturn
```

As we discussed, the call to the static method (with bytecode invokestatic) is actually implemented with a call into the wrapper code of the target native method native_add(). The JIT compiler generates the code for invokestatic in the same way as for calling a static Java method, except the invocation target becomes the wrapper code. When the control flow enters the wrapper code, the runtime stack looks like Figure 7.3, as if a static Java method is entered. The top of the stack is the return address, followed by the two arguments.

The native method native_add(x, y) should be implemented with the following definition. The corresponding stack data right before it is called is shown in Figure 7.4:

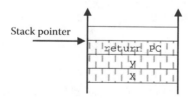

FIGURE 7.3   Stack data right after invoking the Java method.

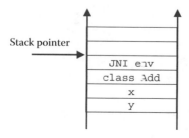

FIGURE 7.4   Stack data right before calling the native method.

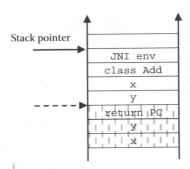

FIGURE 7.5   Stack data with native method arguments.

```
JNIEXPORT jint JNICALL Java_Add_native_1add
                  (JNIEnv *, jclass, jint, jint);
```

It is the wrapper code's responsibility to prepare the stack data accordingly.

Figure 7.3 is the stack the wrapper sees, and Figure 7.4 is the stack the wrapper prepares before calling the native method. Together the data on stack should look like Figure 7.5. In this JNI implementation, the original stack prepared by the Java caller is still kept intact and will be clean when the wrapper returns.

7.2.2 Wrapper for GC Support

In the caller Java method, its callee-save registers may have object references, they should be properly handled before calling the native method. The reasons are

1. When GC happens in the callee native method (or any method in its calling chain), VM needs to enumerate all the root references on stack and registers.

2. Since native code is compiled by other compiler, JVM does not know which callee-save registers from the caller Java method are saved and where they are saved in the native code stack frame.

Saving all the callee-save registers of the caller Java method before calling the native method ensures all the references are kept in a safe place for GC. Assuming the callee-save registers in X86 platform are ebp, ebx, esi, and edi, then the stack should look like Figure 7.6.

The wrapper code then looks like this:

```
// Save callee-saved registers first.
push ebp
push ebx
push esi
push edi
// push native method arguments
push [esp+20]            //push y
push [esp+28]            //push x
```

```
push addr_class_Add      //push class instance of Add
push addr_JNI_Env //push JNI environment var
// call the actual native method implementation
call Java_Add_native_1add
// native method is stdcall, no need to pop arguments
// restore callee-saved registers.
pop edi
pop esi
pop ebx
pop ebp
// return and pop Java arguments (x, y)
ret 8
```

This is a much simplified version, since it does not cover the stack unwinding, garbage collection, synchronization, and exception support. Even for the argument preparation, it does not show the case where single argument may take two stack slots such as `long` and `double` types. We briefly discuss the synchronized native method support here and leave other topics later.

7.2.3 Wrapper for Synchronization Support

When Java method is declared to be "`synchronized`," the compiler generates code in the method prolog for `monitorenter` and in the eplog for `monitorexit`. The site for `monitorenter` is GC safe point so that the current thread does not block GC if it has to wait on the monitor when executing `monitorenter`. When native method is declared "`synchronized`," it has the same semantics as the Java method.

Since native method is compiled by platform compiler, there is no code generation for `monitorenter` and `monitorexit`. The insertion of logics for `monitorenter` and `monitorexit` has to be conducted in the Java-to-native wrapper, which is under VM's control. The example wrapper code for a synchronized native method is given below.

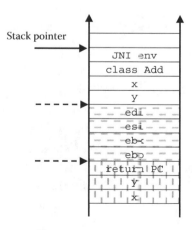

FIGURE 7.6 Stack data with callee-saved registers kept.

```
// Save callee-saved registers first.
push ebp
push ebx
push esi
push edi
//push the monitor object for monitorenter
push addr_class_Add
call vm_object_lock
// push native method arguments
push [esp+20]          //push y
push [esp+28]          //push x
push addr_class_Add    //push class instance of Add
push addr_JNI_Env //push JNI environment var
// call the actual native method implementation
call Java_Add_native_1add
// native method is stdcall, no need to pop arguments
//push the monitor object for monitorexit
push addr_class_Add
call vm_object_unlock
// restore callee-saved registers.
pop edi
pop esi
pop ebx
pop ebp
// return and pop           Java arguments (x, y)
ret 8
```

As a counterpart of the Java method compilation, sometimes we can call the process of generating the wrapper code the "native method compilation." This will not be confused with native compiler's compilation, because there is no native compiler in JVM. Since JIT compiler does not compile native method, "native method compilation" only generates the wrapper code, one for each native method.

Note the calling conventions in other JVM implementations or native language implementations can be different from what we use. The example here is only to demonstrate the design logic.

7.3 BINDING OF NATIVE METHOD IMPLEMENTATION

The wrapper code is generated by JVM. In order for the wrapper code to call a native method, JVM should be able to find the address of the native entry point. The native method can be implemented by the JVM or linked into the JVM statically as a built-in library, or the native method can be built as a dynamically loaded library that is loaded by JVM at runtime.

To locate a native method, JVM can search its native method table(s) that includes the built-in native methods or those registered by the Java application with the RegisterNatives JNI function. If the native method is not known to the JVM, the JVM continues to search in all loaded dynamic libraries with a function name created using one of several mangling schemes, because the native method compiled by native compiler may use name mangling that generates different function name than that declared in Java code. An exception will be thrown if the invoked native method cannot be found and bound. When the native method is located, JVM generates its wrapper code that calls the native method.

After a wrapper is generated, it is treated as JIT-compiled code of the native method, almost in the same way as the JIT-compiled code for Java code. Its entry point is the native method entrance in the eyes of JIT-complied Java code. If the method is virtual, the corresponding entries in vtables are updated.

7.4 TRANSITION FROM NATIVE CODE TO MANAGED CODE

Native method should be able to operate the objects generated by Java method, including both the data access and method invocation.

JNI specification provides APIs for native method to call Java method. These APIs should be implemented by the JVM, such as the following one,

```
jint JNICALL CallStaticIntMethod(JNIEnv* jenv,
                              jclass clazz,
                              jmethodID method,
                              ...)
```

The API allows the native code to call the static method method of certain class clazz with variable arguments and jint type return value. Its function pointer is registered in the JNI environment variable jenv where the native code can find it. An example code for invocation from native method to Java method is given below.

```
// native method Add.native_1add() invokes Add.java_add()
JNIEXPORT jint JNICALL Java_Add_native_add
          (JNIEnv *jenv, jclass clazz, jint x, jint y)
{
    jmethodID mid = (*jenv)->GetStaticMethodID(jenv, clazz,
    "java_add", "(II)I" );
    int sum = (*jenv)->CallStaticIntMethod(jenv, clazz,
    mid, x, 0);
    return sum;
}
```

To support these kinds of APIs, what JVM does basically is to prepare the arguments, call into Java method, and then read the return value. It also checks if there is any exception raised by the Java method execution. There is no need to generate a wrapper for every Java method, because the code path is the same. This is different from the transition from managed code to native code, where a wrapper is generated for every native method.

The reason for the difference is that, JVM does not want to be involved during the transition from managed code to native code. It tries to generate the wrapper code at compile-time and then only the wrapper code is executed in the transition process. If the wrapper code is the same for all native methods, it has to encode the logic that checks if the target native method is static or not, synchronized or not, then goes through different paths for different situations. It also needs logic to check the number and types of each parameter, then prepare the stack arguments accordingly. These logics execution is too slow if involved for every native method call, not mention the stack unwinding and garbage collection support that we will discuss later.

It is much faster if the overhead only occurs once in compile-time, and the runtime path has only the necessary code executed. This design trades memory space for runtime performance by having a separate wrapper for every native method. More importantly, the tradeoff is possible because most of the native method related information is available at compile-time, hence no need to check or query at runtime for every execution. As we mentioned, the wrapper code is considered part of the "compiled" native method.

As a comparison, the transition logic from native to Java is much simpler. More importantly, the native code is compiled by a native language compiler. At its compile-time, the Java method's information is not available to the compiler. It has to use Java's reflection mechanism with JNI APIs to retrieve the method and its signature information. This can only happen at runtime when the native method is executed. That said, it is still possible to generate a wrapper for every Java method for faster native to managed code transition.

When JVM runtime receives the call to JNI APIs like `CallStaticIntMethod`, it does some necessary checks based on Java semantics and then invokes a piece of bridge code. The bridge reverses the operations that a wrapper code does for native method, as given in Figure 7.7 below.

In our example code below, the bridge code is `vm_execute_java_method()`. It prepares arguments according to Java method calling convention and then calls into the actual Java method address. Assuming the to-be-invoked Java method is described in `p_method`, and the arguments are stored in word array `p_args_words`. The return

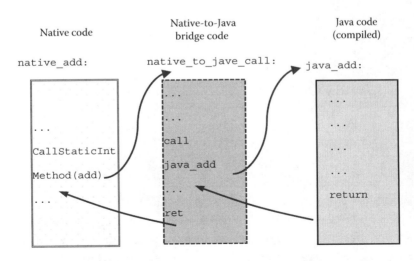

FIGURE 7.7   Bridge from native code to Java code.

value of the Java method invocation is to be stored in a two-word array p_ret in case the return value is double or long type. Then the code skeleton looks like the following.

```
void  vm_execute_java_method(  Method*  p_method,  uint32*
p_args_words, uint32 *p_ret)
{
    //number of words in arguments (not number of arguments,
    //because long/double have two words)
    uint32 n_arg_words;
    java_type ret_type; //return type of Java method
    method_get_param_info(p_method, &n_arg_words, &ret_type);

    void* java_entry;    //entry point of Java method
    java_entry = method_get_entry(p_method);

    uint32 eax_var, edx_var;  //return values in X86
    convention
    native_to_java_call(java_entry, n_arg_words, p_arg_
    words, &eax_var, &edx_var);

    //check if any pending exception
    if(thread_get_pending_exception()) return;

    /* handle return value */
    if ( ret_type == JAVA_TYPE_VOID) return;
    p_ret[0] = eax_var;
    p_ret[1] = edx_var; //useful only for long/double type
}
```

The native_to_java_call is a piece of gluing code that transfers the control into Java method. What it does is to prepare the arguments on the stack and then call the Java method.

```
void native_to_java_call(void *java_entry,
        uint32 n_arg_words, uint32 *p_args_words,
        uint32 *p_eax_var, uint32 *p_edx_var)
{
    __asm {
        // Push all arguments
        mov     n_arg_words -> ecx
        mov     p_arg_words -> eax

loop_more_args:
        or      ecx, ecx            //remaining # arg words
        jz      finished_args       //break if no more
        push    dword ptr [eax]     //push a word
        dec     ecx                 //decrement remaining #
```

```
            add        4 -> eax              //move to next arg word
            jmp        loop_more_args        //loop back to continue

finished_args:
            // All arguments are on the stack, ready to call
            call       dword ptr [meth_addr]

            // In case a value is returned
            mov        p_eax_var -> ecx
            mov        eax -> [ecx]   //store eax to eax_var
            mov        p_edx_var -> ecx
            mov        edx -> [ecx]   //store edx to edx_var
    }
}
```

In the code, the arguments for Java method call are pushed by iterating the arguments passed in by the native code (p_args_words) in a top-down way. That is, the first argument from native code is pushed first, which virtually reverses the arguments order on stack, due to the different calling conventions of native and Java method. The other note is that the argument for static Java method does not include the reference to class instance.

The stack situation is now reversed from that of the Java-to-native transition. Figure 7.8 gives an illustration.

The actual transition from native to Java is more complex that involves GC and exception support, and we will discuss later.

7.5 TRANSITION FROM NATIVE CODE TO NATIVE CODE

So far, we have only discussed the transitions of Java-to-Java, Java-to-native, and native-to-Java. We have not discussed the case of native-to-native. Note the native-to-native here refers to the situation when a native method (of a Java class) invokes another native method (of a Java class), rather than the case between native functions such as when a native method

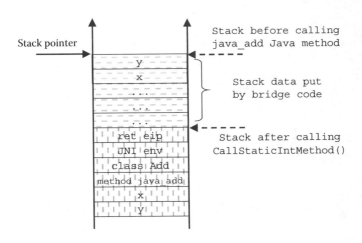

FIGURE 7.8 Stack for native-to-Java transition.

calls a C function. The latter case is just traditional C programming that does not involve VM. For the former case, there are some interesting issues worth discussing.

7.5.1 Native-to-Native through JNI API

A native method can call another native method without using JNI APIs. For example, in the code below, native methods `native_test1` and `native_test2` call another native method `native_add` in two ways. One way is to directly call the native function as C program; the other way calls through JNI APIs.

In Java code Add.java:

```
public class Add{
      public static native int test1(int x, int y);
      public static native int test2(int x, int y);
      public static native int add(int x, int y);
      public static int java_add(int x, int y){
          return add(x, y);
      }
}
```

In native code Add.c:

```
// native method Add.native_add()
JNIEXPORT jint JNICALL Java_Add_add
        (JNIEnv *jenv, jclass clazz, jint x, jint y)
{
        return x+y;
}


// native method Add.test1()
JNIEXPORT jint JNICALL Java_Add_test1
              (JNIEnv *jenv, jclass clazz, jint x, jint y)
{
    jint sum = Java_Add_add(jenv, clazz, x, y);
    return sum;
}


// native method Add.test2()
JNIEXPORT jint JNICALL Java_Add_test2
              (JNIEnv *jenv, jclass clazz, jint x, jint y)
{
    jmethodID mid = (*jenv)->GetStaticMethodID(jenv, clazz,
"add", "(II)I" );
    int sum = (*jenv)->CallStaticIntMethod(jenv, clazz,
mid, x, 0);
    return sum;
}
```

The code for `test1` and `test2` gives same result, but the implication to VM is very different. In case of `test1`, the invocation of `Java_Add_add` does not go through any wrapper code. From VM point of view, it is completely invisible and can be considered as inlined into the caller method `test1`.

However, in case of `test2`, the invocation of `CallStaticIntMethod()` has to go through two transitions in VM, one from native to Java and the other from Java to native.

7.5.1.1 Native-to-Java Transition

JNI API `CallStaticIntMethod()` considers the invoked method as a Java method, although `Add.add()` is a native method. This is nothing wrong, because the Java method here means the method is declared in Java world and defined in JNI conventions. It is not traditional native C function.

We should always distinguish between "native method" in Java world and "native function" in C world. The former requires VM's support and maintains safety properties. It is "complied" by JIT-compiler into "wrapper code." The latter is invisible to VM and compiled by C compiler into binary code.

For the transition from "native world" to "Java world," `vm_execute_java_method()` is used to prepare the stack as to call a JIT-compiled Java method, including pushing arguments and receiving return value in Java convention. The binary code address of the Java method called by `vm_execute_java_method` is the entry point of the method, which for native method is the Java-to-native wrapper code. Once it is called, the control transfers to the Java-to-native wrapper code.

7.5.1.2 Java-to-Native Transition

Once entering the Java-to-native wrapper code, the execution starts to prepare a call from Java code to native method. It does not know that the call actually was initiated from another native method. It only knows the call was from Java world. The stack should look the same as called from `Add.java_add()`.

The control flow looks like Figure 7.9 below.

The stack then looks like the following Figure 7.10.

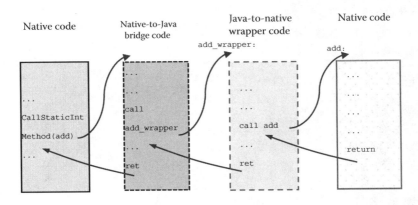

FIGURE 7.9   Control flow from native method to native method.

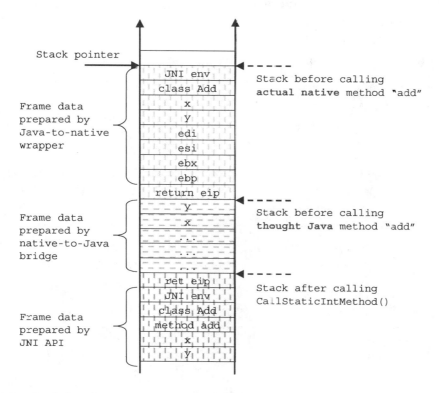

FIGURE 7.10   Stack data for native-to-native method call.

We can see that the arguments have been copied multiple times on the stack.

- First time when making the call to JNI API CallStaticIntMethod();
- Second time when the native-to-Java bridge code prepares the stack for Java method call;
- Third time when the Java-to-native wrapper code prepares the stack for the native method call.

It is possible to have even more than three times, depending on the implementation details. For example, the native-to-Java bridge code may push one more time to facilitate the addition of the "this" pointer to the receiver object before making a Java method call.

When argument repushing happens, the old copy of the arguments become dead, because the method invocation only accesses the newly pushed arguments. It means, in our example implementation, there are at least two copies of arguments are dead. This point is important for GC support that we will see later.

7.5.2 Why JNI API Is Used in Native-to-Native

If the JNI API has to go through two transitions, which are seemingly redundant from the application developer's point of view, the question is why not directly call the native method. The reason is related to Java semantics.

- **Class initialization**: Before calling into a method of the class, the class must be initialized for correctness reason. The transition code in JNI API implementation ensures this semantics.

- **Class inheritance**: When a method of a specified Java class is called, the actual target method can be an overriding method in the target object, whose class inherits the specified class. The transition code in JNI API implementation ensures this semantics by looking up the actual target method.

- **Pending exception**: Native code execution may incur exception that pends for handling. Without checking the pending exception, subsequent native method call may lead to unexpected result.

The example code below shows the necessary operations conducted in JNI API implementation. It calls the `methodID` of target object `obj` with arguments array `args`, and returns an object.

```
jobject JNICALL CallObjectMethodA(JNIEnv * jni_env,
                                  jobject obj,
                                  jmethodID methodID,
                                  jvalue *args)
{
    if ( ExeceptionOccurred()) return NULL;

    Method *method = (Method *)methodID;

    // lookup actual method of the target obj
    if (! method_is_private(method)) {
       char* m_name = method->get_name();
       char* m_desc = method->get_descriptor();
       method = object_lookup_method(obj, m_name, m_desc);
    }

    // target method cannot be abstract
    if (method->is_abstract()) {
        ThrowNew (jni_env, clazz_AbstractMethodError,
                "attempt to invoke abstract method");
        return NULL;
    }

    //ensure target class is initialized
    jclass m_class = method->get_class();
    if (!class_initialize(jni_env, m_class))
        return NULL;
```

```
//add this pointer "obj" as first argument
unsigned nargs = method->get_num_args();
int size_arg = sizeof(jvalue);
int size_nargs = nargs * arg_size;
jvalue *pargs = (jvalue*)alloca(size_nargs);
pargs[0] = (jvalue)obj;
memcpy(pargs + 1, args, (nargs - 1) * size_arg);

//prepare to call java method
jobject result;
jmethodID mid = (jmethodID)method;

//maintain GC-safety invariant
thread_leave_saferegion();
vm_execute_java_method((mid, pargs, &result);
thread_enter_saferegion();

return (jvalue)result;
}
```

In the code, besides the points mentioned above, it also deals with local object handles that we will discuss soon. Another important note is that before and after the execution of Java method, the VM has to maintain the GC-safety invariant. As we have discussed in threading support for GC, the invariant requires that Java code is unsafe and native code is safe. From VM point of view, it does not care whether the target method is native or not, but regards it as a Java-defined method, thus change the GC-safety status from safe to unsafe. This is not a problem even if the target method is native, because the Java-to-native wrapper code will deal with it, which will be explained in Chapter 9.

Now we know how to call methods back and forth between Java and native worlds. This is the code access support in native interface design. The way for data access support, such as to create or manipulate Java objects in native code is not yet discussed, because it needs garbage collection support that we will also discuss in Chapter 9.

CHAPTER 8

Stack Unwinding

STACK UNWINDING REFERS TO the process that the virtual machine (VM) enumerates the stack contents of a target thread. It usually involves the stack frame enumeration that identifies the method frames on the stack, and stack slot enumeration that identifies the contents in every method frame. The process starts from the top of the stack because that is where the current stack pointer points, and we know stack pointer is part of the thread context that can be directly accessed by a thread.

8.1 WHY STACK UNWINDING

Stack unwinding mainly has two use cases, one is for control flow transfer and the other is for stack contents examination.

- Control flow is decided by thread context, which consists of a stack pointer and a program counter, at least. To transfer the control flow of a thread from one place to another, the contents of its thread context should be changed to point to the new locations. Usually, the process pops off the stack frames from current one up till the target one, without keeping the data of the popped-off frames, hence called destructive stack unwinding.

- Stack unwinding can also be used to enumerate the data on the stack, without changing the thread context contents. This use case is also called stack walking or logical stack unwinding, which is nondestructive. There can be other use cases of stack unwinding depending on the needs.

Stack unwinding is needed in exception handling. It requires the runtime to unwind the stack frame recursively till the catch block (i.e., exception handler) is found in a method, or it is an uncaught exception that may be handled by the operating system. The control flow then transfers from the exception-throwing point to the exception-handling point. Exception handling destroy the stack frames above the method of the exception handler if the exception handler is not in the same method of the exception-throwing. No matter if the exception handler is in the same method or not, stack unwinding is needed for the *whole stack* to output the stack trace for the exception. There are similar control-flow transfer use cases in other programming languages such as the `setjmp` and `longjmp` in C and continuation in Scheme.

Object-tracing garbage collector needs stack unwinding to find root references on runtime stack. A debugger needs stack winding to examine the stack contents. Some performance profiling tool also uses stack-unwinding technique to identify the running methods, so as to identify the execution hotspots.

Return of a method call can be considered as a special case of stack unwinding that unwinds one frame and transfers the control from the callee back to the caller. But it is generally not called stack unwinding. Stack unwinding usually refers to the runtime service, while function return in general does not involve runtime but hardware functionality of a return instruction.

To support stack unwinding, stack frames has to be constructed in a way that satisfies two requirements:

- The stack frames are linked through backward pointers so that the runtime can chase after the pointer chain to find every stack frame. This pointer is then called frame-pointer.

- The information of the stack slots have to be bookkept so that the runtime knows how to enumerate the slots. This is not always needed unless the runtime needs to enumerate the stack contents.

In the rest of this chapter, we discuss how to support stack unwinding for stacks with Java and native method frames.

8.2 STACK UNWINDING FOR JAVA METHOD FRAMES

In Java VM (JVM) implementation, the just-in-time (JIT) compiler decides how to chain the Java method frames. It is similar to what native compiler does.

8.2.1 Stack-Unwinding Design

A common implementation uses the frame-pointer as illustrated in Figure 8.1 to form the frame chain.

The frame pointers in the chain starts from current frame-pointer, which points to a stack slot that stores the frame-pointer pointing to the preceding frame, which in turn points to its preceding frame in a recursive way up till the bottom of the stack where the slot for frame-pointer contains NULL. Current frame-pointer can be a dedicate register (such as `ebp` in X86) or stored in a variable in thread-local storage (TLS). It is an addition to the thread context.

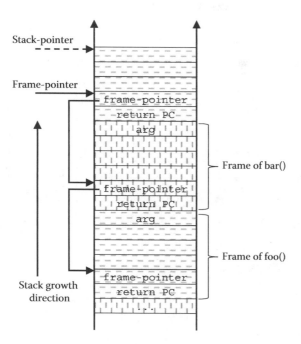

FIGURE 8.1 Stack frames with frame-pointer chain.

It is simple to form such a frame-pointer chain. The JIT compiler only needs to generate following two instructions as the *first* instructions of a method:

```
push frame_pointer
move stack_pointer -> frame_pointer
```

With X86 ISA, they turn into the following two instructions:

```
push ebp
move esp -> ebp
```

Since they are the first two instructions of a method, before they are executed, the last executed instruction is the "call" that invokes current method. At this time point, the current stack top slot pointed by the stack pointer (i.e., esp in X86) is the return PC (i.e., eip in X86). The return PC points to the instruction right after the "call" instruction in the caller code. The current frame-pointer (i.e., ebp in X86) points to the caller frame.

For code sequence below, after "call bar" is executed while before method bar is executed, the program-counter status looks like Figure 8.2.

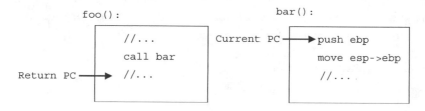

FIGURE 8.2 Snapshot state after executing "call bar" instruction.

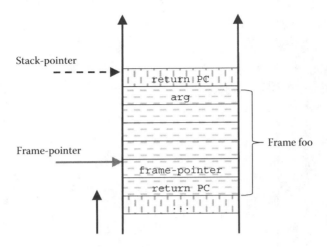

FIGURE 8.3   Stack after executing "`call bar`" instruction.

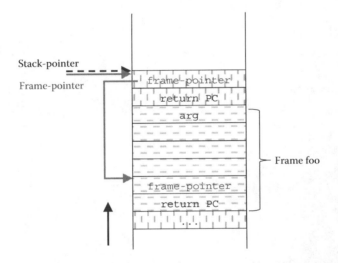

FIGURE 8.4   Stack after the first two instructions of method `bar` are executed.

The stack data at the moment (after executing "`call bar`") look like Figure 8.3. Note the stack pointer and frame-pointer.

After the first two instructions of method `bar` are executed, the stack becomes Figure 8.4. The stack pointer and the frame-pointer point to the same slot, where the old frame-pointer value is stored. The chain of frame-pointer is formed.

To correctly maintain the frame-pointer chain, in the epilog of a method, following instructions have to be executed for method return:

```
pop frame_pointer
return
```

It is the same as following instructions:

```
mov (*frame_pointer) -> frame_pointer
pop     //pop off the stored frame_pointer
return
```

In X86 ISA, they are the following instructions:

```
pop ebp
ret
```

Or in the second form,

```
mov [ebp] -> ebp
ret 4
```

In this way, the frame-pointer register points to the caller stack frame when the method returns.

8.2.2 Stack-Unwinding Implementation

Assuming a frame context data structure holds three register values: frame-pointer, stack pointer, and instruction pointer, then the stack unwinding process looks like this:

```
struct Frame_context{
     uint32 ebp;
     uint32 esp;
     uint32 eip
}

void unwind_stack(VM_Thread* thread)
{
     Frame_context* frame = start_frame(thread);
     while( frame->ebp != NULL){
        //find current frame's method
        uint32 eip = frame->eip;
        Method* method = method_of_pc(eip);
        //operations on the method
        ...
        //find preceding frame context
        frame = find_preceding_frame(frame);
     }
}

// Given a frame, unwind to preceding frame
Frame_context* find_preceding_frame(Frame_context* frame)
{
     frame->eip = frame->ebp - 4;
     frame->esp = frame->ebp - 8;
     //same as "mov [ebp] -> ebp"
     frame->ebp = *(uint32*)frame->ebp;
}
```

A VM implementation may have multiple JIT compilers, or have single JIT compiler with multiple levels of optimizations. Each of them can use different stack frame arrangement. Only the JIT who compiles the method knows exactly how its stack frame is organized. A modular design of stack unwinding needs to identify the JIT compiler for each frame and then delegate the unwinding process to that JIT compiler. The pseudocode looks like the following. An instance of data structure JIT_info is maintained for every compilation unit, e.g., a method. VM can retrieve a JIT_info instance for any generated code address. All the compilation related information can be found through JIT_info instance.

```
struct JIT_info{
      JIT* jit;
      Method* method;
      void* code_addr;
      int code_size;
}


void unwind_stack(VM_Thread* thread){
      Frame_context* frame = start_frame(thread);
      while( frame->ebp != NULL ){
         uint32 eip = frame->eip;
         JIT_info* info = info_of_pc(eip);
         //find current frame's method
         Method* method = info->method;
         //operations on the method
         ...
         //find preceding frame context
         JIT* jit = info->jit;
         frame = jit_find_preceding_frame(jit, frame);
      }
}
```

The function jit_find_preceding_frame() uses the JIT that compiled the method to unwind its frame.

8.3 STACK UNWINDING WITH NATIVE METHOD FRAMES

If the runtime stack has native method frames, stack unwinding is much more complicated, because the native methods are compiled by native compiler whose stack frame chain is unknown to the JVM. In this case, the runtime cannot unwind native frames directly, but it can leverage the native method's wrapper code to work around the issue by working only with the native methods that are called through the wrapper.

8.3.1 Stack-Unwinding Design

As we have discussed, native methods called from Java code or through Java Native Interface (JNI) application programming interface (API) are considered a special part of the Java world. They are called through a wrapper. This is different from the native

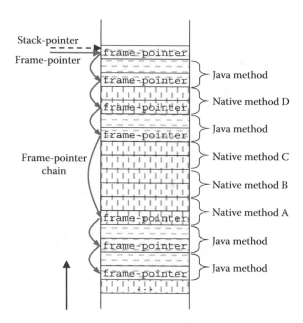

FIGURE 8.5   Stack frame chain with native method frames.

methods that are called directly as a C function. With the wrapper code, there is a chance for the VM to build up the frame-pointer chain, as illustrated in Figure 8.5.

In the figure, native method A is called from Java code, while B and C are called directly without using JNI APIs. In this design, the frames for native method A, B, and C are considered as a single frame, which belongs to method A. Method B and C are considered inlined functions of method A.

Although method B and C do not own any frames on the stack from VM's point of view, they do have from native code point of view. Their native frames are just invisible to the VM, and the native frame-pointer chain in them built by native compiler is ignored by the VM.

In actual implementation, it is complicated to build this frame-pointer chain. The reason is, Java code (i.e., JIT-compiled code) uses dedicated register for its frame-pointer, whose value is not well maintained in the native functions, because the native compiler does not necessarily follow the Java frame's convention.

However, there is no need to use single frame-pointer chain to maintain the stack frames. An idea is to use two levels of chains.

One chain is the original Java frame-pointer chain within a cluster of contiguous Java frames. The Java frame cluster refers to the contiguous Java frames between two native frames, or between stack bottom and first native frame, or between the last native frame and stack top. The frame-pointer chain breaks when it goes to a native method or stack bottom.

The other level of frame-pointer chain links the Java frame clusters, as shown in Figure 8.6. We call this level of frame-pointer "cluster-pointer." In this way, VM can always use the cluster-pointer to find next Java frame cluster and then use Java frame-pointer to find every Java frame within the cluster.

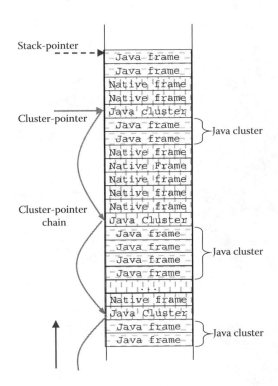

FIGURE 8.6   Java cluster-pointer chain.

Java cluster-pointer chain is started from current "cluster-pointer," which has twofold usage.

- It points to a stack slot containing the cluster-pointer pointing to next Java frame cluster.

- The stack slot it points to has constant offset to the top Java method frame of current Java frame cluster.

This is the same concept as normal frame-pointer, from which the runtime can find both the first slot of current frame and also the next frame.

8.3.2 Java-to-Native Wrapper Design

To support this design, the Java-to-native wrapper code should maintain two pointers, one is the frame pointer and the other is the cluster-pointer. Current frame-pointer is usually kept in a dedicated register (i.e., ebp in X86 ISA) while there is no such a built-in register for cluster-pointer. More importantly, the cluster-pointer should not be touched by native functions, which is difficult to achieve with a register. Since runtime stack is thread-specific data structure, a natural design is to use a thread-local variable in TLS to keep the cluster-pointer.

With this design, the following piece of code should be inserted in the Java-to-native wrapper code right after frame-pointer chain is set up:

```
//get the address of thread-local cluster-pointer
p_cluster_pointer = get_address_of_cluster_pointer();
//push current cluster-pointer on stack to build the chain
push *p_cluster_pointer;
//update current cluster-pointer with stack-pointer
*p_cluster_pointer = stack_pointer;
```

In X86 instructions, they look like the code below:

```
// call result is in eax (p_cluster_pointer)
call get_address_of_cluster_pointer
push [eax]
mov esp -> [eax]
```

After the operation, the stack will look like Figure 8.7 below. From the position pointed by the cluster-pointer, the VM can find the first Java frame of the Java cluster. From the first Java frame, all the rest Java frames in the cluster can be enumerated, till a native frame or stack bottom is reached. (To identify if a frame is Java or native, one way is that the VM can check if the executed code segment of that frame is compiled by JIT or not.)

When the control flow returns to Java code, the following code is needed before returning.

```
//get the address of thread-local cluster-pointer
p_cluster_pointer = get_address_of_cluster_pointer();
//pop the saved cluster-pointer
pop cluster_pointer
//restore the thread-local cluster-pointer
*p_cluster_pointer = cluster_pointer;
```

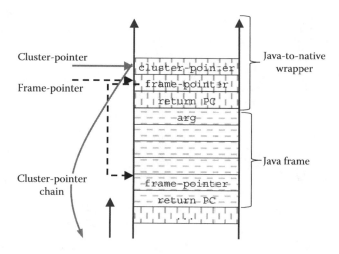

FIGURE 8.7 Cluster-pointer kept in Java-to-native transition.

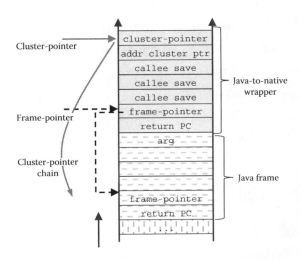

FIGURE 8.8   Stack frame with revised wrapper code with stack-unwinding support.

In X86 instructions, they look like the below:

```
// call result is in eax (p_cluster_pointer)
call get_address_of_cluster_pointer
pop ecx      //pop the saved cluster-pointer to ecx
mov ecx -> [eax]
```

In actual implementation, the address of the thread-local cluster-pointer can be saved on the stack, so as to reduce the function call when the control returns to Java code.

With Java cluster-pointer, the previous example wrapper code for Java-to-native transition should be modified to include cluster-pointer maintenance operations. Note the code pushes some extra data on the stack between the frame-pointer and the cluster-pointer, as shown in Figure 8.8.

```
// Save callee-saved registers first.
push ebp
push ebx
push esi
push edi

//call result is in eax = p_cluster_pointer
call get_address_of_cluster_pointer
//save address, no need to call above func when returns
push eax
//save current value of Java cluster-pointer
push [eax]
//update Java cluster-pointer to point to current one
mov esp -> [eax]
```

```
// push native method arguments
push [esp+28]           //push y
push [esp+36]           //push x
push addr_class_Add     //push class instance of Add
push addr_JNI_Env //push JNI environment var
// call the actual native method implementation
call Java_Add_native_1add
//restore Java cluster-pointer
//get previous value of Java cluster-pointer
pop ecx
//get address of Java cluster pointer
pop ebx
//restore the previous Java cluster-pointer
mov ecx -> [ebx]

// restore callee-saved registers.
pop edi
pop esi
pop ebx
pop ebp
// return and pop Java arguments (x, y)
ret 8
```

The bold face fonts show the modifications we newly introduce for stack unwinding support.

8.3.3 Stack-Unwinding Implementation

To simplify the code, we can group the saved data for the Java-to-native transition into a data structure called M2N_wrapper, referring to the managed-to-native transition data. Its element maps 1 : 1 to the stack entries in Figure 8.8.

```
struct M2N_wrapper{
        M2N_wrapper *jcp;
        M2N_wrapper **addr_jcp;
        uint32 edi;
        uint32 esi;
        uint32 ebx;
        uint32 ebp
        uint32 eip;
}
```

With this data structure, the VM code can access the stack entries in M2N_wrapper through the cluster-pointer jcp.

Now the stack-unwinding process needs to be adjusted to include the cluster-pointer logics, as shown in following pseudocode. Note, in reality, runtime stack always has native frames mixed with Java frames, because the Java main() method is invoked by native code anyway. For this reason, it is not a best solution to determine the bottom the stack by checking (ebp == NULL), since ebp is unlikely NULL at the bottom of Java stack. Instead, the VM can check if the Java cluster-pointer is NULL, which means there is no Java frame any more under current Java cluster. The Java cluster-pointer is set NULL at the beginning when the VM instance is launched.

```
struct Frame_context{
    uint32 ebp;
    uint32 esp;
    uint32 eip;
    M2N_wrapper* jcp; //java cluster-pointer;
}

void unwind_stack(VM_Thread* thread)
{
    Frame_context* frame = start_frame(thread);
    Code_Type type = code_type(frame->eip);

    //iteration through Java frame clusters
    Do {
        //iteration within a Java frame cluster
        while( type == CODE_TYPE_JAVA ){
            Method* method = method_of_pc(frame->eip);
            //operations on the method
            ...
            //find preceding frame context
            uint32 ebp = frame->ebp;
            frame->eip = ebp - 4;
            frame->esp = ebp - 8;
            ebp = *(uint32*)ebp;
            frame->ebp = ebp;
            type = code_type(frame->eip);
        }
        //eip points to native code
        //skip native frames for next java cluster
        M2N_wrapper* jcp = frame->jcp;
        int wrapper_size = sizeof(M2N_wrapper);
        if (jcp != NULL){
            //get the first Java frame in this cluster
            frame->ebp = jcp->ebp;
            frame->eip = jcp->eip;
            frame->esp = jcp - wrapper_size;
            jcp = jcp->jcp;
            frame->jcp = jcp;
            type = code_type(frame->eip);
        }
    }while( type == CODE_TYPE_JAVA)

}
```

The design above enables the fast control-flow transfer between Java and native while supporting runtime stack unwinding. A slower design can keep the meta-data of runtime stack frames in a TLS that is arranged as a shadow stack data structure. Every time when the control transfers to and back from native code, VM can push and pop the meta-data of the native frame in the shadow stack accordingly, to keep the information consistent with the execution status. In this way, stack-unwinding with native frames is possible by retrieving the meta-data from the TLS.

8.3.4 Native Frame versus C Frame

As we mentioned previously, there are cases when a native method invokes another native method through JNI API, which goes through two transitions: one from native to Java and the other from Java to native. The first transition (in `vm_execute_java_method()`) prepares the stack as to call a Java method on top of current native frame. The second transition (in Java-to-native wrapper) does not know it is actually a call from native method, because the stack looks like a call from Java world. The Java-to-native wrapper still maintains the Java cluster-pointer chain as if the preceding stack frame is a Java frame.

To distinguish the native method frame and the traditional C function frame, we use native frame to refer the frame of native method and C frame for traditional function. A C frame can belong to a native method, but the method is called directly from native code, without going through JNI API.

All the native frames are chained by the Java cluster-pointer, even for two consecutive native frames that have no Java frame cluster in between, as shown in Figure 8.9 below.

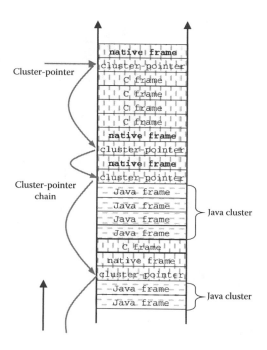

FIGURE 8.9   Stack with consecutive native frames and C frames.

The native-to-native frames do not need extra treatment in stack unwinding. When a native frame is preceded by another native frame, the return code address (`eip`) does not belong to Java method code. Therefore, the VM knows the preceding frame is still a native frame. Then the stack-unwinding routine directly loads next Java cluster-pointer to unwind next native frame.

With the stack-unwinding support, it is possible to design root-set enumeration and exception-throwing. We will discuss them in following chapters.

CHAPTER 9

Garbage Collection Support

W E HAVE DISCUSSED GARBAGE collection (GC) algorithms and the concept of GC safepoint. In this chapter, we discuss the supports virtual machine (VM) provides to garbage collection.

9.1 WHY GC SUPPORT

The main task to support GC in Java code is for the just-in-time (JIT) compiler to generate safepoints Safepoints may include the following sites. They can trigger a collection, block the thread execution, or lead to long-time execution. For each safepoint, a GC-map data structure is needed to support root-set enumeration. It stores information about which locations in the execution context contain references.

1. **Object allocation site**: It is the instruction that may create a new object, such as bytecode new and newarray. When free heap space is insufficient to hold the new object, garbage collection is triggered. This is usually the only place where garbage collection is triggered. A GC-map for the site is definitely needed. On the other hand, when a mutator is allocating an object, a collection may be triggered by another mutator. The first mutator is blocked waiting for the collection to finish, then it can allocate a new object. In this case, a GC-map of the site is necessary too, so that root-set enumeration can be conducted on site.

2. **Call site**: It is the instruction that makes a call into a Java or native method, such as those invoke-family bytecodes. When a collection happens, all the method frames in the runtime stack except the top one are at call sites. So a call site should have GC-map information. On the other hand, the methods can form a recursive call loop that runs a long time. So it is important for the call site to be able to respond to collection requests triggered by other threads with GC polling code.

3. **Blocking site**: It is the instruction, such as monitorenter, that may block the thread execution for an unknown duration. The site should have GC-map information, so that collection can proceed when the current thread is blocked.

4. **Loop back-edge**: It is any place on the back-edge of a loop. The loop that does not include the sites mentioned above may run a long time and is unable to respond to a collection request. It is better to insert GC polling code on the loop back-edge, so that it can poll the collection request and suspend itself if there is a pending request. The polling site should have a GC-map so as to support the collection when the thread suspends in the polling site.

5. **Exception-throwing site**: In Java, many exception-throwing sites do not need to be safepoints, because the exception object has been created for explicit exception-throwing, and the throwing process is a VM service that finishes quickly. But there are some cases when a GC-map is needed.

   - For implicit exceptions that are caught by hardware-fault handler, the handler may have to create some objects for exception object, stack trace, etc., which may cause garbage collection.

   - Sometimes, exception-throwing is used as part of control flow manipulation. Although it is unlikely to form a long-duration execution without any of the sites mentioned above, it may help if some of the exception-throwing sites have GC polling code.

   - If the exception-throwing needs to execute additional code on top of the exception-throwing context, it is just like a call into the additional code. Since the additional code may not have the sites mentioned above, a GC-map has to be built for the exception-throwing site. For example, object creation in exception-throwing usually involves object constructor execution. Another example (not in Java) is the filter expression in Microsoft structured exception handling.

In the list of GC safepoints, the first two sites (object allocation and call site) are mandatory, because GC may happen at object allocation, and call sites are those on stack when GC happens.

The following two sites (blocking site and loop back-edge) are seemingly for optimization purpose, that is, delimiting the response time to collection request. But for some applications, they are also mandatory in order to keep the application moving forward. For example, a thread holding a monitor triggers a collection, while another thread blocks waiting for the same monitor. If the blocking thread does not allow the collection to proceed, the thread triggering the collection can never release the monitor. The situation rarely happens though, so VM implementations exist without supporting the two kinds of GC safepoints.

The last site (exception-throwing) is similar to a call site to a less extent.

For all the GC safepoints, a GC-map should be built. When a colleciton happens, those sites can be on the stack. Call sites and loop back-edges also need to insert GC polling code, so as to break long-duration execution.

In actual implementation, object allocation and blocking operation are implemented as a call into VM service code on memory management and thread management, so they can be covered as call site as well. In this regard, it is ok to say that GC safepoints include only call site and sometimes also loop back-edge.

When GC is triggered, all the threads are suspended at safepoints, with their execution states saved in the respective thread-local storage. The VM then goes through the thread-specific data of every thread (based cn the saved execution state) and global data to find out the root-set. The thread-specific data include runtime stack, register file, and thread-local storage. The globa. data include the loaded classes, interned strings, and global references. The pseudo-code below has been given in Chapter 5.

```
void stop_the_world_root_set_enumeration()
{
    vm_suspend_all_threads();
    for ( each thread thr ) {
      vm_enumerate_root_in_thread( thr );
    }
    vm_enumerate_root_in_globals();  //in global data
}
```

For each thread, the enumeration process is like below. The stack-unwinding details are hidden in the related functions.

```
    void vm_enumerate_root_in_thread(VM_Thread* thread)
    {
        Frame_context *frame = start_frame(thread);
        while(!is_stack_bottom(frame)){
            Code_Type type = code_type(frame);
            if( type == CODE_TYPE_JAVA){
              java_enumerate_root_set(frame);

            }else{ //native code
                native_enumerate_root_set(frame)
            }

            /**
            Here VM can put the class loader of the
            active method's declaring class into
            root references
            **/

            frame = preceding_frame(frame);
        }
    }
```

The root-set enumeration for Java code is conducted by the JIT compiler (or interpreter) and that for the native code is by the VM.

9.2 SUPPORT GARBAGE COLLECTION IN JAVA CODE

In order to enumerate the root-set of Java method, the JIT compiler creates a GC-map data structure for each safepoint of the method it compiles. At the same time, the frame context is designed to support register enumeration in stack-unwinding.

9.2.1 GC-Map

A GC-map at each safepoint book-keeps a bit map for local variables, operand stack, and register file. Each bit represents one variable, a stack slot, or a register. When the entry contains a reference, the corresponding bit is set 1; otherwise it is 0. There are usually three ways to generate a GC-map: runtime update, compile-time generation, and lazy generation.

9.2.1.1 Runtime Update

A GC-map can be maintained dynamically at runtime in a way that every store into the variables, the stack frame or registers, updates the corresponding bit accordingly. A reference stored into an entry originally containing a non-reference means to set the bit, while a non-reference stored into a reference slot means to reset the bit.

This is easy to implement and may be suitable for an interpreter, but it incurs too high runtime overhead to be interesting for JIT.

9.2.1.2 Compile-Time Generation

The runtime update approach does not generate GC-map data for every safepoint ahead of time, but maintains runtime GC-map dynamically for the method under execution. As a comparison, JIT can deduce the GC-map result with data flow analysis before Java code execution. It needs to generate the GC-map only once for each safepoint at compile-time.

To identify the references on stack and in variables, a two-pass analysis is usually needed. A forward pass propagates the type information of the variables, so that the reference variables are identified. A backward pass back-tracks the liveness information from the out-going variables to identify which reference variables are live over which period. Then, for each safepoint, the compiler knows all the live reference variables at that point, and save that information into GC-map of that safepoint. It is the same for the elements in the stack frame. Registers are used mainly to store data from the local variables and stack for faster processing, so the references in registers can be deduced from them and maintained by the register allocation algorithm.

Maintaining the GC-map information for all methods' all call sites causes space overhead. Study shows the extra space needed can be around 10% in size of all JIT-generated information. This approach trades space for runtime efficiency.

9.2.1.3 Lazy Generation

It is possible to lazily generate GC-maps only for sites on the stack when a collection really happens. That is, there is no GC-map information maintained if no collection happens. When a collection happens, the VM checks all the frames on the stack and then generates a GC-map for each frame by recompiling the corresponding method or simulating the method execution up to the current safepoint on the stack. Note that every frame has to be analyzed for its own GC-map, so the same method may be analyzed multiple times, because the same method can be executed by multiple threads or recursively (directly or indirectly) invoked by the same thread. While this approach tries to have a compromise between runtime and memory overhead, it is only useful when runtime efficiency is less critical than memory.

A conceptual implementation of root-set enumeration for Java code may look like below. The GC-map data structure GC_map holds four bit vectors that indicate the corresponding entries holding references. Depending on the actual implementation, it is not necessary to be four bit vectors.

```
struct GC_map{
    bitvector       locals;       //local variables
    bitvector       temps;              //temp vars spilled on stack
    bitvector       registers;   //registers that have refs
    bitvector       args          //outgoing arguments for call
};

struct Safe_point{
    uint32  eip;  //the PC of safepoint
    GC_map* gc_map;
}

struct JIT_info{
    JIT* jit;
    Method* method;
    void* code_addr;
    int code_size;

    //number of safepoints of this method.
    //
    int num_of_safepoints;

    //the array below is actually allocated dynamically
    //to have num_of_safepoints elements
    Safe_point* safepoint[1]
}

void java_enumerate_root_set(Frame_context* frame)
{
    Safe_point* safepoint = safepoint_of_frame(frame);
    GC_map* gc_map = safepoint->gc_map;
    jit_enumerate_locals(frame, gc_map->locals);
    jit_enumerate_temps(frame, gc_map->temps);
    jit_enumerate_registers(frame, gc_map->registers);
    jit_enumerate_args(frame, gc_map->args);

}
```

The code below is an example of enumerating registers. When looking into the code, one can find it is actually not enumerating registers per se, but enumerating the memory slots where registers are saved. We will explain the reason next.

```
//registers are saved on stack before entering GC
void jit_enumerate_registers(Frame_context* frame,
                             bitvector bv)
{
    //find the starting address where registers are saved
    uint32 start_addr = register_saved_start_addr(frame);

    for( int i=0; i< reg_num; i++){
        if( test_bit(bv, i) == 0 ) continue;
        //Bit set means the slot holds a reference
        uint32 root_slot = start_addr + i*slot_size;
        gc_add_root((Object**)root_slot);
    }
}
```

In the conceptual code example, the memory address that holds an object reference is called a root slot, and the address is added into the root-set for GC. As we discussed in the chapter on GC algorithms, when GC needs to traverse the object graph from roots, it dereferences the root slot as follows.

```
Object* root_ref = *(Object**) root_slot;
```

When GC moves the object, it has to update the slot to hold a new reference pointing to the new object location.

```
Object* ref = *(Object**) slot;
//move object from ref to new_ref
Object* new_ref = object_copy(ref);
//update the original slot that holds ref
*(Object**) slot = new_ref;
```

If another memory slot holds a reference pointing to the same moved object, its content should be updated as well to point to the new location. As the slot holds only the old object address, GC needs a way to find the new location of the moved object. A solution is for the collector to save the new address value in the original object, called forwarding pointer, since the original object is no longer useful. Then when GC reaches a slot that holds a reference, it checks a flag in the referenced object whether it has been moved or not. If the object is moved, the collector updates the slot to point to the new location. Otherwise, it moves the object. The logic is something like the code below.

```
Object* ref = *(Object**) slot;
//assuming new address is kept in original object header
//a bit in the header indicating if the object is moved
Object* new_ref = NULL;
if( is_forwarded(ref) ){
    //if it is moved already, load the new location
    new_ref = forwarding_pointer(ref);
}else{
    //move object from ref to new_ref
    new_ref = object_copy(ref);
}
//update the slot that holds root_ref
*(Object**)slot = new_ref;
```

In a parallel GC implementation, it is possible for multiple collectors to reach the same object (from different traversal paths of the object graph) and try to move it, so the object-moving operation has to be mutually exclusive among the competing collectors, and only one collector can move it successfully. The losing collectors will retrieve the object's new location and update their slots accordingly. With transactional memory support, the process can be different, which we will discuss later in Chapter 19.

9.2.2 Stack-Unwinding with Registers

To support GC that moves objects (i.e., moving-GC), GC enumerates the root slots in memory and stack. Then, the question is how GC enumerates registers, since registers are not held in memory and are always actively being used.

At a call site of Java method, JIT usually saves caller-save registers on the stack before calling and leaves the callee-save registers intact. If the callee method needs to use those callee-save registers, it will save them before using and restore them before return.

If a callee-save registers contains an object reference and GC happens during the callee's execution, the reference in the callee-save registers also needs to be updated to the new location if the referenced object is moved.

The solution to register enumeration is simple: Save them on the stack and enumerate the stack slots. After collection, the values are restored to registers before the mutator execution is resumed. This is the same as for a method call.

If all the registers are caller-save registers, before the call instruction, the registers with live data are saved on the stack. Since JIT knows the stack's GC-map at call site, GC has no problem to enumerate them and update their values. After the call, the caller restores the saved data to registers, which then have the latest data.

If some registers are callee-save registers and are to be used by the callee method, they will be saved in the callee's prolog code and restored in the epilog code. In this way, when GC happens in the callee, the callee-save registers stay in the callee's stack frame. (Actually, they are reported as part of the caller stack frame because they keep the data of caller execution status and only the caller knows if they held any object references).

Now we need to modify the data structure of `Frame_context`, so that it does not only hold the important pointers, but also have the stack addresses of the registers saved on the stack. In this way, JIT can enumerate those "register slots" to support moving-GC.

The old design of `Frame_context` is the following:

```
struct Frame_context{
        uint32 ebp;
        uint32 esp;
        uint32 eip;
        M2N_wrapper* jcp; //java cluster-pointer;
}
```

The revised design can be something like below, to include the address of stack slots where registers stay.

```
struct Frame_context {
    uint32 ebp;
    uint32 esp;
    uint32 eip;
    M2N_wrapper* jcp;

    //callee-save registers
    uint32 *p_edi;
    uint32 *p_esi;
    uint32 *p_ebx;

    //caller-save registers
    uint32 *p_eax;
    uint32 *p_ecx;
    uint32 *p_edx;

}
```

When the VM unwinds the stack, it will fill the frame context with the right values, with help from JIT for the registers. Assuming the caller-save registers are saved before the outgoing arguments of the call and the callee-save registers are saved in the beginning of the callee frame, the stack looks like Figure 9.1.

For example, the following pseudo-code unwinds one level stack frame.

```
Frame_context* preceding_frame(Frame_context* frame)
{
    int num_callee_saved = 0;
    uint32 ebp = 0

    Code_Type type = code_type(frame->eip);
    if( type == CODE_TYPE_JAVA ){
```

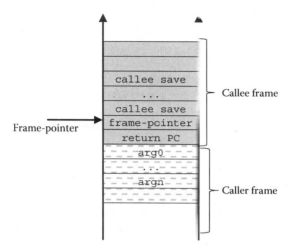

FIGURE 9.1   Stack data before and after a call.

```
        JIT_info* info = info_of_pc(frame->eip);
        //number of callee saved registers in this frame
        num_callee_saved = info->num_saved_callee_regs;

        //find preceding frame-context
        ebp = frame->ebp;
        frame->eip = ebp - 4;
        frame->esp = ebp - 8;
        frame->ebp = *(uint32*)ebp;

   }else{ //eip points to native code
      //number of callee saved registers in M2N_wrapper is const
      num_callee_saved = NUM_M2N_SAVED_REGS;

      M2N_wrapper* jcp = frame->jcp;
      if (jcp == NULL) return NULL;

      ebp = jcp->ebp;
      frame->ebp = ebp;
      frame->eip = jcp->eip;
      frame->esp = jcp - SIZE_M2N_WRAPPER;
      frame->jcp = jcp->jcp;
}

//assume callee registers are always saved in defined order
switch (num_callee_saved){
   case 3: frame->p_edi = (uint32*)(ebp - 12);
   case 2: frame->p_esi = (uint32*)(ebp - 8);
   case 1: frame->p_ebx = (uint32*)(ebp - 4);
   case 0: break;
```

```
    default: assert(0);
 }

 return frame;
}
```

In the example code, it takes care of only the stack slots of the callee-saved registers. The slots of caller-saved registers, as part of the caller's frame, are known to the GC-map at the safepoint of the call site. Here, we assume the callee-save registers are always saved in order, that is, if the callee only saves one callee-save register, it must be `ebx`; if there are two, they must be `ebx` and `esi`.

The frame context includes also caller-save registers. That is used for cases when the frame is not at a call site, but at a hardware exception. The values in caller-save registers are not saved by the method before the exception, but saved by the hardware in exception context that should be enumerated as well.

9.3 SUPPORT GARBAGE COLLECTION IN THE NATIVE CODE

The native method is not compiled by the JIT compiler and cannot use the same technique as the Java method for garbage collection support because of the following two reasons.

- If there is a reference pointer in the native stack frame when a collection happens, the VM is unable to tell exactly if it is a pointer or an integer or other data type because it does not know the native frame layout, and thus cannot support a precise GC.

- Another problem is more serious. If the native code can access the object pointer directly, the native compiler may store it in a physical register or other native-controlled place (we call it "native place") that is unknown to the VM. In this case, even conservative GC is impossible. When an object is moved during a collection while the new location is not updated in the native place, access to the object pointer by the subsequent native code will lead to unexpected results.

The solution to the problems above is to not allow the native code to access object references directly as Java code. Instead, the object pointers should be stored in a separate place that is VM controlled (we call it "managed place") and can be accessed only indirectly by the native code. To the two problems above,

- Since object pointers are stored in a managed place, the VM can precisely enumerate them and support a precise GC;

- Since the native code cannot directly access object pointers, the native compiler has no way to place them into the native place. In this way, the VM guarantees that object pointers are stored in and only in managed places.

9.3.1 Object Reference Access

JNI defines local reference and global reference to allow indirect reference access. Local reference is like a local variable that exists only within a native method scope. Global reference can survive a native-method invocation until it is freed explicitly. It allows the native method to pass and return Java objects, and access and create Java objects while supporting a precise GC. That is, when precise collection happens, there can be native frame(s) in or on top of the stack. JNI does not define how the VM implements local and global references.

An implementation for the indirect object reference access can box object reference in object handle, and object handles are linked together, so that the VM can find all of them. It can be something like Figure 9.2 below.

`Object_handle` data structure can be a simple indirection:

```
struct Object_handle{
    Object* obj;
}
```

`Object_handle` is embedded in `Object_handle_node` for management purpose.

```
struct Object_handle_node{
    Object* obj;
    Object_handle_node* next;
    Object_handle_node* prev;
}
```

The pointer to each object is boxed in an object handle. Native code access `obj1` through `obj_ref1`. Internally, the VM can get the object with the following code.

```
obj1 = obj_ref1->obj;
```

Or,

```
obj1 = *(Object*)obj_ref1;
```

This piece of code cannot be executed when a collection is happening, which is unsafe because GC may move the object leaving an invalid object pointer. It has to be protected by the VM

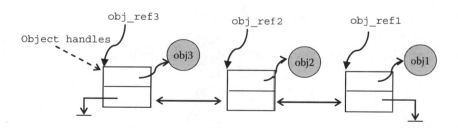

FIGURE 9.2   Object handles arranged as a linked list.

who prevents collection from happening. Conceptually, it should be surrounded with code like below:

```
thread_leave_saferegion();
obj1 = obj_ref1->obj;
//obj1 is valid since GC is disabled
... access to obj1 ...
thread_enter_saferegion();
```

Each method-execution instance has a list of object handles that maintain all the objects that the native code may access. The head of the list is kept in the native method frame, so that GC can find it to enumerate the objects. The object handles (not the objects) are discarded when the method returns. We add an entry in the M2N_wrapper data structure to store the head of the object handle list, as given below.

```
struct M2N_wrapper{
    M2N_wrapper *jcp;
    M2N_wrapper **addr_jcp;
    Object_handle_node *local_obj_handles;
    uint32 edi;
    uint32 esi;
    uint32 ebx;
    uint32 ebp
    uint32 eip;
}
```

When a JNI API function returns an object reference, it has to be wrapped by an object handle, and only the pointer to the object handle is returned.

Method arguments are part of local variables. The arguments of the native method can include object references, as defined in the method signature. They are also accessed through object handles in the native code. When pushing arguments for the native method in Java-to-native transition wrapper code, the wrapper should create object handles to wrap the reference arguments, and push the addresses of object handles as actual arguments to the native code.

The object handles for the method cannot be created when the VM generates the wrapper code of the method, even if the number of reference arguments is known at compile-time. The reason is, as already mentioned, the object handles are dynamic data structures that exist for each method *invocation instance*, just like automatic variables of the method.

With local object handles, it is possible to enumerate the root-set in the native code.

```
void native_enumerate_root_set(Frame_context* frame)
{
    M2N_wrapper* m2n = frame->jcp;
    Object_handle_node* node = m2n->local_obj_handles;
```

```
while(node){
   gc_add_root((Object**)node);
   node = node->next;
}
}
```

Since local object handles are released once the native method returns, it is impossible to keep the referenced object live out of the method scope, or across the invocation instances of the method. The global object handle can help accomplish the goal. The global object handle is implemented in the same way as the local object handle. The only difference is, the head of the object handle list is globally unique in the VM. Object handle nodes in the list are released only explicitly.

9.3.2 Object Handle Implementation

Since every native method should have at least one reference argument (object instance for non-static method or class instance for static method), the wrapper always needs to deal with object handles. The wrapper code example given earlier has to be modified to include this work.

The wrapper code creates the same number of object handle nodes as that of the reference arguments. The number can be computed at compile-time by iterating the arguments on their types. Then the wrapper code links the object handle nodes together and put the head pointer to the M2N_wrapper entry on the stack. Finally, it pushes the arguments for the native method including the object handles for reference arguments and calls the method. When the native method returns, the wrapper code should free all the object handle nodes created for and in this method.

```
// Save callee-saved registers first.
push ebp
push ebx
push esi
push edi

//place-holder for list head pointer to local obj handles
push 0

//construct cluster-pointer chain
call get_address_of_cluster_pointer
push eax
push [eax]
mov esp -> [eax]

//preparing local object handles
push method  // (Method*)method describing native_add
call new_local_obj_handles
//return value eax holds head pointer to handles
```

```
        pop   //pop the input "method"

        // push native method arguments
        push [esp+size_M2N_wrapper]    //push y
        push [esp+size_M2N_wrapper+8] //push x
        push eax      //push class Add's local object handle
        push addr_JNI_Env //push JNI environment var
        // call the actual native method implementation
        call Java_Add_native_1add
        mov eax -> ebx //save return value

        //unhandle the return value if it is reference type
        //i.e., get the actual obj pointer to return
        //do not unhandle if return ref value is null
        //xor ebx ebx
        //je unhandle_done
        //mov [ebx] -> ebx
unhandle_done:
        //free the local object handles
        call free_local_obj_handles
        //restore return value
        mov ebx -> eax

        //restore Java cluster-pointer
        pop ecx
        pop ebx
        mov ecx -> [ebx]

        // restore callee-saved registers.
        pop edi
        pop esi
        pop ebx
        pop ebp
        // return and pop Java arguments (x, y)
        ret 8
```

We still use the same application example as before to illustrate the design. Its native method native_add() is static, so it has a reference argument of the class instance.

```
public class Add{
      public static native int native_add(int x, int y);
      public static int add(int x, int y){
            return native_add(x, y);
      }
}
JNIEXPORT jint JNICALL Java_Add_native_1add
   (JNIEnv *, jclass, jint, jint);
```

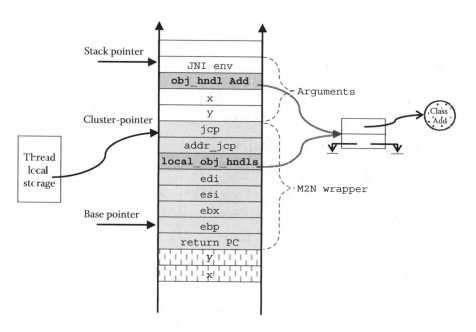

FIGURE 9.3   Stack status before calling into the native method.

In previous discussion on the wrapper design, the class instance's reference is passed to the native code on the stack as an argument. Now the stack should replace it with the object handle pointer, as shown in Figure 9.3.

Note the two added entries in bold face in the figure: one for the object handle of Add class instance and the other for the list head of local object handles. They both point to the same object handle node, which is the only node in the list at the beginning of the native method execution.

The wrapper uses two functions dealing with the creation and releasing of local object handles.

```
Object_handle_node* get_local_obj_handles()
{
   VM_Thread* thread = current_thread();
   M2N_wrapper* jcp = thread->jcp;
   Object_handle_node* handles = jcp->local_obj_handles;
   return handles;
}

Object_handle_node* new_local_obj_handles(Method* method)
{
   Object_handle_node* handles = get_local_obj_handles();
   assert( handles == NULL );
   //generate handles for reference arguments of method
   //linked in order of arguments from head
   handles = ...
```

```
    return handles;
}

void free_local_obj_handles()
{
    Object_handle_node* handles = get_local_obj_handles();
    assert( handles != NULL );
    //free all the object handle nodes
}
```

For performance reason, the functions of creating and releasing local object handles can be replaced with machine code sequence. Since allocating memory in heap is usally more expensive than on the stack, which is thread-local, it is also a performance optimization to allocate the object handles for reference arguments on the stack. The releasing is even faster if on the stack, because it is piggybacked when the wrapper code returns to the caller.

With object handle support, native code can support a precise GC in its execution. In other words, from the application developer's point of view, a precise GC can happen at any place of the native method as long as the JNI Application programming interfaces (APIs) are used, (that is, the native method is a GC safe region), and there is no need to insert safepoint, which is infeasible for the native code.

9.3.3 GC-Safety Property Maintenance

As a contrast, the Java method by itself is GC-unsafe, which needs safepoints inserted to provide opportunities for GC to happen. When a Java method calls a native method, the code becomes GC-safe. Then the question is how the GC-safety state transition is implemented when Java method calls a native method. It is natural to put the transitioning code in the native method wrapper code. The code to enable/disable GC should be inserted before and after the invocation of the native method, as shown below in the modified wrapper code.

```
    // Save callee-saved registers first.
    push ebp
    push ebx
    push esi
    push edi

    //place-holder for head pointer to local obj handles
    push 0

    //construct cluster-pointer chain
    call get_address_of_cluster_pointer
    push eax
    push [eax]
    mov esp -> [eax]
```

```
      //preparing local object handles
      push method  //(Method*)method describing native_add
      call new_local_obj_handles
      //return value eax holds head pointer to handles
      pop  //pop the input "method"

      // push native method arguments
      push [esp+size_M2N_wrapper]   //push y
      push [esp+size_M2N_wrapper+8] //push x
      push eax     //push class Add's local object handle
      push addr_JNI_Env //push JNI environment var
      //enable GC for native method
      call thread_enter_saferegion
      // call the actual native method implementation
      call Java_Add_native_1add
      mov eax -> ebx //save return value
      //disable GC for native method
      call thread_leave_saferegion

      //unhandle the return value if it is reference type
      //i.e., get the actual obj pointer to return
      //do not unhandle if return ref value is null
      //xor ebx ebx
      //je unhandle_done
      //mov [ebx] -> ebx
unhandle_done:
      //free the local object handles
      call free_local_obj_handles
      //restore return value
      mov ebx -> eax

      //restore Java cluster-pointer
      pop ecx
      pop ebx
      mov ecx -> [ebx]

      // restore callee-saved registers.
      pop edi
      pop esi
      pop ebx
      pop ebp
      // return and pop Java arguments (x, y)
      ret 8
```

With the GC enabling/disabling code inserted in the Java-to-native wrapper, the VM ensures the GC-safety invariant when the Java code calls the native method.

9.3.4 Object Body Access

Now we have a solution to object reference access in the native code. We also need a solution to object body access. The VM does not allow the native code to hold a pointer to an object, and therefore, there is no way for the native code to access the object body through pointer arithmetics. It has to be conducted indirectly as well as the object reference access.

An implementation of indirect object body access can introduce a mapping table from a variable index to an object field. When the native code accesses an object reference variable, it actually accesses the variable's index. Then the VM maps the index to the object field address, and finishes the operation requested by the native code. The index can be implemented in anyway as long as it uniquely identifies the field and can be used to reach the field's information.

JNI has defined APIs for this purpose. For example, in Java code, to set the reference field `field` of object `obj` with `value`, it can be as simple as

```
obj.field = value;
```

With JNI API, the native code has to use the following function, where the object field `field` is replaced by an index `fieldID`. The arguments with `jobject` type are reference arguments that are passed with object handles.

```
void JNICALL SetObjectField(JNIEnv * jni_env,
                            jobject obj,
                            jfieldID fieldID,
                            jobject value);
```

The VM should implement the APIs, since ultimately the VM has to access the object field directly to manipulate it. The question is how the VM can guarantee the safety and portability properties, and support precise GC. The answer is that the VM has to disable GC when it enters a potentially GC-unsafe region or when the code is probably GC-unsafe. Disabling GC prevents GC from happening so as to ensure no object is moved. Here is the example implementation of the JNI API above.

```
//VM code accessing an object field of an object
jobject GetObjectField(JNIEnv *env,
                       jobject jobj,
                       jfieldID fieldID)
{
    //convert field ID to VM's field description
    Field *fld = (Field*)fieldID;
    if (!class_initialize(env, fld->get_class()))
        return NULL;

    if (ExceptionCheck(env))
        return NULL;
```

```
    //same as vm_disable_gc()
    thread_leave_saferegion();

    //access the Java object field
    Object* java_ref = (Object_handle)jobj->obj;
    //get the offset of the field in object
    uint32 offset = fld->get_offset();
        Object_handle* new_handle = NULL;

    Object* fld_obj = *(Object**)(java_ref + offset);
    if( fld_obj != NULL ){
        //for non-NULL reference, box it
        new_handle = allocate_local_obj_handle();
        if (new_handle != NULL) {
            new_handle->obj = fld_obj;
        }
    }

    //same as vm_enable_gc()
    thread_enter_saferegion();

    return (jobject)new_handle;
}
```

The VM leave/enter safe-region functions ensure that no collection happens between them when the VM code is accessing the object. If a collection is triggered before the code leaves the safe region, the thread calling `thread_leave_saferegion()` will block in the function and not proceed until the collection finishes. It has been discussed in the chapter on threading design.

With JNI APIs, an application can develop the following code to access an object's field. The field's name and type are fname and ftype, respectively.

```
//application code accessing a reference field of an object
jobject ReadObjectField(JNIEnv *env,
                        jobject obj,
                        const char * fname,
                        const char * ftype,)
{
    1: // Get object handle of obj's class instance
    jclass clazz = (*env)->GetObjectClass(env, obj);

    2: // Get field description with its name and signature
    jfieldID fid = (*env)->GetFieldID(env, clazz, fname, ftype);
    if (fid == NULL) return NULL;
```

```
3: /* Load the field data (a reference) to object handle */
jobject fobj = (*env)->GetObjectField(env, obj, fid);
return fobj;
}
```

The types of jclass, jobject, and jfieldID are opaque to the application code. The application developer should not assume their actual definitions.

Like their Java counterparts, variables of type jclass and jobject, as object handles, keep the referenced objects live in the object handles' live range, which is defined by the native language semantics. In this case, they are live from the point they are declared until the point the method returns. That means, if there is a collection happening between the statements 1 and 2, the access to clazz is still valid.

9.3.5 Object Allocation

Besides accessing the Java object, the native code can also create a Java object and return it to Java code. The object is boxed in local object handle when it is created in the native method and should be unboxed when it is returned to the Java world. The unboxing (or unhandling) operation is conducted in the wrapper code of the native method, which has been shown in the wrapper code above.

Below is the example code showing how the new object is created in the VM code. It is the implementation of JNI API NewObjectA(). The parameters meth and args are the object's constructor and its arguments.

```
jobject JNICALL NewObjectA(JNIEnv * jenv,
                           jclass clzz,
                           jmethodID meth,
                           jvalue *args)
{

    if (ExceptionCheck(jenv) || clzz == NULL ) return NULL;

    Class* clss = jclass_to_Class(clzz);

    if(clss->is_interface() || clss->is_abstract()) {
        // Cannot instantiate interface or abstract class.
        char* cname = clss->get_name()->bytes;
        ThrowNew(jenv, Clazz_InstantiationException, cname);
        return NULL;
    }
    if (!class_initialize(jni_env, clss)) {
        return NULL;
    }

    thread_leave_saferegion();
    //allocate an object with clss type
```

```
Object* new_obj = gc_alloc_object(clss);
//allocate an object handle to box new object later
Object_handle handle = allocate_local_obj_handle();
if (new_obj == NULL || handle == NULL) {
    //cannot allocate either obj or its handle, quit
    thread_enter_saferegion();
    return NULL;
}
//box with object handle
handle->object = new_obj;
thread_enter_saferegion();

//call the constructor with arguments
CallNonvirtualVoidMethodA(jenv, handle, clzz, meth, args);
if ( ExceptionCheck(jenv) ) return NULL;

return handle;
}
```

The function call `gc_alloc_object()` returns an object reference, so it is a GC-unsafe operation, which has to be operated in a GC-unsafe region. On the other hand, if the heap is low, it may trigger a GC event. That is not a problem, because `vm_trigger_gc()` assumes to happen in a GC-unsafe region.

Besides local object handles, there are some other thread-local objects that should be enumerated as well, such as the exception object that is not yet handled by an exception handler, or a blocked monitor object, depending on the VM implementation.

Obviously, the runtime overhead in the native code is much higher than in Java code. This is the cost of supporting GC in the native code, and is needed to maintain the safety and portability semantics. The API hides all the details of object implementation from the native code (and native compiler). Only the VM knows the details and conducts actual operations upon the object on behalf of the native code.

9.4 SUPPORT GARBAGE COLLECTION IN A SYNCHRONIZED METHOD

It is worth mentioning how a synchronized method supports GC.

9.4.1 Synchronized Java Method

In the prolog and epilog of the synchronized Java method, the following code should be inserted respectively after/before dealing with callee-save registers push/pop.

Code in prolog:

```
//pushed callee-saved registers
//push the monitor object for monitorenter
push monitor_obj
call vm_object_lock
```

Code in epilog:

```
//push the monitor object for monitorexit
push monitor_obj
call vm_object_unlock
//to pop callee-saved registers
```

Functions vm_object_lock() and vm_object_unlock() are runtime functions for monitor enter/exit. The execution of vm_object_lock() may block waiting for the monitor, when the thread should not prevent a collection from happening.

In Java code, although the call site is a safepoint, it is no longer GC-safe once the control goes out of the safepoint or enters the Java callee method. In case the thread is blocked by the monitor, the VM should provide GC support here.

The code below is the pseudo-code for the slow path of monitor entering. Slow path means the thread may be blocked if it cannot acquire the lock. We have discussed the code in the chapter on threading design. Here the code is modified in two places:

1. The thread puts its sleep-waiting period in a safe region to allow a collection to happen.

2. If a collection indeed happens when the thread is sleeping, the monitor object may be moved. Then after the thread wakes up from sleeping, it needs to reload the monitor object from the enumerated slot.

```
void lock_blocking(Object* jmon)
{
    VM_Thread* self = thread_self();
    //try to hold the lock
    while( !lock_non_blocking(jmon) ){
        //cannot hold the lock, go to sleep
        //record the blocked lock
        self->blocked_lock = jmon;
        self->status = THREAD_STATE_MONITOR;

        //sleep waiting for wakeup in safe-region
        thread_enter_saferegion();
        wait_for_signal( self->SIG_UNLOCK, 0);
        thread_leave_saferegion();
        //reloading the jmon object after potential GC
        jmon = self->blocked_lock;

        //wake up by a thread that unlocks the monitor
        self->status = THREAD_STATE_RUNNING;
        self->blocked_lock = null;
```

```
        //loop back competing for lock again
    }
    //finally hold the lock and then return
    return;
}
```

In the VM's enumeration code for each thread, we should add the following:

```
VM_Thread* self = current_thread();
gc_add_root((Object**)&(self->blocked_lock));
```

This ensures the monitor object (blocked_lock), actually the slot holding its reference, is enumerated during a collection.

There are a few other objects in the VM that are not in mutators' execution context. They all can be handled in a similar way.

9.4.2 Synchronized Native Method

If it is a synchronized native method, the compiler should insert the monitor enter/exit code in Java-to-native wrapper, right before/after it enables/disables GC, as given below.

```
//process M2N_wrapper on stack
//push native method arguments
push [esp+size_M2N_wrapper]          //push y
push [esp+size_M2N_wrapper+8]        //push x
push eax      //push class Add's local object handle
push addr_JNI_Env //push JNI environment var

//push the monitor object for monitorenter
//save the monitor object in esi for monitorexit
mov [eax] -> esi
push esi
call vm_object_lock

//enable GC for native method
call thread_enter_saferegion
// call the actual native method implementation
call Java_Add_native_1add
mov eax -> ebx //save return value
//disable GC for native method
call thread_leave_saferegion

//push the monitor object for monitorexit
push esi
call vm_object_unlock
```

```
//unbox the return value if it is reference type
//free the local object handles
//restore return value
//restore M2N_wrapper saved data
//return and pop Java arguments
```

This works because when the current thread blocks in vm_object_lock() and GC happens, all the reference arguments are kept in local object handles that GC will enumerate. The only missed root is the monitor object, which will be enumerated separately and correctly.

To enumerate the monitor object specifically is not a general solution. A more general solution is to box the monitor object in an object handle, so that it can be enumerated in a unified way together with other object handles. This is easy to implement for a synchronized native method which already has local object handles initialized before calling vm_object_lock(). Then the code snippet for the thread waiting on the monitor becomes the following. The object handle is automatically linked into the list of local object handles initialized by the native method.

```
void lock_blocking(Object* jmon)
{
    VM_Thread* self = thread_self();

    Object_handle* hndl = allocate_local_obj_handle();
    hndl->obj = jmon;

    //try to hold the lock
    while( !lock_non_blocking(jmon) ){
        //cannot hold the lock, go to sleep
        //record the blocked lock
          self->blocked_lock = jmon;
          self->status = THREAD_STATE_MONITOR;

          //sleep waiting for wakeup in safe-region
          thread_enter_saferegion();
          wait_for_signal( self->SIG_UNLOCK, 0);
          thread_leave_saferegion();
          //reloading the jmon object after potential GC
          jmon = hndl->obj;

          //wake up by a thread that unlocks the monitor
          self->status = THREAD_STATE_RUNNING;
          self->blocked_lock = null;
          //loop back competing for lock again
    }

    free_local_obj_handle(hndl);
```

```
    //finally hold the lock and then return
    return;
}
```

The solution with a local object handle works for the synchronized Java method as well. Although the Java method does not have the local object handles setup in its prolog, this newly created object handle will be linked to the list of object handles set up by the last native frame pointed by the current Java cluster-pointer. It is then freed before vm_object_lock() returns.

With that said, vm_object_lock() cannot be directly invoked by the Java code for bytecode monitorenter implementation or directly called by JNI API function MonitorEnter(). It is related to runtime helper design, which we will discuss later in Chapter 10.

9.5 GC SUPPORT IN TRANSITIONS BETWEEN JAVA AND NATIVE CODES

We have discussed GC supports in Java code and in native code; the remaining part is with the transitions between Java and native codes. The processes of transition have been discussed. Here is a summary from GC's point of view.

9.5.1 Native-to-Java

When calling the Java method from the native method, the native code calls JNI APIs such as CallObjectMethodA to invoke the method defined in the Java class. The method invocation APIs then call the bridge code (i.e., vm_execute_java_method()) to prepare the stack for the Java method call. The bridge code needs to unbox reference arguments and push object references on the stack, including the target object of the call (i.e., the method-declaring class for the static method or the receiver object for the virtual method). These operations touch objects and are GC-unsafe, so the JNI APIs implementation should leave/enter the GC saferegion before and after calling the bridge code vm_execute_java_method(). We need to modify the previous implementation of the bridge code to reflect the process of object handles unboxing for input arguments and boxing for return value of reference type.

```
void vm_execute_java_method( jmethodID* mid,
                             jvalue* pargs,
                             jvalue* ret)
{
    //thread leaves safe-region before calling this function
    assert( !thread_in_saferegion() );

    Method* method = (Method*)mid;
    //number of words in arguments (not number of arguments,
    //because long/double have two words)
    char* desc; //method descriptor
    java_type ret_type; //return type
```

```
method_get_param_info(method, &desc, &ret_type);

//process input values.
uint32 nargs = 0;
for(++desc; (*desc) != ')'; desc++) {
   java_type type = (java_type)*desc;
   switch( type ){
      case JAVA_TYPE_CLASS:
      case JAVA_TYPE_ARRAY:

         //unbox reference arguments in place,
         //replace object handle to object reference
         Object_handle* hndl;
         hndl = (Object_handle*)pargs[nargs];
         pargs[nargs] = (jvalue)(hndl ? hndl->obj : NULL);

         while(type == '[') desc++;
         if( type == 'L' )
             while( type != ';' ) desc++;
         nargs++;
         break;

      case JAVA_TYPE_LONG:
      case JAVA_TYPE_DOUBLE:
         nargs+ = 2;
         break;

      default:
         nargs++;
   }
}

//get entry point of Java method
void* java_entry = method_get_entry(method);

uint32 eax, edx;     //return values
native_to_java_call(java_entry, nargs, pargs, &eax, &edx);

//check if any pending exception, clear return value
if(thread_get_pending_exception()){
   *ret = (jvalue)0;
   return;
}

// process return value.
if ( ret_type == JAVA_TYPE_VOID) return;
```

```
((uint32*)ret)[0] = eax;
//second word useful only for long/double type
((uint32*)ret) [1] = edx;

//box return value if it is reference
if( ret_type == JAVA_TYPE_CLASS ||
    ret_type == JAVA_TYPE_ARRAY )
{
    if( eax != NULL ){
    Object_handle* hndl = allocate_local_obj_handle();
    hndl->obj = (Object*)eax;
    *ret = (jvalue)hndl;
    }
}
return;
}
```

The stack data prepared by the bridge code are input arguments for the Java method, and hence part of the Java method stack frame. The method's GC-map encodes the reference information. The stack data before the input arguments may include object references put by the unsafe code of the bridge code. Although this case can be avoided by delicate design of the bridge code, it is not a problem actually, because those items on the stack by the bridge code are dead data that no code accesses anymore. The Java code only accesses the data in its method frame, and the native code after the Java method returns only accesses local object handles, including the returned reference value from the Java method.

9.5.2 Java-to-Native

In the discussion of local object handle, we know the native method accesses objects through object handles. Any unsafe accesses should be protected by the pair of leaving and entering the GC safe region. The Java code prepares arguments on the stack and invokes the Java-to-native wrapper that re-pushes the arguments for the native method, where reference arguments are boxed in local object handles. The stack data before the items pushed by the wrapper code belong to the preceding Java frame, and the reference information is maintained in its (the preceding Java frame) GC-map.

There is a GC safepoint at the call instruction in the Java code before it calls the native method, and then the GC-safety state becomes unsafe when the call instruction is executed and the control enters the Java-to-native wrapper code. The wrapper turns the state back to GC-safe right before it calls the native method, after it prepares the local object handles. When the invocation to the native method returns to the wrapper, the GC-safety state then turns back to unsafe. The wrapper unboxes the return value if it is an object reference and puts the object reference to the return register of the Java method.

9.5.3 Native-to-Native

This is the case when a native method calls another native method with JNI API. Although it looks only involving the native method, the transition actually is from native to Java and then from Java to native. In other words, it is the combination of the two cases above. The implication to GC is a little different from a simple combination.

In the native-to-Java transition, the object reference values in the native frame pushed by the bridge code are ignored, because the reference arguments are re-pushed on the stack for the Java frame and recorded by Java frame's GC-map if the target is really a Java method. When the target is not a Java method and then the control continues with Java-to-native transition, the arguments are re-pushed one more time for the native method call and are boxed with local object handles.

When GC happens, the reference arguments can be enumerated through local object handles, and those pushed before the Java-to-native wrapper code are ignored, because they are no longer useful, as shown in Figure 9.4 below, which still uses the previous application code as example.

The native method is in safe region. When it calls the Java method, the native-to-Java transition leaves the safe region before the invocation. When it encounters the Java-to-native wrapper, the GC-safety state is set back to the safe region before calling the native method. The code in the returning path does exactly the opposite. In this way the GC-safety invariant is ensured, as shown in Figure 9.5.

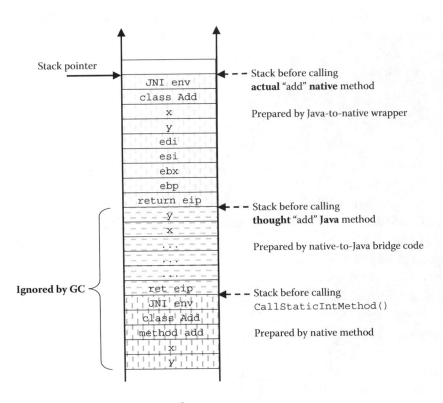

FIGURE 9.4   Stack data in the transition frames.

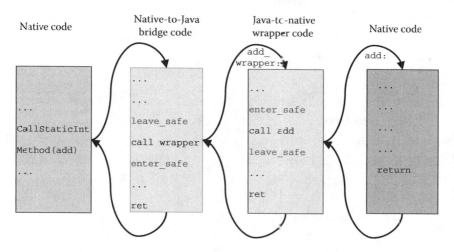

FIGURE 9.5   GC-safety invariant maintained across transitions.

9.6 GLOBAL ROOT-SET

The VM maintains many global data structures that may hold live objects. They are not always able to be reached from thread-local root references and should be enumerated seperately during GC.

- **Class loaders**: Except the bootstrap class loader, the VM may have additional custom class loaders. If the VM does not support class unloading, all the custom class loaders should be enumerated, including their loaded classes. If the VM supports class unloading, the class loaders should not be enumerated as roots, because the liveness of the class loaders should be defined by reachability from the liveness of its defined classes. If any of its defined classes is live, the class loader is live.

- **Classes**: The classes loaded by custom class loaders are treated similarly as above. A class is live only when it has live object instance or when it has an active method on the stack. So if the VM supports class unloading, classes are not enumerated. Otherwise, they should be enumerated. Even when classes are not enumerated as roots for class unloading support, they should be enumerated as weak roots, in order to process them when they are unreachable.

    There may be some resolution errors that are represented as exception objects and kept in the class data structure. They should be enumerated as well in this case. All the classes defined by a bootstrap class loader should be enumerated, including their static reference fields.

- **Global object handles**: They keep the referenced objects alive and should be added to the root-set.

- **Objects to be finalized**: Unreachable objects that have finalizers to execute should be enumerated to avoid being garbage collected. We will discuss this later in Chapter 12.

- **Weak-Reference objects to be enqueued**: When the Weak-Reference family objects' referents are unreachable, the Weak-Reference objects will be enqueued. They should be enumerated before they are enqueued. We will discuss the details later in Chapter 12.

- **Interned strings**: Interned strings are managed in the VM, so that same string literals are represented by same string objects. They are more like cached copies and do not necessarily be enumerated separately as roots since their liveness is defined by reachability from live objects. But as with class unloading, if the VM wants to recycle interned strings, they should be enumerated as weak roots.

In most VM implementations, interned strings are not recycled, because their life time is a little different from other objects'. When a class of the running application has a string literal, the corresponding interned string can be regarded live. In other words, a string literal is considered a live "reference" although it is not until the class containing it is loaded.

CHAPTER 10

Runtime-Helpers

Now we know the transition between Java and native code. Before we discuss more about the control-flow transition in virtual machine (VM) execution, especially when it throws exception, it is worth discussing runtime-helpers.

10.1 WHY RUNTIME-HELPERS

In Java virtual machine (JVM), there are roughly two kinds of running code, classified according to the used languages: Java code and native code. As we have seen, it actually has more subtleties than just this classification. Below is a summary of the different types of code run in JVM. Here, we assume the VM is developed in the same language as the native method. We will discuss the case when they use different languages later, but the key concepts remain the same.

- Java code (bytecode): It is the only purpose of JVM to run applications written in Java. A more accurate statement is to run Java class file, since JVM cannot see Java code.

- Native methods: The native method code can come from the application or from the VM. The VM needs to implement some built-in native methods that are closely dependent on the VM internals such as to support `java.lang.reflect`, `java.lang.System`, and others. The native method is garbage collection (GC)-safe.

- VM code: The vast majority of the native code in a VM implementation is not native method code, but other supporting components such as a just-in-time (JIT) compiler, garbage collector, and threading library. They can do all kinds of low-level operations at platform level without worrying about Java's safety and portability requirements. Actually, VM code is the gluing layer between safe-language and the underlying platform, which is usually unsafe.

The three types of code constitute the main body of the executed code in JVM. Since they have different properties on calling convention, GC safety, and platform access, the Java code, native methods and VM code cannot simply call each other. They have to depend on the following additional code types or components to work together.

- Java Native Interface (JNI) functions (JNI APIs [Application Programming Interfaces]): These are the functions providing native methods the APIs to access the Java world and maintain safe-language properties, such as to call a Java method, to throw an exception, or to synchronize with monitor. JNI functions follow native method programming rules, except that they may have GC-unsafe operations.

- Glue code: Glue code refers to the code for control flow transition or manipulation. For examples, the native-to-Java bridge code and the Java-to-native wrapper code are all glue code. It can be written in assembly code (or hand-written machine code). Assembly code is useful when VM wants precise control over the stack or register operations. Sometimes assembly code is also used for performance.

- Hardware exception handler (or signal handler): When a hardware exception happens, the registered handlers are invoked by the operating system. Exceptions can happen in both native and Java code, while the handlers are written in native code.

Glue code is necessary. The native world (written in native language) is compiled by a native compiler, and the Java world (written in Java bytecode) is compiled by the JIT compiler, which is usually a JIT. Normally, the two compilers know nothing about each other. When the control needs to go from one world to another, gluing code is needed. The VM developer should not and cannot assume the calling conventions of the two worlds be the same. At least, object references cannot automatically be boxed into object handles when Java code calls native code, or unboxed from object handles when native code calls Java code. (So it is easy to understand that even interpreter-based VM can hardly avoid handwritten machine code.)

Transitioning between Java and native worlds can happen in many places, and not only for explicit method calls. As long as a potential cross-world transition may happen, glue code is needed.

As we mentioned earlier, VM code can be considered as providing runtime services which we call VM-services. Java code and native methods are the clients of the services. Java code needs glue code to access the VM-services. The native method needs JNI APIs (JNI functions) for the access. We call the gluing code from Java to VM-services "runtime-helpers." The relation between different code types can be illustrated as Figure 10.1 below.

In the calling relation graph, all the calls are in the direction from Java code to native code, except one situation that goes in the other direction, that is, the native-to-Java bridge. The native-to-Java bridge needs only a single piece of code, the function `vm_execute_java_method()`. This is reasonable, because JVM is designed to support Java APIs and semantics, and not the reverse.

So far in this book, we have discussed (sometimes briefly) the implementations of all the code types except runtime-helpers and hardware exception handlers, which we will discuss in this and the next chapter, respectively.

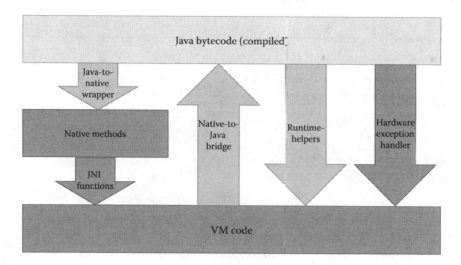

FIGURE 10.1   Calling relation between different types of code.

10.2 VM-SERVICE DESIGN WITH RUNTIME-HELPERS

During Java code execution, it has to access various VM-services. Here are a few examples when VM-services are needed:

- Java bytecode invokes a Java method (the `invoke`-series), while the latter has not yet compiled. The calling then triggers the VM to invoke the "compiler" to compile the Java method just-in-time. The original entry point of the called method is actually a piece of trampoline code that triggers the target method compilation and then jumps to the compiled code. (It is virtually the same for the native method, which the compiler does not compile into binary code, but generates the Java-to-native wrapper code as the compilation result).

- Java bytecode executes monitor code (`monitorenter` or `monitorexit`), which may involve thread blocking and waking-up operations. "Threading" needs low-level platform-specific services that can be conducted only in the native code.

- Java bytecode creates a new object or array (the `new`-series). The operation may trigger "garbage collection" due to insufficient free heap space; then the execution has to trap into the VM for the service.

- Java bytecode throws "exceptions" (`athrow`). It has to depend on the VM code to find the matching handler, which may involve stack-unwinding and control-flow transference. Other Java bytecodes that may throw exception will also need trap into VM code.

When Java code execution needs the VM-services, a runtime-helper is called that helps transition the control from the Java world to the native world. To some extent, runtime-helpers are like system calls in operating system design, which provide kernel services that are not available in the user space. Here, kernel is the VM code, and user space is the Java world.

With this analog in mind, it is easy to understand that the VM only needs to provide a limited number of runtime-helpers that summarize and represent all the necessary VM-services. For example, exception-throwing is a service provided by the VM. The VM does not need to provide a runtime-helper for every Java bytecode that may throw exceptions. Those bytecodes only need to call the same VM-service for exception-throwing.

10.2.1 Operations of Runtime-Helpers

To design the runtime-helper, the first thing to understand is why not to develop the VM-services as native methods. If they can be developed as native methods, there is no need to write dedicated code for the runtime-helpers. Native methods have a unified mechanism to access. In other words, it is like using a unified system call mechanism for all kernel services. This is possible, but unnecessary, mainly for performance reason in the VM design. The runtime-helper for native method access is the Java-to-native wrapper, which has additional operations compared to a normal Java method call. Not all of them are needed for every VM-service.

1. The following operations are needed for both GC and exception handling because the VM does not know how the native compiler lays out the stack frame.

   - **Callee-save registers**: The wrapper needs to push all callee-save registers on the stack. In compiled Java code, which register to push relies on the JIT compiler's decision. For a native method that is compiled by a native compiler, it is unknown which callee-save registers will be used by the native compiler. Some of them may contain object references that have to be enumerated during GC, so the VM needs to put them in a known place. The wrapper also restores all the callee-save registers by popping the stack upon the native method return.

   - **Java cluster-pointer chain**: The VM has to work around the traditional C frames for stack-unwinding by using the Java cluster-pointer. It needs to maintain the chain for the current native method before and after calling it.

2. The following operations are needed in order to support GC in the native method. Java code is GC-unsafe, so it can directly access objects, which is not allowed for the native code.

   - **Local object handles**: The wrapper needs to create local object handles for the current native method so that the native method can access Java objects. This is necessary even if the native method does not access any Java objects, because the VM knows nothing about the native method internals, and the native method actually always has at least one Java object in its arguments.

   - **Boxing/Unboxing arguments and return value**: If the native method has reference arguments, the wrapper needs to box them in local object handles, and then free the local object handles upon the native method return, so as to clear the references (and avoid memory leak if object handles are not allocated on stack).

If the native method returns a reference value, the wrapper also needs to unbox it for Java world to access, since the native method returns an object handle.

- **Enable/Disable GC**: The wrapper needs to enter a safe region before and leave the safe region after calling the native method, because Java code is GC-unsafe, while the native method is GC-safe. This is a requirement of native method semantics.

3. The following operations are needed if the calling conventions are different between the JIT compiler and the native compiler.

- **Re-prepare the arguments**: If the JIT compiler uses left-to-right pushing order for method arguments, the wrapper has to re-push them right-to-left to follow C function's argument order.

4. The following operations are needed because the VM knows nothing about the native method execution.

- **Exception**: The wrapper should process any pending exception that is either thrown by the native method or passed over from a callee in its call chain. When the wrapper code is generated, the VM does not know whether the native method execution would raise any exception or not. It has to check and process accordingly. (This part will be discussed later in Chapter 11.)

Not all of the additional operations above are necessary for runtime-helpers. Although VM-services are compiled by the native compiler, their code is known to the VM since they are part of the VM code. Then it is possible to omit some operations to improve the performance of VM-services, which in turn accelerates the Java code execution. For example, if we know a VM-service does not access Java objects, there is no need to create local object handles in its runtime-helper. If we know a VM-service finishes quickly without causing GC or throwing an exception, its runtime-helper does not need to enable/disable GC or maintain the Java cluster-pointer chain, and others. Here, we use examples to discuss runtime-helper implementations.

10.2.2 Runtime-Helper Implementation

Bytecode monitorenter throws an exception when the monitor object reference is null; otherwise it proceeds to lock the monitor.

The JIT compiler can generate the following code (in pseudo-code) for monitorenter.

```
//obj is the monitor to enter
if( obj == NULL ){
    runtime_throw_exception("NullPointerException");
}else{
    runtime_monitor_enter(obj);
}
```

In the conceptual code, the JIT generates calls to two different runtime-helpers. One is to runtime_throw_exception(), the other is to runtime_monitor_enter().

Although the VM has implemented vm_object_lock() for locking a non-null monitor, the JIT cannot generate code directly calling it. The reason is, function vm_object_lock() may block in lock_blocking() if the monitor is held by another thread. Invocation to vm_object_lock() has to support GC so that the blocking thread does not prevent GC from happening. For this purpose, a runtime-helper runtime_monitor_enter() is used to conduct the following three pieces of work:

- Save/restore callee-save registers, so that when GC happens, the object references kept in those callee-save registers can be enumerated and updated.

- Maintain the Java cluster-pointer chain for stack-unwinding support, so that all the root references on the stack can be enumerated.

- The runtime-helper also needs to re-push the argument.

The runtime-helper does not need to enable/disable GC, because vm_object_lock() is not a native method, but a pure C function, which is GC-unsafe. Internally, it enables/disables GC right before/after the thread sleeps waiting for the lock.

It does not box/unbox reference argument and return value, because the reference argument is boxed within vm_object_lock(). As a result, the runtime-helper does not need to create local object handles either. If vm_object_lock() needs local object handles, it can create when needed.

The pseudo-code for runtime_monitor_enter() can look like the following.

```
void runtime_monitor_enter(Object* obj)
{
    __asm {
    // Save callee-saved registers first.
    push ebp
    push ebx
    push esi
    push edi

    //place-holder for head pointer to local obj handles
    push 0

    //construct cluster-pointer chain
    call get_address_of_cluster_pointer
    push eax
    push [eax]
    mov esp -> [eax]

    // re-push native method arguments
    push [esp+size_M2N_wrapper]    //push obj

    call vm_object_lock
```

```
    //restore Java cluster-pointer
    pop ecx
    pop ebx
    mov ecx -> [ebx]

    // restore callee-saved registers.
    pop edi
    pop esi
    pop ebx
    pop ebp
    // return and pop Java argument (obj)
    ret 4
        }
    }
```

The code in bold face before and after the call to vm_object_lock() is actually the same code for all similar runtime-helpers, so we can put them into a code generator or macro that can generate the same sequence when needed. They can be regarded as push/pop M2N_wrapper data structure on/off the stack. Then the modularized runtime_monitor_enter() becomes the following.

```
void __stdcall runtime_monitor_enter(Object* obj)
{
    __asm{
        //macros M2N_wrapper processing
        push_M2N_wrapper
        // re-push native method arguments
        push [esp+size_M2N_wrapper]    //push obj
        call vm_object_lock
        pop_M2N_wrapper
        ret 4
    }
}
```

A question is, why in the prolog of a synchronized method, it is not a problem to call vm_object_lock() directly, as we saw earlier. The reason is, the GC support for the synchronized method has been prepared by either the JIT compiler if it is a Java method or the Java-to-native wrapper if it is a native method. There is no need to do the separate preparation for vm_object_lock() again.

10.2.3 JNI API as Runtime-Helper

JNI functions also provide APIs for native methods to access VM-services. As an analog to the runtime-helpers that provide VM accesses to Java code, JNI functions can be regarded as runtime-helpers for the native code. The difference from Java code access is that, when the native code calls JNI functions, the code is in GC safe-region and the reference arguments are already boxed in local object handles.

For example, the JNI function `MonitorEnter` is provided as a JNI API for the native method to use.

```
jint JNICALL MonitorEnter(JNIEnv * jenv, jobject jobj)
```

It accesses the VM code `vm_object_lock()` in a slightly different way due to the different assumptions between the native method and Java code. What the JNI function `MonitorEnter()` needs to do is to leave the safe region and unbox the reference argument. Below is the example code.

```
jint JNICALL MonitorEnter(JNIEnv * jenv, jobject jobj)
{
    if ( ExceptionCheck() )
        return -1;

    vm_leave_saferegion();
    Object* obj = (Object_handle)job->obj;
    vm_object_lock(obj);
    vm_enter_saferegion();

    return 0;
}
```

Since `MonitorEnter()` is also a native method, if we do not focus on performance, we can use it to implement Java bytecode `monitorenter`. Then the dedicated runtime-helper `runtime_monitor_enter()` is unnecessary, and Java code can call the native method `MonitorEnter()` through the standard Java-to-native wrapper. As we have mentioned previously, the Java-to-native wrapper actually needs to be generated for every native method due to different input arguments and different target native methods. So a unified wrapper approach does not save the VM a piece of runtime-helper code. The difference is the unified wrapper code is automatically generated by the VM, while the dedicated runtime-helper is manually developed and has better performance.

10.3 VM-SERVICE DESIGN WITHOUT RUNTIME-HELPER

Another example of VM-services is the support for bytecode `instanceof`. It is to check if the given object is an instance of the specified class. It is implemented in VM code as `vm_instanceof()`.

```
int __stdcall vm_instanceof(Object *obj, Class *clss)
{
    if( obj == NULL ) return 0;
```

```
    Class* sub = class_of_object(obj);
    bool is_subtype = class_is_subtype(sub, clss);
    return is_subtype;
}


bool class_is_subtype(Class *sub, Class *clss)
{
    if(sub == clss)    return TRUE;

    if( class_is_array(sub) ) {
        if ( clss == class_java_lang_Object ||
             clss == class_java_io_Serializable ||
             clss == class_java_lang_Cloneable_Class)
           return TRUE;

        if( !class_is_array(clss) ) return FALSE;

        sub = class_of_array_element( sub );
        clss = class_of_array_element( clss );
        return class_is_subtype(sub, clss);

    } else { //not array
        if( !class_is_interface(clss) ) {
            sub = class_get_super_class(sub);
            do{
                if( sub == clss ) return TRUE;
                sub = class_get_super_class(sub);
            }while(sub);

        }else{ //is interface
            do{
                unsigned n_intf = number_of_interfaces(sub);
                for(unsigned i = 0; i < n_intf; i++) {
                    Class* intf = class_get_interface(i);
                    if( class_is_subtype(intf, clss)) {
                        return TRUE;
                    }
                }
                sub = class_get_super_class(sub);
            }while(sub);
        } //interface
    } //array

    return FALSE;
}
```

We can see that `vm_instanceof()` is a function that does not throw exception, or trigger GC, or block. It is a VM-service because its implementation relies on VM implementation details.

This function is GC-unsafe, similar to Java code. Java code can directly call it without going through a runtime-helper, as long as the JIT compiler prepares the input arguments ready. In order to keep the calling conventions consistent across platforms, `vm_instanceof()` is modified with `__stdcall`, as other VM-services.

The benefit without a dedicated runtime-helper is that the execution overhead incurred by the extra work in the helper can be eliminated, and the corresponding programming and maintenance efforts on the VM developer can be largely reduced.

It is possible for the JIT compiler to generate the whole code sequence for `instanceof` that implements the same logics of `vm_instanceof()`. In that case, there is seemingly no trap into the VM-service. That, however, does not change the nature that the code sequence is still part of VM logics, because it is definitely not part of Java application/library code, nor the compiler's logic. It is still coded by the VM developer and provided as a compiler intrinsic. The key difference from a true compiler intrinsic is that the code logic relies on the VM implementation, for example, how the VM retrives the class pointer from an object, how the VM gets the element class of an array class, and others.

On the other hand, `vm_instanceof()` still needs a compiler to generate its machine code for runtime execution. To program `vm_instanceof()` does not have to use C language. It can be any language that allows programming VM-services. If the compiler of VM-service code can generate IR (intermediate representation) that is known to the Java JIT compiler, the JIT compiler may inline the small but frequently executed service code into the compiled Java code, thus improving the performance significantly.

10.3.1 Fast-Path of Runtime-Helpers

Based on the observation on `vm_instanceof()` and `runtime_monitor_enter()`, we may consider a way to use direct call for VM-services, as much as possible, for better performance.

For a VM-service that may trigger GC or exception-throwing or be blocking, an intuitive common practice to improve its performance is to partition the execution into a fast path and a slow path. The fast path does not need a runtime-helper, while the slow path with a runtime-helper takes care of the extra work for GC and exception support. The execution goes to the fast path first without a runtime helper and only executes the slow path when the fast path is not viable. The criteria for the partitioning are the following:

- The fast path does not trigger exception-throwing or garbage collection, and never blocks.

- The fast path is inherently part of the target VM-service.

- The fast path is the common path for most invocations of the VM-service.

- If the fast path returns successfully, the slow path will not be taken.

Using vm_object_lock() as an example, the fast path can be the case when the monitor is free and locked successfully, while the slow path deals with all the other cases. The code for runtime_monitor_enter() can be changed as below.

```
void runtime_monitor_enter(Object* obj)
{
    //fast-path first
    __asm{
      push [esp+4]   //push obj
      call lock_non_blocking
      test eax eax
      jz FAILED
      ret 4
    FAILED:
    //slow-path if fast-path fails
      push_M2N_wrapper
      // re-push native method arguments
      push [esp+size_M2N_wrapper]   //push obj
      call vm_object_lock
      pop_M2N_wrapper
      ret 4
    }
}
```

The new implementation can significantly improve the performance of many Java applications when entering a free monitor is the common case. Note that the fast path still can call into VM-service function, as long as the function does not lead to garbage collection, exception, or blocking.

10.3.2 Programming for Fast-Path VM-Services

The fast path of VM-services is expected to be executed with high frequency. Since the code for the fast path is developed in native language, a call is needed from compiled Java code to the native-compiled service code. This is not efficient. It would be desirable if the fast-path code can be compiled into the same intermediate language that is known to the JIT compiler, and then the fast path can be inlined into the compiled Java code, thereby enabling more compilation optimizations. Then a question is why not directly develop the fast-path VM-services in Java code.

It is impossible to write VM-services in Java code, since the existence of VM-services is solely to provide low-level supports to Java. Using Java to write VM-services leads to circular dependence. That is, the Java application accesses the VM-services for low-level resources, while the VM-services written in Java need another layer of lower-level VM-services to accomplish the goal.

On the other hand, it is possible to use a Java variant to accomplish the goal. Apache Harmony uses an "unsafe Java" library for some of the fast-path service development. The library provides a few special Java classes that are recognized by the compiler as intrinsics.

For example, Java class `Address` in the library represents a memory address, which provides an interface "`dereference()`" to load the value from the address. When the JIT compiler compiles the bytecode that invokes the `dereference()`, it does not really generate a method call; instead, the JIT compiler replaces it with a pointer dereference. The upside of using "unsafe Java" is that it can be uniformly processed by the same VM infrastructure (including JIT); going through the same class loading, front-end compilation, and so on, processes as normal Java code. The downside is that it is not as straightforward as the native code, which need not rely on the JIT compiler to generate the desired code.

The inlining and optimization of the VM-services are only feasible to the fast-path, which can be considered an extension of the Java bytecode that they implement. The slow-path of the VM-services that is hard to implement in "unsafe Java" still needs runtime-helper. As we have seen, the runtime-helpers use assembly code extensively to glue the code compiled by JIT and that compiled by the native compiler. This is true for all the situations when the VM needs delicate code sequence to connect the Java and native worlds, such as in wrapper code, bridge code, and stub code.

It is tedious to write and maintain the assembly code sequence for multiple different micro-architectures. It is possible to write them with other more convenient languages that can be compiled into the expected code sequence. For example, Apache Harmony uses a "domain-specific languages" called LIL to write the gluing code. LIL is a platform-neutral low-level intermediate language that can express low level semantics like runtime stack manipulation and register operations. The compiler (or parser) of LIL can generate the expected assembly code for different micro-architectures. Note LIL is not for performance benefit, but for development benefit, while "unsafe Java" has the benefits of both.

10.4 TYPICAL VM-SERVICES

The main VM-services used in a JVM are the following. All of them need to access the implementation details of VM, including JIT and GC. Most of them may trigger GC, exception, or blocking operations, and therefore, runtime helpers are needed. If a VM-service may call into Java code, then all the factors (such as GC, exception, blocking) exist. In the list below, we mark explicitly the VM-services that do not need a runtime-helper.

1. Compilation related:

   - **Compile a method**, with the method data structure as input parameter. The method can be Java or native method. This service may throw exceptions, execute Java code (class initializer, exception constructor), and hence may trigger GC.

   - **Load a constant String**, with parameters of the declaring class, and the index of the string literal in the constant pool. It may trigger GC when generating the String object. It may execute Java code for string interning. This service is to support the implementation of bytecode ldc.

2. Exception related:

- **Throw an exception**, with parameter of a reference to the exception object, corresponding to the `athrow` bytecode. This function does not return, because it transfers the control to the exception handler or the nearest native caller method.

- **Throw a linking exception**, with parameters of constant pool index to the item that are causing linking exception, declaring class, and the exception object. The exception object has been installed during class loading.

- **Throw an access exception**, such as those caused by invoking an abstract method and accessing a private method.

3. Threading related:

- **Get the pointer to thread-local storage**, with no argument. It needs to access VM implementation details. It does not need a runtime-helper.

- `Monitorenter`, with parameter of the monitor object. It may be blocking.

- `Monitorexit`, with parameter of the monitor object. It throws exceptions if the thread unlocks a monitor that is not held by it.

4. Class-support related:

- **Initialize class**, with parameter of the class to initialize. It executes the class initializer Java code. It may be blocked waiting for another thread initializing the same class. It should be called before `putstatic` and `getstatic` at runtime unless the class is known initialized.

- **Find java.lang.Class object from its counterpart in VM** (i.e., the corresponding VM's Class data structure), with parameter of a pointer to the VM's Class data structure. Each class has a data structure maintained by the VM and also an instance of `java.lang.Class`. When the VM does not store them together, the VM-service is needed to find from one to another. This service is used, for instance, when JIT generates argument for the monitor instructions of a synchronized static method, where the argument is the `java.lang.Class` instance of the method's owning class. It does not need a runtime-helper.

- **Get interface vtable of object**, with parameters of the object and an interface class. It loads the interface's vtable, with method entries for the implementation of that interface by the actual class of the object. It may trigger exception if the vtable cannot be found. It is to support the implementation of bytecode `invokeinterface`.

5. Type checking related, which is part of the class support above:

- **Checkcast**, with parameters of the object and the class type to cast. It checks if the object is of the given type. If it is not, throw an exception. It is to implement bytecode `checkcast`.

- **Instanceof.** It is the same as checkcast, except that it does not throw an exception but returns 0 if the object is not of the given type. It is to implement bytecode `instanceof`.

- **Aastore**, with parameters of the array object, the element index, and the element object. It stores element object into the specified index of the array. It may trigger exception when the object is not of the array element type. It is to implement bytecode `aastore`.

6. Garbage collection related:

- **Allocate object**, with arguments of object size and its class. It may trigger collection if heap is low. It may throw exception when out of memory.

- **Allocate one-dimension array** (i.e., vector), with parameters of array length and its class. It may trigger GC and exception.

- **Allocate multi-dimensional array**, with parameters of its class, number of dimensions, and length of every dimension. This function has variable number of arguments, hence using `__cdecl` calling convention. It may trigger GC and exception.

- **Get object hashcode**, with parameter of the object. This function returns the object associated identity hashcode. This relies on VM implementation details. It does not need a runtime-helper.

- **GC write-barrier**, with parameters of the host object, the field address in host object, and the guest object reference that is to be written into the field. It also includes an operation type parameter to indicate what kind of heap write it is. It needs to access GC implementation details. It does not need a runtime-helper.

- **GC read-barrier**, with parameters of the object and its field to read. It needs to access GC implementation details. It does not need a runtime-helper.

- **Call GC safe-point**, with no argument. It may be blocking.

7. JVMTI related:

- **JVMTI callbacks.** They are a group of VM-services for JVMTI events: method enter, method exit, field access, and field modification. Each is a call to a native method of JVMTI agent when the respective event happens.

8. Lazy resoluton related:

- **Lazy resolutions.** They are a group of VM-services for class-related operations with lazy resolutions: new object, new array, initialize class, get non-static field offset, get static field address, checkcast, instanceof, get entry point address of invokestatic, invokeinterface, invokevirtual, and invokiespecial.

There are some additional helper functions into which Java code calls, while we consider them compiler intrinsics rather than VM-services. Those include, for example, arithmetic operations such as 64-bit divide operations or operand type convertions from float to double. They are not necessarily classified as VM-services because they do not rely on specific VM implementation internals, so different JITs can have their own implementations. Sometimes they are called JIT-helpers as compared to the runtime-helpers.

CHAPTER 11

Exception-Throwing

T HE PURPOSE OF EXCEPTION-THROWING is to transfer the control out of normal flow in order to handle the *exceptional* situation.

An exception can be thrown from both Java and native codes, explicitly or implicitly. Explicit exception throwing refers to the case when one of the "throw" application programming interfaces (APIs) in Java or Java Native Interface (JNI) is used, while implicit exception throwing is when a certain condition (usually meaning something wrong) is triggered by the application execution, such as "out of memory" and "class not found." For implicit cases, the virtual machine (VM) throws the exceptions for the application. From the VM's point of view, the difference between explicit and implicit is nonessential because the implicit throwing becomes explicit to the VM.

An exception can be synchronous or asynchronous. Synchronous exception is triggered as a result of the thread executing certain instruction, where the VM throws an exception on the spot when needed, such as an exception due to a null-pointer dereference. All the explicitly thrown exceptions are synchronous exceptions. Asynchronous exception is not known on the spot by the VM, which can happen at any arbitrary time point, such as an internal error.

An exception is thrown only within a single thread. There is no way to transfer the control flow of one thread to another, which is contradictory to the definition of thread. A thread may trigger conditions that cause another thread to throw an exception, such as a thread stop or interrupt request by another thread, which is also an asynchronous exception. In this case, it is similar to the signal mechanism in the operating system (OS).

In general, to throw an exception, the VM needs to have the following four steps:

- Step 1. Save the exception-throwing context, which tells the execution state when the exception happens;

- Step 2. Save the stack trace. This step can be considered as part of step 1;

- Step 3. Find the exception handler;

- Step 4. Transfer control to the exception handler.

In some languages, there is a step 5. After an exception is processed by a handler, the control resumes to the original site where the exception was thrown. It is like the default signal handling for a SIG_SEGV in Linux. In Java, there is no such continuable exception.

11.1 SAVE CONTEXT OF EXCEPTION-THROWING

When an exception is thrown, the first thing the VM does is to find the execution state that can be used for the VM to understand why, where, and what exception is thrown. Then the VM can use the information to unwind a stack or create a stack trace that can be output to users. For the purpose, the major information in the execution state is the register file content.

11.1.1 VM-Saved Context

For explicit exception, the VM can save the execution state on spot when it throws the exception. For some synchronous exception that may be triggered by the execution of a bytecode such as "integer divided by zero," "null pointer dereference," and "out of bound access to array," the VM can check the variable in question proactively and decide whether an exception should be thrown, thus turning some implicit exception into explicit, whose execution context is easy to get. For example, for monitorenter, the compiler generates the following pseudo code: (the actual code is in machine code)

```
//obj is the monitor to enter
if( obj == NULL ){
    Object* exc = runtime_new_object(NullPointerException);
    runtime_throw_exception(exc);
}else{
    runtime_monitor_enter(obj);
}
```

Function runtime_throw_exception() is a runtime-helper that calls VM service vm_throw_exception(). As we discussed in Chapter 10 runtime_ throw_exception() needs to save the context when it prepares the Java-to-native transition.

```
void __stdcall runtime_throw_exception(Object* exc)
{
    __asm{
    push_M2N_wrapper
    // re-push arguments
    push [esp+size_M2N_wrapper]
    call vm_throw_exception
    //should never come here
}
```

11.1.2 OS-Saved Context in Linux

Some synchronous exceptions can be detected by hardware, such as "integer divided by zero" and "null pointer deference" on X86 architecture. There is no need for the VM to check the variable value every time for an integer division or dereference operation, which is much slower than hardware detection. When a fault occurs, a hardware exception is thrown by the processor that is handled by the OS kernel. The OS kernel then saves the CPU execution state and delivers an OS event with the state in the event context. For example, for null-pointer access, the OS event in Linux is signal SIG_SEGV, while that in Windows is exception EXCEPTION_ACCESS_VIOLATION.

First of all, the VM needs a data structure as temporary storage for the execution state.

```
//data structure to store execution-context
struct Registers {
    U_32 eax;
    U_32 ebx;
    U_32 ecx;
    U_32 edx;
    U_32 edi;
    U_32 esi;
    U_32 ebp;
    U_32 esp;
    U_32 eip;
    U_32 eflags;
}
```

In Linux, the VM needs to register a signal handler for SIG_SEGV; then it can obtain the execution context in the signal handler with the following code. The signal handler loads the execution-context information from an event-context data structure that is prepared by the OS kernel.

```
//initialize signals
int initialize_event_handlers()
{

    struct sigaction sa;

    sigemptyset(&sa.sa_mask);
    sa.sa_flags = SA_SIGINFO | SA_ONSTACK;
    sa.sa_sigaction = null_ref_handler.
    sigaction(SIG_SEGV, &sa, NULL);

    //other processing
    ...

}
```

```
//signal handler for SIG_SEGV
void null_ref_handler(int signo, siginfo_t* info, void* context)
{
    VM_Thread* self = current_thread();
    Registers* regs = self->context_regs;

    //context is prepared by OS kernel for the event
    ucontext_t* uc = (ucontext_t*)context;
    regs->eax = uc->uc_mcontext.gregs[REG_EAX];
    regs->ecx = uc->uc_mcontext.gregs[REG_ECX];
    regs->edx = uc->uc_mcontext.gregs[REG_EDX];
    regs->edi = uc->uc_mcontext.gregs[REG_EDI];
    regs->esi = uc->uc_mcontext.gregs[REG_ESI];
    regs->ebx = uc->uc_mcontext.gregs[REG_EBX];
    regs->ebp = uc->uc_mcontext.gregs[REG_EBP];
    regs->eip = uc->uc_mcontext.gregs[REG_EIP];
    regs->esp = uc->uc_mcontext.gregs[REG_ESP];
    regs->eflags = uc->uc_mcontext.gregs[REG_EFL];

  //other processing
    ...
}
```

11.1.3 OS-Saved Context in Windows

In Windows, it is very similar to Linux but using the vectored exception handling (VEH) mechanism.

```
//initialize VEH
int initialize_event_handlers()
{
    //...
    AddVectoredExceptionHandler(0, null_ref_handler);

    //other processing
    ...
}

//exception-handler
LONG CALLBACK null_ref_handler (LPEXCEPTION_POINTERS winexc)
{
    VM_Thread* self = current_thread();
    Registers* regs = self->context_regs;

    PCONTEXT context = winexc->ContextRecord;
    regs->eax = context->Eax;
    regs->ecx = context->Ecx;
    regs->edx = context->Edx;
```

```
regs->edi = context->Edi;
regs->esi = context->Esi;
regs->ebx = context->Ebx;
regs->ebp = context->Ebp;
regs->eip = context->Eip;
regs->esp = context->Esp;
regs->eflags = context->EFlags;

//other processing
...
}
```

11.1.4 Synchronous versus Asynchronous Exception

The VM does not always know when an exception is thrown. For asynchronous exceptions such as "thread stop," after it receives the request, the current thread should throw an exception whenever it has a chance. There is no strict timing requirement for when the asynchronous exception has to be handled.

11.1.4.1 Context

The current thread may check if there is a pending "thread stop" request at every garbage collection (GC) safe point. If there is one, the thread throws an exception before it leaves the safe point. The execution context then reflects the state of the safe point. Similar to `runtime_throw_exception()`, safe point is also called through a runtime-helper that saves the execution context.

As we mentioned previously on "Thread suspension support for GC," a safe point can be implemented by using OS–specific supports on event handling. It is possible to use similar techniques to implement some asynchronous exception triggering. A thread can deliver an event to another thread that has registered an event handler to process the event. The execution state is then in the event context that is saved by the OS kernel.

To summarize, the exception can be thrown proactively by the VM with a runtime-helper or passively in an event handler due to a hardware exception. In the former case, the exception object is usually created before calling the runtime service. In the latter case, the exception object has to be created in the event handler before it is thrown. In both cases, the exception happens in compiled Java code.

To distinguish the exceptions thrown proactively or passively, the VM can use a flag. For example, when it is thrown proactively, the context registers can set empty or with some special value because the frame context can be constructed from the Java cluster-pointer.

11.1.4.2 GC Safety

When the VM proactively throws an exception, the call site to the runtime-helper is by default a GC safe point, but it is not a good idea to set the exception-throwing process in a safe region when the VM needs to manipulate the stack. If it is a safe region and a collection happens, GC may be confused when it works on the stack. The exception object is also easier to directly access if GC is disabled. However there can be some short-period safe regions within the process when appropriate.

When the exception is thrown in an event handler, the instruction causing the hardware exception should be a GC safe point with GC-map information. The creaton of the exception object may trigger a collection, and the object constructor has to be executed as common Java code.

We have not discussed the case when an exception is thrown in the native method, which is the topic of the next section.

11.2 EXCEPTION HANDLING IN AND ACROSS THE NATIVE CODE

A Java virtual machine (JVM) deals with exceptions differently in Java and native code. In the Java world, whenever there is an exception thrown, the control flow immediately transfers to the exception handler, or the thread will terminate if no handler is found. In the native world, however, the VM does not assume anything on the native language's exception support, which is in line with the philosophy of JNI support. Instead, the VM provides JNI functions (APIs) for exception operations such as `Throw()`, `ExceptionOccurred()`, and `ExceptionClear()`.

11.2.1 Exception Handling in the Native Code

When an exception is thrown in the native code, the control flow does not immediately transfer to the exception handler, because the native language may not have such an "exception handler" concept at all. The VM keeps the exception only internally in a thread-local storage. Then the native code can use JNI APIs to check if there is any exception occurring (i.e., by checking the thread-local storage that indicates an exception happening) and decides if it wants to handle it. The APIs allow the native code to do various actions on exceptions, such as to clear the existing exception, leave it intact, or throw a new exception (i.e., to save a new exception in the thread-local storage).

The only things the VM needs to do for native code exception handling is to implement a few JNI functions that deal with exceptions. For example, the code below implements JNI API `Throw()`, which throws an exception `jobj`.

```
jint JNICALL Throw(JNIEnv* jni_env, jthrowable jobj)
{
        if( !jobj ) return -1;

        VM_Thread* self = current_thread();
        //jobj is an object handle pointer.
        vm_leave_saferegion();
        self->exception_obj = jobj->obj;
        vm_enter_saferegion();

        return 0;
}
```

Although the API is named Throw(), the implementation does not really "throw" the exception or transfer control; instead, the exception object is saved in the thread-local storage. The execution of the native method continues rather than complete abruptly. The actual "throwing" process is continued in the Java frame when the native method returns to its Java caller. Note that the saved exception object in the thread-local storage (TLS) should be enumerated during a collection.

When the native code returns to the Java world, the pending exception in the thread-local storage will continue to be processed in the Java world as thrown from the current Java frame. In this way, the native code has almost the full capability of Java exception handling, including to pass the exception to its Java exception handler and to program the "native exception handler." The name is quoted because it is not the same as the Java exception handler.

In Java code, a "catch" block is invoked automatically by the VM when a matching exception is thrown in its corresponding "try" block. In JNI native code, an exception handling can be something like below, which does not have any visibility to the VM because the native code is not compiled by the VM.

```
jthrowable exception = ExceptionOccurred(jenv);
if( exception ){
   //exception-handler
}
//...
```

The JNI API ExceptionOccurred() checks the thread-local storage for any saved exception object. In the "native exception handler," the native method can call JNI API ExceptionClear() to clear the exception object in thread-local storage (TLS), thereby finishing its throwing process.

11.2.2 Java Code with Exception Returns to the Native Code

When the exception is thrown in the Java code, the VM unwinds the stack to find the exception handler. Since there is no VM-visible exception handler in the native code, the stack–unwinding process cannot simply continue at a native frame. The VM does not know whether there is any exception handling in the native method or not. Although the VM could skip the native frame and keep unwinding the stack with the Java cluster-pointer, it is not the right way of exception handling, because skipping the native frame also skips the possible "native exception handler" in the native method.

The correct way is that the stack-unwinding process should stop at the native frame and resume the execution of the native code as if the Java callee just returns, though abruptly, to the native method. It is then the native code's responsibility to go through its logic of exception handling.

We have discussed the transition from native code to Java code. The native code calls a JNI API for method invocation such as CallVoidMethod(), which in turn calls function vm_execute_java_method() to accomplish the native-to-Java transition, as shown below.

```
void vm_execute_java_method( jmethodID* mid,
                             jvalue* pargs,
                             jvalue* ret)
{
     //thread leaves safe-region before calling this function
     assert( !thread_in_saferegion() );

     Method* method = (Method*)mid;
     //number of words in arguments (not number of arguments,
     //because long/double have two words)
     char* desc; //method descriptor
     java_type ret_type;      //return type
     method_get_param_info(method, &desc, &ret_type);

     //process input values.
     uint32 nargs = 0;
     for(++desc; (*desc) != ')'; desc++) {
        java_type type = (java_type)*desc;
        switch( type ){
           case JAVA_TYPE_CLASS:
           case JAVA_TYPE_ARRAY:

               //unbox reference arguments in place,
               //replace object handle to object reference
               Object_handle* hndl;
               hndl = (Object_handle*)pargs[nargs];
               pargs[nargs] = (jvalue)(hndl ? hndl->obj : NULL);

               while(type == '[') desc++;
               if( type == 'L' )
                   while( type != ';' ) desc++;
               nargs++;
               break;

           case JAVA_TYPE_LONG:
           case JAVA_TYPE_DOUBLE:
              nargs+ = 2;
              break;

           default:
              nargs++;
       }
    }
```

```
        //get entry point of Java method
        void* java_entry = method_get_entry(method);

        uint32 eax, edx;  //return values
        native_to_java_call(java_entry, nargs, pargs, &eax, &edx);

        //check if any pending exception, clear return value
        if( thread_get_pending_exception() ){
          *ret = (jvalue)0;
          return;
        }

        // process return value.
        if ( ret_type == JAVA_TYPE_VOID) return;

        ((uint32*)ret)[0] = eax;
        //second word useful only for long/double type
        ((uint32*)ret) [1] = edx;

        //box return value if it is reference
        if( ret_type == JAVA_TYPE_CLASS ||
              ret_type == JAVA_TYPE_ARRAY )
        {
          if( eax != NULL ){
            Object_handle* hndl = allocate_local_obj_handle();
            hndl->obj = (Object*)eax;
            *ret = (jvalue)hndl;
          }
        }
        return;
}


void native_to_java_call(void *java_entry,
        uint32 n_arg_words, uint32 *p_args_words,
        uint32 *p_eax_var, uint32 *p_edx_var)
{
    __asm {
        // Push all arguments
        mov      n_arg_words -> ecx
        mov      p_arg_words -> eax

loop_more_args:
        or       ecx, ecx              //remaining # arg words
        jz       finished_args //break if no more
        push     dword ptr [eax]      //push a word
        dec      ecx                  //decrement remaining #
```

```
        add        4 -> eax              //move to next arg word
        jmp        loop_more_args //loop back to continue

finished_args:
        // All arguments are on the stack, ready to call
        call       dword ptr [meth_addr]

        // In case a value is returned
        mov        p_eax_var -> ecx
        mov        eax -> [ecx]   //store eax to eax_var
        mov        p_edx_var -> ecx
        mov        edx -> [ecx]   //store edx to edx_var
    }
}
```

When an exception in the called Java method has no matching exception handler and the exception-throwing process hits the native code, the Java method completes abruptly and the control flow returns to the instruction right after the Java method call.

```
        call       dword ptr [meth_addr]
```

When the execution finishes the call to native_to_java_call(), the VM checks if there is any pending exception set by the exception-throwing process. If there is one, the VM clears the return value.

```
//...
uint32 eax, edx;   //return values
native_to_java_call(java_entry, nargs, pargs, &eax, &edx);

//check if any pending exception, clear return value
if( thread_get_pending_exception() ){
    *ret = (jvalue)0;
    return;
}
```

The VM code above returns to the JNI API of "call method," such as CallVoidMethod(), which in turn returns to the native method that calls the Java method through the JNI API. The native method then can continue the exception processing.

When the native code returns to the Java code, and if there is an exception remaining, the VM restarts the stack-unwinding process, as described above, with Java frames.

This exception-throwing process finishes in any of following three conditions:

1. Find an exception handler in the Java method and the control transfers to it with the exception as the argument. If the exception handler rethrows the exception or throws a new exception, a new round of exception-throwing starts.

2. The exception is cleared by a native method. If the native method rethrows the exception or throws a new exception, a new round of exception-throwing starts.

3. The exception is not handled by any method, and the thread terminates.

To summarize, the stack-unwinding process for an exception actually is a mix of Java frame unwinding and native code execution. The key reason for this design is that the VM has no elegant and portable way to find a matching exception handler in the native code. It has to delegate that work to the native code itself. The stack-unwinding process is illustrated in Figure 11.1 below; the dashed line in native frames means it is not stack unwinding per se, but acting as part of the process, assuming there is no exception handling in the middle.

Based on this design, to implement exception-throwing in the VM for the native code is relatively simple because it virtually does nothing else but letting the native code to execute as usual.

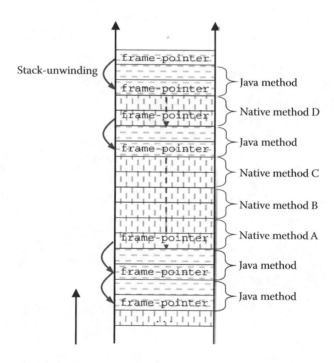

FIGURE 11.1 Exception handling with native frames.

11.2.3 Native Code with Exception Returns to the Java Code

When a native method returns to the Java world, it actually returns to the Java-to-native wrapper. The wrapper code checks if there is any exception pending in the thread-local storage. If there is one, the wrapper code invokes VM service to throw it as from the Java frame. The code is conceptually shown below.

```
//operations shown in comments below
__asm{

    //push_M2N_wrapper
    //create local object handles if has reference argument
    //push native method arguments
    //monitorenter for synchronized method
    //enable GC for native method
    //call the actual native method
    //save return value
    //disable GC for native method
    //monitorexit for synchronized method
    //unhandle the return value if it is reference type
    //free the local object handles

    //check if TLS has the saved exception-object
    call thread_get_pending_exception
    //check if return value has non-zero value (an exception)
    or eax,eax
    //zero value, done with exception processing
    je EXCEPTION_DONE
    //call VM-service to continue the exception-throwing
    call thread_rethrow_pending_exception
    //control-flow should never come here
    int 3 // <- a break-point, purely for debugging purpose
  EXCEPTION_DONE:

    //restore return value
    //pop_M2N_wrapper
    //return and pop Java arguments
}
```

The related functions are implemented as follows:

```
void thread_set_pending_exception(Object* exc)
{
  VM_Thread* self = current_thread();
  self->exception_obj = exc;
}

Object * thread_get_pending_exception()
```

```
{
  VM_Thread* self = current_thread();
  Object* exc = self->exception_obj;
  return exc;
}

void thread_rethrow_pending_exception()
{
  Object* exc = thread_get_pending_exception();
  thread_clear_pending_exception();
  vm_throw_exception( exc );
  //never comes here
}
```

When the execution returns to the Java-to-native wrapper, the code is back to the Java world, where rethrowing the exception will transfer the control and hence the wrapper code never returns. In this case, the exception rethrowing is also proactive as in other non-hardware exception cases. The stack status is similar to that of throwing the exception with a runtime-helper, while the current stack is prepared by the Java-to-native wrapper. Thus, the VM does not need to distinguish if the proactive exception-throwing is from the native code or from the Java code. The stack trace saved in the exception object will tell where this exception originates, which is the topic of the next section.

11.3 SAVE STACK TRACE

Once it gets the exception-throwing context, the VM can optionally find the stack trace and save it in the exception object. It is good to save the stack trace now before the control transfers to the exception handler, when the stack-trace information may be lost.

The stack trace is usually obtained by unwinding the stack from the spot of exception-object creation. Sometimes it is desirable to get the stack trace at the spot where the exception is thrown. The two spots, exception-object creation and exception throwing, can be different. An exception object can be created and passed to other methods to throw. (There is nothing preventing the exception to be passed even to other threads, though it is usually a bad practice.) The implication is a little different from the two cases. If the stack trace is allowed to be obtained when the exception is thrown, there is a chance to create the exception object lazily. In the JVM, a stack trace is mandatory to be saved in an exception object and is generated in the exception object's constructor.

In many cases, the exception handler does not really need the exception object itself, but leverages the exception-throwing mechanism for control-flow manipulation or to catch exceptional running condition. In those cases, the exception object is used only to help find the matching exception handler. Once the exception handler is found, the exception object is virtually dead. To match the exception handler, what the VM needs is actually the class of the exception object, rather than the object per se. Based on this observation, it is possible to omit the exception-object creation, and hence there is no associated stack-trace creation either. This is a significant saving of runtime operations, not to mention the potential garbage collections caused by those object creations.

One solution is to create the exception object lazily. That is, by default the VM generates the exception-object only when one of the following conditions is met.

- Case 1: The execution of the exception-object constructor causes potential side effects, like writing into other objects than the exception object, throwing exception, or entering monitor.

- Case 2: The target exception handler accesses the exception object.

- Case 3: The stack-unwinding process hits a native method frame before reaching a matching exception handler.

In Case 1 above, the exception object has to be created as usual, that is, eagerly at the exception-throwing time. In the other two cases, the VM can either eagerly or lazily create the exception object. Lazy creation means the VM can delay the creation up to the point when it finds the matching exception handler or the stack unwinding hits a native frame. Otherwise, the exception object can be omitted. Condition of Case 3 is needed because the VM knows nothing about how the native method would deal with the exception object.

To generate the stack trace, the stack-unwinding process is conducted from the execution context saved in in the exception object. It can be started from the native frame set up by the runtime-helper or from the Java frame that caused a hardware exception. A frame can be identified with a stack base pointer (for Java frame) or a Java cluster-pointer (for native frame). We use the instruction pointer as a flag to indicate the frame type of the throwing context.

```
Frame_context* start_frame(VM_Thread* thread)
{
    Registers* regs = thread->context_regs;
    Frame_context* frame = vm_alloc(sizeof(Frame_context));

    frame->jcp = thread->jcp;
    frame->eip = regs->eip;

    //Here eip value is multiplexed as a flag
    if( regs->eip != 0xFFFFFF )
        frame->ebp = regs->ebp; // hardware exception in Java code

    return frame;
}

Stack_frame* vm_get_thread_stacktrace(VM_Thread* thread)
{
        Frame_context* frame = start_frame(thread);
        Stack_frame* trace = stacktrace_create();
```

```
while(frame){
    Stack_frame* method;
    Code_Type type = code_type(frame);
    if( type == CODE_TYPE_JAVA){
        method = get_java_stackframe(frame);

    }else{ //native code
        method = get_native_stackframe(frame)
    }

    stacktrace_add_frame(trace, method);
    frame = preceding_frame(frame)
}

return trace;
}
```

In the example code above, the instruction pointer (eip) is used to indicate the top frame type: Java or native. The reason is that when the exception was caused by a hardware fault, the instruction-pointer value saved by hardware points to the exact faulting instruction in the Java code. If the exeption was not caused by a hardware fault, the exception is thrown by the VM proactively with the runtime-helper. Then the instruction-pointer value at the throwing spot is not interesting, which points to certain native code. That is why the instruction-pointer entry in the saved exception context can be used as a flag.

Actually, according to the implementation preference, the start frame identified from the saved exception context may not be the first frame of the exception-throwing, because the top few frames may be introduced by the exception-throwing process, and they were not on the stack when the exception happened. If the exception is caused by hardware fault in the compiled Java code, the unwinding process is started from the method that caused the hardware fault, which is exactly the start frame identified from the saved exception context, and hence there is no need to skip it.

To make the output more elegant, the VM may also ignore some reflection frames in the middle that were used to invoke other methods. To some extent, the reflection method invocation is like the native-to-Java bridge or Java-to-native wrapper that is not necessarily user interested if the developers care only about the method call chain.

11.4 FIND THE EXCEPTION HANDLER

According to JVM specifications, each Java method has zero or more exception handlers installed. Each exception handler specifies the range of code in the method that this handler is associated with and the type of exception that the handler catches. When an exception is thrown in the method, if the spot where the exception is thrown falls in the range of an exception handler and the exception type is assignable to the exception handler's catch type, then the exception matches the handler and the control flow should transfer to the handler.

In case the current method does not have a matching exception handler, the current method completes abruptly, with its frame popped off the stack. That makes the stack into a state like right before (or after) the method is called. Then the exception is rethrown in the caller's context, like it is caused by the call instruction.

If the caller is a Java method, the process described above repeats. The VM keeps searching for a matching exception handler in the caller for the exception thrown at the call instruction. If the caller is a native method, the VM transfers the control to the native code as if the Java callee just returns to the native caller and the return value is cleared.

Before the throwing process completes a method abruptly, the thread should exit all the monitors it has entered in the method.

- If the thread enters a monitor due to a synchronized block and an exception is thrown from the block, then by default, there must be an exception handler in the method to catch the exception. This default handler exits the monitor it holds and rethrows the exception.

- If the thread enters a monitor because the method is synchronized, there is no exception handler specifically for the monitor exit. It is the VM's responsibility to exit the monitor when it needs to complete the method abruptly (because of no matching exception handler).

The VM goes this way recursively up the method call chain until a matching handler is found, or a native frame is reached, or the thread is terminated for an uncaught exception.

Actually for an uncaught exception, the JVM provides final chances for the application to handle. Every Java `Thread` and `ThreadGroup` can register an "uncaught exception handler" to whom the uncaught exception thrown by the thread will be passed, first to the `Thread`'s handler, then to the `ThreadGroup`'s handler if the thread does not register its handler. The `Thread` can also register a "default uncaught exception handler" that will handle the uncaught exception if neither the `Thread` nor the `ThreadGroup` has registered their handler.

The pseudo-code for searching the matching exception handler looks as shown below. This process is destructive, meaning the unwound frames will be popped off.

```
Exc_handler* thread_find_exception_handler(Frame_context* frame,
                                           jobject exc_obj)
{
    //skip the first frame if it is native frame.
    //it is setup by runtime-helper of throwing exception
    Code_Type type = code_type(frame->eip);
    if( type != CODE_TYPE_JAVA ){
        free_local_obj_handles();
        frame = preceding_frame(frame);
    }

    while( !is_stack_bottom(frame) ){
        type = code_type(frame->eip);
```

```
        if( type != CODE_TYPE_JAVA ){
            //condition 1: native frame,
            //store exception in thread-local storage
            thread_set_pending_exception( exc );
            return NULL;
        }

        //Java frame
        JIT_info* info = info_of_pc(frame->eip);
        int num_handlers = info->num_exc_handlers;
        for(int i=0; i<num_handlers; i+-){
            Exc_handler* handler = info->exc_handler[i];
            if( !handler ) continue;
            if(ip_in_range(handler, frame->eip) &&
                   exc_is_assignable(handler, exc_obj) ){
                //condition 2: find matching exception-handler
                return handler;
            }
        }

        frame_monitor_exit(frame);
        frame = preceding_frame(frame);
    } //while

    //condition 3: past stack bottom, i.e., uncaught exception
    return NULL;
}
```

In this example code, the function returns in three cases:

- Case 1: Hitting a native frame, represented by a NULL return value (i.e., no Java handler found), and the frame is not past the bottom of the stack;

  ```
  (handler == NULL && !is_stack_bottcm(frame))
  ```

- Case 2: Finding a matching handler, represented by a returned handler, and the corresponding frame context;

  ```
  (handler != NULL && !is_stack_botton(frame))
  ```

- Case 3: Reaching the bottom of the stack, represented by a NULL return value, and the frame is past the bottom of stack.

  ```
  (handler == NULL && is_stack_botton(frame))
  ```

The VM will decide the next step based the cases. Ncte that in Case 1, when a native frame is hit, the VM does not need to free the local object handles of the frame here, because they are still used by the native method. The Java-to-native wrapper will handle that right before the native method returns to the Java world.

When a frame is past the bottom of the Java runtime stack, it is not a Java frame or a native frame. It is a traditional C frame, which starts the Java thread by calling a Java method or a native method through the native-to-Java bridge. It can use JNI API "call method" family functions.

If a frame is a Java frame, the code type is Java type. If it is a native frame, there is a valid Java cluster pointervalue, which points to the M2N_wrapper data structure on the stack that is set up by a Java-to-native wrapper. So the function to check if a frame is past the bottom frame can look as shown below.

```
bool is_stack_bottom(Frame_context* frame)
{
    Code_Type type = code_type(frame->eip);
    if( type == CODE_TYPE_JAVA || frame->jcp != NULL)
        return FALSE;

    return TRUE;
}
```

11.5 TRANSFER THE CONTROL

When the VM finishes searching the matching exception handler, it will transfer the control accordingly.

11.5.1 Operations of Control-Transfer

As we mentioned, control transfer happens only in the Java code. Within the Java method that throws an exception, there are two cases for control transfer:

- Case 1. The control goes to the matching exception handler in the same method, with the exception object as the argument; or

- Case 2. If there is no matching handler in the same method, the method completes abruptly and returns to its caller.

In Case 2, the control continues to transfer in the caller method recursively until it hits one of the following cases.

- Case 3. If it finds a matching exception handler in a Java method, the VM transfers control to the handler, as if a jump within that method to the entry point of the handler code, with the operand stack cleared but the exception object on it.

- Case 4. If it hits a native frame, the VM transfers control to the native method, as if the execution completes abruptly from the Java callee and returns to the native-to-Java bridge code, with return value cleared and the exception-object kept in the thread-local storage.

- Case 5. If it is past the bottom of the runtime stack, that is, the preceding frame before the first-invoked Java method or native method of this thread, the VM handles it in the same manner as that for a normal native frame in Case 4. The VM resumes the execution to the native code as if the control returns from the first Java method or native method, with return value cleared and the exception object kept in the thread-local storage.

There is no control-transfer within the native method and the control transfer never crosses the native frame.

To summarize the cases, we can consider the design of control transfer according to their operational semantics. All the cases can split their operations into one or more of the following actions.

- Action 1: Transfer control to the exception handler. This action is internal to a Java method.

- Action 2: Complete abruptly from a Java method callee. This action returns from the Java method.

- Action 3: Resume execution.

Case 1 transfers the control to the matching handler and resumes execution.

Case 2 completes abruptly from the Java method. Note that this does not finish the full control-transfer process. It has to be continued by other actions.

Case 3 completes abruptly from Java methods one by one until it finds a matching exception handler; then it transfers the control to the handler and resumes execution in Java code.

Case 4 completes abruptly from Java methods one by one until it hits a native frame, where it resumes execution in the native code.

Case 5 completes abruptly from Java methods one by one until it hits the bottom of the Java stack, where it resumes execution in the native code.

The actions included in different cases are given in Table 11.1. We do not include Case 2 since it is not a complete process. Mark "X" in a cell means the action of the column is included in the case of the row. All of them have Action 3: "resume execution." From the table, we can see that Case 4 and Case 5 are actually the same process.

TABLE 11.1   Operations Involved in Control Transfer

Operations	Transfer to Handler	Complete Abruptly	Resume Execution
Case 1	X		X
Case 3	X	X	X
Case 4		X	X
Case 5		X	X

We can implement the control transfer by designing the three actions. In actual design, only the action of "resume execution" really changes the application's execution. The other two actions, "transfer to handler" and "complete abruptly," only involve VM operations, whose main task is to prepare the execution context for the final execution resumption.

11.5.2 Registers for Control Transfer

To resume the execution at the target code, the VM needs to set up the execution context for the target, which includes the following two categories of information:

1. **Control registers**

- **Data for thread context**: The thread context includes the stack pointer and the instruction pointer. Here we also include the stack data. These are the most basic data to identify a thread of control. They should always be restored by the VM for exception control transfer. In X86, they are `esp`, `eip`, and the exception object. If the target is in the native code, the exception object is saved in thread-local storage. If the target is Java code, the exception object is put on the operand stack as the only element of the current frame.

- **Stack frame pointers**: They are the frame base pointer and the Java cluster-pointer, which are necessary for the VM to resume the right stack frame for the Java frame and the native frame, respectively. The data should always be restored by the VM for exception control transfer. In our discussion, they are `ebp` and `jcp`.

  Since the control transfer happens only in Java frames, it seems that `jcp` is untouched. But in real implementation, the source of the control transfer is usually in the VM code that has a `M2N_wrapper` in the top frame. It will be popped off, hence `jcp` is touched. It should be restored to point to the next Java frame cluster or set `NULL` if the current Java frame cluster is the last one.

2. **Data registers**

- **Callee-save registers**: If the target is native code, the last action before resuming execution is the abrupt completion of a callee Java method. Then the callee-save registers are assumed live at the target code, since it is the callee's responsibility to restore the data when the call returns. If the target is Java code, it is the JIT compiler's responsibility to decide the callee-save register restoration. In our discussion, the callee-save registers include `ebx`, `edi`, `esi`, and `ebp`.

- **Caller-save registers**: If the target is native code, the caller-save registers are handled by the caller before the call to a Java method and are not assumed live after the call site. So there is no need to restore the caller-save registers for the target code. If the target is Java code, it is the JIT compiler's responsibility to decide the caller-save register restoration. In our discussion, the caller-save registers are `eax`, `ecx`, and `edx`.

The VM cannot simply restore all the needed register values by only looking at their contents in the target frame. Control registers, that is, `esp`, `eip`, `ebp`, and `jcp`, can be restored in the same way as stack unwinding, which we have discussed. For other registers, more work is needed.

11.5.3 Data Register Restoration

We discuss the data register restoration in two actions: abrupt completion of the Java method and control transfer to the exception handler.

11.5.3.1 Abrupt Completion of the Java Method

In the action of Java method abrupt completion, the control flow looks like going to the code right after the call to the abruptly completed Java method (the callee). The callee may save the callee-save registers according to its use of them. It may not save any of them if it does not use callee-save registers. Some of the unsaved callee-save registers might be saved by the callee's callee, or even further up the stack, until the top frame (i.e., the exception-throwing frame). In the top frame, all the callee-save registers are saved for sure.

- When the control-transfer source is a runtime-helper, all the callee-save registers are saved in `M2N_wrapper` on the stack by the Java-to-native wrapper.

- When the control-transfer source is a hardware-fault handler, all the callee-save registers are saved in the exception context by the OS and passed to the fault handler.

In order to restore all the callee-save registers, the VM has to restore them from the top frame when it starts the stack unwinding. When the top frame is popped off, all the callee-save registers have been assigned values. Note that the values are not really loaded into the registers. The frame context has pointers pointing to the stack slots of those saved registers. The registers are loaded only when the Action 3 "resume execution" happens.

When control-transfer logics continue the abrupt completion of Java methods one by one, the VM conducts destructive stack unwinding. Some registers restored from the earlier popped frames may be overwritten by those from the latter popped frames, while some others may be kept valid and used by the target code.

The stack-unwinding process ensures that the callee-save registers are correctly restored. It simulates not only the method return operation from the top frame down to the target frame but also the callee-save registers restoration operation. (The simulation of method return operation actually restores the control registers.)

Figure 11.2 shows the final frame-context status when the VM finishes stack unwinding for the control transfer. It identifies the registers data for the target frame to resume execution. The frame context contains the pointers to the saved registers in the stack.

The process above is implemented in the stack-unwinding process that we have discussed in GC support. There we showed sample code in `preceding_frame()`, which GC also needs to enumerate all the callee-saved registers for possible object references.

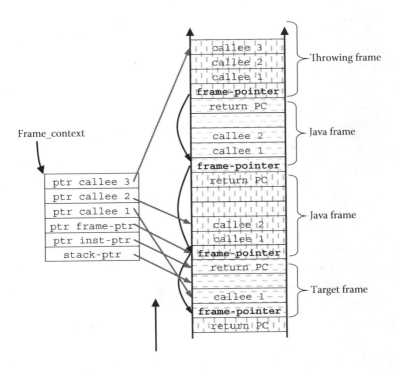

FIGURE 11.2   The frame-context status when stack unwinding finishes.

11.5.3.2 Control Transfer to the Exception Handler

For the action of control transfer to the matching exception handler, the VM needs to ask the JIT compiler which registers to restore and from where to recover the values. It is different from simulating a method return. Since this action happens within a method, the JIT knows all the details of data dependence between the exception handler and its corresponding try block.

- If the exception is triggered by a hardware fault in the same method, all the exception context is saved on the faulting spot. The VM can provide them to the exception handler in case they are needed.

- If the exception is triggered by a proactive throwing through runtime-helper, the situation is the same as a method invocation, where all the callee-save registers can be restored from the helper's frame.

For example, Apache Harmony, by default, uses eax register to pass the exception object to the exception handler, rather than on the runtime stack, and the other caller-save registers are free to use in the exception handler.

If the exception is thrown from a method other than the target one, the action of "control transfer to exception handler" follows the "abrupt complete of Java method" action. The control flow looks like the exception is thrown by the abruptly completed method in the try block of the target exception handler in the same method.

11.5.4 Control-Register Fixing

When the target exception handler is identified, the contents of the frame context cannot be used directly to resume the execution, because it only reflects the context of a method abrupt return. Using it directly only resumes the execution right after the method call.

The VM should modify the frame context to reflect the need of the exception-handler execution. The VM asks the JIT compiler to adjust two registers in the frame context: one is the instruction eip, which should point to the exception-handler entry point, and the other is the stack pointer esp, which should point to the stack position for the exception handler to start with. These two registers define the thread of control.

Once the target frame is identified by function thread_find_exception_handler(), the VM needs the following operations:

```
Exc_handler* handler;
handler = thread_find_exception_handler(frame, exc_obj);

if( handler ){ // a matching exception-handler is found
      //get handler's stack top address
      uint32 ebp = *(frame->p_ebp);
      uint32 stack_depth = handler->entry_stack_depth;
      frame->esp = ebp + stack_depth;

      //get handler's entry point
      frame->eip = handler->entry_code_address;
}

//pass exception-object to handler through eax
frame->p_eax = (uint32*) &exc_obj;
VM_Thread* self = current_thread();
self->jcp = frame->jcp;
```

The function finds the stack top slot and exception-handler entry address, and assigns them to the thread-context registers (esp and eip) Finally, it assigns the address of the exception object to eax and then sets the current Java cluster-pointer.

11.5.5 Resume the Execution

With the frame context prepared, the VM can transfer the control to the context, resuming the execution at the native method or exception handler. Different sources of exception-throwing use different ways to resume the execution.

11.5.5.1 Resume for Proactive Exception

When the exception is proactive from a runtime-helper, the following logic can be used to transfer the control. It directly assigns all the registers and finally jumps to the target code.

```
void vm_transfer_control(Frame_context* context)
{
    //callee-save registers
    uint32 ebx_var = *(context->p_ebx);
    uint32 edi_var = *(context->p_edi);
    uint32 esi_var = *(context->p_esi);

    //caller-save registers
    uint32 eax_var = *(context->p_eax)

    //frame and thread of control
    uint32 ebp_var = *(context->p_ebp);
    uint32 esp_var = context->esp;
    uint32 eip_var = context->eip;

    //restore the registers
    __asm{
    mov ebx_var -> ebx
    mov edi_var -> edi
    mov esi_var -> esi

    mov eax_var -> eax

    mov ebp_var -> ebp

    //now take effect
    mov esp_var -> ecx
    mov eip_var -> edx
    mov ecx -> esp
    jump edx
    }
}
```

To change the current execution flow, there are usually three ways in today's processor design, mapping to three kinds of instructions: call, jump, and return. For exception control transfer, the "call" instruction is not suitable, because it pushes a redundant return address on the stack, which the target code knows nothing about and does not want to deal with. Both "jump" and "return" instructions can be used for exception control transfer. The code above uses "jump." To use the "return" instruction, the target instruction pointer is put on the stack top; then the last four instructions (in bold face) above can become the following.

```
    //now take effect
    //ecx has stack-pointer
    mov esp_var -> ecx
    //edx has instruction-pointer
    mov eip_var -> edx
    //push return eip on stack
```

```
sub 4 -> ecx
mov edx -> [ecx]
mov ecx -> esp
ret
```

Using the "return" instruction has a minor benefit in that the VM does not need to occupy the two caller-save registers ecx and edx when it transfers the control. This is convenient if all the registers, including the caller-save registers, have to be restored. In some platforms, the "return" instruction can also be simulated with a "pop" instruction that pops the stack top element into instruction pointer.

11.5.5.2 Resume for Hardware–Fault Exception

If the exception is thrown from a hardware-fault handler, the VM can reuse the hardware-faulting mechanism for control transfer. Modern operating systems provide developers a chance to process hardware fault with a fault handler. They provide the fault context (contents of all registers) to the fault handler, and then the handler can check what happens by examining the fault context. The handler can also change the fault context when needed.

When the fault handler returns, the control flow can resume to the state specified by the fault context. For example, if the fault handler changes the return instruction pointer in the context, the execution resumes to the new position pointed by the new instruction pointer. It is a common practice for the fault handler to decrement the return instruction pointer to point to its preceding instruction, so as to re-execute the faulting instruction after the faulting problem is resolved, for example, the faulting page is loaded.

The mechanism can be used by the exception-throwing process in the hardware-fault handler. The VM can modify the fault context to meet the needs of the exception-throwing target code. Then returning from the fault handler automatically transfers the control to the target code. The example code is as follows. The fault handler calls the function event_transfer_control() to modify the context.

Linux version:

```
void event_transfer_control(Frame_context* target_context,
                            void* fault_context)
{
    ucontext_t* resume = (ucontext_t*)fault_context;
    Frame_context* target = target_context;

    resume->uc_mcontext.gregs[REG_EAX] = *(target->p_eax);
    resume->uc_mcontext.gregs[REG_EDI] = *(target->p_edi);
    resume->uc_mcontext.gregs[REG_ESI] = *(target->p_esi);
    resume->uc_mcontext.gregs[REG_EBX] = *(target->p_ebx);
    resume->uc_mcontext.gregs[REG_EBP] = *(target->p_ebp);
    resume->uc_mcontext.gregs[REG_EIP] = target->eip;
    resume->uc_mcontext.gregs[REG_ESP] = target->esp;
}
```

Windows version:

```
void event_transfer_control(Frame_context* target_context,
                            PCONTEXT fault_context)
{
    PCONTEXT resume = fault_context;
    Frame_context* target = target_context;

    resume->Eax = *(target->p_eax);
    resume->Edi = *(target->p_edi);
    resume->Esi = *(target->p_esi);
    resume->Ebx = *(target->p_ebx);
    resume->Ebp = *(target->p_ebp);
    resume->Eip = target->eip;
    resume->Esp = target->esp;
}
```

From the discussion on exception handling in JVM, we can see that the runtime over-head can be high, mainly due to stack unwinding and exception-handler matching. The stack unwinding may undergo twice: once for exception stack trace and once for exception-handler searching. There are possibilities to optimize them into one pass of stack unwinding.

Another optimization is to cache the stack-trace or stack-unwinding result after an earlier exception-throwing. Then the later exception-throwing can possibly reuse the data by searching the cache for a given instruction pointer, assuming the stack keeps stable between the two exception-throwing instances.

It is also possible to avoid the stack unwinding at all if the compiler can determine that the thrown exception is to be caught by the handler in the same method. Then a direct execution path can be established by the compiler from the throwing spot to the catching spot.

11.5.6 Uncaught Exception

When the exception cannot find a matching exeption handler and finally hits the stack bottom, the execution returns to the state before any Java/native method is invoked. In this case, the VM essentially terminates the current Java thread.

As we mentioned, there is an "uncaught exception handler" that might be registered by the thread or an "default uncaught exception handler" installed. They will be invoked when the Java thread is detached from the VM, with the uncaught exception object as argument. Since the uncaught exception handler is a Java or native method, the invocation virtually restarts the Java-thread execution. The execution may cause another exception, but it will not lead to circular exception handling, because the VM ensures the execution come back to the Java thread detaching process, no matter whether the uncaught exception handler throws an exception or not.

For example, the Java code for `Thread.detach()` can be as follows. This method is called by the VM through the JNI API when the target thread is going to terminate.

```
//uncaught exception is the argument
void detach(Throwable uncaught) {
    try {
        if (uncaught != null) {
        //invoke the registered handler
            getUncaughtExceptionHandler().invoke(this, uncaught);
        }
    } finally {
        //remove current thread from ThreadGroup
        group.remove(this);
        synchronized(this) {
            //set current thread to dead
            isAlive = false;
            notifyAll();
        }
    }
}
```

Any exception triggered in getUncaughtExceptionHandler().invoke() is ignored, and the execution goes to the finally block to terminate the current this thread.

CHAPTER 12

Finalization and Weak References

FINALIZATION AND WEAK REFERENCES are two tricky topics to many Java and virtual machine (VM) developers. They are closely related to the memory management and threading interactions.

12.1 FINALIZATION

Java requires to execute the `finalize()` method of any object that overrides the default method in `java.lang.Object`, after it becomes unreachable and before it is reclaimed. The idea is to provide the application developers a chance to do some wrap-ups when they know the objects become unreachable. The logics in VM to support finalization are like the following.

1. When a class is loaded, the VM checks if it or its superclass has the `finalize()` method implemented. If it is implemented, the VM marks this class as having a finalizer.

2. When an object of certain class is allocated, the garbage collector (GC) checks if the class has a finalizer. If it does, the object is linked into a list, the "finalizer object list."

3. When a collection starts and marks all the reachable objects, before GC reclaims dead objects, it goes through the "finalizer object list" to check the objects' aliveness status. If an object is dead, then GC removes it from the "finalizer object list" and adds to another list, the "finalizable object list." If the object is live in the "finalizer object list," the pointer to the object may need to be updated to point to the new location if GC moves it. In other words, both live and dead objects in the original "finalizer object list" are retained by GC, but in two different lists.

4. After the step above is done, GC *resurrects* the dead objects in the "finalizable object list." It traverses the list for every object, marks it live, and recursively marks all its

reachable objects live. For a trace-copy GC, marking a live object means to forward the object to a new location and update all references to them to the new location. Then the "finalizable object list" is passed to the VM.

5. When mutators are resumed, all the objects in the "finalizable object list" are ready for `finalize()` method execution. It is the VM's decision when and how to execute them. Usually the VM uses dedicated "finalizing" thread(s) for the execution. They are regarded as mutators since they execute Java methods. (This means GC should suspend them and enumerate them as with normal application threads.)

6. Right before an object is finalized, that is, executing its `finalize()` method, the object is removed from the "finalizable object list." The finalization operation might make the object reachable again, for example, install its reference into a field of a reachable object.

7. When a finalized object becomes unreachable again some time later, GC will directly reclaim it, without checking if it has a finalizer or not, because it is not in the "finalizer object list." Any object with a finalizer can be put into the "finalizer object list" only when it is born. Once it is removed from the list, the object becomes a normal object as if without a finalizer.

8. When the VM is shut down, it tries to finish all the object finalizations.

The logics are simple. Only one thing worth mentioning is when and how to execute the `finalize()` method. There is no specification in Java on the time or deadline of finalization. If the application code acquires a resource in an object's initializer and releases the resource in its finalizer, there is no guarantee that the resource will be released timely. The resources may be retained for a long time, causing serious resource leak, including the memory leak caused by the finalizable objects themselves. So it is not suggested to release the critical resource in a finalizer. Instead, the use of a finalizer should better be avoided, or only for a backup solution to check if any resource that should have been released has not been released yet and then release them.

Using dedicated mutators for finalization after mutators resumed from a collection has some implications. First of all is the potential correctness issue. Finalizers may execute in parallel with each other, and with other application code, and hence synchronization is needed if they access a shared resource.

Some VM implementation may finalize all the finalizable objects identified by a collection in the same collection context before resuming mutators. This may avoid some concurrency complexity, but may incur more serious problems. The lock that is needed by a finalizer may be held by a mutator thread that is suspended for the collection. The lock can only be released after the collection resumes the mutators. This is a deadlock.

When there are lots of finalizable objects waiting to be finalized, they may take lots of heap space. In order to release the heap space, the finalizers should be executed. Executing the finalizers may take many processor cycles. A balance is needed between memory consumption and processor overhead. It is desirable to finalize the objects at a speed that is proportional to that of finalizer-object generation.

When the finalizer objects are created faster than the speed of their finalization, one solution is to increase the number of dedicated finalizing threads to accelerate the speed of finalization. The other solution is to slow down the generation of finalizer objects while keeping the number of finalizing threads stable. The former solution may have too many mutators competing for the CPU against each other, while the latter solution may block some application threads so that they can give CPU to the finalizing threads. As above, the latter solution may incur a deadlock situation.

When the finalizable objects are moved to the "finalizable object list," they are not reachable from the application in this collection cycle, although some of them may be reachable to other finalizable objects. Resurrection cannot make the application-unreachable objects reachable, but helps keep the unreachable objects in a heap without being recycled by GC.

When the next collection cycle starts, some of the objects on the "finalizable object list" may have been finalized and removed from the list, while some others have not. For non-finalized finalizable objects, some of them may become reachable to the application again because of the finalization operations. Those application-unreachable finalizable objects should be enumerated by GC as known to be "resurrected" and kept in heap without being recycled.

To keep those finalizable objects "resurrected," one solution is to copy the "finalizable object list" to a Java data structure and pass it to the finalizing threads. Since the finalizing threads are Java threads, the objects linked in the live data structure are automatically live. The other solution is for GC to explicitly enumerate the "finalizable object list" when a collection cycle starts.

12.2 WHY WEAK REFERENCES

In high-level languages, objects' lifetime is managed automatically by garbage collectors. It is impossible or not encouraged for a programmer to know if an object is dead. Based on reachability analysis, if the object is referenced by the application, it is live. When an object is dead, there is no reference in the application to the object. In other words, when the application queries for the liveness of an object, the object must be live, since the application should hold a reference to the object for the query. If the object is dead, the application never knows that fact, since the application can never query on that without a reference to the object.

Finalization is an approach that presumably can tell if an object is unreachable, since the object can define `finalize()` that is executed when the object is unreachable. But it has a serious drawback that, to execute `finalize()` means the object has to be kept reachable. So while `finalize()` can be sometimes useful to clean up some resources that have been used and still retained by the object, it is not suitable for the goal of "managing object lifetime." The fundamental reason is, `finalize()` is a method "inside" the object. To manage objects' lifetime, it is better to use some approach "outside" the object. Here are three examples where finalizer is not enough.

Example 1: Page Cache of a Browser

Sometimes it can be convenient if the application knows an object's liveness and if the programmer can check the dead objects. An example is a browser's "page cache." A browser keeps a cache for the visited pages, so that when one of the pages is visited again, its contents can be loaded directly from the page cache if they have not expired. The cached contents are virtually dead in the sense that they can be cleaned without any problem. But the browser still holds references to them, so that they can be resurrected when needed. For this purpose, a language construct is needed that can express the "dead but still referenceable" semantics.

Example 2: URL and Page Snapshot

Even for resource management purpose, `finalize()` is not always effective. Sometimes the resource is not used by an object, but only associated with the object's lifetime, so that the resource never survives the object. Still using browser as an example, the developer can associate a page `Snapshot` object with the corresponding `URL` object. When the `URL` object is dead, the `Snapshot` should die as well. It might be easy to implement such semantics if the `URL` object keeps a singleton reference to the `Snapshot` object, but this is often impossible in reality, for example, when the `URL` object is defined as final.

It is also impossible to implement the semantics by aggregating the `URL` and `Snapshot` objects in a third object, say `Page` object. The `Page` object keeps a reference to the `URL`, which keeps the `URL` always reachable unless the `Page` object itself is dead. That virtually moves the problem of `URL` management to that of the `Page` object, rather than solving the problem.

Nullifying the `Snapshot` reference in `Page` with the `finalize()` of `URL` seems to solve the problem, since the `finalize()` is only invoked when `URL` is unreachable. But the problem is that there is not guarantee that the finalized object `URL` will be recycled.

Example 3: Tab Object of a Browser

Yet another lifetime management problem is how the program knows an object is indeed dead, that is, not only unreachable but also finalized and not resurrectable. Let us take browser development as an example again. When a browser user closes an old tab, the tab page object may stay in memory for a long time, taking significant heap size. It should be recycled when the heap is low. When developing the browser, the developer may want to know if an old tab is surely to be recycled before a new tab is allowed to open. This is obviously not possible to implement with `finalize()`, since `finalize()` cannot tell if the object has been finalized.

Java introduces "reference-object" to give programmers an explicit way to manage objects' lifetime from "outside" of the object. A reference-object can be regarded as a pointer to an object, but this pointer itself is represented as an object. This reference-object has a field holding a reference to the target object. The target object here is called *referent*. The purpose of a reference-object is to keep a reference to the referent, while this reference does not keep the referent alive. In other words, the reference-object is a "pointer" that only keeps the pointed object referenced, but cannot keep the pointed object alive. The code may retrieve the object from the "pointer" even after it is considered dead.

If an object can be reachable only through a reference-object, this object is virtually dead and subject to GC's discretion, although the object is still reachable by the application. In this situation, the object is called "weakly reachable." The traditional "reachable" is called "strongly reachable" in this context. The application can access the weakly reachable object before GC reclaims it. To access the referent, "get()" action is invoked upon the reference-object. The referent of a reference-object can be set to null when action "clear()" is called on the reference-object.

A reference-object can solve the problems in browser development.

On Example 1: Page Cache of a Browser

When a browser manages its page cache, it can use reference-objects to hold the cache contents of previously visited pages. The cache contents can be regarded as dead and available for reclamation when the system memory is low. When the same page is visited again, the browser can check the reference-objects to see if the cache contents are still available as their referents. If they are, the contents can be loaded into the browser and become strongly reachable again. This page cache feature is only an optimization to reduce the page loading time. The time when to reclaim the cache contents does not impact the browser's correctness. To implement the page cache without reference-objects, the browser then has to decide when and how to reclaim the cache according to the system memory status which conflicts with the original purpose of programming in high-level languages that have GC.

On Example 2: URL and Page Snapshot

When the browser manages snapshots for its URLs, it can aggregate URL and Snapshot objects in a third object Page, while the third object Page references the URL through the reference-object. Whenever the URL object is no longer reachable to the application, the aggregation object will know the condition and consequently nullify the Snapshot reference as well.

We will discuss Example 3 later since it needs deeper understanding of reference-object.

The idea to implement reference-objects is straightforward. Since it is basically only about reachability, the implementation details are mainly in GC component. During object tracing, reference-objects are treated differently than normal ones. When a reference-object is reached and scanned, GC does not mark its referent as usual. Only when the referent is reached from a path that has no reference-object can it be marked live. So reference-object processing mainly has two steps.

1. During object tracing, mark all reachable objects except referents live, unless the referent is reached from a path without reference-object. Record all the reachable reference-objects in a list.

2. After object tracing, go through the live reference-object list. For those reference-objects whose referents are not marked live, the referent fields are set null, that is, `clear()`-ed, so that the referenced object is nonreachable.

The two steps are not enough to meet the needs of object lifetime management because there are subtle differences in real usage of reference-objects. For example, the page cache problem wants to keep the "dead but still referenceable" objects in cache as long as the memory allows, while the `URL-Snapshot` problem wants to recycle the `URL`s and `Snapshot`s together as soon as the `URL` becomes unreachable. The old tab problem wants to know not only when the old tab object is unreachable but also when the object is surely to be recycled (i.e., finalized and no longer resurrectable).

12.3 OBJECT LIFE-TIME STATES

To meet the needs of reference-objects in different scenarios, Java language provides three reference-object classes: `SoftReference`, `WeakReference`, and `PhantomReference`. A reference-object can be an instance of any of them or an instance of a subclass of them. We use "soft-reference," "weak-reference" and "phantom-reference" to represent the respective types of the reference-objects. They define the strengths of (weak) reachability in a finer granularity. From strongest to weakest, the strengths of weak reachability are defined as the following.

- An object is *softly reachable* if it is not strongly reachable, but reachable through at least a path that has a soft-reference. A softly reachable object may be reclaimed at the discretion of GC. When memory is low, GC **may** `clear()` the soft-reference objects so that their referents can be reclaimed, but it is not mandatory.

- An object is *weakly reachable* if it is not strongly reachable or softly reachable, but reachable through at least a path that has a weak-reference. When GC determines that an object is weakly reachable, all weak-reference objects that refer to that object **should** be `clear()`-ed. After that, the object becomes **finalizable**.

- An object is *phantom reachable* if it is not strongly, softly, or weakly reachable, but there is at least one path to the object with a phantom-reference. Phantomly reachable objects are objects that have been **finalized**, but not yet reclaimed. `Get()` operation on a phantom-reference object always returns null, meaning a phantomly reachable object is **unreachable** to the application. This is different from softly and weakly reachable objects that can be `get()`-ed before GC `clear()` their reference-objects.

In order to make our discussion easy, we use *nonstrongly reachable* to cover any of the three cases above.

12.3.1 Object State Transition

Some states of an object's lifetime can be illustrated in Figure 12.1. Note for the sake of focused discussion that the graph is correct but not complete, since it omits many other states and transition arrows.

In the figure, the dashed arrows are for the objects that have only default finalizers. We will discuss them later. The other transitions in the figure are the following:

- A: The object is new-ed (optionally with a nondefault finalizer).

- B: The object's constructor has been executed.

- C: The object's reference is stored in the application context.

- D: All strong references to the object are nullified. The object becomes softly reachable through a path with a soft-reference.

- E: All strong references to the object are nullified. The object becomes weakly reachable through a path with a weak-reference.

- F: All softly reachable paths to the object are cleared. The object is still reachable from a weak-reference.

- G: All softly reachable paths to the object are cleared. It is ready to be finalized if it has a nondefault finalizer.

- H: All weakly reachable paths to the object are cleared. It is ready to be finalized if it has a nondefault finalizer.

- I: A strongly reachable object becomes finalizable directly because it has no non-strongly reachable path.

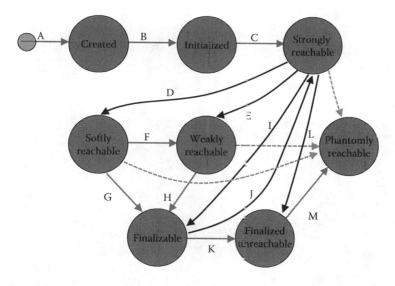

FIGURE 12.1   Possible state transitions in an object lifetime.

- J: A finalizable object may become strongly reachable again after finalization.

- K: A finalized object that is not reachable to the application.

- L: A strongly reachable object that was resurrected and finalized, and becomes application-unreachable again.

- M: The application-unreachable object is phantomly reachable through phantom-reference.

The arrow M makes phantomly reachable different from other two kinds of weak reachability. Objects unreachable from other reference-objects may become reachable due to finalization. But that is impossible for phantom-reference. Once an object becomes phantomly reachable, it is no longer reachable to the application. For objects with nondefault finalizers, there is no transition directly to phantomly reachable from either softly or weakly reachable.

For the objects that have only default finalizers, there is no step of "finalizable" or "finalized unreachable." The transition looks like Figure 12.2 below:

The dashed arrows are:

- O: A strongly reachable object becomes unreachable to the application, while phantomly reachable through phantom-reference.

- P: All softly reachable paths to the object are cleared. The object is still phantomly reachable through phantom-reference.

- Q: All weakly reachable paths to the object are cleared. The object is still phantomly reachable through phantom-reference.

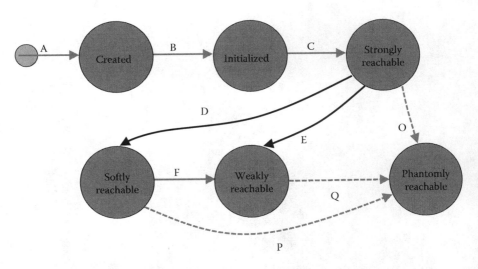

FIGURE 12.2   State transitions for objects without default finalizers.

Obviously soft-reference is most suitable to develop the mentioned page-caching mechanism, because it is up to the GC whether to reclaim the softly reachable objects. GC can retain them as long as the heap space is enough.

Weak-reference can be used to associate other objects' lifetime with the target referent object, so that references to other objects can be nullified when the referent becomes unreachable from the applicaiton. The time point is known to the application. We will explain how it knows next. Weak-reference is hence a handy tool for the URL-snapshot problem.

12.3.2 Reference Queue

Java application programming interface (API) defines a reference queue class, ReferenceQueue. When a reference-object is created with an instance of ReferenceQueue (or its subclass) registered, the reference-object will be put into the queue by the VM automatically with enqueue() action when its referent is unreachable to the application. That is, soft- and weak-reference objects are placed in their respective reference-queues after they are clear()-ed, while phantom-reference objects are placed in their reference-queue after their referents become phantomly reachable, but before their referent field is clear()-ed. In any case, the get() operation on the reference-object returns null when it is enqueue()-ed. Reference-queue helps the application to know when the interested objects become unreachable, thus taking corresponding actions. The application can use poll() or removed() upon the queue to dequeue the reference-objects.

Reference-queue makes phantom-reference useful for its purpose. The existence of the phantom-reference gives the application a chance to perform postfinalization processing that requires the object to be unreachable or to perform some operation that is only expected when the target object is known dead for sure. It is supposed to replace the finalization mechanism but with a much more flexible way, by collaborating with a reference-queue.

Phantomly reachable objects are under a reclamation process and have been finalized. The phantom-reference simply prevents the object from being reclaimed until the phantom-reference is finally clear()-ed or the phantom-reference itself becomes unreachable. A phantom-reference is enqueue()-ed when the referent is phantomly reachable, and then the application can dequeue the phantom-reference to know the fact that the referent is no longer reachable to it. Now we have a solution to the old tab problem in browser design.

On Example 3: Tab Object of a Browser

Phantom-reference is suitable for the old tab problem. When the browser finds the phantom-reference that holds the old tab object was enqueue()-ed, it knows the old tab is dead for sure. It can remove the phantom-reference object from the queue, conduct all the needed operations, and then drop the final reference to the old tab object. Now it is ready to open a new tab.

A reference-queue is needed for a phantom-reference to be useful, since the only purpose of phantom-reference is to know certain objects are surely dead. It does not make sense to create a phantom-reference object without registering a reference-queue.

12.3.3 Reference-Object State Transition

A reference-object has a different life cycle than the referent object. A reference-object is created for a referent and `enqueue()`-ed when the referent is not strongly reachable. A reference-object *cannot* be created without a referent. Since a reference-object exists for its referent, it does not make much sense to keep a reference-object reachable for a long time without the referent being strongly reachable, except for one reason: telling the application that the referent is unreachable. This is why the reference queue exists. It collects the reference-objects whose referents' reachability is interesting to the application. Once the reference-objects are dequeued from the queue by the application, they are no longer reachable from the queue, and it is the application's responsibility to deal with them. But since the application can never set a new referent to the reference-object, after knowing its referent is indeed unreachable, it makes no sense to keep the dequeued reference-object any more.

Based on the discussions above, the life cycle of a reference-object looks like Figure 12.3 below.

The transitions are the following:

- A: A reference-object is created (with argument of a referent and optionally a reference-queue for nonphantom-reference).

- B: A reference-object becomes reachable when its reference is stored in the program context. Its referent is strongly reachable.

- C: The referent of the reference-object becomes not strongly reachable.

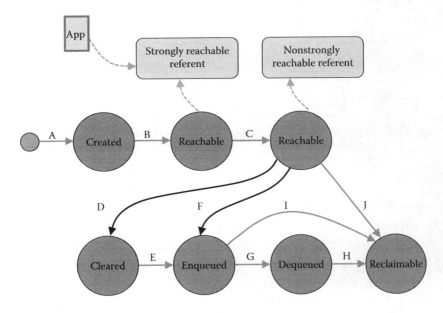

FIGURE 12.3   State transitions of a reference-object.

- D: If the reference-object is not phantom-reference, the reference-object is cleared and the referent becomes either finalizable (with a nondefault finalizer) or reclaimable (without a nondefault finalizer).

- E: If the reference-object is not phantom-reference, the reference-object is enqueued. If it was created with a reference-queue registered, the reference-object is put into the queue. Otherwise, the enqueuing operation does nothing.

- F: If the reference-object is phantom-reference, it is enqueued directly before cleared.

- G: The reference-object is dequeued from the reference-queue. It is referenced by the application code that dequeues it.

- H: The reference-object becomes unreachable to the application, ready to be reclaimed. If it is phantom-reference, the application may or may not clear it before it is reclaimed. If all the phantom-reference objects to the same referent are cleared, the referent becomes reclaimable immediately. Otherwise, the phantom-reference and the referent become reclaimable together.

- I: If the reference-object was created without a reference-queue registered, the reference-object is not in any queue and becomes unreachable.

- J: The reference-object becomes unreachable directly, since the application loses its reference.

The state transitions for normal objects and reference-objects help us to implement the reference-object supports.

12.4 REFERENCE-OBJECT IMPLEMENTATION

A typical flow of VM supports of Java reference-objects includes the steps given below, which are much more complicated than the two earlier-mentioned steps, but the same design principles still apply. The steps are integrated in GC and VM components.

1. When a class is loaded, the VM checks if it or its superclass is of any reference type. If yes, the VM tags this class with certain reference type: soft-reference, weak-reference, or phantom-reference.

2. Process reference-objects during heap tracing. GC marks all the reachable objects except the referents. For the marked reference-objects, GC builds three checklists—one list for each reference type.

3. Process soft-reference objects after heap tracing. GC traverses the checklist for soft-reference objects. For this collection, GC has to decide how to deal with soft-reference-objects: whether they should be treated as normal objects or as reference-objects.

- If a soft-reference object is treated as a normal object, GC removes it from the soft-reference checklist, and marks it and all its recursively reachable objects, including the reached soft-reference objects.

- If a soft-reference object is treated as a reference-object, the referent of the soft-reference-object is checked if it is marked. If it is not, it means the referent is unreachable to the application, and the soft-reference object is `clear()`-ed; otherwise, the soft-reference object (holding a live referent) is removed from the soft-reference checklist;

4. Process weak-reference objects always as reference-objects, either `clear()`-ed (when the referent is not marked) or removed from the list (when the referent is marked).

5. Process finalizable objects. GC traverses the "finalizer object list." (Objects in the list were added when they were created.) GC traces the heap from the objects in the list to resurrect all reachable objects from them. The finalizable objects (dead but now resurrected in the "finalizer object list") are removed from the "finalizer object list" and put into the "finalizable object list."

   - Note the resurrection process may resurrect some reference-objects. There is no specification telling whether or not the resurrected reference-objects should be added in the reference-object checklists. It is an implementation decision. When a reference-object is resurrected, its referent is not. In other words, the resurrected reference-objects are `clear()`-ed. This is necessary because otherwise the newly resurrected reference-objects would have missed the processing in previous steps. The reachability of the referents should not rely on the resurrection of their reference-objects. For phantom-references, their referents are not available to `get()` anyway. To ensure consistency, it is suggested not to put the resurrected reference-objects back to the checklists.

6. Process phantom-reference objects in a little different way from other reference types. The phantom-reference checklist is traversed to find if any referent is marked. If the referent is marked, meaning it is strongly reachable, the phantom-reference object is removed from the checklist. Otherwise, if the referent is not strongly reachable, it is not cleared as other reference types.

   - There is no specification telling whether the referent should be resurrected when its phantom-reference is resurrected and whether the resurrection includes all the objects recursively reachable from the referent. The author does not see any problem to `clear()` the phantom-reference.

   - Phantom-reference processing is ordered after finalization because it must treat the resurrected objects as live ones. This is important so that the system has a broader view on live objects, including those accessible only to finalizers.

7. All the remaining items in the checklists have live reference-objects. The phantom-reference objects are not `clear()`-ed, while others are. GC removes them from the

lists. If there is a registered reference-queue wher the reference-object was created, it will be enqueue()-ed into that reference-queue. This usually is executed by dedicated thread(s). If there is no registered reference-queue, the reference-object becomes reclaimable.

After the reference-objects are enqueued, they are no longer handled specially by the VM (compared to other normal nonreference-objects). When and how they are dequeued is the application's decision. It is common for the application to check the death of the referent by dequeuing the reference-queue and then drop the reference-object for GC's disposal.

Note that although we use clear() and enqueue() to refer to specific actions in reference-object processing, GC does not actually call the clear() and enqueue() methods of the reference-objects when it does those actions. GC conducts the operations *directly*. For clear(), GC nullifies the referent field in the reference-object, and for enqueue(), GC puts the reference-object in the reference-queue, both directly without calling the methods. The Java methods clear() and enqueue() are only for application code to call. The reason for this is to avoid expected behavior implemented in clear() and enqueue() because they are public methods hence can be overridden by the application code. GC does not want to risk with user-defined semantics. But this may cause confusions for the application developer. An application may call enqueue() before the referent is unreachable when the application expects the same result as if the referent is unreachable. A reference can only be enqueue()-ed once, so the semantics can be kept consistent.

As in the finalize() method, there is no specification in Java on the time or deadline of enqueue() method execution.

If the application code associates some important resource with an object and expects to release the resource once the object dies, the application should better not rely on the enqueue() operation (by checking the reference-queue). In other words, the resource is better to be arranged in a way that once the target object is nonstrongly unreachable, the resource becomes unreachable at the same time automatically, no matter whether the reference-object is enqueue()-ed or not. In this case, the application can use weak-reference to manage the target object, try to get() it to check the death of the target object, and then deal with the associated resource.

Without depending on the reference-queue, there is a potential risk that the developer may get() the target object and accidently keep the reference, thereby keeping the object live while releasing the associated resource. Using phantom-reference prevents get() from returning the target object, but it never returns the object, so the application cannot check the death by get()-ing it.

Different from finalization, the enqueue()-ing operation by GC is not Java code execution, and thus there is no need to use Java threads for enqueuing. It can be conducted before or after mutators are resumed. Similar as finalization, the number of enqueuing threads and load balance have to be considered.

When the reference-objects are moved to the reference-queue, they are reachable from the application even if the application loses the direct references to them, until they are dequeued and their references are nullified by the application.

12.5 REFERENCE-OBJECT PROCESSING ORDER

The design decision on the soft-reference objects processing is implementation specific. There is no specification on this. There are multiple choices when the VM runs an application:

- **Partial-normal**: Within one collection, treat some soft-reference objects as normal objects and some others as reference-objects.

- **Collection-normal**: In one collection, treat all soft-reference objects as normal objects; in another collection, treat all soft-reference objects as reference-objects.

- **Always-normal**: Always treat all soft-reference objects as normal objects.

- **Always-reference**: Always treat all soft-reference objects as reference-objects.

We will show that "partial-normal" is error prone and should be avoided. Any of the other three choices is compliant to the specification.

A common design usually chooses "collection-normal." A minor GC can treat all soft-reference objects as normal objects, and a major collection treats all of them as reference-objects. A minor collection is named relative to major collection, where the former only collects part of the heap for higher collection efficiency and the latter usually collects the whole heap. Since the referents of soft-references expect stronger reachability than those of other two kinds of reference-objects, it makes sense to retain them during minor collection. This is not necessarily the only design choice but is recommended. For this design, the steps above need some adjustments as given below. In minor collection, there is no separate processing for soft-reference objects. Their processing is merged in heap tracing, together with other normal objects.

1. The VM tags the reference type of a loaded class.

2. Process reference-objects during heap tracing.
   In a minor collection, GC marks all the reachable objects except the referents of weak-reference and phantom-reference objects. In other words, the soft-reference objects are treated as normal objects, and softly reachable objects are marked as strongly reachable. For the marked weak-reference and phantom-reference objects (not their referents), record them in two checklists—one list for each reference type;
   In a major collection, mark all the reachable objects except the referents. For the marked reference-objects, build three checklists to record them—one list for each reference type;

3. Process soft-reference objects as reference-objects in a major collection. After heap tracing, the checklist for soft-reference objects is traversed. Every referent of the soft-reference object is checked if it is marked. If it is not, it means the referent is unreachable to the application and the soft-reference object is clear()-ed; otherwise, the soft-reference object (holding a live referent) is removed from the soft-reference checklist.

4. Process weak-reference objects as reference-objects. In a minor collection, it is processed after heap tracing. In a major collection, it is processed after soft-reference processing.

5. Process finalizable objects.

6. Process phantom-reference objects.

7. Pass all the remaining items in the three checklists to the VM.

8. VM enqueue() the reference-objects.

Note that weak-reference processing is always after soft-reference processing. This is exactly because some VM implementation may have different treatments for soft-reference and weak-reference objects in a collection, which is the case in "collection-normal" and "always-normal" designs. The order is to ensure correct handling of the cases of multiple nonstrongly reachable paths to the same referent or chained nonstrongly reachable paths to a referent.

Figure 12.4a shows the situation when the same referent is reachable from multiple nonstrongly reachable paths, where one path is softly reachable and another path is weakly reachable. When the collection treats soft-reference objects as normal objects, the softly reachable path marks the referent R as strongly reachable during heap tracing and then the weak-reference processing removes the weak-reference object W1 from its checklist as the referent is reachable. This has no problem.

If the processing is in the reverse order, the weak-reference processing first considers the referent R as unreachable and clears it, and then the soft-reference processing considers it strongly reachable, which is contradictory. The weak-reference object W1 is enqueued later, leading the application to believe the referent R is dead, and hence cleans up some associated resources that should only be cleaned up when the referent R is unreachable. When the collection treats soft-reference objects as reference-objects, there is no difference caused by different processing orders.

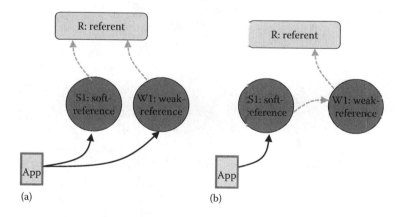

(a)   (b)

FIGURE 12.4   Reference types processing order: (a) multipath reference and (b) chained-path reference.

Figure 12.4b shows the situation when a referent itself is a reference-object. When the collection treats soft-reference objects as normal objects, the weak-reference object W1 is first marked live with soft reachability. Then the weak-reference processing finds the referent R is unreachable and clears it. This is not a problem.

If the processing order is reversed, the weak-reference processing at first does not process the weak-reference object W1, because it is not marked by GC due to the fact that it is only reachable through a reference-object. Then the soft-reference processing finds the weak-reference object W1 and marks it strongly reachable. Now that the referent R is not marked reachable, the get() operation on the live weak-reference W1 may cause unexpected errors. When the collection treats soft-reference objects as reference objects, there is no difference caused by different processing orders.

Actually the same problem may happen when both the reference-objects are soft-reference objects in a "partial-normal" design, where soft-reference objects are treated differently in one collection. For example, in Figure 12.5 below, when S1 is a soft-reference object and is treated as a normal object, while S2 is a soft-reference object and treated as a reference-object, the different processing orders of S1 and S2 can lead to inconsistent results, and sometimes incorrect results. That is why a "partial-normal" design is not recommended. Furthermore, it is not recommended to generate the case of multiple-path or chained-path nonstrongly reachability in the first place.

To summarize, the order of object processing has to be from strong to weaker reachability, and not the reverse in any case. Since phantom-reference retains the phantomly reachable referents rather than clears them, it might be considered by some as a stronger reachability than other reference types that clear their referents (i.e., softly reachable and weakly reachable). This understanding is actually incorrect. By retaining the referent, phantom-reference does not cause any problem as above, because the referent of phantom- reference is not accessible to the application. The retention of the referent does not change the strength of its reachability.

In a reference-counting system, the biggest challenge is cyclic reference, which is formed when two or more objects form a reference cycle, so that none of them has zero reference count. To break the cycle, a reference-object can be used for one link of the reference cycle. This technique can also solve the "lapsed listener" problem.

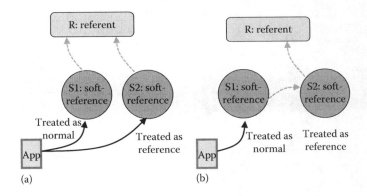

FIGURE 12.5 Potential erroneous conditions when soft-reference objects are treated differently in one collection: (a) multipath reference and (b) chained-path reference.

CHAPTER 13

Modularity Design of VM

N ow that we have discussed the important components in virtual machine (VM) design, it is time to briefly discuss the architectural design of VM implementation.

13.1 VM COMPONENTS

As we have discussed in Chapter 10, the calling relation between different code types can be illustrated as the Figure 13.1.

In the figure, the dashed-line boxes are application code, and the rest are implemented by the VM. To support all the Java and native methods, the VM has to implement the following components. Note that the list does not cover all the VM components, but only the major ones.

- **VM core:** This is the core of a VM implementation, mostly for class-support. It has all the core data structures and operation logics around classes. Especially, all the class data have detailed description so that they can be reflected, including the class, interface, field, and method. This is necessary for the VM to implement the semantics of the virtual instruction set architecture (ISA), such as dynamic class loading and linking. The logics in class support mainly include class loading, linking, initialization, and reflection. The VM core includes the VM's initialization and shutdown, and also provides interfaces for the components to talk to each other.

- **Native support:** This component supports a native interface between managed code and native code, including the Java Native Interface (JNI) application programming interface (API) that rely on the VM core. The JNI APIs need to access class support for reflection. They also need support from other components such as exception and threading that are provided through the VM core interfaces.

- **Runtime-helpers:** This component provides VM services to the Java method, including the same services provided to native methods through JNI APIs. The implementations of the same VM service can be different for the Java method and the native

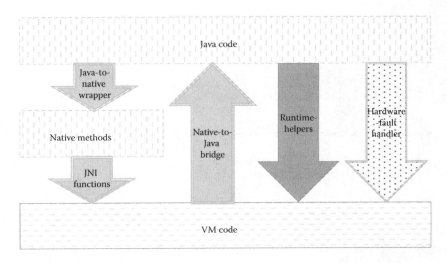

FIGURE 13.1   Calling relation between different types of code.

method due to the different properties of the two worlds. Exception-throwing is one obvious example.

- **Kernel classes**: The VM has to provide implementation of certain Java classes that access VM internals, which is unavailable to a VM-independent class library. Examples include reflection, reference-object, threading, object, and atomics. Java reflection needs to access the properties of class, field, method, and others, that are provided in the VM core. Java reference-objects have to be VM-specific because the VM needs to keep the semantics consistent between the Java class and garbage collection (GC) reference-object processing, for example, for clear() and enqueue() operations. Java threading has to map to operating system (OS) threading support. Basically, all the OS features embedded in Java APIs have to be provided by the VM, which maps them to OS features.

- **Exception support**: This component provides the exception-throwing implementation for both native and Java methods. It also includes the processing logics for hardware fault.

- **Threading support**: The system has to provide threading support that can bridge the semantic gap between the virtual-ISA VM and the underlying platform, including thread creation, scheduling, and synchronization.

- **Execution engine**: This is the component that executes the bytecode, including the just-in-time (JIT) compiler and/or interpreter. There can be multiple JIT compilers and multiple interpreters. They can be managed by an execution driver (or execution manager), so that the execution engines (EE) can be switched at runtime for different methods or different parts of the same method.

- **Garbage collector**: GC manages the object allocation and heap usage, including partial supports to reference objects and finalization. There can be multiple space

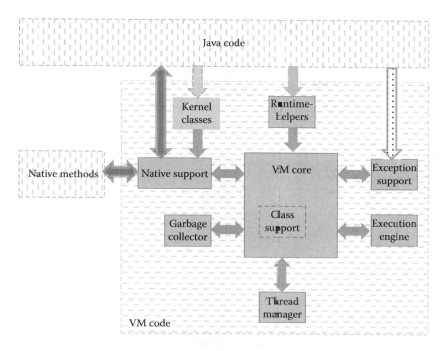

FIGURE 13.2   Major components of VM implementation.

collectors, managed through a GC manager. The multiple space collectors can collaborate to collect different spaces of the heap or be applied to the same space at different collections. The object hash-code feature is usually supported by the GC component as well.

The components described above are illustrated in Figure 13.2, which keeps the original structure in Figure 13.1.

From the nature of the virtual-ISA VM, it is easy to understand why these components are needed.

- An application distributed in virtual-ISA instructions is not executable, which has to be interpreted or compiled in the VM, and hence the need for the "Execution engine"

- Safety requires the application not to touch memory, but delegates to the "Garbage collector" for object allocation and memory management

- In order to execute the application, the VM has to schedule and manage the execution entity. In a VM for control-flow-based language, the execution entity is thread, and the VM uses "Threading manager" to manage threads

- The managed code needs to access platform resources to accomplish meaningful tasks, so the VM needs a native interface to provide the access. "Native support" provides the interface between Java world and native world

- For the language that provides exception-throwing and catching features, the VM needs "Exception support" to implement the features. The exception support also handles hardware faults and OS events/signals

- The language depends on the VM to provide key runtime services for some of its semantics such as creating object and throwing exception. "Runtime helpers" provide access from the language to the VM services

- The core part of the library for the language has to be relying on the VM implementation such as for the reflection and stack trace, and hence the need for the "Kernel classes" provided by the VM.

In all the major components, the EE is the only component that does not provide direct service to the managed code. In other words, the managed code does not know the existence of the EE. The EE is always invoked implicitly.

When developing a virtual machine, it is good to keep the common practice of software engineering for modularity and portability. Modularity here means the components should better have a well-defined interface, and are not tightly coupled with each other, so that the developers of different components do not have to maintain the code or interactions in other components. Portability here means the VM should try to keep the platform-specific part abstracted in a layer underneath other components, so that most engineering work does not have to consider the platform-specific issues, and the VM can be easily ported across different platforms. Since portability is a traditional topic that has lots of discussions available already, we only focus on the modularity design topic, using Apache Harmony as a reference.

13.2 OBJECT INFORMATION EXPOSURE

Only the VM core knows the details of an object. Almost all the information about an object can be obtained from its class data structure (say `VM_class`). In this sense, other components can have the opaque pointer (`void*`) to the class data structure and then query VM core for all the needed information. For examples, following are some VM core interfaces.

- `bool class_has_finalizer(void* clss)`

  Returns TRUE if the class has a nondefault finalizer method;

- `bool class_is_reference_type(void* clss)`

  Returns TRUE if the class is of reference-object type;

- `bool class_is_array(void* clss)`

  Returns TRUE if the class is an array;

- `bool class_has_reference_fields(void* clss)`

Returns TRUE if the class has a field that is an object reference;

- `unsigned int class_instance_size(void* clss)`

  Returns the memory size used by an instance of the given class;

- `unsigned int array_get_length(void* arry)`

  Returns the array length;

- `void* array_get_element_addr(void* arry, unsigned int i)`

  Returns the address of the ith element of array;

The opaque class pointer must be accessible from the object reference, so that the other components can find it given the object reference. It is convenient to put the first field of an object in memory to be the opaque pointer to its class data structure, as follows.

```
struct Object {
  void* clss; //The opaque class pointer of the object
  ...          //other fields of the object
}
```

The VM can put the virtual method dispatching table (vtable) together with the class data structure. The VM can also choose to put them separately. They have 1 : 1 mapping, so either way is fine. Putting them separately gives a chance for the VM to put all the vtables in a consolidated memory area, so that accessing a vtable may have better cache locality.

In Apache Harmony, vtable and class data structure are put separately. They link to each other so that the VM can always find one from another. Then the question is whether the object header should include the opaque pointer to the class or to the vtable. From a performance perspective, the compiled Java code mostly accesses an object's instance fields at runtime and accesses its vtable for virtual-method dispatching. It is uncommon for the Java code to access the class data structure. It makes sense to keep the vtable pointer in the object header.

```
struct Object {
  void* vt; //The opaque vtable pointer of the object
  ...          //other fields of the object
}
```

Since both the vtable pointer and the class pointer can represent the type of the object, we sometimes use "type pointer" for both of them.

Besides the type pointer stored per object, there are some other per-object metadata needed by the VM components. For example, the thread manager needs per-object data for monitor implementation; GC needs per-object data for collection operations so as to indicate if an object is marked, moved, or dirtied. These per-object metadata are convenient to be encoded in the object directly, rather than using a separate storage. Apache

Harmony uses an additional pointer-sized field in the object header for them. The object layout becomes the following.

```
struct Object {
  void* vt; /The opaque vtable pointer of the object
  Obj_info obj_info; //important per-object metadata
  ...          //other fields of the object
}
```

These two fields are all what the VM components need to have on an object's layout. There is no need to define object layout details (i.e., the instance fields) for the components, except the VM core. Other components only need to know the object header definition.

```
struct Object_header {
  void* vt; //The opaque vtable pointer of the object
  Obj_info obj_info; //important per-object metadata
}
```

Although the object header is enough for other components, this is not the best for performance. For example, if GC has to call the VM core interface methods every time for object information, the overhead can be high. A better way is to expose some important object information to GC, so that accessing them does not have to go through the interface calls. The most frequently used object information by GC is the following.

- **Array flag**: It is a flag to indicate whether the object is an array or not. The information is needed when GC scans the object for references. The way to access an array element is different from the object field;

- **Finalizer flag**: It indicates if the object has a nondefault finalizer. If it does, it should be added to the "Finalizer object list" when allocated;

- **Reference-object flag**: It indicates if the object is of any reference-object type. If it is, it should be treated specially when GC traces the object connection graph. GC also needs to know the offset of the referent field in the reference object, so that it can scan it and `clear()` it;

- **Reference field flag**: It is a flag to indicate if the object has any reference fields. The information is needed for GC to scan an object for its reachable objects.

The information can be provided to GC when a class is loaded and prepared. Then GC can cache the information to a place that it can access directly without querying the VM. Later when GC does allocation and collection, it can get the information quickly. For nonperformance-critical information, GC still can query the VM core with the opaque class pointer.

For this data–caching purpose, a GC interface is provided to the VM core.

- `void gc_class_prepared(void* clss)`

The VM core calls this function after a new class has been prepared. In the function, GC queries the VM core for all the performance-critical information and caches them locally.

In Apache Harmony, the information obtained from gc_class_prepared() is stored in a data structure GC_info that is pointed by the pointer in the vtable header, so that GC can access them from an object pointer easily, as shown below.

```
struct Vtable_header {
    GC_info* gc_info; //pointer to GC cached class information
}

struct Object_header {
    Vtable_header* vt; //The opaque vtable pointer of the object
    Obj_info obj_info; //important per-object metadata
}

GC_info* object_get_gcinfo(Object_header* obj)
{
    return obj->vt->gc_info;
}
```

In the following sections, we discuss how to design modular GC and JIT components.

13.3 GARBAGE COLLECTOR INTERFACE

A GC component can be built as a dynamically linked library with a well-defined interface. There are only a small number of interfaces that are essential for the VM to invoke upon GC without sacrificing functionality, flexibility, and performance. The above-mentioned gc_class_prepared() is one of them and is important for performance.

Thread-related APIs: The following interfaces support the interactions between mutators and collectors.

- void gc_mutator_init ()

    API for a mutator to call when it is created. It initializes the mutator allocator and other mutator-specific data structures in GC, including a list the mutator is linked in.

- void gc_mutator_destruct ()

    API for a mutator to call when it is exiting. It cleans up the mutator-specific data structures.

Allocation API: GC needs to provide an interface for the Java code and the native method to allocate an object.

- Object_header* gc_mutator_alloc(unsigned size, Vtable_header* vt)

- `Object_header* gc_mutator_alloc_fast(unsigned size, Vtable_header* vt)`

  API to allocate an object that has total `size` bytes. The object vtable pointer `vt` is given to indicate the type of the object. GC needs the type information to identify if the object has a nondefault finalizer, is of reference-object type, and so on. This function may trigger a collection, so the code that calls it has to be a safe-point or in a safe region.

  API to allocate an object that has total `size` bytes. The object vtable pointer `vt` is given to indicate the type of the object. It is the fast path of `gc_mutator_alloc()` and only for common allocation cases where a collection is not triggered. When there is a risk to trigger a collection, the API returns NULL.

  In the runtime helper for object allocation, the code calls `gc_mutator_alloc_fast()` first; if it returns NULL, the code then prepares the M2N_wrapper on the stack and calls `gc_mutator_alloc()`. The purpose of `gc_mutator_alloc_fast()` is to avoid the M2N_wrapper preparation and cleanup, which is expensive. This API is only for performance and hence optional.

Read/Write-barrier APIs: GC needs to provide interfaces to support read/write barriers.

- `Barrier_Type gc_requires_barriers ()`

  API to indicate if GC needs the VM (including the JIT compiler and interpreter) to insert read/write barriers. It returns the types of barriers to insert.

- `void gc_heap_write (Object_header* dst, Object_header** dst_slot, Object_header* src, Op_Type op)`

  API to call when object reference `src` is to be written into object `dst` in heap at address `dst_slot`. The API includes the situation of single-object field store, array copy, and object clone. It uses `op` to tell GC what situation the write is.
  The heap write itself is conducted in the API, because GC may want to have a barrier before or after a write, or in the middle of multiple writes, for example, in array copy. So this API is a combination of heap write and write-barrier. This API can be split into a few separate APIs for different operations.

- `Object_Header* gc_heap_read_barrier (Object_header* src, Object_header** src_slot)`

  API to call when object `src` or a reference field `src_slot` of object `src` is to be read. It returns the right reference for object access. This read-barrier is used in concurrent copying collection with to-space invariant. It does not conduct the actual object reading, but returns the right reference for object reading. It is called before any object access.

Note that the read/write-barrier interfaces here are only examples. The actual VM implementation can choose different designs.

Programming APIs: The following interfaces are required to implement the programming APIs in Java.

- `void gc_force_gc ()`

  API for the VM to force a GC, typically in response to a call to `java.lang.Runtime.gc`.

- `long int gc_total_memory ()`

  API for the VM to determine the current GC heap size, typically in response to a call to `java.lang.Runtime.totalMemory`. The return value is "long int" type to indicate that it has to be the same size integer as a pointer size of the platform.

- `long int gc_max_memory ()`

  API for the VM to determine the maximum GC heap size, typically in response to a call to `java.lang.Runtime.maxMemory`.

- `long int gc_free_memory ()`

  API for the VM to get an approximate view of the free space, typically in response to a call to `java.lang.Runtime.freeMemory`.

- `int gc_get_hashcode (Object_header* obj)`

  API for the VM to get the hashcode of the object, typically in response to a call to `java.lang.Object.hashCode`.

- `bool gc_is_object_pinned (Object_header* obj)`

  API for the VM to know if the target object is nonmovable. It can be optionally used in JNI functions `GetXXXArrayElements`, where `XXX` stands for a primitive type.

GC lifecycle APIs: The VM initializes and shuts down the GC component.

- `void gc_init()`

- `void gc_destruct()`

  APIs for VM to initialize and shut down the GC component.

Root-set enumeration APIs: GC provides the VM an API to add a root-set entry.

- `void gc_add_rootset_entry(Object_Header** p_ref)`

    API for the VM to add a root-set entry. This is a callback when GC asks the VM core to enumerate a root-set. The VM suspends mutator threads to enumerate the root-set and report every root-set entry to GC by calling this API.

GC components need to access many VM core APIs, which can be classified into two categories. One is for general class information query. The other is for root-set enumeration. It is reasonable to put the core function of root-set enumeration in the VM core because the process needs to interact with other components such as garbage collection, EE, threading support, and native support. The root-set-enumeration-related APIs provided by the VM core are the following.

- `void vm_suspend_thread (VM_thread* mutator)`

- `void vm_resume_thread (VM_thread* mutator)`

    GC calls this method to request the VM to suspend/resume an individual thread.

- `void vm_enumerate_thread_rootset (VM_thread* mutator)`

    GC calls this function for the VM to enumerate a thread, which was suspended using `vm_suspend_thread()`.

- `void vm_enumerate_global_rootset ()`

    GC calls this function for the VM to enumerate the global root-set.

Note that the supports to GC safe point and safe region are not implemented by the GC component, but by the thread manager. GC interacts with them through the VM core.

The GC interface given here is for one GC component (i.e., a dynamically linked library). A VM implementation may have multiple GC implementations, each in one GC component. In one instance of VM execution, only one GC component can be loaded. It does not limit the flexibility of GC implementation, because one GC component can implement multiple collection algorithms. In this case, how the multiple algorithms collaborate with each other is completely internal to the GC component, since the GC component supports the VM with the single set of interface described above. This design choice has been proven to be powerful because different GC developers can easily develop their own independent GC components. At the same time, they have all the flexibilities to accommodate any collection algorithms in their own GC components.

13.4 EXECUTION ENGINE INTERFACE

The EE is largely hidden from other VM components. It may access other components frequently, but is rarely accessed by other components. The main reason is that the EE, conceptually together with the managed code, uses the services from the VM and not the other way round. Looked from the application's point of view, there is no Java programming API that relies on the EE.

There can be multiple JIT compilers implemented in one VM. All of them can be wrapped in one EE. As with GC, it is possible to develop multiple EE components, while only one of them is loaded by an instance of the VM.

Following are the major interfaces exposed by an EE.

EE lifecycle APIs: The VM initializes and shuts down the EE component.

- `void ee_init()`

- `void ee_destruct()`

    APIs for the VM to initialize and shut down the EE component.

Execution APIs: This the only purpose for which the EE exists.

- `void ee_invoke_method(Method* method)`

    API to invoke a method, either Java or native method, assuming the arguments to the target method are ready on the stack. If it is the first time to invoke a virtual method, the JIT compiler will install the "compiled method code" entry address into the method's declaring class' vtable. If the target is a native method, the API has to call the VM core to prepare the Java-to-native wrapper code as the "compiled method code." Before the first invocation of the target method, the vtable entry is a pointer to a piece of stub code that calls this API through a runtime helper. The arguments to the target method are prepared by the caller method, either a Java method or a native one.

    This API is not necessarily exposed.

Stack APIs: Only the EE knows the compiled code stack layout. The APIs are necessary for stack-trace preparation, exception-throwing, and root-set enumeration.

- `Code_info ee_get_code_info(void* ip)`

    API for the VM to get the code information pointed by program pointer `ip`. The information includes whether the code is compiled Java code or native code, the method it belongs to, the corresponding bytecode info if it is compiled Java code, etc.

- `void ee_unwind_stack_frame(Frame_context* frame)`

    API for the VM to unwind the stack by one frame.

- `Exc_Handler* ee_find_match_exception_handler(Frame_context* frame, jobject Exception_obj)`

    API for the VM to find the matching exception handler in the Java method. The API also fixes the frame context, so that it represents the catch handler's context. After this API is called, the control can transfer to the handler based on the information saved in the frame context.

- `void ee_enumerate_rootset(Frame_context* frame)`

  API for the VM to enumerate the root-set entries in the current stack frame. It calls the VM interface to report the entries to GC.

We can see that the EE APIs are mostly related to runtime-stack processing. This is probably the only part where the VM needs helps from the EE.

Above, we have given only two examples of modularity design. Other components can follow the principle to define their own interfaces.

13.5 CROSS-COMPONENT OPTIMIZATIONS

A strict modular design may limit some optimizations that require additional contract between the components. For example, if the JIT compiler knows how to find a class' `java.lang.Class` object from its `VM_class` data structure, the JIT does not need to generate a runtime helper call to the VM core for the service. Instead, the JIT compiler can directly generate the code sequence. The original code sequence is as follows:

```
push pointer_to_vmclass
call runtime_get_jlC_from_vmclass
```

The pointer to a class' `java.lang.Class` object is stored in its `VM_class` data structure. Assuming that the JIT compiler knows the offset where the pointer is stored in `VM_class`, the new code sequence will be the following.

```
mov pointer_to_vmclass -> eax
mov [eax + jlC_offset] -> eax
```

Here constant `jlC_offset` is the offset where the pointer to a class' `java.lang.Class` object is stored in `VM_class`. The new code sequence can save the overhead of a function call.

There are a few ways to achieve this optimization. One way is for the JIT compiler to cache the `jlC_offset` value in `jit_class_prepared()` when a class is loaded and prepared, similar to how `gc_class_prepared()` does for the GC component. The limit of this solution is that it actually not only exposes the offset information to JIT, but also requires the pointer to the `java.lang.Class` object be put at a fixed offset in `VM_class` data structure.

Another optimization is for the VM core to provide the function with an assembly version that is delicately programmed, so that the overhead of function call is kept as small as possible.

Yet another optimization is to allow the JIT compiler to inline the call to a runtime helper or VM service so as to eliminate the call overhead as we have mentioned in Chapter 10.

This can be achieved by introducing additional compiler infrastructure that allows the runtime helpers to be programmed and compiled into the same intermediate representation (IR) as the JIT uses.

For example, the `gc_mutator_alloc_fast()` interface is the most frequently accessed GC API for object allocation. It returns NULL if the fast path is not suitable for the requested allocation. The typical code is as follows (for a bump-pointer allocator):

```
Object_header* gc_mutator_alloc_fast (int obj_size,
                                      Vtable_Header* vt)
{
   //class has finalizer, leave it to slow path gc_mutator_alloc
   if( vt_has_finalizer(vt))
      return NULL;

   //object size is too big, leave it to slow path
   if ( obj_size > GC_LARGE_OBJ_SIZE_THRESHOLD )
      return NULL;

   //get the thread local allocator for the mutator
   Allocator* allocator = (Allocator*)gc_get_mutator_allocator();
   long free = allocator->free;
   long ceiling = allocator->ceiling;
   long new_free = free + obj_size;

   //if there is enough free space, allocate it
   if (new_free <= ceiling){
      allocator->free= new_free;
      obj_set_vt((Object_Header*)free, vt);
      return (Object_Header*)free;
   }

   //not enough free space, leave it to slow path gc_mutator_alloc
   return NULL;
}
```

The function can be implemented in "unsafe Java" that the JIT compiler recognizes the special classes like Address as intrinsics and compiles them as memory address operations. Since it is compiled by the JIT compiler as application code, the function can be inlined and more optimizations can be enabled.

The version of `gc_mutator_alloc_fast()` looks like below in "unsafe Java." Here, GC_Helper is a Java class that includes all the GC services that are written in "unsafe Java."

```
private static Address mutator_alloc_fast(int objSize, Address vt)
{
    if( GC_Helper.VT_has_finalizer(vt)
```

```
        return null;

    if( objSize > GC_Helper.GC_LARGE_OBJ_SIZE_THRESHOLD )
        return null;


    Address allocator = GC_Helper.get_mutator_allocator();
    Address free_addr = allocator.plus(FREE_OFFSET);
    Address free = free_addr.loadAddress();
    Address ceiling_addr = allocator.plus(CEILING_OFFSET);
    Address ceiling = ceiling_addr.loadAddress();

    Address new_free = free.plus(objSize);

    if (new_free.LE(ceiling)) {
        free_addr.store(new_free);
        GC_helper.obj_set_vt(free, vt);
        return free;
    }

    return null;
}
```

With unified IR, cross-component optimizations are made easy. The problem is that writing an "unsafe Java" version of runtime helpers is tedious and nonintuitive. There has been research trying to compile C/C++ code and Java code into the same IR, so that the runtime helpers written in native code can also be inlined into compiled Java code, while it requires to deploy the components in source code or IR format.

IV

Optimizations of Garbage Collection

CHAPTER 14

Optimizing GC for Throughput

WITH THE UNDERSTANDING OF all the important components in a virtual machine (VM) implementation, it is time to discuss more than just the functionalities, but also the optimizations. In the development of a VM, basic functionalities can be accomplished relatively easily and then major efforts are usually made to optimize the VM for better performance, including throughput, scalability, and responsiveness. We will discuss various techniques to optimize VM components, and start with garbage collection.

We have discussed the common garbage collection (GC) designs in Chapter 5. The algorithms used in a VM often include reference-count, mark-space, semi-space, trace-forward, and mark-compact. In the chapter on "Modularity design," we mentioned that one VM implementation can have multiple GC components, while one instance of VM execution can load only one GC component, and the one component can have multiple GC algorithms. The benefit of having multiple GC algorithms in one component is that they can provide flexibility of using different algorithms for different situations.

One important note is that GC performance is largely decided by the application behavior. None of the techniques discussed in this chapter is generally applicable to all applications. Instead, the techniques only give hints to VM developers on the optimization methodology.

14.1 ADAPTATION BETWEEN PARTIAL AND FULL-HEAP COLLECTIONS

A round of garbage collection can collect the full heap or only part of it. Full-heap collection usually is in-place collection, that is, it does not require any free region available in the heap before the collection (or requires only small free space remaining), hence is desirable when the VM wants to fully utilize the heap space. The common in-place collection algorithms are reference-count, mark-sweep, and mark-compact.

Partial-heap collection can collect the specified region in-place by applying a full-heap collection algorithm but only on the collected region. If there is free-space available in other region, partial-heap collection can also move the surviving live objects in the collected region to the free-space, that is, copying collection, which is non-in-place collection. Typical copying algorithms are semi-space, trace-forward, and mark-copy.

There is no strict boundary between in-place and non-in-place collections. In an in-place collection, the reserved free-space can be as small as a single seed page, where the collection moves live objects to the free page and hence empties some used pages for next round of live objects moving. In this design, the non-in-place collection achieves "in-place" effect.

In-place full-heap collection needs to deal with all the heap objects, and has various disadvantages. For example, the mark-compact algorithm needs multiple passes across the entire heap. The often used slide-compact algorithm has four passes:

```
void mark_compact()
{
    pass1:
     traverse_object_graph();
    pass2:
     compute_new_locations();
    pass3:
     repoint_object_references();
    pass4:
     compact_space();
}
```

Each of the four passes needs to go through the entire heap, which brings high memory-access overhead. It also makes parallelization of the algorithm inefficient because it requires all the collectors to synchronize at the start of every pass. Note multiple-pass compaction can be optimized into fewer passes with delicate design and auxiliary date structure support, which we will discuss later.

Mark-sweep has two passes only, but it cannot solve the heap fragmentation problem, so it is actually not widely used as a main algorithm in commercial VM implementations except for special cases like large object space (LOS) GC or concurrent GC.

In addition to the multiple passes, the full-heap algorithm cannot benefit from the fact that, in most applications, the newly allocated objects may die young, while the survived objects may stay long. The full-heap algorithm processes the new and old objects uniformly, while the old objects may largely be still alive, so the collection can benefit much less from processing old objects than from processing new objects. This is the fundamental hypothesis of generational GC, where usually only the new objects are processed.

A partial-heap collection can choose the heap region that has least live objects to collect. The collection time then can be much shorter. Although the partial-heap collection has its benefit, its downside is that it only recycles part of the dead objects in the whole heap, so its benefit has a limit. At the same time, a collection, no matter if it is partial-heap or full-heap, incurs similar operations to suspend thread, enumerate root-set, etc. If the overhead is too high, the time spent in these supporting operations may become dominant in a collection, which may compromise the benefit of the partial-heap collection. The question then is how to compare the collection efficiency of partial-heap and full-heap collections, and when is a good time to collect the partial-heap or full-heap.

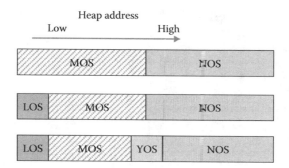

FIGURE 14.1   Heap layout of a common GC design.

In a common GC design, the heap usually is partitioned into spaces, to benefit from the partial-heap collection. New object space (NOS) is introduced for new object allocation. When it is full, a partial-heap collection is conducted on it. The surviving objects are moved to mature object space (MOS) so that the NOS is cleaned up again for new object allocation. The heap layout is given in Figure 14.1.

Different spaces apply different collection algorithms.

- NOS usually uses copying-GC that moves the surviving objects to MOS.

- MOS usually uses in-place moving-GC such as mark-compact that compacts the live objects into one end of the space.

Allocation happens only in NOS.

To facilitate the NOS-MOS management, and avoid moving large live objects from NOS to MOS, sometimes a third space, LOS, is introduced for allocating objects that are larger than a threshold. LOS usually uses nonmoving GC such as mark-sweep to avoid moving large objects. In this section, we do not include LOS in the discussion for brevity, without impacting the conclusions. Sometimes, there might be yet another space between NOS and MOS as young object space (YOS) so that NOS objects are promoted to YOS first, and when YOS is full, its objects are promoted to MOS. We will discuss more about it later.

NOS size can be a constant or variable. If it is constant, NOS cannot fully use the free space for allocation even when the heap is largely empty at the beginning. The choice of a right size of NOS is also a question. Constant NOS size sometimes is used for generational GC that has two generations. Another better way we use here is to allow the NOS to use as much as possible the available free space in the heap for object allocation, as long as there is enough reserved free region in MOS to accommodate the NOS survivors. We will discuss the space size adaptation algorithm later. In this section, we discuss how GC decides which space (NOS or MOS) to collect in a collection.

In a minor collection, only NOS is collected. In a major collection, all the spaces are collected. The minor collection is a partial-heap collection, and major collection is a full-heap collection. Minor collection moves live objects to MOS reserved free region. In the first time collection, only NOS has objects. MOS is empty and only reserved for NOS collection.

The total free space in the heap becomes less and less with rounds of minor collections. That means the minor collection has to be triggered more frequently. Finally, when the NOS size is too small, a major collection is triggered. Major collection recycles the dead objects in MOS hence frees up some space in MOS; thus, minor collection can be conducted again in following collections.

The question is when the allocation space (NOS) is considered too small to trigger a major collection. An intuitive design is to have a constant minimum size like 4 MB or 16 MB. But this is not necessarily a good one.

Here we discuss another adaptive strategy that has been proven effective. The goal of the adaptive strategy is to find the optimal minimum free space size when a major collection should be triggered, hence to achieve maximum overall *collection throughput*.

Collection throughput of a GC algorithm for an application is measured as the ratio between the sum of the all produced free region sizes in all the collections and the sum of all the collections' times, in one execution of the application, that is,

```
Throughput = (∑ Size_of_freed_space) / (∑ Time_of_collection)
```

Assume the free space size in the whole heap after a major collection is `Fmax`, and the threshold free space size in the whole heap that triggers a major collection is `Fmin`. If `Fmin` is close to 0, it means GC triggers a major collection only when the free space is not enough to hold minor collection survivors. If `Fmin` is close to `Fmax`, GC always uses major collection. The target of the adaptive design is to find a right `Fmin` that can achieve maximum GC throughput.

We define a collection super-cycle to be the period from the point right after a major collection finishes to that of next major collection. The collections in a super-cycle include one major collection and all the minor collections between two major collections. If a strategy can get maximum collection throughput for a super-cycle, then probably the application can get the overall maximum collection throughput with the same strategy. So our focus is only on the throughput of one super-cycle.

Assume after each minor collection, the sum size of the surviving objects from NOS is `dS`, then the free space size in the heap is reduced by `dS`, compared to the free space size after last minor collection. This means, after a major collection, the count of consecutive minor collections that can be conducted is `(Fmax - Fmin)/dS`, before next major collection. Then the free space size in the heap becomes `Fmin`, and a major collection has to happen.

If each minor collection takes time `Tminor`, and each major collection spends time `Tmajor`, the total time spent in all the collections in a super-cycle is:

```
T_super-cycle = ((Fmax - Fmin)/dS) * Tminor + Tmajor
```

The total free region size produced during this period is:

```
F_super-cycle =
     Fmax - dS +           //after first minor collection
     Fmax - 2*dS +         //after second minor collection
```

```
      ... +
      Fmax - (n-1)*dS +      //after (n-1)-th minor collection
      Fmin +                 //after n-the minor collection
      Fmax                   //after a major collection
```

It adds up to:

$$F_{super-cycle} = (Fmax + Fmin)*(Fmax - Fmin + dS)/(2*dS)$$

The throughput of a collection super-cycle is then:

$$TP_{super-cycle} = F_{super-cycle}/T_{super-cycle}$$

Since Fmax, dS, Tminor, and Tmajor can be measured at runtime as a, b, c, d, the formula above becomes a function of Fmin:

$$TP(X) = (((a-X)/b)*c+d)/((a+X)*(a-X+b)/(2*b))$$

The maximum TP(X) can be reached by solving the differential equation, and the solution to X is Fmin. The Fmin value is computed at the end of every collection. When the remaining free region size after a minor collection is no more than Fmin, a major collection should be conducted for next collection.

With the well-known Java benchmark SPECJBB, when the Fmin is a constant 16 MB, the throughput curve of the intuitive design is shown in Figure 14.2. The value of a major collection is shown as "M," and that of a minor collection as "m."

In a collection super-cycle, the throughput of minor collection initially can be high since there is enough free region right after a major collection. Then it goes lower and lower till the reserved free region is not enough and triggers a major collection.

With the heuristic design, major collection can be triggered much earlier, even when there is still enough free region. The overall throughput line is higher than the intuitive design, as shown in Figure 14.3.

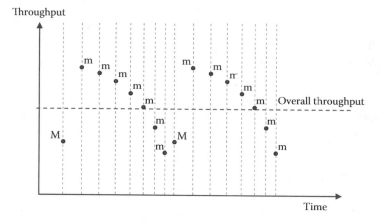

FIGURE 14.2 The throughput curve of collections in an intuitive design.

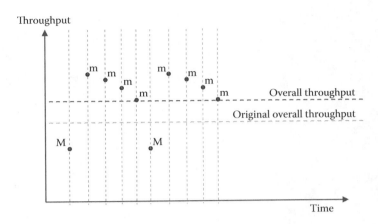

FIGURE 14.3   The throughput curve of collections in the heuristic design.

The heuristic developed in this section is valid only for the applications whose behavior roughly matches the described model. That is, the surviving size in a minor collection, the collection time of minor collections, and that of major collections are roughly stable or linearly varying in a collection super-cycle.

With concurrent collection, it is possible to conduct the major collection concurrently, then the strategy to trigger it can be different. Specifically, some GC design allows the major collection and the minor collection to happen at the same time to collect their respective MOS and NOS spaces. In this case, the collection scheduling policy can be largely independent for major and minor collections.

14.2 ADAPTATION BETWEEN GENERATIONAL AND NONGENERATIONAL ALGORITHMS

When the heap is partitioned into NOS and MOS, partial-heap collection on NOS has two design choices regarding how to find the live objects. One choice is to start from root-set and traverse the entire heap, but only collect NOS. It moves the live objects of NOS to MOS, while keeping the existing objects in MOS untouched. Although MOS objects are not collected, the collector has to traverse MOS, because some live objects in NOS are reachable only through paths that have objects in MOS. If the collector does not traverse MOS, those objects would not be marked live, which is wrong. In this design, although the collector needs to traverse the entire heap, the partial-heap collection throughput can possibly be higher than the full-heap one, because NOS may have only small number of live objects for the collector to promote, while the recycled free space size (NOS size) can be big.

The other choice is generational design. It does not traverse MOS but uses remember-set, which keeps all the references from MOS to NOS. Those references pointing from old generation (MOS) to young generation (NOS) called cross-generation references. The collector only needs to traverse NOS from root-set and remember-set. When a reference goes to MOS, the collector just ignores it.

To record all the references from MOS to NOS, write-barrier is needed. During mutator execution, whenever there is a heap write that stores a reference in an object, write-barrier checks if the reference is from an object in MOS to an object in NOS. If yes, the heap slot where the reference is written is recorded in remember-set.

Note in some GC algorithms, remembering the slots during mutator execution is not enough. Those cross-generation references may also be created during collector execution too. If a collection on NOS does not promote all live objects to MOS, that is, NOS still keeps some live objects after the collection, there can be some references from the promoted objects pointing to the nonpromoted objects. These cross-generation references should be recorded in remember-set as well. When the collection finishes and mutator execution is resumed, the remember-set already has some members. Together with the cross-generation references newly recorded during mutator execution, they are used by next collection. The remember-set is cleared after being consumed for object graph traversal, and new remember-set might be generated again.

A typical write-barrier implementation code is given below for the heap in Figure 14.4.

```
gc_write_barrier(Obj_header* src, Obj_header** slot, Obj_header*
dst)
{
    *slot = dst;

    if( src >= nos_boundary || dst < nos_boundary )
        return;
    gc_add_remset_entry(slot);
}
```

Write-barrier has runtime overhead in both time and space, because it needs to check every reference-store in heap, and record every slot that contains cross-generation reference. There have been good techniques to reduce the runtime overhead in some GC designs. For example, card-table sometimes can save the spatial overhead. Card-table does not remember every heap slot, but mark the heap region (a card) that contains cross-generation references. When a collection happens, the collector scans the marked regions to find the cross-generation references. Card-table trades the card scanning time for remembers-set space. We use remember-set to refer both the slot-set and card-table in our discussion, unless explicitly stated otherwise.

Remember-set has another problem. Although it guarantees a collection never miss marking a live object, it may also lead to many objects marked in NOS that are actually dead.

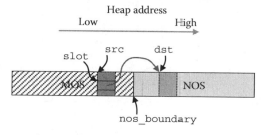

FIGURE 14.4   Write-barrier illustration.

The reason is, the objects in MOS that contain those slots in remember-set may have been dead themselves. The collector cannot know that fact without traversing MOS. The incorrectly marked dead objects are retained as floating garbage, and the amount can be big enough that offsets the benefit of generational collection.

Sometimes the throughput of generational partial-heap collection may be lower than its nongenerational counterpart. There are mainly three factors impacting the balance: the overhead of write-barrier, the amount of floating garbage, and the amount of live objects in MOS (i.e., working set size). For example, in the early phase of an application execution, MOS contains no or a few live objects. Nongenerational collection is apparently more effective, because then the NOS collection does not waste much time in traversing MOS.

With Java benchmark SPECJBB, the throughput curve with nongenerational collection looks like Figure 14.5.

The curve of its generational counterpart looks like Figure 14.6 in double-line and darker color. The square dots are the throughput value points. In this experiment, the NOS size is a constant, because bigger NOS size usually means more floating garbage retained by remember-set. The throughput may not benefit from a bigger NOS size (in a two generation layout).

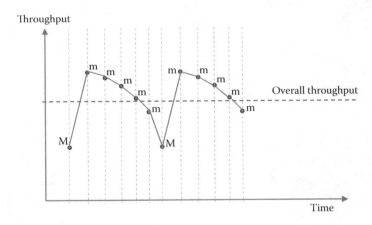

FIGURE 14.5   The throughput curve of nongenerational collections.

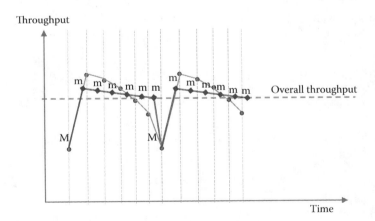

FIGURE 14.6   The throughput curve of generational collections.

Note the throughputs of major collections are the same in both curves, since major collections are full-heap collection, hence not impacted by generational or not. When we are talking about generational collection, we only refer to minor collection. The nongenerational data in round dots are shown together in Figure 14.6 for a comparison.

For this benchmark, the generational collections have linear throughputs that are lower in the first stage of a collection super-cycle, then higher in the second stage. In this case, an adaptive strategy choosing the suitable collection between generational and nongenerational can help the overall throughput.

The idea is to make the throughput curve to take the higher parts of both nongenerational and generational curves, and the overall throughput of the adaptive design is higher than either of them, as shown in Figure 14.7. The black curve is a combination of generational curve and nongenerational curve. Note there are applications where generational collections are always better than nongenerational, or the opposite. For those cases, there is no need to switch between the two modes of collections.

The question for such an adaptive design is to find the right time to switch between the modes. It should have the just-in-time (JIT) compiler to insert write-barrier for every heap write so that generational mode is possible. In the write-barrier, there is one more check than before on the collection mode. It simply returns doing nothing if the mode is not generational. The pseudo-code for the write-barrier is:

```
void gc_write_barrier(Obj_header* src, Obj_header** slot, Obj_
header* dst)
{
    *slot = dst;
    if( collection_mode != GC_GENERATIONAL )
        return;

    if( src >= nos_boundary || dst < nos_boundary)
        return;
    gc_add_remset_entry(slot);
}
```

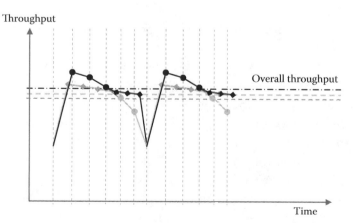

FIGURE 14.7 The throughput curve of adaptive collections between generational and nongenerational.

When written in "unsafe Java," and inlined to compiled Java code, the overhead of write-barrier in nongenerational mode due to the mode checking is negligible. Then it is not an issue to insert the write-barrier no matter whether the collection is going to be generational.

In order to be able to enable generational mode at any collection, the decision to switch the mode should be made during current collection before mutator execution is resumed so that the write-barrier can remember the cross-generation references. At the same time, current collector should remember the cross-generation references in case GC decides to switch to generational mode in next collection.

In order to know which mode has higher throughput, the adaptive strategy has to run both modes at certain times. The design can take the first super-cycle for the initial data collection. GC runs nongenerational mode in the first few minor collections and then generational mode is following minor collections. Another way is to run nongenerational minor collection all the way until the heuristic decides to run a major collection next, then GC switches to the generational mode minor collection instead of a major collection, till the reserved free space is not enough and a major collection is triggered. Either way GC knows the maximum, minimum, and average throughputs of both modes after the first super-cycle.

If in the first super-cycle profiling none of the nongenerational collections has higher throughput than the maximum generational collection, all the collections in next super-cycle will run generational mode, till GC makes another decision in next major collection. Otherwise, GC will run the first collection in nongenerational mode for the next super cycle. This is the common case, because in the initial stage of application execution, nongenerational mode is often better because there are only a small number of live objects in MOS. Right after a major collection, there is big free space. The free space can be big enough that it can support the application to run long time, and then most of the newly created objects in it become dead before next garbage collection, while generational mode may retain lots of them as floating garbage, especially in a two-generation heap layout (NOS and MOS). We will discuss more about this point later.

Now that GC decides to run nongenerational mode in the first collection of next super cycle, it needs to know when to switch to generational mode. GC will predict the throughput of next collection by end of current collection. A simple model is to use the current throughput as the predicted value of next one. GC continues to be nongenerational collection till the predicted throughput is lower than the average throughput of generational mode that was got in the first super-cycle. Then GC switches to generational mode till major collection. It does not switch back to nongenerational mode in this super-cycle, because the collection throughput curve tells that it is unlikely for a nongenerational mode becomes better later in the same super-cycle. The reason is understandable: there are usually more live objects in MOS, and there is smaller free space size to recycle.

Starting from the third super-cycle, if there is nongenerational collection in last super-cycle, the new super-cycle will always start with nongenerational collection, and follow the heuristic above. If there are only generational collections in last super-cycle, GC will check the survival rate of its major collection to decide the mode of the first collection in next super-cycle. The major collection is the last collection of a super-cycle.

Survival rate is defined for a collected space as the ratio between the total size of surviving objects in the space and the space size. That is,

```
Survival_rate(space) = (Σ size(live_object ∈ space))/ size(space)
```

The survival rate of a major collection is computed in the following formula.

```
Survival_rate(heap) = (Σ size(live_object ∈ heap))/size(heap)
```

The survival rate of a minor collection is computed in the following formula.

```
Survival_rate(NOS) = (Σ size(live_object ∈ NOS))/size(NOS)
```

Survival rate is complementary to mortality rate.

```
Mortality_rate(space) = 1 - survival_rate(space)
```

Survival rate is an important data item that reflects how fast the application's objects die. When survival rate is low, the application does not have lots of live objects surviving the collection. The application is able to achieve high collection throughput. Furthermore, it means two points for a minor collection. First, most of the allocated objects in NOS are garbage; second, the amount of live objects in MOS is not big. The first point means, if the minor collection uses generational mode, then the floating garbage retained by remember-set may not lead to the same level of survival rate. The second point means, traversing MOS space for live objects may not incur high overhead. Put together, a low survival rate implies that nongenerational mode may achieve better collection throughput than generational mode.

When all the collections in last super-cycle use generational mode, there is no chance to run nongenerational mode and compare the throughputs. There is a chance to use the data from major collection to deduce the potential benefit of nongenerational mode, because major collection is nongenerational too. When the survival rate of a major collection is lower than the average survival rate of previously sampled nongenerational collections, it is worth to give the nongenerational mode a try in the first collection of the new super-cycle, just in case it could bring higher throughput.

Again, the heuristic strategy is not generally applicable to all applications. GC optimization is nothing but application behavior investigation and tries to find algorithms and strategies that are adaptive enough. For specific applications, additional tuning usually can help achieve more improvements.

14.3 ADAPTION OF SPACE SIZE IN HEAP

When an application is started, it is a question for VM to decide how big size the heap should be committed at the beginning. Apparently the heap size is the bigger the better, since then the application does not trigger any collection, and all application time is spent in mutator computation. But this is not necessarily always a good choice. For one thing, it is impossible to commit infinite heap size, so there must be a size limit.

14.3.1 Space Size Extension

There is no need for the VM to commit a big size heap at the beginning, because the application may not allocate lots of objects in its life time; or even if it allocates lots of objects, the working set size (amount of live objects) at any time can be small. So it is natural to choose a reasonably small heap size at the beginning, and then adjust it during the execution, based on system memory availability and the application behavior.

The initial heap size is an experience value. GC then decides the new heap size after every collection, based on the remaining free space size and survival rate. In reality, the heap size may only be adjusted after a major collection to avoid frequent adjustment overhead. The other reason is that major collection has the information of the whole heap to help the adjustment decision.

Usually the VM has maximum heap size that is given by the application runner, or decided by the system platform. At the beginning the maximum size is reserved, but only the initial heap size is committed. That is, the virtual space of maximum size is reserved but only the physical space of initial size is committed. Space reservation is not mandatory, while it is useful to have a contiguous address space reserved. Later when physical space is committed, it is known to be mapped at the expected contiguous virtual address. Large object allocation needs contiguous virtual space, and it also helps cache locality if the cache is virtual-address indexed, which is the case in most modern processors.

The code to reserve, commit, decommit, and release memory can use following system calls. On Windows:

```
Reserve:
     VirtualAlloc(start_addr, size, MEM_RESERVE, PAGE_READWRITE);
Commit:
     VirtualAlloc(start_addr, size, MEM_COMMIT, PAGE_READWRITE);
Decommit:
     VirtualFree(start_addr, size, MEM_DECOMMIT);
Free:
     VirtualFree(start_addr, 0, MEM_RELEASE);
```

On Linux:

```
Reserve:
     mmap(0, size, PROT_NONE, MAP_PRIVATE|MAP_ANONYMOUS, -1, 0);
     mmap(start_addr, size, PROT_NONE, MAP_FIXED|MAP_PRIVATE|MAP_
     ANONYMOUS, -1, 0);
Commit:
     mprotect(start_addr, size, PROT_READ|PROT_WRITE);
Decommit:
     mprotect(start_addr, size, PROT_NONE);
Free:
     munmap(start_addr, size);
```

Linux now has mremap that can shrink or extend a mapped region that is also handy for commit and decommit implementation. Windows can use Address Windowing Extensions (AWE) to lock down the allocated memory that will not be paged out.

A simple heuristic to extend or shrink heap size can use the following formula:

```
For extend:
      if ( survival_rate > max_survival_rate )
          new_heap_size = surviving_object_size/
      expected_survival_rate
For shrink:
      if ( survival_rate < min_survival_rate )
          new_heap_size = surviving_object_size/
      expected_survival_rate
```

The threshold minimum, maximum, and expected survival rates are experience values that can be, for example, one-third for the maximum eighth for the minimum, and one-fifth for the expected rate. They mean that if more than one-third of the heap, or less than one-eighth of the heap is taken by surviving objects, GC should adjust the heap to make it take only one-fifth of the size. Figure 14.8 illustrates the heap extension scenario.

The logic to extend the heap when the survival rate is high is that many newly allocated objects should have long enough time to die between two collections. For a better heuristic, the ratio between the time of collection and mutation (the time between two collections) can also be considered. If collection time is too small compared to the mutation time, there is no need to extend the heap because the application may not allocate object intensively. In other words, the heap is not the scarce resource for this kind of applications to achieve good performance.

14.3.2 NOS Size

Once the heap size is decided, a follow-up question is how much size to assign to new object allocation. Since one-pass object trace-forwarding has much higher throughput than multiple-pass in-place collection, it is common to use trace-forward algorithm whenever possible for the newly allocated objects. The requirement is there is enough reserved-free region

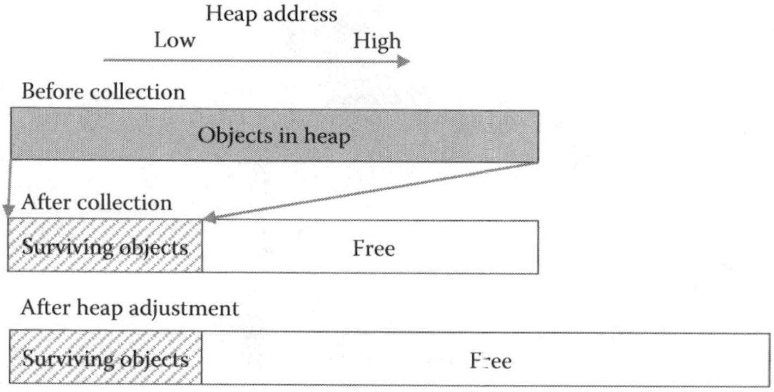

FIGURE 14.8   Heap extension when the survival rate is higher than a threshold.

for the object promotion. In a heap that has NOS and MOS layout, the assigned NOS size should satisfy the following inequality:

```
nos_size * nos_survival_rate <= reserved_free_size
```

Since,

```
reserved_free_size = free_size - nos_size
```

It deduces the NOS size:

```
nos_size <= free_size/(1+nos_survival_rate)
```

The NOS size can be adjusted every time after a collection before the mutator execution is resumed. Since minor collection does not collect MOS, the available space for NOS becomes smaller and smaller till a major collection. As we have discussed, it does not make sense to keep doing minor collection until the available space is run out. A major collection can be triggered much earlier for maximum overall throughput. Figure 14.9 illustrates the progress.

Some generational GC design does not employ variable NOS space. With a fixed size NOS, it is possible to extend the heap gradually by growing MOS space when surviving objects are promoted. One more important reason for using fixed size NOS is that a generational GC with two generation layout may not get better throughput with bigger NOS size.

In a two-generational GC design, as shown in Figure 14.9, all the newly created objects that are live are promoted to MOS in a minor collection. Since the objects created in a short time usually reference each other, when mutator execution is resumed and starts to allocate objects in NOS, the promoted new-born objects in MOS and the fresh new-born objects in NOS likely have references to each other. When many of those new-born objects

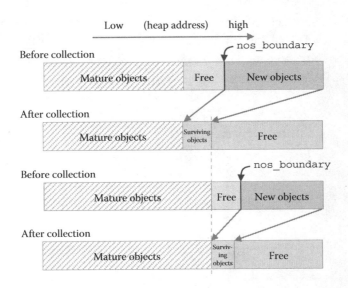

FIGURE 14.9   Space assigned to new object allocation.

die after a while, the cross-generation references keep the objects in NOS alive in a generational minor collection. Furthermore, those dead-but-retained fresh new-born objects in NOS keep even fresher new-born objects alive. As a result, lots of floating garbage is retained. That incurs big overhead in object graph traversal and live object moving. Those floating garbage is promoted to MOS and stay there till a major collection, which makes the heap become full more quickly, hence shorter super-cycle period. The point is bigger NOS size may not bring better collection throughput in a two-generational design.

14.3.3 Partial-Forward NOS Design

A better way for NOS design is to introduce one more generation, and therefore give the new-born objects more time to mature. For example, in a minor collection, only the live objects in the older half of NOS are promoted (called the "promoted-half"). In next minor collection, those in the other half are promoted, as shown in Figure 14.10. This design is called "partial-forward," which can benefit from bigger NOS size.

Partial-forward is an improvement over a simple two-generational design, by promoting new objects after collection. It effectively reduces the number of floating garbage. But it is not without shortcomings. One problem is that the nonpromoted-half does not recycle dead objects, whose quantity can be big and take the space, although this half participates in the object graph traversal and the dead objects are known. In other words, the throughput of the minor collection could be negatively impacted with less freed space and longer traversing time. The other less problem is, when the nonpromoted-half is bordering with MOS, the NOS boundary cannot shift to NOS side to give MOS more reserved free region. It may have to either trigger a major collection early or reserve more than needed in last minor collection when the promoted-half neighbors to MOS. Neither way is a good solution.

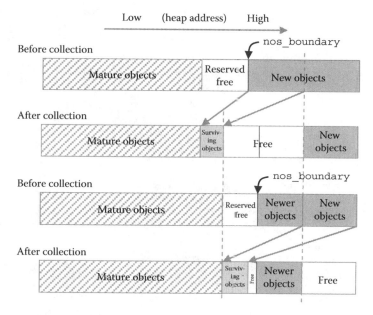

FIGURE 14.10   Partial-forward illustration.

14.3.4 Semi-Space NOS Design

Another design different from partial-forward is to promote all the live objects in NOS, but not to MOS. They are promoted to the reserved free region in NOS instead, to avoid moving the new-born objects to MOS. This can be considered as a semi-space algorithm with generational control. That is, NOS is partitioned into two halves, one of which is for allocation, the other is reserved free region for first-time live-object promotion in a minor collection.

We define age to be the times of an object surviving collections. In a minor collection, the live objects younger than age one are promoted to the reserved NOS free region. Those older than age one can be promoted to MOS reserved space, or moved to the NOS reserved space again to longer aging. At what age the live objects will be promoted to MOS is a design decision. In a common design, GC promotes the live objects of age one to MOS without aging them longer. The process is illustrated in Figure 14.11. We call it "generational semi-space."

In this design, the reserved free region in NOS acts as an additional generation within NOS. Since there are no new-born objects promoted to MOS, this design can achieve the same result as partial-forward, but it does not solve the key problem of partial-forward. The allocation half of NOS space is shared with one-year-old objects, only less than half of the NOS space is used for object allocation, which is even worse than partial-forward. Since a minor collection needs to scan one-year-old objects, the tracing time is the same as partial-forward.

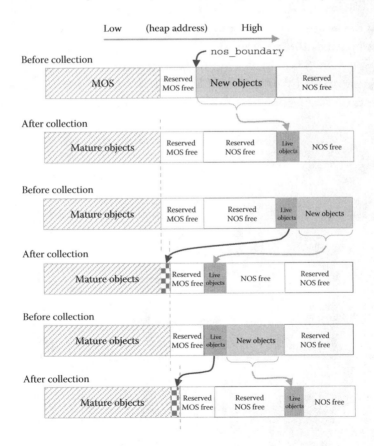

FIGURE 14.11 Generational semispace illustration.

14.3.5 Aged-Mature NOS Design

Generational semi-space has lower space efficiency than partial-forward, because it reserves too much free region in NOS than necessary. The reserve space is good enough as long as it can accommodate the new objects promotion. Based on this observation, we can have the following design.

This design introduces a middle-generation in NOS. The middle-generation has two halves. One is reserved for new objects promotion in next minor collection (called "reserved-half"). The other keeps the promoted objects in last minor collection (called "promoted-half"), who will be promoted to MOS in next minor collection. As in semi-space, the design can choose to move the objects in promoted-half to the reserved-half as well in next minor collection, and only promotes them to MOS when they are aged enough. In our experience, one-year-old promotion to MOS usually is good enough. Note the middle-generation is within NOS, so the remember-set only records the references that cross-NOS-MOS boundary.

This design is a variant of generational semi-space. The difference is the allocation space size is variable here, and as big as possible. Since the NOS free region for allocation always borders with MOS, it is very easy to adjust the NOS boundary so as to leave enough room to MOS reserved free region. We call this design "aged mature." The process is shown in Figure 14.12.

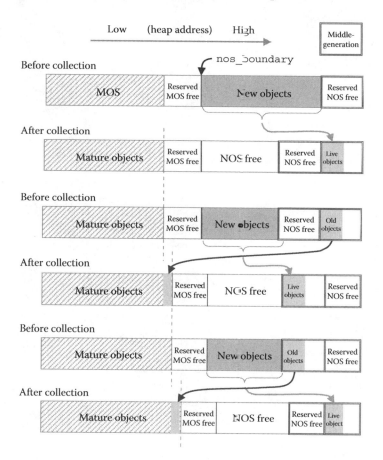

FIGURE 14.12   Aged-mature illustration.

With aged-mature, the space is more utilized than partial-forward or generational semi-space. The middle-generation in NOS can be small, as long as it can accommodate the promoted new objects in twice minor collections. The space left for new object allocation has the following size:

In aged-mature,

```
allocation_space_size = nos_size - 2*nos_size*nos_survival_rate
```

In partial-forward or generational semispace:

```
allocation_space_size = nos_size/2
```

In the following condition, aged-mature has bigger allocation space.

```
nos_size - 2*nos_size*nos_survival_rate > nos_size/2
```

It deduces the following requirement for aged-mature to achieve higher throughput. This requirement is the common case with normal applications.

```
nos_survival_rate < 1/4
```

In reality, the size of the reserved-half in middle-generation should be a little conservative, so as to guarantee enough space for new object promotion. However, the remaining free region in the promoted-half can be used for allocation as well without any problem, as in semi-space, shown in Figure 14.13.

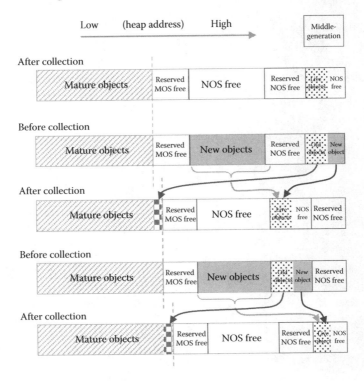

FIGURE 14.13 Fully utilize NOS space in aged-mature.

14.3.6 Fallback Collection

With reserved free regions in both NOS and MOS that are computed based on survival rates and some conservative headroom, the design can operate well in most collections. But still it needs to address the potential situation when the survival rate in a collection is significantly higher than the predicted one.

If the reserved free region in NOS is not enough, the remaining live objects can be moved to MOS directly instead of the middle-generation. If the reserved space in MOS is not enough, a fallback in-place collection has to be triggered over the whole heap. That is, it switches to major collection on the fly in the middle of the unfinished minor collection. Note when the reserved space is inadequate, it should not trigger an exception for out-of-memory. Garbage collection should never trigger out-of-memory exception, because all the objects have been existing before the collection. If a collection requires more memory than available, the algorithm is flawed.

The fallback collection algorithm usually is mark-compact, though not mandatory. Because fallback collection needs to operate on the existing heap organization that was for a minor collection, it is easier if the fallback collection and the minor collection use similar heap organization. Since minor collection uses moving-GC, it is natural to use mark-compact for the fallback collection that is also a moving-GC. Another in-place algorithm mark-sweep usually has very different heap organization, for example, with size-segregated lists. Although it is still possible to use mark-sweep for the fallback collection, the design is not intuitive.

Fallback collection is like a major collection, but is more complicated than a normal major collection. All the forwarded objects have two copies: the original one in the NOS allocation space and the new one in the reserved space of either NOS or MOS. We cannot simply remove either copy, because both may be referenced by other live objects when fallback happens.

It is possible to remove the new copy by restoring all the information in the old copy, and then repoint all the references to the new copy back to the old copy. Those references may come from other objects, root-set, and remember-set. This approach tries to keep only the old copy of live objects, because some live objects do not have the new copy yet when fallback collection happens. Actually, to guarantee the correctness of fallback collection, GC does not necessarily use only the old copy. The following algorithm is more efficient. As a major collection, fallback collection first needs to traverse the heap to mark reachable objects. When the collector reaches an object, it scans all the objects' reference fields. If there is any reference pointing to the original copy of a forwarded object, the collector updates the reference to the new copy. Then after the tracing phase, the heap status becomes consistent: all the references can only point to one copy of a live object. The fallback collection may have to use different bit in object header to indicate a marked live object from the bit used in the unfinished minor collection, and then the collector is not confused by the obsolete copy.

The full-heap collection may not be able to move all the live objects to MOS. This is not a problem, because the whole heap is treated as a single space now. When the collection finishes, GC partitions the heap into NOS and MOS again in preparation for next minor collection.

14.4 ADAPTION BETWEEN ALLOCATION SPACES

In a NOS/MOS heap layout, GC has only the NOS for object allocation, so the space adaptation is mainly between the allocation space for new objects and other space(s) for surviving objects. Then the survival rate is the main factor in the adaptation heuristic. When a GC has more than one allocation space, the allocation spaces compete for the free heap space, and they are no longer tied through the survival rate. New heuristic is needed to assign heap space to them.

It is common to manage large objects in a separate space, though not mandatory. Large object refers to the object whose size is bigger than a predefined threshold. There are usually two reasons for a GC to employ an LOS.

One is that, by default a moving-GC (especially a copying-GC) has better throughput than a nonmoving GC, but that is true only when the object moving cost is relatively lower than other collection cost such as object graph traversal. Large objects incur high-moving cost that may cancel the advantage of a moving-GC.

The other reason is that a moving-GC usually arranges its space in equal-size units such as blocks, to achieve better data locality, or better OS support on space management, or easier task parallelization for multiple collectors. Some large objects can be bigger than the predefined block size, which requires special GC design.

In addition to the case of large objects for additional allocation space, some GC may support pinned objects. Pinned objects are not moved during collections. To put pinned objects together with nonpinned objects in a same space complicates the design of a moving-GC. It is possible to put the pinned objects into a separate space. Yet another case is that some GC may separate an "immortal space" for immortal objects who are always alive once born.

When a GC has more than one allocation spaces, for instance LOS and non-LOS, heap space assignment between the two becomes a challenge. In an ideal design, they can share the same free region for allocation. When the free region is run out, a collection is triggered that can collect both LOS and non-LOS, or only one of them, based on the strategy. In this way, LOS and non-LOS spaces are not mixed. The situation can be illustrated in Figure 14.14.

Since the free region is now a shared resource between LOS and non-LOS allocations, it has to be protected for mutual exclusive access. In order to avoid too frequent expensive atomic operations, non-LOS allocation does not allocate new objects in the free region directly; instead, it allocates a block every time from the free region, and then only allocates new objects in the grabbed block. LOS allocation may have to allocate every object from the free region, because it does not know a proper block size to allocate.

This solution has a limit that it can only solve the problem of two allocation spaces in GC. If there are more, they cannot grow toward each other. In that case, at least one allocation space has its own separate space that does not share the same free region with others.

FIGURE 14.14 Two allocation spaces share same free region.

FIGURE 14.15   Two allocation spaces have separate free regions.

Whenever one of the allocation spaces is full, a collection has to be triggered. Still using LOS and non-LOS heap as an example, the situation is illustrated as Figure 14.15.

When a collection is triggered by one space while the other space is sparsely filled, the heap is not fully utilized. Consequently, it leads to more frequent collections and lower application performance.

The key question here is why one space can get full before the other one does. It is because one space allocates objects faster than the other. That is, within the same amount of time, a higher fraction of one space's free region is consumed than that of the other.

If both spaces allocate the same fraction of its free region within a same amount of time, then both spaces may be full when garbage collection is triggered. Based on this observation, GC can dynamically monitor the allocation speed, which is defined as the size of objects allocated per unit time (e.g., bytes/seconds), of different spaces, and utilizes this information to adjust the heap partitioning. Thus, in the ideal case, if the free sizes of LOS and non-LOS are set proportionally to their respective allocation speeds, then both spaces become full at the same time. Then the free region size assigned to LOS can be computed in the following way.

$$FreeSize_{LOS} = TotalFreeSize*AllocSpeed_{LOS} / (AllocSpeed_{LOS}+AllocSpeed_{non-LCS})$$

The computation of allocation speed can be flexible. For example, it can be the total allocated bytes from last collection if the space is flat (i.e., does not have any nested spaces), or the average value of the speeds in last few collections. In our experience, it is good enough to use the allocated bytes from last collection.

Sometimes, the allocation speed computation may be related to the GC algorithm, in order to be precise. For example, if an allocation space includes nested space, such as the non-LOS can include MOS and NOS inside, the allocation speed cannot be computed using the allocated bytes over certain time. GC should compute the allocation speed of the nesting space, that is, the non-LOS as a whole, rather than any of its nested spaces. The free region partitioning is at the non-LOS level between LOS and non-LOS, rather than at the NOS or MOS level. In this case, the allocated bytes of non-LOS should be computed as the total object size difference between two collections, that is, after last collection and before this collection. Since the collections at the non-LOS level are major collections, non-LOS allocation speed can be approximated by computing the MOS size difference right after last major collection and right before this major collection, over the time between the two collections.

The heuristic strategy can be extended to multiple allocation spaces, but it is very cumbersome. Even with a delicate design, the heap is hard to be fully utilized. A better solution is to share same free region but does not require linear contiguous address. Contiguous address is mainly for allocating large object, and for thread-local bump-pointer allocation of normal object. It is also useful for fast write-barrier execution in a generational collection where the collected and non-collected spaces stay on the opposite sides of the boundary.

Contiguous address can be achieved by using OS' memory remapping facility that can map a physical page from current virtual address to another specified virtual address.

For this purpose, it is possible to manage the heap in two levels. First level manager partitions the heap into blocks, and only manages the memory at inter-block level, that is, in units of one block or multiple contiguous blocks (multiblocks). The second level manager operates at intra-block level. A space in the heap is no longer a contiguous address space, but a linked list of blocks or multiblocks. We call them virtual spaces. When a space is a linked list of blocks, its address is ordered in block's linking order. Collections and allocations are operated upon the blocks. For example, a heap with LOS and non-LOS in blocks can look like Figure 14.16.

The non-LOS list points to the first normal object block in the heap, and this block contains a pointer that points to the next normal object block, and so on. Hence, it is easy to find all normal blocks through this virtual non-LOS list, and then form the virtual non-LOS space. Similarly, the virtual LOS list points to the first large object, and this large object contains a pointer to the next large object, and so on. The virtual LOS list and the blocks of large objects form the LOS. Note in this example, a large object occupies one or more blocks.

The Free Pool manages all free blocks in the heap, and it is actually a table of linked lists indexed by the number of contiguous blocks. Each linked list in the Free Pool manages all free regions with a certain number of contiguous blocks. For instance, slot 1 of the Free Pool contains a pointer to the first free block that has no other contiguous free block. Slot 3 of the Free Pool contains a pointer to a region of three contiguous free blocks, which, in turn, has a pointer pointing to the next region of three contiguous free blocks. For all free regions that contain more than 32 free continuous blocks, they are linked by a list starting from the slot >32. With this design, the virtual spaces can grow based on need, and garbage collection happens only when the whole heap is fully utilized.

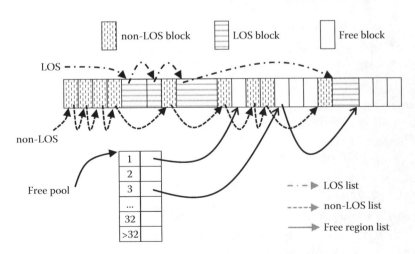

FIGURE 14.16 Virtual spaces arranged in block lists.

To allocate normal objects, the mutator grabs a free block from the Free Pool as thread-local block, then allocates the objects in the block till the block space is run out. Then the mutator grabs another free block. To guarantee fast normal object allocation, a mutator only allocates thread-local block from slot 1 or slot >32 in the Free Pool. It first checks if slot 1 is null. If not, it allocates from slot 1; otherwise, it allocates from the last slot, slot >32.

In these cases, it only requires one atomic operation for each thread-local block. When picking the thread-local block from slot 1, one atomic operation is enough to grab a node from a shared list. For thread-local block allocation in slot >32, instead of removing a region, the mutator simply decrements the number of blocks of a region in the last slot list to secure its acquisition of a block. This decrement operation should be atomic; thus, it guarantees thread-safe block allocation and only one atomic operation is needed.

However, if both slot 1 and slot >32 are null, then the mutator scans down the table from slot 2 and tries to allocate a free block from the first non-null slot. In this case, the mutator needs to pick off the region, allocates a block, and puts back the rest into the corresponding slot, which requires two atomic operations.

Different from normal objects, each large object occupies one or more blocks. Thus, a mutator directly allocates large objects in the Free Pool. When there is an allocation request, the mutator first checks the number of blocks requested, *block_count*. Then it searches the Free Pool down from slot with index of *block_count*, checking whether there is any region in the pool. If there is a hit in slot *block_count* or slot >32, one atomic operation is needed to pick off it. Otherwise, it needs two atomic operations.

If a mutator cannot find a needed free region, garbage collection should be triggered. The neat point is although the free area is shared by different virtual spaces, it does not prevent different virtual spaces to apply different collection algorithms, be it moving or nonmoving, generational or nongenerational. The moving-GC can move live objects within the virtual space. The generational GC requires to remember all the cross-generation references. This can be easily achieved by modifying the write-barrier into the following code.

```
gc_write_barrer(Obj_header* src, Obj_header** slot, Obj_header* dst)
{
    *slot = dst;
    Block_header* src_blk = block_of_object(src);
    Block_header* dst_blk = block_of_object(dst);

    if( block_in_nos(src) || block_in_mos(dst) )
        return;
    gc_add_remset_entry(slot);
}
```

When the contiguous free space in the heap is not big enough to hold a large object, and the total size of the non-contiguous free blocks is bigger than the large object, GC can try to compact the heap to leave enough contiguous free space. For a block that holds live objects,

GC can remap the virtual address of the block to a new location (virtual address) without really copying the block data. The overhead of OS memory remapping should be compared with the memory copying overhead, and then GC can choose the cheaper approach. The other solution is to remap the noncontiguous free blocks to a continuous virtual address range if the virtual address space is large enough. This solution does not need to copy the block data that we will discuss Chapter 15.

The application programming interfaces (APIs) for memory remap in Linux is mremap(). In Windows, it is not as convenient as in Linux. It uses AWE. One can reserve two regions of virtual memory, then maps the first to a physical memory region at a time, and maps the second to the same physical memory region at another time. Or one can reserve single virtual memory region but maps different segments of it to the same physical memory region at different time. Sample code for Windows looks like the following (based on example code from Microsoft MSDN).

```
BOOL bResult;              // generic Boolean value
ULONG_PTR NumberOfPages;   // number of pages to request
ULONG_PTR *aPFNs;          // page info; holds opaque data
PVOID lpMemReserved1;      // AWE window. Virtual addr 1
PVOID lpMemReserved2;      // AWE window. Virtual addr 2
int PFNArraySize;          // memory to request for PFN array

NumberOfPages = MEMORY_REQUESTED / sysPageSize;
// Calculate the size of the user PFN array.
PFNArraySize = NumberOfPages * sizeof(ULONG_PTR);
aPFNs = (ULONG_PTR *)HeapAlloc(GetProcessHeap(), 0,
PFNArraySize);
    bResult = AllocateUserPhysicalPages(GetCurrentProcess(),
&NumberOfPages, aPFNs);
    lpMemReserved = VirtualAlloc(NULL, MEMORY_REQUESTED, MEM_
RESERVE | MEM_PHYSICAL, PAGE_READWRITE);
    lpMemReserved2 = VirtualAlloc(NULL, MEMORY_REQUESTED, MEM_
RESERVE | MEM_PHYSICAL, PAGE_READWRITE);
    // map
    bResult = MapUserPhysicalPages(lpMemReserved1, NumberOfPages,
aPFNs);
    // unmap
    bResult = MapUserPhysicalPages(lpMemReserved1, NumberOfPages,
NULL);
    // remap
    bResult = MapUserPhysicalPages(lpMemReserved2, NumberOfPages,
aPFNs);
    // Free the physical pages.
    bResult = FreeUserPhysicalPages(GetCurrentProcess(),
&NumberOfPages, aPFNs);
```

```
// Free virtual memory.
bResult = VirtualFree(lpMemReserved1, 0, MEM_RELEASE);
bResult = VirtualFree(lpMemReserved2, 0, MEM_RELEASE);
// Release the aPFNs array.
bResult = HeapFree(GetProcessHeap(), 0, aPFNs);
```

Before using AWE in Windows, the user account of the application has to get the "lock page in memory" privilege.

14.5 LARGE OS PAGE AND PREFETCH

In addition to the algorithm designs, there are lots of other optimizations that can help the throughput of garbage collection. For example, large page is commonly used by VM to reduce TLB misses. It asks OS to allocate memory in bigger page size than normal 4 KB. Depending on the OS specifics, large page size can range from 64 KB to 4 MB or even bigger, which effectively reduces the TLB entry count when VM allocates the same size of memory.

Prefetch is another common technique to accelerate garbage collection that can reduce cache misses. Prefetch can be implemented explicitly or implicitly. Explicit prefetch means to insert instructions that are purely for performance rather than functionality. The instruction can be a hardware-specific prefetch instruction or a memory access that effectively loads the accessed memory data into cache. Implicit prefetch does not insert any specific instructions, but relies on the GC code's memory access pattern to load data into cache for future access. In other words, implicit prefetch tries to exploit the GC algorithm's data locality.

One example of data prefetch is in the tracing algorithm design. When the collector traverses heap to mark the reachable objects, it needs to access the live object data. The first touch of a live object (by the microprocessor pipeline through a load instruction) is usually to load the object header and check if it is marked. If the live object is not in cache yet (or "fresh"), the microprocessor needs to load the data into the cache. In our study, the first touch may take more than half of the cache misses in the tracing process. How to prefetch the fresh objects into cache before they are actually accessed is then an interesting question.

The object connection graph can be traversed in depth-first or breadth-first, or hybrid order. The locality benefit of different orders depends on the application behavior. Usually, the more the object traversal order matches their heap layout order (which is also largely the object allocation order), the more locality benefit can be achieved. Studies show that depth-first order may benefit most to common applications. It reflects the fact that most applications allocate objects in the same order as the object depth-first connection order. When the collector loads the data of one live object into cache for marking and scanning, the neighbor object is usually the next object to mark and scan, whose data are now loaded into the cache together with current object. This locality benefit can be achieved in implicit prefetch. Explicit prefetch is also possible. For example, the collector can use hardware prefetch instruction to load next object reference in the mark stack, and load its referenced object data.

Note object allocation performance is also important or even more important sometimes. GC optimization should never ignore object allocation. For example, prefetch technique can also be applied to object allocation, so that when a new object is allocated, its data are in cache already, and then the mutator accessing to the object does not incur many cache misses.

CHAPTER 15

Optimizing GC for Scalability

T HE HIGH-THROUGHPUT GARBAGE COLLECTION (GC) algorithms we discussed in the last chapter can run on a platform of single core or multiple cores. Ideally, a design should double its throughput on a dual-core platform compared to that on single-core, that is, with linear scalability. It means the throughput on a platform of N cores is N times of that on a single-core platform, assuming all other factors are the same. It can be expressed in the following equation, where throughput is expressed as a function of the number of cores.

```
Throughput(N) = N*Throughput(1)          //linear scalability
```

If the GC algorithm is the same, the freed memory size of a collection desirably should not be impacted by the number of cores used in the collection. Since,

```
Throughput = Size_freed_memory / Time_collection
```

Then the formula above becomes the following,

```
Time_collection(N) = (1/N)*Time_collection(1)    //linear
                                                   scalability
```

To achieve linear scalability, the algorithm has to be fully parallel. That is the operations can be assigned to different cores with balanced loads, and they do not waste time for synchronization with each other. This may be achievable in certain phase of a collection algorithm while it is extremely difficult to achieve it in the full collection process. In this chapter, we will discuss the design of parallel collection algorithms. Load balance and synchronization are two constant topics throughout the discussions.

Parallel collection is conducted by multiple collectors. When a collection starts, GC may decide to launch multiple collectors on a multi-core platform. In a stop-the-world collection, the number of collectors is usually the same as the number of cores available to the virtual machine (VM). The optimal number of collectors depends on system tuning.

All the collection algorithms start from root-set enumeration phase. It is possible for the collector to enumerate all the mutators' root-sets, or the mutators can enumerate their own root sets and report to the collector. Since this phase involves mutators suspension that is expensive operation, and the root-set enumeration is usually fast, it is not critical to parallelize this phase; instead, the tasks after this phase should try to be parallelized.

15.1 COLLECTION PHASES

When the number of collectors is big, barrier synchronization across all of them between collection phases can be expensive and should better be avoided whenever possible. In this regard, the number of barriers in a collection algorithm is an important factor in its design consideration.

As we have discussed, live-object marking is the second phase after root-set enumeration. Trace-copy collection can conduct the object forwarding at the same time of object graph traversal, so it does not need barrier synchronization between the marking phase and moving phase.

Mark-sweep collection has two stages: live-object marking and dead-object sweeping. It has to have a barrier between the two stages because the dead objects are only known to the collectors after the tracing phase finishes. In actual implementation, the sweeping phase can be deferred to allocation time.

Mark-compact collection has challenge to be conducted without a barrier due to its nature of in-place moving collection. Object graph traversal is in order to object connection, while compaction is usually in order of the object addresses. It has to compact the heap after all the live objects are marked, to avoid the moved objects overwriting other live objects.

Besides the consideration on collection algorithm phases, GC may have to include barriers for other reasons. When a GC is designed to have more than one collection spaces, the collectors may have to synchronize between collecting different spaces. Finalization, reference-object processing, class unloading, etc. usually need separate phases, so barriers may be needed as well. However, although these phases have barriers, if the VM implementation can execute them concurrently with respect to mutator execution, then the barrier overhead is not necessarily a serious issue.

15.2 PARALLEL OBJECT GRAPH TRAVERSAL

Object graph traversal is usually the most time-consuming phase in a collection. It can be purely marking the reachable objects, or can include copying the marked object to a free space. In the traversal process, an auxiliary data structure, mark-stack (or mark-queue) is usually used, although this is not mandatory. The stack is initially stuffed with root references (or slots containing root references). The collector pops a reference from the stack, marks the referenced object, and scans its fields that contain references. The reference (or the slot containing the reference) of every unmarked object that is found during object scanning is pushed onto the stack. When the mark-stack is empty, all the reachable objects are marked.

The whole tracing process can be viewed as iterations over the mark-stack elements. At first glance, it is trivial to parallelize it because of the perfect iterative property.

A straightforward parallelization can simply let the collectors to share the mark-stack in a synchronized way. That is, each collector pops an element from the stack, marks and scans it, and pushes unmarked reachable objects onto the stack. The stack accesses (pop and push) are synchronized so that they are atomic between the collectors. The problem of this solution is that the intensive synchronization accesses to the mark-stack mean high overhead and low scalability. In other words, the task sharing granularity is too small to be only a single-object reference processing. When the number of collectors is big, the accesses to the shared mark-stack can be a performance bottleneck.

To avoid the high synchronization overhead, it is natural to partition the tracing tasks among the collectors. A solution is to partition the initial root references evenly to the collectors, and then each collector can largely operate independently with its own mark-stack, starting from the assigned root references. The collectors do not exchange tasks throughout the object graph traversal. The problem of this solution is that the object graph structure is arbitrary, so the initial even partitioning of the root references does not necessarily lead to even distribution of the tracing tasks across the collectors. Load balance is an issue. There should be a method to share or exchange the tracing tasks among the collectors dynamically.

15.2.1 Task Sharing

One way to share tracing tasks is "task sharing," where the tracing tasks are grouped into blocks and the collectors share the tasks in block granularity. One tracing task is represented by an object to be scanned, and one block has multiple object references (or reference slots). The algorithm is illustrated in Figure 15.1 below.

- Step 1. At the beginning, all the root references are put into equal-sized blocks (task block), and all the task-blocks are put in a task-pool that is a global data structure.

- Step 2. Every collector grabs a task-block from the task-pool through synchronized access to the pool.

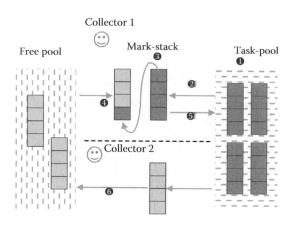

FIGURE 15.1 Task-sharing among collectors for tracing tasks.

- Step 3. Each collector uses the task-block as a mark-stack and operates on it as in a sequential tracing process.

- Step 4. If the mark-stack is full, the collector pushes the new tasks to a new mark-stack and continues tracing task on the new mark-stack.

- Step 5. The collector puts back the old full mark-stack to the task-pool.

- Step 6. When a mark-stack is empty, the collector puts it back to a free block pool and grabs another task-block from the task-pool until the pool is empty.

This solution solves both synchronization granularity and load balance problems. It is not a perfect solution though, because sometimes one collector may keep busy with its local mark-stack for a long time while another collector is idle waiting some collector puts a task block to the task-pool. The synchronization over the pool access is another issue.

15.2.2 Work-Stealing

To avoid the problem of unbalanced mark-stack tasks, "work-stealing" can be a solution. The idea is for the idle collector to steal some tasks from the busy collector's mark-stack. The idle collector does not need to wait for a block put back by a busy collector who overflows its mark-stack. The operations can be illustrated in Figure 15.2 below.

- Step 1. Each collector has a thread-local mark-stack. At the beginning, root references are partitioned evenly to all the collectors and pushed onto the respective mark-stacks. Each collector operates on its mark-stack as in a sequential tracing process.

- Step 2. When a collector runs out its mark-stack, it steals the last entry of another collector's mark-stack. Since the last entries of the mark-stacks are globally accessible, the access to them has to be synchronized for all the collectors. When the last entry is stolen, the pointer to the last entry is modified to the second last entry.

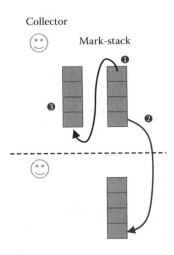

FIGURE 15.2 Work-stealing among collectors for tracing tasks.

- Step 3. If a mark-stack is full, the collector creates a new mark-stack for the over-flowed object references and continues its operations on the new mark-stack.

Work-stealing essentially makes the last entry of every mark-stack to be the task-pool that is shared by all the collectors. In an actual implementation, the last entry can be the last couple of entries, or the half of the remaining stack entries. The stack can be a double-ended queue. Work-stealing can be combined with task sharing so that a collector only steals a task when the task-pool is empty.

Work-stealing guarantees that, as long as there are enough tasks, the tasks can be distributed to multiple collectors to achieve load balance. But this solution still needs synchronization for the last entry access. Yet another solution "task-pushing" can help to eliminate the synchronization at all.

15.2.3 Task-Pushing

The idea of task-pushing is to use a separate task-queue data structure for the task exchange between collectors. The queue is like the task-pool in task-sharing, where a collector puts some of its spare tasks voluntarily. The shared task, as in work-stealing, is taken by the collector from the last entry of its own mark-stack and put to the task-queue.

The idea can be illustrated in Figure 15.3 below.

- Step 1. Each collector has a thread-local mark-stack. At the beginning, root refer-ences are partitioned evenly to all the collectors and pushed onto the respective mark-stacks. Each collector operates on its mark-stack as in a sequential tracing process.

- Step 2. When collector pops a task from its mark-stack, it checks if the task-queue is empty. If yes, it drips a task from the bottom of its mark-stack and pushes to the

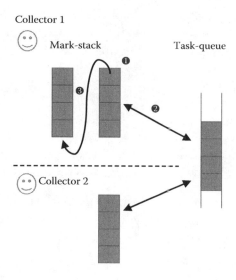

FIGURE 15.3 Task-pushing among collectors with task-queue for tracing tasks.

task-queue. When the mark-stack of a collector is empty, it checks if task-queue has task. If yes, it dequeues the task and pushes to its mark-stack and continues.

- Step 3. If a mark-stack is full, the collector creates a new mark-stack for the overflowed object references and continues its operations on the new mark-stack.

Task-pushing is a hybrid of task sharing and work-stealing. The difference from task sharing is, task-pushing puts only one task to the task-queue, rather than a block to the task-pool. Since the last entry of the mark-stack usually is root node of a subtree to be traversed, one task is not necessarily a small task. The difference from work-stealing is task-pushing uses a separate data structure for task exchange and only the accesses to the task-queue need to be synchronized, which makes the algorithm implementation easier.

A special queue design can eliminate the synchronization on the queue accesses. It is called single-producer, single-consumer (SPSC) queue. A multi-producer, multi-consumer (MPMC) queue can be composed of SPSC queues in a way that every pair of producer and consumer employs an SPSC queue.

In task-pushing, an SPSC queue for producing-collector i and consuming-collector j is represented as *queue[i, j]*. Collector i sends its spare task to collector j by enqueuing the task in *queue[i, j]*. Collector j then dequeues the task from the queue. In order for all the N collectors to exchange tasks to each other, a matrix of $(N - 1)*(N - 1)$ SPSC queues are needed to compose the MPMC queue. This MPMC queue is used by task-pushing as the task-queue.

If SPSC queue can be designed to eliminate the need of synchronization, the MPMC queue does not need synchronization either. SPSC queue utilizes the inherent atomicity property of word-aligned memory access, which is available in all known modern processors. All the entries in MPMC queue are required to be word aligned, thus their loads and stores are guaranteed to be atomic. Since object reference is word-size, this requirement can be trivially satisfied.

SPSC queue uses value NULL (or any value that is not a valid task identifier, that is, object reference) to indicate a vacant entry. Any non-NULL entry holds a task. Once an entry is dequeued, the consumer stores a NULL into the entry. Before a producer enqueues, it checks whether the current entry value is NULL. The queue has a head and a tail pointer that always point to the first filled and first unfilled entry, respectively, that is, the two ends of the tasks in the queue. Task-pushing with MPMC task-queue can be illustrated in Figure 15.4.

- Step 1. Each collector has a thread-local mark-stack. At the beginning, root references are partitioned evenly to all the collectors and pushed onto the respective mark-stacks. Each collector operates on its mark-stack as in a sequential tracing process.

- Step 2. When collector x pops a task from its mark-stack, it checks if any of its output queues *queue[x, *]* has vacancy. If yes, it drips a task from the bottom of the mark-stack and pushes to the vacant output queue.

- Step 3. When the mark-stack of collector y is empty, it checks if any of its input queues *queue[*, y]* has task. If yes, it dequeues the task and pushes to its mark-stack and continues.

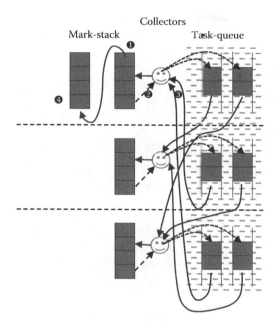

FIGURE 15.4 Task-pushing among collectors with multiproducer, multiconsumer (MPMC) queues for tracing tasks.

- Step 4. If a mark-stack is full, the collector creates a new mark-stack for the overflowed object references and continues its operations on the new mark-stack.

In reality, the size of each SPSC queue needs to be only one or two entries. Longer queue does not bring better performance, because that means a collector drips tasks faster than they are consumed.

Task-pushing algorithm needs to have a correct design to ensure the process terminate correctly. A collector cannot locally determine if it should exit the tracing phase. Empty mark-stack and empty input queues of a collector do not necessarily mean the collector has no more tasks, since other threads may pass new tasks to it soon. Interested readers can refer the "task-pushing" paper by the author.

15.3 PARALLEL MARKING OF OBJECTS

In a parallel collection, it is possible for more than one collectors reach same object and try to mark it at the same time. Some GC uses mark table, where one bit maps to one word in the memory. When an object is reachable, the corresponding bit in the mark table to the first word of the object is set to indicate the object is live. If the word width is 32 bit, 1/32 of heap size is used for mark-bit table, which is not a big overhead. The problem is, when there is more than one bit in a word corresponding to respective live objects, to set them concurrently may require atomic operation if bit setting on the processor is not atomic by default, which is the common case in modern processors. Atomic operation is expensive.

One solution is to use a byte-size flag to indicate the object's liveness, if byte-size operation is automatically atomic in the processor. It is unlikely to use one byte to map one word because of the too high space overhead. GC can map one byte to the object alignment unit.

For example, the GC can choose to align the object at 16-byte address boundary, then 1 byte can map to 16 bytes, and it is impossible for two objects being mapped into same byte. With this solution, the atomic operation overhead is eliminated, while the space overhead is not negligible.

To reduce the space overhead, the flag can be mapped to bigger piece of memory, such as 256 bytes. When the flag is set, all the objects in the mapped area are considered live; otherwise, they are dead. When a collector traverses the heap, the flag is set whenever an object in the mapped area is reached. This design does not need atomic operation and has low space overhead, but it cannot tell exactly which object is live in a marked area, hence retains floating garbage. It trades floating garbage for small mark table.

The byte in mark table and the words in heap are mapped mutually. That is GC can find the mapped object from the byte flag, and vice versa. One way to do it is to allocate a big chunk of memory for mark table that maps to the whole heap. Since the base addresses of the mark table and heap are known, the offset mapping between an object and its flag can be deduced easily. Assuming 1-byte flag maps to 16-byte memory, then,

```
offset_flag = offset_object << 4;
addr_flag = addr_table_base + (addr_object - addr_heap_base) >> 4;
addr_object = addr_heap_base + (addr_flag - addr_table_base ) << 4;
```

Here `addr_object` is the address of an object, and `addr_flag` is the address of the mapped marking flag.

To preallocate a big piece of memory for mark table is not always a best solution because VM may never use the assumed heap size throughout its instance life time. More importantly, the heap space may not be contiguous. It is not convenient to make up mark-table segments to map the heap segments. A solution is that the mark table for one heap area stays together with that area, and the mark table is only allocated when the heap area is allocated, then the mark table and its mapped heap area always have same base address.

To be more convenient, the heap area can be allocated in block of constant size that is two's power, and the block base address is aligned at the size boundary. In this way, the base address of the heap area can be deduced from any address in this area. Assuming the mark table takes `TABLE_SIZE` space in each block header, then,

```
block_base = addr_object & ~(BLOCK_SIZE - 1);
addr_flag = block_base + (addr_object -block_base - TABLE_SIZE) >> 4;

block_base = addr_flag & ~(BLOCK_SIZE - 1);
addr_object = block_base + TABLE_SIZE + (addr_flag -block_base) << 4;
```

Putting mark table in block header for each block is usually better than putting it in a separate single piece of memory for the entire heap. The mark table still can use bit or byte or other size flag to map word or other size in the block body based on its need. A tracing algorithm can be designed to be that one block is only traversed by same collector, so that the mark table in the block header is only modified by one collector, hence no requirement for atomic operation.

Mark table has a merit that the flags of live objects stay together, and it is easy for a collector to find all the live objects in heap by scanning the mark table. For mark-sweep collection, this is useful to sweep the dead objects.

For trace-copy GC, mark table is not so useful, since a collector marks and forwards the live objects at the same time in one pass, thus there is no need to scan the mark table to find live objects. In this case, the mark table can be reused as a target table that holds forwarding address, and one live object maps to a forwarding address. Or a trace-copy GC may not use the extra mark table at all by putting the liveness flag directly in object header.

15.4 PARALLEL COMPACTION

Compaction refers to in-place moving collection that squeezes free space out of a fully allocated heap. It produces a continuous large free space, so that allocation can be done by bumping pointer, and large objects can be successfully accommodated. Surviving objects are compacted together, thus the access locality is improved too.

15.4.1 Parallel LISP2 Compactor

Ideal compacting collection is "slide-compact," where live objects are shifted to one end of the heap in the original order. Sequential LISP2 compactor implements slide-compact collection in a straightforward way. Figure 15.5 below shows the steps in a LISP2 compactor.

The explanations of the steps:

- Step 1. Live-object marking. Collector traverses the heap by tracing from root-set to mark all the reachable objects.

- Step 2. Object repointing. Scanning from the heap start to end in sequential order, collector computes target addresses for all live objects in the heap. The target address of a live object is its new location after compaction. When computing a new location for a live object, the collector has to know the new locations of other live

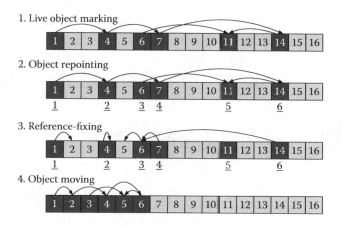

FIGURE 15.5 Sequential LISP2 compactor.

objects ahead of it in the heap to maintain the slide-compact property. The target address of every live object is kept in its object header or a separate place.

- Step 3. Reference-fixing. Collector traverses the heap and repoint all the object references in the heap to the target addresses of the referenced objects. The traversal can be heap scanning in order from begin to end, or heap tracing by following the object connection graph. In some design, this step is called remapping, reference updating.

- Step 4. Object moving. Collector moves the live objects sequentially in order from heap start to end. When an object is moved to its new location, the original live objects in the new location have been moved earlier, hence no data loss in the process.

It is easy to find that step 1 and step 3 can be executed with multiple collectors as in parallel heap tracing. Step 2 and step 4 have ordering requirement that needs additional design. The conceptual sequential algorithm of step 2 and step 4 are like below. The loop-carried dependence based on heap order is obvious.

```
Step 2:
    new_addr = heap_start;
    next_obj = next_live_object_from(new_address);
    while (next_obj != NULL){
    target_address(next_obj) =  new_addr;
        inc_size = object_size(next_obj);
        new_addr += inc_size;
        next_obj = next_live_object_from(next_obj + inc_size);
    }
Step 4:
    next_obj = next_live_object_from(heap_start);
    target_addr = target_address(next_obj);
    while (next_obj != NULL){
        object_copy(target_addr, next_obj);
        inc_size = object_size(next_obj);
        next_obj = next_live_object_from(next_obj + inc_size);
        target_addr = target_address(next_obj);
    }
```

One simple solution to parallelize LISP2 compactor is to partition the heap into subareas and then compact the subareas independently in parallel. This solution fragments the heap. With virtual address remapping, the fragmentation probably is not an issue.

Another solution is to build a dependence relation between the objects; therefore, the collectors can follow the dependence relation so as to maintain the required order.

15.4.2 Object Dependence Tree

The idea to build object dependence relation is, if a live object is going to be overwritten by other live objects, a dependence between the to-be-overwritten object and overwriting object is built, with an edge going from the former to the latter. If an object has an incoming edge, the object will be moved to overwrite the object where the edge comes. If an object is going to overwrite itself, an edge is also built pointing from and to itself. Thus a dependence tree is formed among all the live objects. The tree is used with the following rules:

1. Only the objects that have no incoming edges are ready to be overwritten. When all the incoming edges to an object are removed, the object becomes ready.

2. When an object finishes its overwriting on another object, the edge from the latter to the former is removed, since there is no more dependence between the two objects.

To really build such a dependence tree is troublesome. In actual implementation, the heap is arranged in constant size blocks, so the dependence tree can be built between the blocks. A block S is another block T's source block if a live object in block S will be moved to block T. (At the same time, block T is block S' target block.) Due to the nature of compaction, the target-source relation has the following properties:

1. Every target block has one or more source blocks, since there can be dead objects in source blocks.

2. Every source block has one or two target blocks. In most cases, one source block has only one target block. In some other cases, when a target block has multiple source blocks, the last source block (in heap address order) may not be able to move all its live objects to the target block. Some of them have to be moved to a second target block. The last source block then has two target blocks.

3. A block can depend on itself, when some of its live objects are to be moved to same block. For example, the first block at the heap-start has to compact live objects within itself. The second block probably has half of its live objects moved to first block, and the other half to itself.

Following Figure 15.6 shows a dependence tree example of a heap that has 12 blocks.

The dependence tree is built during step 2 when the collectors compute new addresses for the live objects. Executing in parallel, all the collectors compete grabbing a source block and a target block in heap order (or block index order). This is to ensure the slide-compact property.

To describe the rules with more details, we need to define the block states and their transitions.

- UNHANDLED: This is the initial state of all blocks. The block is not an src (source) block or a dest (target) block.

- IN_COMPACT: The block is an src block of a collector, that is, the target addresses of the live objects in it are under computing;

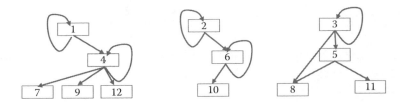

FIGURE 15.6   Dependence tree among blocks.

- COMPACTED: The target addresses of the live objects in it have been computed. The block is not an src block or a dest block.

- TARGET: The block is a dest block of a collector.

The rules for block state transitions are the following, with illustration in Figure 15.7.

1. All the blocks are UNHANDLED at the beginning;

2. The collectors compete for an UNHANDLED block in heap order. If a block is grabbed, it becomes the source block of the winning collector, and its state is set IN_COMPACT. The failing collectors then compete for next source block in heap order till the heap end.

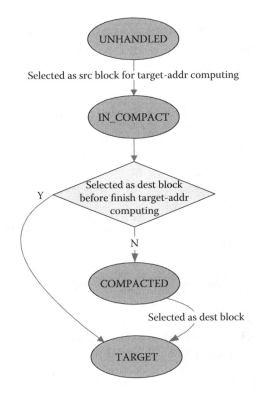

FIGURE 15.7   State transitions of blocks in parallel compactor.

3. When a collector finishes the target address computation for all live objects in its source block, it sets the block state to be COMPACTED, and the collector continues to grab a new source block going to step 2.

4. At the same time, all the collectors compete for a COMPACTED block in heap order. If a block is grabbed, it becomes the target block of the winning collector, and its state is set TARGET. If a collector fails to grab a COMPACTED block in heap order before reaching its source block, the collector uses this source block as its target block and sets its state from IN_COMPACT to TARGET (i.e., the same block is both source and target block of the collector).

In this way, every collector always holds a source block and a target block at the same time. For every live object in its source block, it computes a new address in its target block. For every target block, it has a linked list to link all its source blocks. This is the representation of the dependence tree. Figure 15.8 below shows the internal representation of dependence tree, corresponding to the dependence tree in Figure 15.6 above. Every block has a counter that records the count of target blocks depending on it, that is, the count of target blocks that the live objects of this block will be moved to. The number is either 0, 1, or 2. Number 0 means the block has no live objects for compaction.

With the dependence tree and the new addresses of all the live objects, the collectors can move the objects in step 4. To execute step 4 in parallel, GC uses a shared task-pool to coordinate the load balance between collectors. One task in the pool is represented by a block that has no incoming edges in the dependence tree except itself, that is, the root node in the dependence tree, such as block 1, 2, and 3 in Figure 15.6. The task is to move all the live objects from its source blocks to it. Initially, the task-pool has all the

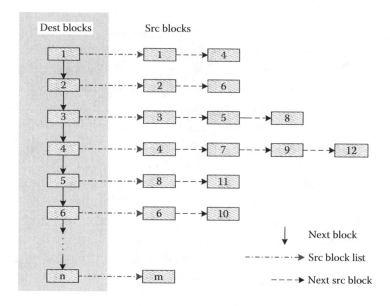

FIGURE 15 8   Internal representation of dependence tree

root nodes of the dependence tree. The idea is the tasks represented by the root nodes can be processed in parallel by the collectors without synchronization because there is no dependence in those tasks.

When the live objects of a source block are copied to its target block, the dependence edge from the target to the source block is removed from the dependence tree. This may make some previous child nodes to be new root nodes. These root nodes are then put into the task-pool as new tasks. Since the computation amount is decided by the size of moved live objects, one task by one target block means the computation amount of each task is a constant across the collectors. The load is balanced except the rare case when the dependence tree is too deep and there are not enough root nodes available in the task-pool.

When the number of root nodes in the task-pool is small, GC can break a deep tree into subtrees with temporary root nodes. GC selects one of its inner nodes in the middle of the tree, say block S. It is the source block of some parent node(s) and the root node of a subtree. GC copies the content of block S to a temporary empty block T, and let block T to replace block S as the source block of S' original parent node(s). Now block S is a new root node and can be put into the task-pool. Once the compaction is done, the data in temporary block T are copied to block S. In this way, GC can break a deep tree into multiple subtrees, and they can be processed in parallel.

There are also more parallelisms in one task. For example, when a target block is taken from the task-pool, there is no need to copy from all its source blocks with single collector. The design can be like this: when a target block has multiple source blocks, if itself is also a source block, the collector can move the live objects in itself first. Then the remaining free space is for other source blocks. The multiple source blocks can be processed in parallel by multiple collectors, since there is no data dependence in all the object movings.

15.4.3 Compactor with Target Table for Forwarding Pointer

LISP2 compactor does not have to strictly follow the four steps if the target addresses of live objects are kept in an auxiliary data structure (such as a target table) rather than the object header. The reason for the four steps of LISP2 compactor is that it keeps the forwarding pointer in object header and uses that for reference-fixing. LISP2 compactor can only overwrite an object after all the references in the heap to the object are fixed.

If the forwarding pointer is saved in target table, and the mapping relation can be established between the object and its forwarded location, the order of the object-moving phase and the reference-fixing phase can be arbitrary or together in one stage.

The target table cannot take too much memory, so it is unlikely to map one address in target table to the minimum object size in heap. An intuitive solution is to map the address to a section of the heap. Then the section is viewed as a "macro-object," and its forwarding pointer is stored in the target table. Since GC still marks live objects individually, the collectors can identify the individual live objects in a section. This is different from using section for live-object marketing, where, if one section is marked live, all the objects in it are considered live.

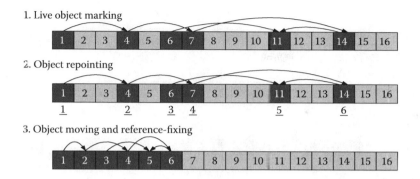

FIGURE 15.9   An improvement of LISP2 compactor with target table.

With the target-table design, objects can be moved (step 3) together with the reference-fixing (step 4). The steps of this algorithm are illustrated in Figure 15.9.

The explanations of the algorithm are as follows:

- Step 1. Live-object marking. Collector traverses the heap by tracing from root-set to mark live objects.

- Step 2. Object repointing. Scanning from the heap start to end in sequential order, collector computes target addresses for a section of live objects in the heap. The target address of every section is kept in a target table.

- Step 3. Object moving and reference-fixing. Starting from the heap start, collectors move live sections in heap order and repoint all the object references in the section to the target addresses of the referenced objects by looking up the target table.

The algorithm does not change the parallelization strategy but reduces one synchronization barrier. This is an improvement in the parallelization efficiency, with the cost of additional memory requirement to store the target table.

If the GC design uses a mark table to map every object in heap (and hence implicitly encoding object size), the object repointing (step 2) can be done purely based on the data in the mark table, without scanning the heap. Then only step 3 here needs a pass of heap scanning.

However, in the LISP2 compactor, if objects are moved (step 4) before the reference-fixing (step 3), then object moving (step 4) can be conducted together with the new address computation (step 2), with the help of target table. The steps of this algorithm are illustrated in Figure 15.10.

The explanations of the algorithm are as follows:

- Step 1. Live-object marking. Collector traverses the heap by tracing from root-set to mark live objects.

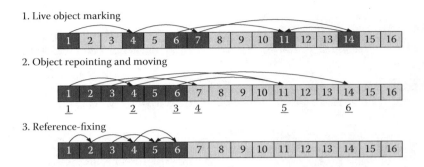

FIGURE 15.10 Another improvement of LISP2 compactor with target table.

- Step 2. Object repointing and moving. Scanning from the heap start to end in sequential order, collector computes target addresses for a section of live objects in the heap and moves it to the new location. The target address of every section is kept in a target table. In some design, this step is called relocation.

- Step 3. Reference-fixing. Starting from the heap start, collectors repoint all the object references in the section to the target addresses of the referenced objects by looking up the target table.

This design also reduces a synchronization barrier while keeping the parallelization strategy. It needs two passes of heap scanning: one for object moving and the other for reference-fixing.

15.4.4 Compactor with Section of Objects

The target table in a parallel compactor can be an array of addresses, where one address maps to a section of the heap, and vice versa. When there is a single live object in the section, the whole section is considered live. In this way, the variable-sized object compaction problem is converted into a constant-size section compaction problem.

Since now a section is treated as a single object, the efficiency of the target-table-based compaction design depends on the following assumptions:

- Many sections have no live objects in them, that is, the heap has many dead sections.

- Every live section is hopefully filled densely with live objects.

The choice of section size is then important; otherwise, some application may have small ratio of dead sections and sparsely filled live sections. If GC uses an operating system (OS) page as a section, virtual memory property can be leveraged.

If there is a single object alive in the page, the page is alive; otherwise, the page is dead and can be recycled. One way to compact the heap is to move the live pages to one end of the heap as usual. The other way, due to the OS page nature, is to unmap the dead pages. If GC unmaps the dead pages, there is no need to move the live pages (i.e., the macro-objects), hence no

1. Live object marking

2. Free pages unmapping and remapping

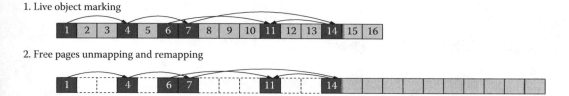

FIGURE 15.11   Compaction based on mark-sweep and page mapping.

need for object repointing and reference-fixing either. Then the compaction can be achieved by unmapping the dead pages in the heap and remapping new pages to one end of the heap.

This design can also be regarded as an extension of mark sweep at page granularity. The operations are given below, as illustrated in Figure 15.11.

Step 1. Live-object marking.

Step 2. Unmap the pages that have no live objects inside and remap new pages to one end of the heap.

Apparently step 1 and step 2 can be easily parallelized, and this design reduces one more synchronization barrier. But this design may have big space overhead because it cannot recycle the dead objects in live pages. When the intrapage fragmentation is big, a fallback compaction is needed.

15.4.5 In-Place Compactor in Single Pass

A natural question is whether it is possible to further merge the steps in an in-place compactor. First of all, it is impossible to merge the live-object marking with other steps. As in-place compaction, the dead objects are only known and then can be recycled after all the live objects are identified. This is different from trace-forward collection that does not directly recycle dead objects but only process the live objects.

It is possible to merge the object-repointing step and the reference-fixing step into a single step. Reference-fixing can only finish after object repointing finishes; otherwise, the former does not have new addresses of all the live objects to update references. The key to conduct the two operations in one step is that the collector should be able to find all the references to a live object when it is moved.

This can be achieved by chaining the fields that have references to same object X before X is moved. The head of the chain is in the target-table entry that maps to object X, so the chain can be found and updated when object X is really moved. Before X is moved, the chain needs to be maintained valid when other objects are moved.

When X is moved, the target-table entry is changed to the new address of object X. Later, when other object that has a reference to object X is moved, the collector can find the new address from target table and update the reference. The idea is based on Jonkers and Morris' threaded pointer algorithm, but it allows to merge the object repointing and reference-fixing in one step.

Figure 15.12 below shows the compacting operations after live-object marking. We call it "thread-compact" collection.

The explanations are the following:

1. The initial state after live object marking. The target-table entry has 1:1 mapping to an object (or section) in the heap.

2. When a live object is moved, its fields are scanned. All the fields of the object that contain references pointing to the right-hand side are linked into their respective threaded reference chains. A threaded reference chain links all the fields in the moved objects that contain same reference that points to an unmoved object. The unmoved object O has a corresponding entry E in the target table, which is the head of threaded reference chain for object O. When a live object T is moved and it has a slot R containing a reference to O, the slot R is then linked into O's threaded reference chain, being inserted atomically right after the head E.

3. When another live object is moved, if it has a field that contains a reference pointing to right side, this field is linked into that reference's chain, by atomically updating the target-table entry. The chained reference fields do not need to store the reference value, because the target-table entry address is mapped to the reference value.

4. When a live object is moved, all the chained reference fields of that object are updated to point to the new location of the object, including the target-table entry.

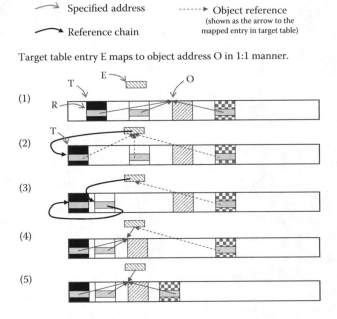

FIGURE 15.12   Operations of thread compact.

5. When a live object is moved, its fields are scanned. All the fields that contain reference pointing to objects on the left side are updated to point to the value in corresponding target-table entries.

Thread-compact implements in-place compaction in two steps.

Step 1. Mark live objects

Step 2. Compact live objects

Both of the steps can be parallelized. The part that processes objects on the right side of a live object is the same as other target-table-based compaction, since the object's new address is known. The only part worth noting is the reference chain's building. When multiple collectors are moving objects that contain references to same object to the right, they need to update the same reference chain. Every collector tries to insert its reference field to the chain right after the head, that is, the target-table entry. They should use atomic operation to change the target-table entry.

CHAPTER 16

Optimizing GC for Responsiveness

S TOP-THE-WORLD (STW) GARBAGE COLLECTION (GC) has an obvious shortcoming. The application has to be paused during the collection. This is a problem in server system where transaction processing latency is critical to business, and it is also not welcome in the client system where responsiveness is critical to user interaction. Reducing the collection pause time is one of the hottest topics in the GC community.

The common technology to reduce collection pause time is to make the collection and mutation run concurrently. They can be interleaved execution or parallel execution. With parallel execution, collectors and mutators can run at the same time in different threads on different cores in a multicore platform. With interleaved execution, collectors and mutators do not run at the same time but alternately.

Interleaved execution partitions a single collection into a few smaller phases, hence reducing a single application pause into a few shorter pauses. Parallel execution allows the mutators to run when collection is ongoing, hence removes the application pause caused by collection.

From the perspective of a full collection cycle, that is, from root-set enumeration to dead objects recycled, both interleaved and parallel execution are concurrent collection. From design point of view, to make collectors and mutators run in parallel is a superset to make them run in an interleaved manner. In the GC community, the former (parallel execution) is usually called "concurrent GC," whereas the latter (interleaved execution) is called "incremental GC," referring to the fact that a collection is finished incrementally with multiple pauses of the mutators' execution. An orthogonal term "Parallel GC" refers to the collection that is conducted by multiple collectors in parallel, and the collection can be concurrent/incremental.

If a concurrent collector and a mutator are running in parallel on a single-core platform, the operating system (OS) thread scheduler makes their execution automatically interleaved. Incremental GC, however, schedules the collector and mutator autonomously.

Since virtual machine (VM) knows more details about the collection and mutation tasks than the OS scheduler, sometimes an incremental GC can achieve some benefits that are hardly achievable through OS' blind scheduling. The case of incremental GC is somehow similar to implement a user-level thread scheduler, which is less interesting with more cores in modern platforms, or only interesting in specific domains. In this chapter, we mainly focus on the concurrent GC.

16.1 REGIONAL GC

In reality, complete removal of pause time is difficult, so the community is mainly striving for a balance between pause time and overall system performance. For example, to reduce the pause time, regional/generational GC we mentioned early can help. Regional GC partitions the heap into multiple regions. One collection collects one or a few regions. There can be multiple design choices regarding live object marking and dead object recycling.

To collect a region, the collector needs to know the live objects in the region. In a tracing GC, live objects can be got by either full-heap or partial-heap traversing. When it is partial-heap traversing with one region, the cross-region references from other regions to this region should be maintained in a remember set.

Figure 16.1 below is an example that shows all the references from root-set and across region.

As any collection, there are always two tasks to consider for a regional collection.

Operation 1. Find live objects: To find all the live objects in the region, the collector can traverse the whole heap or only the region.

To trace the whole heap may take much longer time than only traversing the region, while whole-heap traversal can find all the live objects in the heap, including other

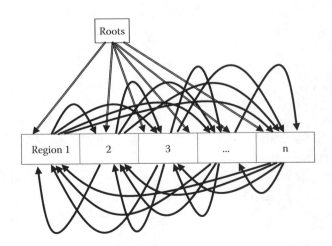

FIGURE 16.1   All the references from root-set and across region.

regions. Knowing all the live objects gives the collector flexibility to decide which region(s) to recycle. It is possible for the collector to choose the region(s) that has least live objects so as to achieve highest throughput. This is a tradeoff to make in the GC design. The long tracing time with whole heap may not be always a problem if it is concurrent tracing, which we will discuss in next section.

To trace only specified region requires not only root-set but also remember set that includes all the incoming references from other regions. This information is maintained by write-barrier that track mutators' updates on any references in heap. If a full collection cycle wants to collect the whole heap by recycling one region after another, the write-barrier needs to remember all the cross-region references, to support regional collection on every region. This would incur big mutator overhead. Sometimes, the cross-region references may retain lots of floating garbage. The smaller a region is, the more floating garbage there will be.

Operation 2. Recycle dead objects: After finding the live objects in the region, the collector can sweep the dead objects leaving a fragmented region, or move the live objects to another region leaving an empty contiguous region.

If it is a moving collection, the GC should preserve enough free space for the relocated objects or just compact in-place within the region, and then all the incoming references to the region have to be updated to point to the new locations. The incoming references can be got from the write-barrier execution and/or built on-the-fly by the collector during object tracing/moving. The former is called "mutator remember set" and the latter is called "collector remember set," as we have discussed.

Moving object in one or a few regions usually can be fast enough that makes the STW pause time acceptable. Otherwise, the GC can choose to move the objects concurrently while mutators are running. In the latter case, the GC then has to solve the problem of race condition, whereas both mutator and collector are accessing an object at the same time and one of the accesses is modification, which we will discuss in later sections.

Note the two operations above (find live objects and recycle dead objects) can be conducted together in one pass in a trace-copy GC, as we discussed before.

Figure 16.2 shows the states before and after a regional collection, assuming the live objects in region 3 are moved to the reserved region.

In the figure, the incoming references are represented with double-line arrows. If we consider the collected region as one generation and the rest regions the other generation, the figure is almost the same as a generational semispace collection. As we discussed in adaptive GC design, it is not necessarily to use equal size for both halves of the semispace, the collector can move live objects of multiple regions to one reserved region. The risk is the reserved region may not be enough to hold all the survivors. Then a backup solution has to be designed, such as using a fallback in-place compaction.

Before collection:

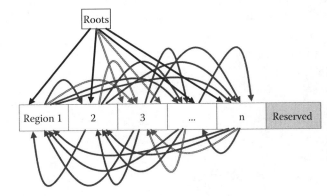

After collection:

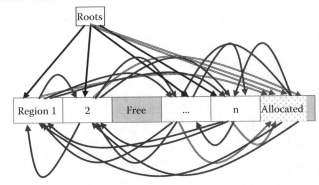

FIGURE 16.2   Incoming references are updated before and after a moving collection.

16.2 CONCURRENT TRACING

Finding live objects is one of the two major tasks of the GC. When the number of live objects to mark is relatively big, the tracing time can be too long to be acceptable if it requires to pause the application. Concurrent tracing can help to reduce the pause time, usually with the cost of lower throughput.

Assuming the collectors have enumerated all the root-set in mutators' stacks, registers, global variables, and the mutators continue their execution, the collectors start to trace the heap from the root-set concurrently. (The step on how to get the root-set concurrently is the topic of next section.)

A tracing design is valid as long as it meets the following three properties.

1. Correctness property: The GC does not lose any live object.

2. Progress property: The GC does not retain any dead object for too long. It is fine to retain some floating garbage for one or two collection cycles.

3. Termination property: The tracing phase is guaranteed to finish.

In this section, we discuss the concurrent tracing algorithms.

16.2.1 Snapshot-at-the-Beginning

With a STW tracing GC, all the objects reachable in the object connection graph from root-set are live objects, and the rest are dead. We assume the live object set at the beginning of tracing phase is L, and the dead object set is D. The problem with concurrent tracing is that, when the mutators continue execution, the object connection graph is changing while the collectors traverse it. With an initial set of roots, the object connection graph is changed in two ways:

- Mutators write to the reference fields of objects, which may change a live object dead. In live object set L, assume the objects that are still reachable is set ΔL. We have $L \supseteq \Delta L$.

- Mutators create new objects, which may stay reachable or become dead along with mutators execution. Assume the newly created object set during the tracing phase is N, and the reachable ones of them by end of the tracing phase is set ΔN. We have $N \supseteq \Delta N$.

Then the live object set after the tracing phase L' becomes,

$$L' = \Delta L + \Delta N$$

The relation can be illustrated in Figure 16.3.

A concurrent tracing design should try to find the sets of ΔL and ΔN. Since $L \supseteq \Delta L$ and $N \supseteq \Delta N$, we have the following relation:

$$\Delta L + \Delta N \subseteq L + N$$

That means, if the concurrent tracing design can find the sets of $L + N$, which is a superset of all the reachable objects by end of the tracing phase, the design meets the correctness property. As long as it meets other properties, it is a valid design.

- Set L is the live objects at the beginning of tracing phase. Although mutators change the object connect graph, set L still can be restored by using write-barrier that catches every heap write into a reference field. With the write-barrier, collectors know the original reference value thus to restore the original object connection graph.

- Set N is the newly created object set during tracing phase. It can be caught by the allocation routine. That is all new objects are marked live directly.

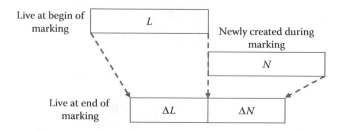

FIGURE 16.3   The sets size relation through the course of concurrent tracing.

The idea of this design is called "snapshot-at-the-beginning" (SATB) because it tries to find all the live objects at the beginning of the tracing phase, as a snapshot of the object connection graph. Together with the newly created objects being marked as live, this tracing algorithm effectively find a superset of the live objects by end of the tracing phase. It meets the correctness property of a tracing algorithm design.

With SATB tracing, some live objects in the snapshot or newly created objects may become dead during tracing phase, and they are retained. This is not a problem because they will not appear in the snapshot of next collection cycle, hence for sure to be recycled.

Since the snapshot is a fixed set of objects, and the write-barrier does not generate new object, the tracing phase is guaranteed to terminate when all the objects in the snapshot are reached.

16.2.1.1 Slot-Based SATB

There are two representative implementations of SATB tracing algorithm. One is slot-based and the other is object-based. The difference is minor and mainly in the write-barrier code for every reference field write. In slot-based, write-barrier records the original reference value that is to be overwritten by the mutator write, so as to be a loyal implementation of SATB concept. A later write to the same object needs to be caught again, since it may be a write to a different reference field. In object-based design, write-barrier logs all the reference fields' values of the object on the first time of mutator writing to the object's reference field. A later write to the same object will not record any more information but executes the field write itself.

The write-barrier pseudocode for slot-based is,

```
write_barrier_slot(Object* src, Object** slot, Object* new_ref)
{
    old_ref = *slot;
    if( !is_marked(old_ref) ){
        remember(old_ref);
    }
    *slot = new_ref;
}
```

The remembered original reference (`old_ref`) is recorded in remember set. Since write-barrier catches heap writes when collectors are tracing the heap from root-set, the elements in the remember set are pushed to the mark stack for tracing as well. When the stack is empty, the tracing phase terminates. Figure 16.4 is an illustration of the write-barrier result after a mutator executes two object field writes.

In the figure, the reference to object B (i.e., the old value of A.f1) is stored to variable a in the runtime stack. Without write-barrier remembering its reference, object B may be incorrectly considered as a dead object.

The write-barrier does not generate any new tracing task beyond those objects in the snapshot. It is possible for a mutator to write to same field multiple times. The later writes

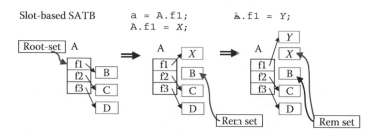

FIGURE 16.4   Slot-based snapshot-at-the-beginning (SATB) concurrent tracing.

also trigger the write-barrier execution and lead to remember reference values that were not original in the object's snapshot.

As shown in Figure 16.4 above, reference X is a value written to an object field f1, and later X is overwritten by another value, then reference X is remembered by write-barrier. This reference either points to an object that is in the snapshot, or to a newly created object which is marked by default and does not cause a new tracing task. So after the snapshot is traversed, the condition check `is_marked(old_ref)` always returns TRUE, and no new task can be generated.

Note that the write-barrier of slot-based design does not check if the object to be written is marked. If it is marked, all its reference fields have been scanned, hence no need to remember any of them. It is fine to add the checking as the code in bold face below while it does not bring much benefit.

```
write_barrier_slot(Object* src, Object** slot, Object* new_ref)
{
    old_ref = *slot;
    if( !is_marked(src) && !is_marked(old_ref) ){
        remember(old_ref);
    }
    *slot = new_ref;
}
```

Ultimately, whether to generate a new task (i.e., `remember(old_ref)`) is decided by whether `old_ref` has been scanned. If it is not scanned, it makes sense to add it to the mark stack even if the object `src` has been marked. (This happens when a marked object is updated with a reference to an unmarked object.)

Another concern is whether the write barrier for writes on a newly created object may generate lots of redundant work, if without checking its marking status. Again, this does not bring actual difference since the overall task amount is decided by the number of live objects in the snapshot at the beginning. In any case, slot-based design ensures that any object in the connection graph snapshot is scanned and only scanned once.

On the other hand, with the additional check, it may bring some benefit for certain applications. The reason is not because the additional checking can reduce any actual work, but because the is_marked(src) might be a local data access while is_marked(old_ref) be a remote data access, which have different data cache localities. If object writes are very intensive, the benefit may be visible.

16.2.1.2 Object-Based SATB

The write-barrier pseudocode for object-based is,

```
write_barrier_object(Object* src, Object** slot, Object* new_ref)
{
    if( !is_marked(src) && is_clean(src) ){
        remember(snapshot of src); //remember all references
        dirty(src);
    }
    *slot = new_ref;
}
```

The remembered original references in the snapshot of an object (snapshot of src) are pushed to the mark stack for tracing as well. When the stack becomes empty, the tracing phase terminates. Figure 16.5 below is an illustration of the write-barrier result after a mutator executes two object field writes.

A deeper look reveals that object-based is more a loyal implementation of SATB tracing than slot-based. It takes a snapshot of an object right before it is written and ensures to trace those references. When an object has been scanned, write-barrier will not take its snapshot, since the scanned data is the same as the snapshot. If the object has been taken a snapshot (i.e., dirty), later write-barrier will not take it again. In this way, object-based makes sure that every reference field of the object in the snapshot connection graph is scanned and only scanned once.

Note that the write-barrier of object-based design does not set the dirtied object as marked. Here an object is marked means the object has been scanned. When all the references have been remembered, it is virtually the same operation as the collector scanning the object. So it is fine to add the code in bold face as shown below, while this does not bring essential difference.

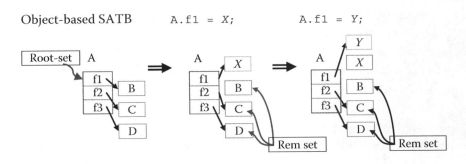

FIGURE 16.5   Object-based snapshot-at-the-beginning (SATB) concurrent tracing.

```
write_barrier_object(Object* src, Object** slot, Object* new_ref)
{
    if( !is_marked(src) && is_clean(src) ){
        remember(snapshot of src); //remember all references
        dirty(src);
        mark(src);
    }
    *slot = new_ref;
}
```

No matter if the object is marked or not, write-barrier takes snapshot of it only once. Setting it marked here avoids the collector to mark it later, which can save the collector scanning the object again. On the other hand, since this object is written, it has one field updated that contains a new reference value that may point to an unmarked object. The mutators may write this object multiple times, hence installing multiple new references. Since this object is live, the objects pointed by those new references are live as well (in the snapshot connection graph or as being new objects). Not marking this object here gives the collector a chance to find those unmarked objects from this object and avoid the mutators to copy snapshots of those unmarked objects later in write-barrier, which is a save of mutator work.

16.2.1.3 SATB Discussions

That slot-based and object-based algorithms are virtually the same, and both return the same set of live objects, including floating garbage, decided by the snapshot. It is worth mentioning that they do have difference in performance implication. Object-based write-barrier touches only the data of the object to be written, which normally results better data cache locality. Slot-based needs to check the marking status of the referenced object (new_ref), which can be remote to the written object. A slot-based implementation is known as "DLG"* algorithm, and an object-based implementation is called "snapshot" algorithm in literatures.

Multiple mutators writing to same object at the same time do not have any correctness problem. It is possible for multiple mutators to execute the write-barrier code in an interleaved way so that they all read the same old value, or only one mutator reads the old value. This is fine as long as the old reference value is read hence the SATB nature is kept. This property is same for both slot-based and object-based write-barrier.

SATB tracing can also be implemented with OS/hardware support. That is to replace the write-barrier with a page-fault handler. At the beginning of heap tracing, all the heap is page protected. Whenever there is a write into the page, a fault is triggered and the page data is copied that includes all the old references in the page. This design has too high overhead of page faulting and data copying, hence is probably only theoretically interesting.

16.2.2 Incremental-Update

Different from SATB, another way for concurrent tracing tries to catch all the current live objects.

---

* DLG is the name initials of the three authors of the algorithm, D. Doligez, X. Leroy, and G. Gonthier.

16.2.2.1 INC by Remember Reference

Whenever there is a write to a reference field, instead of remembering the old value, the write-barrier remembers the new value. The pseudocode of the write-barrier can be the following. We call it "remember-reference" INC write-barrier.

```
write_barrier_ref(Object* src, Object** slot, Object* new_ref)
{    *slot = new_ref;
     if( is_marked(src) )
         remember(new_ref);
}
```

The write-barrier remembers the new reference if the object has been marked. The remembered references are pushed to collector's mark stack for concurrent tracing. There is no need to remember the new reference before the object is marked, since the new reference will be traced when the object is marked if it has not been overwritten yet. If the object has been marked, it will not be scanned again, so the new reference written to it should be remembered and traced.

If all the reference updates in the system (including heap, execution context, global variables) can be remembered, this design has no correctness problem. In the GC community, this idea is called "incremental-update" (INC), because it incrementally modifies the object connection graph to keep it up to date. As a comparison, SATB maintains the snapshot.

INC tracing does not need to mark the new objects alive by default, whose liveness is decided by the tracing algorithm, same as the existing objects. If an object is live, its reference must be written somewhere in the system and can be caught by the write-barrier.

16.2.2.2 Second-Round Tracing for INC

The problem with INC design is, during the concurrent tracing, although all the references to live objects are written somewhere in the system, some of them may not be written to objects in heap. For examples, they can be written to runtime stacks and registers. There is no efficient way to track the updates to them.

Without tracking the out-of-heap updates, INC design cannot ensure the correctness property. A case of lost reference in INC tracing is shown in Figure 16.6 below.

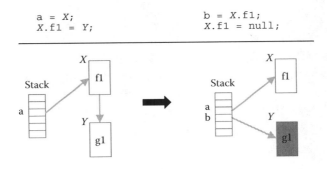

FIGURE 16.6   A case of missed live object in INC tracing.

To correct the problem of potentially missing live object in INC algorithm, the GC has to conduct another round of non-INC live object marking after the INC tracing. It can use STW tracing or any other known correct method such as SATB. A design that combines INC with STW for the second-round tracing is known as "mostly concurrent," since it is not fully concurrent.

The second-round live object marking does not need to retraverse the full heap to find all the live objects. It does not trace the objects that have been marked live by the first-round concurrent tracing. The second-round tracing aims to find only the live objects that have not been marked in first round because they were only reachable from root-set during INC tracing. In other words, those first-round missed live objects should be found even without scanning the first-round marked objects.

Looking from another angle, if a live object Y can only be reachable from a first-round marked object X, then Y should never be missed in the first-round tracing. If Y's reference exists in X at the beginning of the first-round tracing and is not overwritten during the tracing, the tracing process should be able to reach Y from X and mark it. If Y's reference exists in X due to mutator writing value Y into a field of X, the write-barrier will remember Y and the collector will mark it for sure.

So the second-round tracing does not need to scan the first-round marked objects, and no live objects will be lost. Correctness property is maintained by the combination of two rounds of complementary tracing.

In some GC designs, the second-round tracing is also used as the root-set enumeration of the next collection. In this kind of designs, GCs are connected back-to-back and never finish. The root-set enumeration stage is used to complete the last collection and start the current collection.

In SATB design, the number of remembered references has an upper limit that is decided at the beginning of tracing. In slot-based SATB, the number of remembered references is no more than the number of the live objects in the snapshot. In object-based SATB, the remembered object snapshots are no more than the number of the live objects in the snapshot that are written by the mutators before marked by the collectors.

In INC design, the number of remembered references is the number of references written to the heap objects after the objects are marked. This number has no upper limit. As long as the tracing is ongoing, the number increases since the mutators are executing at the same time. This means there is no natural termination point to the concurrent tracing. A scheduling algorithm has to be in place to decide when is the best point to stop the INC tracing and start the second-round tracing. The latter must have an algorithmic inherent termination point.

16.2.2.3 INC by Remember Root

Note that INC write-barrier does not check if the object is dirty. If an object is written after it is marked, it becomes dirty, which means there is a new reference in the object that should be remembered. After an object becomes dirty, any later reference writes to it (even to the same slot) should be remembered.

For a slot that is written by the mutator, INC design really should remember only the final reference value in the slot right before the second-round tracing. All the previous values written to the slot are not needed because only the final reference values form the most updated object connection graph. To remember all of the slot updates can become a big overhead in both space and time. The ultimate goal of tracing is to find all the live objects by the end of tracing phase, rather than all the temporarily live objects in the course, since many of them die by the end of the INC tracing phase.

Based on this observation, a variant of the INC write-barrier can be designed to remember the dirty object instead of every new reference written to it. Then later the remembered objects are added to the root-set of the second-round tracing for rescanning. We call it "remember-root" INC design.

```
write_barrier_root(Object* src, Object** slot, Object* new_ref)
{
    *slot = new_ref;
    if( is_marked(src) && is_clean(src) ){
        dirty(src);
        remember(src);
    }
}
```

With remember-root INC write-barrier, when a reference is written to a marked live object, the object is set dirty, indicating that this object contains new reference that should be rescanned later. In this way, the INC design does not need to remember all the new references written to the heap but only flag the heap areas that need rescanning in second-round tracing.

The write-barrier supports parallel execution by multiple mutators. The same object might be dirtied more than once, which does not cause any correctness issue.

16.2.2.4 INC Discussions

The relation between remember-root and remember-reference in INC design is similar to that of card-table and remember-set in the generational GC, and also similar to that of object-based to slot-based in SATB design.

For INC design, remember-root is not necessarily better than remember-reference, although it does not need to remember all the intermediate reference writes. Which write-barrier is better all depends on the application's behavior. If there are not a huge number of reference writes or overwrites, remember-reference can be more efficient because it does not need to accumulate and then add the remembered references to root-set for the second-round tracing. They can be traced by the collectors once remembered. The remaining ones in the remember set that are not traced yet before the second-round tracing, however, need to be added to the root-set.

The GC can also choose to rescan the remembered roots once they are remembered instead of adding them to the root-set for the second-round tracing. In this case, if any of them are rescanned before the second-round starts, they must be reset to be clean, so that the new writes to those objects can be caught again by the write-barrier.

Since INC tracing may miss live objects and depends on a correct tracing round to make it up, it is fine to have more rounds of INC tracing before the final correct tracing. An intermediate INC tracing round can start from root-set or the remember set or both. It does not matter, because the INC tracing round does not try to improve the tracing preciseness (or correctness), but help to find more live objects so as to save the time of the final-round correct tracing.

If it is remember-root INC, then any rescanned remembered objects should be set clean. Then the later updates to this object will dirty it again. In any case, according to our theory, the remember set before final-round correct tracing should include all the marked objects whose updates have not been scanned, including the root-set.

Performance-wise, in INC tracing, new objects are created unmarked. This may significantly reduce the floating garbage for common applications that create lots of short-lived objects.

Although INC tracing needs additional round of correct tracing, it does not mean INC tracing has to incur more pauses, because less floating garbage helps the collection throughput, thus defers triggering the next collection.

16.2.3 Concurrent Tracing in Tricolor Terminology

Now, we discuss the concurrent tracing in another angle.

After collectors traverse part of the graph G, say, ΔG of G has been scanned, and the other part, $(G - \Delta G)$, has not. When mutators write the heap and change the structure of G, it has two potential effects.

1. It may make some already-scanned objects (in ΔG) dead thus retained as floating garbage.

2. It may also make some unscanned objects in $(G - \Delta G)$ only connect to the scanned objects in ΔG while losing their original connections in $(G - \Delta G)$.

The first case will not cause any correctness issues, while the second case may do. The second case is shown in Figure 16.7 below.

Using tricolor terminology, the scanned objects are black in ΔG, the unscanned objects are white in $(G - \Delta G)$, and the objects on the border (wave-front of the tracing process) are gray. Gray objects are referenced by black objects but not yet scanned. In other words,

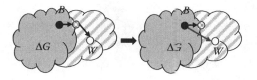

FIGURE 16.7   A potentially lost object during concurrent tracing.

the gray objects are known reachable, but their referenced objects are unknown yet. There is no reference directly from black object to white object.

Assuming a reachable white object W is connected in $(G - \Delta G)$, it is pointed by a reference in slot S of a gray object or a white object. If a mutator reads the reference to object W from slot S, installs it into a black object B, and overwrites the original slot S with another value, then the mutator creates an edge from a black object to a white object. The operations causing the changes in Figure 16.7 are like below:

```
1:      a = *S;     //S contains reference pointing to W
2:      B.f = a;    //the reference to W is written to B
3:      *S = b;     //the original reference in S is overwritten
```

The reachable object W might be lost if without SATB or INC write-barrier, because the already-scanned object B will not be rescanned.

With SATB write-barrier, the original reference to object W is caught when the original slot S is overwritten.

With INC design, the situation is a little different. Since INC only remembers the newly written references, rather than the original overwritten references, it should catch the new edges (shown in double-line arrow in Figure 16.7).

With INC design, the cause of the potentially lost objects comes from three sources:

- Case 1. Objects originally reachable in $(G - \Delta G)$ are now only reachable from already-scanned objects in ΔG. These objects are tracked by INC write-barrier.

- Case 2. Objects originally reachable in $(G - \Delta G)$ are now only reachable from non-heap locations such as runtime stacks, registers, and so on. These locations are where root-set is located and not tracked by write-barrier.

- Case 3. New objects created after INC tracing starts are now only reachable from the already-scanned objects in ΔG or from nonheap locations. This case is covered by case 1 and 2 above.

Based on this observation, the second-round tracing is necessary for INC design. The second-round tracing should trace the object connection graph from the remembered set (for case 1) and root-set (for case 2). Actually, the nonheap locations can be regarded as a virtual object that is constantly updated by the mutators.

16.2.4 Concurrent Tracing with Read-Barrier

Concurrent heap tracing can be done with read-barrier as well. For example, whenever a reference is loaded into a mutator's execution context, it is pushed into mark stack for tracing if the referenced object is not marked yet. At the same time, collectors concurrently trace the heap by pushing root references to the mark stack. This design does not need to remember the old reference values that are overwritten by mutators as SATB does, because

- If the overwritten reference is the only path to an object, the overwriting makes the object dead, hence no need to remember it;

- If there is other path to the object from the root-set, it will be reached by a collector;

- If the overwritten reference was the only path and the mutator installs the reference to somewhere else (runtime stack, register, a marked object, or unmarked object), the read-barrier can catch it.

This seems to be a much simpler solution than the write-barrier-based solutions. The problem is read-barrier for every reference access brings too much overhead. It is seldom used in the actual GC design if only for concurrent heap tracing. But the idea is widely used in concurrent moving-GC, where live objects are moved while mutators are executing. There can be two copies of same object. When a mutator loads an object reference for object read or write, it has to know which copy it should access: the original or the relocated one. Read-barrier then can be very useful to dynamically find the right copy. We will discuss more on it when discussing concurrent moving-GC.

16.3 CONCURRENT ROOT-SET ENUMERATION

In the discussion of concurrent tracing, we have not mentioned how the root-set is enumerated, because concurrent root-set enumeration is a superset of concurrent tracing.

The theory of SATB requires to have a snapshot of root-set. The straightforward way to get its snapshot is to stop the world. That is to suspend the mutators and enumerate the root-set before resuming any mutator. In this way, we consider the whole root-set of all mutators as a virtual object.

When there are many mutators, this STW root-set enumeration can cause obvious application pause. We do not want the enumeration of one mutator to block another mutator. The root-set from one mutator can be regarded as one virtual object, including its runtime stack and registers that can be enumerated independently from other mutators. This is concurrent root-set enumeration.

The GC can suspend the target mutators one by one to take the snapshot of everyone mutator's root-set. When one mutator is suspended, other mutators can keep executing.

The other way is that the GC sets a global flag to indicate that it is time for root-set enumeration, all the mutators respond to the flag by enumerating themselves at a GC safe point and reporting the root-set to the GC. In this case, no thread suspension is needed, but synchronization through flags between mutators and the GC, that is, hand-shaking, is needed.

In both cases (suspension or handshake), the root-set of a mutator is enumerated as a snapshot, or atomically, regarding to the mutator execution. The mutator has to pause its execution for its root-set enumeration. In other words, the mutator does not change its stack or registers when its root-set snapshot is taken. (It is possible to enumerate a mutator's root-set without completely pausing its execution. We will discuss that later.)

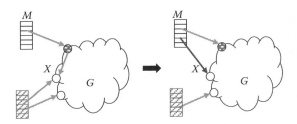

FIGURE 16.8   A potentially lost object during concurrent enumeration.

The GC can wait till all the mutators' root sets are got before starting the live object marking. It can also start live object marking at the same time when starting root-set enumeration. We discuss the former case first.

16.3.1 Concurrent Root-Set Enumeration Design

When the GC has the root-set snapshot of mutator M, some other mutators may be in any status of executing application code before or after root-set enumeration or under root-set enumeration.

Similar to tracing the object connection graph, there can be an object X's reference written to the first mutator M's stack after its snapshot has been taken. If there is no reference to object X existing in other locations of the system, that is, heap or other mutators' execution context or global variables, this object X will not be found by the GC, and then considered dead. This is the case similar to what we discussed on object connection graph, as shown in Figure 16.8 below.

In tricolor terminology, a mutator's root-set is always gray before it is enumerated, if we consider it as a virtual object. The reason is root-set is always known reachable while their referenced objects are unknown before root-set is enumerated.

Before the object X's reference is written to M's stack, as a reachable object, it has to be in one or more of the following four states. To avoid losing the reference to object X, concurrent enumeration has to be able to catch the reference in any of the cases.

Case 1. Object X's reference was in the heap, now only exists in mutator M's context.

After mutator M root-set is enumerated and before the GC starts the live object marking, the object field containing reference X is overwritten by other value. The reference can be caught with write-barrier that remembers the old reference value in the updated field, similar to SATB slot-based write-barrier. The pseudocode for write-barrier is the following. "IS_ENUMERATING" is a global flag indicating if the system is under concurrent enumeration.

```
write_barrier_enum_only(Object* src, Object** slot, Object*
new_ref)
{
    old_ref = *slot;
    if( IS_ENUMERATING ){
```

```
            remember(old_ref);
    }
    *slot = new_ref;
}
```

Different from SATB slot-based write-barrier (code shown below), the concurrent enumeration write-barrier does not check if the old referenced object has been marked, because heap tracing is not started yet. That is why it is named `write_barrier_enum_only`(). It only checks if enumeration is started. We will discuss the case when heap tracing is started in later section.

```
write_barrier_slot(Object* src, Object** slot, Object* new_ref)
{
    old_ref = *slot;
    if( !is_marked(old_ref) ){
        remember(old_ref);
    }
    *slot = new_ref;
}
```

In tricolor terminology, to remember a reference is to mark the object gray. If possible, the GC should avoid remembering the same reference more than once.

Case 2. Object X's reference is in a global variable, now only exists in mutator M's context.

Before GC scans the global variable, it is overwritten by other value. The reference can be caught by tracking the old values in global variables as in heap.

Case 3. Object X's reference is in the context (stack or registers) of another mutator N, now only exists in mutator M's context.

Before the snapshot of this mutator N's root-set is taken, mutator N removes reference X from its context. Since Java does not allow a mutator to directly write another mutator's stack, the reference must be written in either heap or global variable before mutator M can read it and write to its stack.

When reference X uses heap for the intermediate transition, it is a new reference value written to the heap, which cannot be caught by the SATB slot-based write-barrier that only catches old values. But this is fine if reference X stays in heap, then it will be scanned by heap tracing since it is live.

If the object containing X becomes unreachable (or if the field containing X is overwritten) and the reference in M's stack is the only copy of X, there is no problem either, since the overwritten references can always be caught by the write-barrier as old values, if the write-barrier execution is atomic.

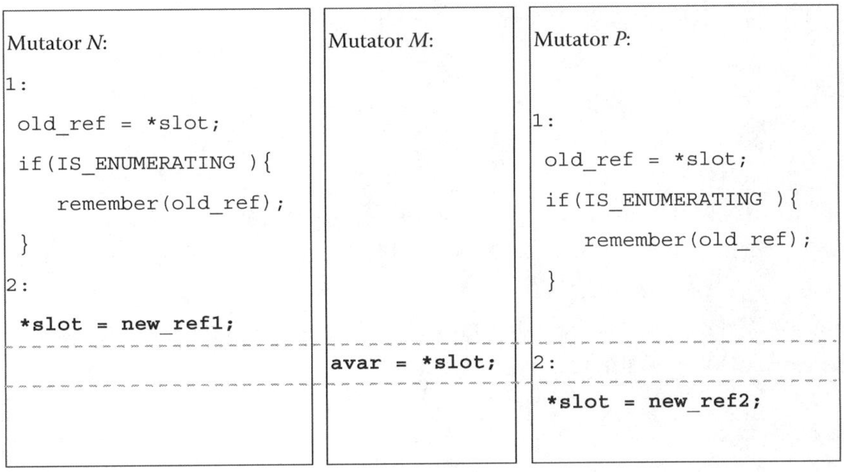

Mutator *N*:	Mutator *M*:	Mutator *P*:

`1:`
 	
`old_ref = *slot;`
 	
`if(IS_ENUMERATING ){`
 	
   `remember(old_ref);`
 	
`}`
 	
`2:`
 	
`*slot = new_ref1;`
		`1:`
		
		`old_ref = *slot;`
		
		`if(IS_ENUMERATING ){`
		
		   `remember(old_ref);`
		
		`}`

	`avar = *slot;`	`2:`
		
		`*slot = new_ref2;`

FIGURE 16.9   Race condition when a reference is missed by write-barrier.

The problem is the slot-based write-barrier is not atomic operation. When two mutators *N* and *P* write to the same object field, their execution of the write-barrier code may be interleaved, as shown in Figure 16.9.

Both mutator *N* and *P* read the same old value in statement 1 and write different new values in statement 2. It is possible that mutator *N* writes reference *X* as the new reference, and then mutator *M* reads reference *X* from heap and writes it to *M*'s stack. Then mutator *P* writes another new reference in the same field overwriting *X*.

In this scenario, mutator *M* installs reference *X* (i.e., `new_ref1`) in its stack, while the write-barrier only remembers `old_ref`.

To avoid this problem, the write-barrier in concurrent enumeration should remember the new reference as well as in INC write-barrier. The pseudocode looks like below.

```
write_barrier_enum_race(Object* src, Object** slot, Object*
new_ref)
{
    old_ref = *slot;
    if( IS_ENUMERATING ){
        remember(old_ref);
        remember(new_ref);
    }
    *slot = new_ref;
}
```

The key reason for the new write-barrier is that, there is no strict "old" or "new" ordering in the heap field writes in multithreaded execution. This is different from SATB write-barrier where the "old value" is accurately defined by the snapshot.

Here the "old value" is defined by heap write ordering: any value in a slot that is overwritten is considered an old value. Object-based SATB write-barrier does not meet the need either, because it only remembers the first time overwritten values in an object, but we need to remember the old values every time when an overwriting happens.

The problem described above in Figure 16.9 happens when two mutators write to same slot. In a race-free application, the problem should never happen.

With `write_barrier_enum_race`, the remember set essentially includes all the reference writes in the heap during the root-set enumeration process with all mutators. Its intention is to remember all the overwritten references that disappear in heap when the full root-set enumeration finishes. The final reference values that stay when root-set enumeration finishes do not need to be remembered, because they can be scanned by the tracing process right after root-set enumeration.

This rule should be applied to the global variables too.

Case 4. Object X is a new object created by mutator M, whose reference now only exists in mutator M's context.

M directly writes reference X in its context after creating the object. This reference can be caught if new object allocation is remembered.

Based on the discussions above, concurrent enumeration is possible. When there is no race condition in object write, that is, write-barrier execution with respect to each other is atomic (or noninterleaved), the write-barrier needs to remember only the overwritten values. Otherwise, both new and old values should be remembered.

To start the tracing process, the GC takes all the root sets together with the remember set caught by write-barrier as a "coherent snapshot of root-set" and then traverses the heap from it using whatever heap tracing algorithm.

16.3.2 Trace Heap during Root-Set Enumeration

If the GC starts traversing the object connection graph once the first mutator's root-set is available, without waiting for all the mutators' root sets ready, then one more case needs to be considered for write-barrier design.

Case 5. Object X's reference is written not to an already-enumerated stack (black stack) but to a marked object (black object).

Before all the root sets are available, part of the object connection graph has been marked (i.e., the ΔG in figure below). The situation is the similar to what we discussed in INC concurrent tracing: during concurrent root-set enumeration, the reference of a white object is written in a black object while removed from its original reachable path(s). The difference from the INC discussion is that in INC discussion, a reachable path to the white object must go through a border object (gray object); now with concurrent

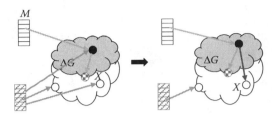

FIGURE 16.10   A potentially lost object when enumeration and tracing are in parallel.

enumeration, a reachable path can also come from an unenumerated stack (virtually gray), as the object X shown in Figure 16.10. By remembering old reference only in heap is not enough to catch this case because here the removed old reference was only in stack.

To avoid losing the object, an INC write-barrier is needed for heap write that remembers the new reference installed in a marked object. Combined with the requirements in cases above, the write barriers have to be a combination of INC (for case 5) and SATB (for case 1), that is, it should remember both old and new references. That is,

```
write_barrier_enum(Object* src, Object** slot, Object* new_ref)
{
    old_ref = *slot;
    if( IS_ENUMERATING ){
        remember(old_ref);
        remember(new_ref);
    }
    *slot = new_ref;
}
```

This write-barrier is the same as the one for case 3 (`write_barrier_enum_race`) while for different reasons. The reason to include INC write-barrier now for cast 5 is that concurrent root-set enumeration does not have a single global snapshot for all the root sets. In other words, it does not take the global root-set snapshot atomically but take every mutator's root-set snapshot separately. Different root sets of the mutators (i.e., virtual gray objects) are scanned (i.e., marked black) separately, which is an incremental process.

As a result, if the GC starts tracing when it has a mutator's root-set, there is no "snapshot" of the object connection graph available. The collectors can only mark the object connection graph "incrementally," hence the INC write-barrier.

To summarize it, `write_barrier_enum_race` wants to catch all the written references except the final ones (that stay live) before the object is scanned, while `write_barrier_enum` wants to catch only the final values (that are potentially lost) after the object is scanned. Their code looks same because there is no way for the write barriers to know when is the "final" write to a slot before all root sets are enumerated. Although the code may look same, the intentions are very different.

In some GC literatures, the root-set enumeration phase is called "marking" phase, while the live object marking phase is called "tracing" phase. In some other literatures, marking phase includes both root-set enumeration and live object marking. Using marking phase to include both is convenient in the case when root-set enumeration and heap tracing are allowed to conduct simultaneously as in case 5, where there is no clear-cut boundary between root-set enumeration and heap tracing. We do not strictly define the term usage in our text but clarify the actual meaning of the terms in their using contexts.

There are some implementations of concurrent root-set enumeration available from the community. When applied with concurrent heap tracing, the design is called on-the-fly GC or sliding-view GC in literatures.

16.3.3 Concurrent Stack Scanning

Concurrent root-set enumeration treats the root-set of each mutator separately, rather than atomically for all mutators in STW design. The granularity in concurrent root-set enumeration is single mutator's execution context. Actually, the granularity can be even smaller.

A mutator's root-set locates in its runtime stack and local registers. In Java semantics, a mutator only actively operates on the top frame of the stack and with registers. The rest of the stack frames are stable. With this observation, it is possible to treat the stack frames separately in enumeration. For example, the collectors can enumerate the stack from bottom up till the top frame is met where the mutator is actively operating. The top frame and the registers will be enumerated by the mutator itself. Since the purpose is to have a snapshot of the stack, when the mutator finishes enumerating the top frame, the snapshot is achieved together with the frames enumerated by collectors. In this design, the interrupt of the mutator execution is to enumerate the top frame and registers, whose duration can be shorter than that of enumerating the whole stack. Some other solution suggests to enumerate the stack in a top-down direction.

Since mutator keeps operating on the stack, the key in concurrent stack enumeration is to synchronize the operations between the mutator and collectors. One solution is to protect the memory pages of the stack except the first page where stack top stays. The collectors are designed to be able to process the memory-protected stack pages without worrying about the racing with the mutator's execution. Whenever there is a write to the protected page by the mutator, a page fault is trapped and then the fault handler can scan the frame where the faulting page stays. This solution virtually installs a write-barrier to stack access.

The other solution is to use "return barrier." Return barrier is a piece of VM code that is executed by a mutator when it returns from a method to the caller method. In machine code, return address is the first instruction in caller method that will be executed after the mutator returns. The return address is usually stored on the stack as the parameter to the return instruction. Return barrier uses its entry point to replace the return address on the stack, so that when the method returns, the control flow goes to the return-barrier code. The return barrier saves the original return address in its context. When it returns, the control flow goes back to the original return target in the caller method.

Return barrier is usually installed at runtime to the stack, so that it only impacts the execution when necessary. The first return barrier can be installed by the mutator because only it has a stable view of the stack. To achieve that the collector can set a flag. When the mutator checks the flag at its GC safe point, it knows the collector's requests for return-barrier installation and then installs one.

16.4 CONCURRENT COLLECTION SCHEDULING

Once all the mutators' root sets are enumerated, the GC continues with the heap tracing stage. Heap tracing could have been started before all root sets are available.

16.4.1 Schedule Concurrent Root-Set Enumeration

The starting set of references for heap tracing is a "coherent view of root-set" that includes all the root sets and the remember set got by the concurrent root-set enumeration. The difference from a root-set snapshot that is got with STW enumeration is that the coherent view of root-set may contain outdated references, hence retaining floating garbage.

The GC can use this coherent view as the starting set for any collection algorithm, even an STW one. That is, after concurrent root-set enumeration finishes with all the mutators, an STW algorithm can start. Depending on the design, the STW algorithm can be moving or nonmoving, parallel, or sequential. The progress looks like Figure 16.11 below.

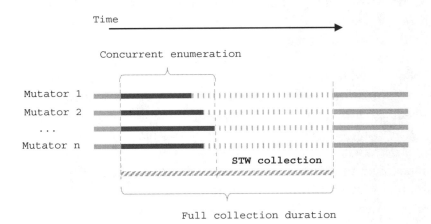

FIGURE 16.11   Concurrent root-set enumeration and stop-the-world (STW) collection.

The interaction between mutators and GC need synchronization protocol or handshake.

The pseudocode in GC is like the following. The global flag gc_phase and thread-local flag enumeration_done are the interaction flags.

```
void garbage_collection(){
    // GC starts a new round collection from root-set enumeration
    // GC turns on enumeration write-barrier code
    gc_phase = IS_ENUMERATING;
    // GC waits for enumeration done by all mutators
    for(every mutator t){
        while( !t->enumeration_done )
```

```
          thread_yield();
    }
    // All mutators suspends themselves
    // GC turns off enumeration write-barrier code
    gc_phase = IS_TRACING;
    gc_stw_collection();
    // GC finishes collection
    gc_phase = IS_IDLE;
    gc_resume_mutators();
    }
```

Before a mutator reaches a GC safe point, it executes the write-barrier as expected. When it reaches a safe point, the mutator enumerates its root-set and suspends itself for STW collection. The pseudocode in mutator's GC safe point is like the following:

```
void vm_safepoint(){
    VM_Thread* self = current_thread();
    // Mutator checks if it is time for root-set enumeration
    if( gc_phase == IS_ENUMERATING ){
        // Mutator enumerates its root-set and reports to GC
        mutator_enumerate_rootset();
        self->enumeration_done = TRUE;
        // Mutator suspends itself waiting for GC resumption
        mutator_suspend();
        self->enumeration_done = FALSE;
    }
}
```

In actual implementation, it is common to follow root-set enumeration with concurrent tracing, which can be a pure live object marking phase or include also object moving. In this chapter, we focus on nonmoving GC and leave the case of object moving to next chapter.

16.4.2 Schedule Concurrent Heap Tracing

To connect concurrent root-set enumeration with concurrent heap tracing, the mutators do not need suspend themselves after enumerating root sets. After the concurrent tracing, the mutators may suspend, for example, for a parallel compaction, or the mutators can continue with concurrent sweeping phase to accomplish a fully concurrent collection.

The collection progress with concurrent heap tracing may look like Figure 16.12, when using an STW recycling phase.

To implement the collection with concurrent enumeration and concurrent tracing, the write-barrier needs to support both. The following pseudocode gives a sketch of the collection code, mutator GC safe point, and write-barrier.

The collection code uses a collection phase flag (including its global and thread-local variables) to indicate the phases and also serve for thread interactions. The function

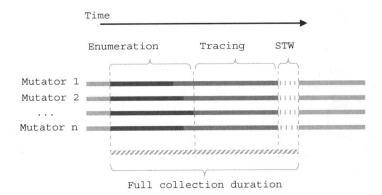

FIGURE 16.12   Concurrent root-set enumeration and heap tracing.

gc_wait_mutators() waits for all the mutators to reach the same collection global phase as a barrier before moving on.

```
void garbage_collection()
{
    // GC starts a new round collection from root-set enumeration
    // GC turns on concurrent enumeration write-barrier code
    global_gc_phase = IS_ENUMERATING;
    gc_wait_mutators();
    // All mutators have finished root-set enumeration
    // GC turns on concurrent marking write-barrier code
    global_gc_phase = IS_TRACING;
    gc_trace_heap();
    //GC finishes tracing, starts recycling
    global_gc_phase = IS_RECYCLING;
    gc_wait_mutators();
    //All mutators are suspended
    gc_stw_collection();
    // GC finishes collection
    global_gc_phase = IS_IDLE;
    gc_resume_mutators();
}
```

The GC safe-point code invoked by mutators implements the handshake protocols between mutators and collectors, including the collection phase flag setting, and required operations like root-set enumeration and thread suspension.

```
void vm_safepoint()
{
        VM_Thread* self = current_thread();
        // Mutator checks if global gc phase changes
        if( global_gc_phase != self->gc_phase ){
            if (global_gc_phase == IS_ENUMERATING){
                mutator_enumerate_rootset();
```

```
      }else if(global_gc_phase == IS_RECYCLING){
          self->gc_phase = global_gc_phase;
          mutator_suspend();
      }

      self->gc_phase = global_gc_phase;
    }
}
```

The write-barrier code supports both concurrent root-set enumeration and SATB tracing. It checks the collection phase flag. If it is in enumeration phase, write-barrier remembers both old and new references. If it is in tracing phase, write-barrier remembers only old value. The key in the design is that, when the collection phase transitions from enumeration to tracing, all the mutators' root-set enumerations have finished, so that write-barrier does not miss any new reference that is only remembered during enumeration phase.

```
void write_barrier_enum_slot(Object* src, Object** slot, Object*
new_ref)
{
    old_ref = *slot;
    if( gc_global_phase == IS_ENUMERATING ){
        remember(old_ref);
        remember(new_ref);
    }else if( gc_global_phase == IS_TRACING ){
        remember(old_ref);
    }

    *slot = new_ref;

}
```

Now that heap tracing is started, it is good to check if the referenced object is marked before remembering it, so as to reduce the number of remembered references. In tricolor terminology, when an object is scanned, it is black. If it is remembered (or pushed to mark stack), it is gray. Otherwise, it is white. Write-barrier does not want to remember the objects that have been either scanned or remembered. So the remember() function can be implemented in the following code:

```
void remember(Object* src)
{
    if( obj_is_white(src)){
        enqueue(src);
        obj_set_gray(src);
    }
}
```

The write-barrier code can be rearranged in the following way, where the old value and new value are remembered in different conditions.

```
void write_barrier_enum_slot(Object* src, Object** slot, Object*
new_ref)
{
    old_ref = *slot;
    if( gc_global_phase == IS_ENUMERATING ||
            gc_global_phase == IS_TRACING){
        remember(old_ref);
    }

    if( gc_global_phase == IS_ENUMERATING ){
        remember(new_ref);
    }

    *slot = new_ref;

}
```

Based on this new code arrangement, the slot-based write-barrier above can be substituted with object-based write-barrier for the same goal.

```
void write_barrier_enum_object(Object* src, Object** slot, Object*
new_ref)
{
    if( gc_global_phase == IS_ENUMERATING ||
            gc_global_phase == IS_TRACING){
        if( !is_marked(src) && is_clean(src) ){
            remember(snapshot of src); //remember all references
            dirty(src);
        }
    }

    if( gc_global_phase == IS_ENUMERATING ){
        remember(new_ref);
    }

    *slot = new_ref;

}
```

The write barriers above only support SATB tracing. To support INC tracing, the write-barrier should remember new reference values or dirty the modified objects for GC rescanning. We will not give all the details here.

16.4.3 Concurrent Collection Scheduling

The logics given above can be extended to support various concurrent GC designs while it does not mention how a collection is triggered. It is understood that VM should trigger GC as rarely as possible since collection consumes system resources like processor cycles and memory. Even if there is enough free central processing units (CPUs) and dynamic random-access memory (DRAM) banks in the system, GC still impacts mutators' execution due to GC safe-point, write-barrier, read-barrier, return barrier, synchronization with collectors, and so on that are conducted by the mutators. There is research work trying to turn GC to be beneficial to the application's execution rather than be only overhead, for example, by improving data locality by laying out live objects in collection. But overall, GC is still a tradeoff for better safety, portability, and productivity. For this reason, VM expects to trigger a collection as late as possible.

On the other hand, a collection may not want to be triggered too late. One reason is, as what we have discussed in adaptive collection, sometimes triggering a collection earlier can achieve better throughput or shorter pause time. The other reason is specifically for concurrent collection where mutators execute in parallel with collection. In this case, new objects keep being created and consume more heap space. The heap may become full before the concurrent collection recycles enough space for mutator's object allocations. Then the mutators have to be blocked waiting for the collection to free up enough memory. It effectively turns the concurrent collection to an STW collection, which is contrary to the design goal.

In an ideal case, a collection is triggered so that, when it finishes identifying all the dead objects, the allocation space becomes full. That means right before the mutators cannot allocate new objects due to inadequate free space, GC is able to find new free space.

Assuming the collection time is `Time_collection`, and mutators allocate objects at speed of `Rate_allocation`, then the total size of objects allocated during collection is:

```
Size_allocation = Time_collection * Rate_allocation
```

This means if the mutators do not want to pause due to out of free space, a collection has to start when the free space size is still more than or equal to size `Size_allocation`.

Collection is normally triggered by a mutator when it allocates object, because the heap consumption status only changes by new object allocation. In an STW setting, the mutator only needs to trigger a collection when it fails to allocate object. For concurrent collection, the mutator may trigger a collection with the free space size is no less than `Size_allocation`.

To compute free space size in every allocation can be expensive, especially when there are many mutators. The other way is to estimate the time point to start collection. If current free space size is `Size_current_free`, the mutator should start collection after duration ΔT:

```
∆T = (Size_current_free - Size_allocation)/Rate_allocation
```

To avoid inaccurate prediction, the mutator can check the free space size again and redo the prediction after duration $\Delta T/2$, in a way of binary approximation.

16.4.4 Concurrent Collection Phase Transitions

When there are multiple mutators, they may trigger collection at the same time. Synchronization is needed to ensure that only one mutator triggers the collection. An actual GC implementation may have multiple collectors that can work in parallel and on-demand. "On-demand" here means that, the number of activated collectors can change dynamically to meet the collection need. For example, if the allocation rate becomes higher, more collectors are needed to catch up. Otherwise, if the allocation rate becomes lower, less collectors are used to reduce system burden.

To coordinate the operations of multiple collectors and mutators, the mutators do not only trigger collection but trap into the collection scheduler that schedules all the phases' transitions. So the pseudocode may look like below.

```
Object_header* gc_mutator_alloc(int size, Vtable_header* vt)
{
  //check the expected type of next collection
  if( collection_is_concurrent() ){
     gc_schedule_collection();
  }
  //normal allocation logic
  ...
}


void gc_schedule_collection()
{
  switch (global_gc_phase){
    case GC_IDLE:
      bool should_start = gc_check_start_condition();
      if( !should_start ) return FALSE;
      //all mutators try to transition the phase, only one succeeds
      bool state = gc_phase_transition(GC_ENUM_START);
      if( !state ) return;
      //only one mutator comes here
      gc_start_enum(); //install write-barrier and enum functions
      break;

    case GC_ENUM_DONE:
      bool state = gc_phase_transition(GC_TRACE_START);
      if( !state ) return;
      //only one mutator comes here
      gc_start_trace(); //launch multiple collectors
      break;

    case GC_TRACE_DONE:
      bool state = gc_phase_transition(GC_SWEEP_START);
```

```
    if( !state ) return;
    //only one mutator comes here
    gc_start_sweep(); //trigger lazy sweep or start sweeping
    break;

  //other state transitions
    ...

  } //end of switch

}

bool gc_phase_transition(GC_Phase next)
{
    GC_Phase old = global_gc_phase;
    GC_Phase curr = CompareExchange(&global_gc_phase, old, next);
    return (old == curr);
}
```

In this design, every mutator can trap into the collection scheduler code. Normally only one of them drives the state transitions and conducts corresponding pre- and postoperations. For example, when the global GC phase reaches GC_ENUM_DONE, one mutator will transition the stage to GC_TRACE_START and then launches multiple collectors on demand for concurrent heap tracing. All the collectors are started by the scheduler, and they synchronize with each other to accomplish the assigned tasks. When they finish the tasks, the global GC state is changed to next phase.

Based on the discussion above, the work flow for a fully concurrent mark-sweep collection may look like Figure 16.13 below.

The states in Figure 16.13 are the following:

- State 1: collection idle;

- State 2: enumeration;

- State 3: heap tracing;

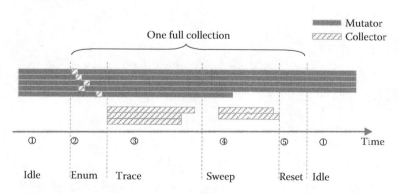

FIGURE 16.13 Garbage collection (GC) phases in a fully concurrent mark-sweep collection.

- State 4: heap sweeping;

- State 5: collection wrap-up;

Since the collection scheduler is unlikely to always avoid STW collection, we also have an additional state for STW collection:

- State 6: STW collection.

To support the state transitions, following phases can be defined:

```
enum GC_Phase{
  GC_IDLE;
  GC_ENUM_START;
  GC_ENUM_DONE;
  GC_TRACE_START;
  GC_TRACE_DONE;
  GC_SWEEP_START;
  GC_SWEEP_DONE;
  GC_RESET;
  GC_STW
}
```

The state transition flow is given in Figure 16.14. Since there are multiple collectors, it is convenient to allow the collectors to change the global state to indicate they all have done the assigned job. For example, TRACE_DONE and SWEEP_DONE are transitioned

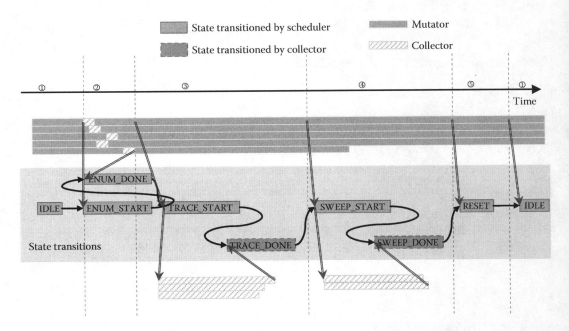

FIGURE 16.14 Garbage collection (GC) phases transition in a fully concurrent mark-sweep collection.

by collectors to their respective next phase. When the collection scheduler detects the change, it transitions the phase again to next phase and may launch another round of multiple collectors. There is no collector running in the duration between collector's transition and mutator's transition. In actual implementation, the design may allow one collector to run at that time. This is useful that gives GC a period for single-threaded operations.

There is a state that does not show up in the flow graph, that is, GC_STW, which is used for STW collection. Note even if a collection is started as a concurrent collection, it may have to transition into STW state if the collection cannot finish before the heap space is run out. On the other hand, a flexible GC design should allow the user to specify which stage to be concurrent or STW. In both cases, the scheduler should be able to transition a collection to STW. The state transition graph among all the phases is given in Figure 16.15:

The explanations to the transitions are:

- ①→① Heap has enough free space, hence no need to trigger a collection.

- ①→② It is time to trigger a concurrent root-set enumeration.

- ①→⑥ It is time to trigger an STW collection.

- ②→③ Concurrent enumeration is done. Collection transitions to concurrent heap tracing.

- ②→⑥ Heap becomes full, or concurrent enumeration is done; collection transitions to STW heap tracing.

- ③→④ Concurrent tracing is done. Collection transitions to concurrent sweeping.

- ③→⑤ Concurrent tracing is done. Collection transitions to wrap up for lazy sweeping.

- ③→⑥ Concurrent tracing is done. Collection transitions to STW collection, such as compaction.

- ④→⑤ Concurrent sweeping is done. Collection transitions to wrap up.

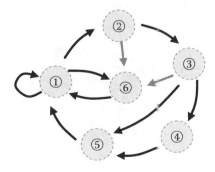

FIGURE 16.15   State transition graph of a garbage collection (GC) design.

- ⑤→① GC finishes concurrent collection, returns to idle.

- ⑥→① GC finishes STW collection, returns to idle.

For concurrent collection, termination process is not as obvious as STW collection because it may have multiple data structures that contain tasks at the same time. All of them should be cleaned up. The actual design depends on the data structures and threading design that we do not discuss here.

CHAPTER 17

Concurrent Moving Collection

A S WE HAVE SEEN the benefit of moving garbage collection (GC), it is desirable to allow concurrent moving collection, that is, moving live objects when mutators are executing. The challenges to support concurrent object moving are mainly the followings:

- **Racing access by the collector and the mutator:** When an object is moved by a collector, it might be accessed by mutators. Protocol is needed to ensure object data's consistence.

- **Reference-fixing:** When an object is moved, there may be references pointing to its old location. These references should be fixed to point to the new location.

- **Termination:** As in the discussion of concurrent heap tracing, concurrent moving algorithm needs to guarantee its termination in a timely fashion.

For a copying-GC, some free space is needed to move live objects into. We call the free space "to-space," and the recycled space "from-space." The free space can be reserved before the collection happens or be produced during the collection by evacuating nonfree space. For example, a semispace reserves half heap for copying collection. In-place compaction does not reserve free space, but it has to traverse the heap first to find the live objects. Then it knows where the free space is to move in the live objects. We will discuss concurrent copying GC first and then compacting GC.

17.1 CONCURRENT COPYING: "TO-SPACE INVARIANT"

When root-set is known, a copying collection starts to copy the reachable objects to the free space. Once an object is copied, a forwarding pointer is installed in the original object header, or in a target-table, so as to map the addresses between the original copy and the new one. Then the first question is how to deal with the root-set references. During a stop-the-world (STW) collection, all the root references are fixed to point to the new copies before the mutators are resumed. If GC wants to copy the objects concurrently when the mutators are executing, the question is, should the mutators be able to see only new copies, or old copies, or both? Different answers to the question lead to different solutions.

17.1.1 Slot-Based "To-Space Invariant"

One solution allows the mutators to see only the new copies. This is called "to-space invariant."

17.1.1.1 Flipping Phase of "To-Space Invariant"

The first phase of a collection in this design is similar to an STW copying collection. That is, during root-set enumeration, the mutators are suspended. All the objects that are directly reachable from root-set are copied to to-space, and the root references are updated to point to the new copies. Different from traditional copying collection, the STW phase finishes here in concurrent copying collection. It leaves the system in a state that all the mutators see only objects in to-space, while all the rest live objects are still in from-space. All the references in heap objects point to the objects in from-space, including those references in the new copies in to-space. At the moment, all the mutators are resumed to continue execution.

The pseudocode for the process described above is given below.

```
void concurrent_copying_to()
{
    gc_suspend_mutators();
    Set* rootset = gc_enumerate_rootset();
    for( each slot in rootset ){
        Object* obj = *slot;
        *slot = obj_forward(obj);
    }
    gc_resume_mutators();
    //collection work below is in parallel with mutation
    ...
}
```

The process of the STW phase is illustrated in Figure 17.1.

This phase is usually called "flipping" step because it flips all the root references from pointing to from-space to to-space.

17.1.1.2 Copying Phase of "To-Space Invariant"

After mutators are resumed, when a mutator loads an object field F in to-space that contains a reference R, it checks if the reference points to from-space. The checking result can be following cases:

Case 1. If the referenced object is in from-space and has been copied to to-space, the mutator needs to do the following:

1. Load the forwarding-pointer P

2. Replace the old reference R in F with P

3. Finally, use the reference P in execution context instead of R

Before collection:

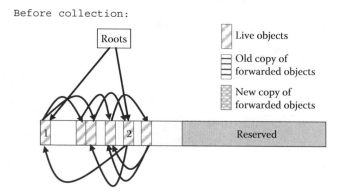

After the STW phase of collection:

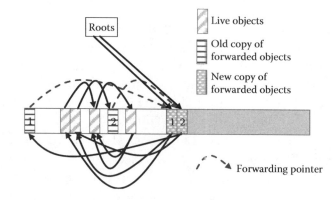

FIGURE 17.1   Concurrent copying collection before and after the stop-the world (STW) phase.

Case 2. If the referenced object is in from-space and not copied, the mutator needs to do following operations:

1. Copy the R referenced object to to-space, say at new location P

2. Install the forwarding-pointer P in the old copy in from-space

3. Replace the old reference R in F with P

4. Finally, use the reference P in execution context instead of R

Case 3. If the reference points to to-space, the mutator does nothing

These operations are implemented by GC as "read-barrier" that is executed when a mutator loads a reference into its execution context. Read-barrier ensures that there is no reference in its context pointing to from-space. After the reference is loaded in its context, the mutator can then read or write the referenced object in to-space. In this way, the design maintains "to-space invariant." This design was firstly proposed by Baker, and lots of other concurrent moving algorithms may trace back to his original work. The pseudocode of read-barrier for "to-space invariant" is given below.

```
// read-barrier on loading ref in "slot" of object "src"
Object* read_barrier_slot(Object* src, Object** slot)
{
    Object* obj = *slot;
    if( in_from_space(obj) ){
        if( !is_forwarded(obj) ){
            obj_forward(obj);
        }
        obj = forwarding_pointer(obj);
        *slot = obj;
    }
    return obj;
}
```

The read-barrier is executed when a mutator loads reference field "slot" of object "src." Object "src" is in to-space. The read-barrier is not only for object data read but also for write. In some literature, this kind of barrier is called "load-barrier," referring to the fact that the barrier is executed whenever a reference is loaded into mutator's execution context. The read-barrier code above is slot based, since it loads the reference from a slot.

If live objects are only copied by read-barrier, the collection may take too long time or never terminate. The reason is some live objects are not accessed by mutators soon enough after the collection starts. They do not get chance to be copied to to-space. Since the root-set is known to GC, it is possible for the collectors to trace and forward all the reachable objects to to-space, in parallel with the mutators.

When mutators are resumed, collectors can at the same time traverse the heap and forward all the references. The operations of a collector loading a reference are the same as a mutator does with read-barrier. The difference is mutators load references for program execution, while collectors load references to trigger object forwarding or reference-fixing.

However, the mutators can do more collection work if that is desirable. For example, the mutators can piggyback a few objects scanning to every object allocation. Every read-barrier can also push a reference to mark-stack that points to an unmarked object so as to accelerate heap tracing, as code shows below.

```
Object* read_barrier_slot(Object* src, Object** slot)
{
    Object* obj = *slot;
    if( in_from_space(obj) ){
        if( !is_forwarded(obj) ){
            obj_forward(obj);
        }
        obj = forwarding_pointer(obj);
        *slot = obj;
    }
```

```
    if( !is_marked(obj) ){
        remember(obj);
    }
    return obj;
}
```

17.1.2 "To-Space Invariant" Properties

As a comparison to concurrent heap tracing, the "to-space invariant" concurrent copying seems to be similar to snapshot-at-the-beginning (SATB) algorithm. A deeper look reveals that they are different because "to-space invariant" does not maintain the "snapshot invariant" as SATB does. In STAB design, write-barrier is needed to remember old reference values that are overwritten, so as to maintain the "snapshot" of object connection graph, hence the correctness. The reason is the overwritten reference may point to a white object. After it is overwritten, the reference may be stored in a black object or runtime stack that will not be scanned again. Although the referenced object is still reachable, GC cannot find it.

In "to-space invariant" copying collection, the objects in to-space are either black (i.e., all the object's references have been loaded and forwarded) or gray (i.e., not all its references have been forwarded). The objects in from-space are white. Whenever a reference to a white object is loaded, the object will be forwarded (i.e., grayed). It is impossible to install a reference to a white object into a black object or runtime stack. In other words, the read-barrier semantics have guaranteed the correctness of the design.

One may wonder why it is possible to install a white pointer to a black object in SATB and INC (incremental-update) design. The reason is they do not use read-barrier, thus cannot catch all loaded references. Especially, a reference to a white object can be loaded by a mutator by following the reference chain, with only object reading. The mutator then installs the white pointer to its runtime stack or a black object. SATB write-barrier cannot catch either case, and INC write-barrier cannot catch the case of writing to runtime stack.

The key reason for the difference is that the read-barrier in "to-space invariant" design uses "mutator access" to decide an object's aliveness. Accessed objects are surely live, and a live object will sooner or later be accessed (since never-accessed live objects can be considered dead), which is actually a stricter definition of object aliveness than reachability. The read-barrier does not depend on a separate reachability analysis, hence avoid the most common problem in concurrent collection design, where the object connection graph is changing. Or in other words, the changes of object graph themselves are introduced by mutators. There is no race condition between the mutator's read-barrier execution and its self's application execution. Reachability analysis and object graph mutation are inherently the same procedure. Loaded reference is live reference. A copied object may become dead before the collection finishes, but it is surely live when copied.

When concurrent collector is used besides the read-barrier, the situation is a little bit different. If the collectors trace the heap (hence forwarding the reachable objects) faster than mutators' accesses, that is, collectors copy objects before they are accessed by mutators, all the copied objects are then the same as those marked in an STW heap tracing. No live object is lost, even if some of them may become dead after a while.

If mutators access some objects before collectors copy them, the mutators may write to them and overwrite some references pointing to white objects in from-space. This may cause some of those white objects unreachable if they have no other reachable path. Although they are part of the STW snapshot, they are not forwarded, since they are no longer live now. The faster the mutators access references to the objects in from-space (compared to the speed of collectors tracing wave front), the less floating garbage will be retained by the collectors.

In other words, when the collectors push forward the tracing wave front, the mutators effectively cut some paths from the wave front to the white objects (i.e., from-space). The collectors take the current wave front (i.e., gray objects) as the current "new roots" and try to get a snapshot starting from them in the remaining part of object connection graph (i.e., objects in from-space), as illustrated in Figure 17.2 below. We call the snapshot reachable from the wave front a "wave-front snapshot."

In the figure, the arrows under crosses are cut by mutators. The current snapshot does not include those white objects that are no longer reachable, although they were part of the wave-front snapshot before the mutators writes. In a "to-space invariant" collection, along with mutators' execution, the current wave-front snapshot becomes smaller and smaller.

As part of the "to-space invariant," new objects should be put in to-space since they are allocated (hence accessed) by mutators. This is similar to SATB design. Looked from another angle, it is necessary to treat new objects as alive. In extreme case, as we already knew, "to-space invariant" design achieves the same result as STW snapshot, where new objects are not part of the snapshot of object connection graph. New objects do not need to be scanned because any reference written into new objects must be caught by read-barrier.

When comparing the equality of two object references, mutator can do that directly because it only loads the reference to to-space, and the references to same object are always identical.

Termination is not a problem for "to-space invariant" collection, since the size of from-space is fixed when a collection starts. From graph traversal point of view, the collection converges faster than STW collection since the remaining snapshot monotonically becomes smaller.

1.Remaining snapshot   2. Mutator writes   3. Current snapshot

FIGURE 17.2   Collaboration between mutators and collectors in "to-space invariant" collection.

17.1.3 Object Forwarding

When multiple threads, no matter if they are mutators or collectors, access same object, there is no problem as long as the copying is only committed by one thread. When a thread tries to forward an object and finds the object is under copying by another thread, it waits for the copying to finish, then accesses the data. The pseudocode for object forwarding is given below. It uses atomic operation to ensure only one thread forwards the object. This routine is used by both mutator and collector threads.

```
//last two bits of object header are reserved for forwarding
//object address always aligned at 4 (i.e., last two bits are 0s)
#define FORWARDING_BIT 0x1
#define FORWARDED_BIT  0x2
#define FORWARD_BITS (FORWARDING_BIT | FORWARDED_BIT)

Object* obj_forward(Object* obj)
{
    Obj_header header = obj_header(obj);
    if( !(header & FORWARD_BITS) ) {
        // the object is not forwarded or under forwarding
        // lock the FORWARDING_BIT in object header
        bool success = lock_forwarding(obj);
        if( success ){
            //successfully locked the object
            //copy the object to new addr
            Object* new = obj_copy(obj);
            //install forwarding pointer
            header = new | FORWARD_BITS;
            obj_set_header(obj, header);
            unlock_forwarding(obj);
            return new;
        }
    }
    // forwarded or under forwarding by other thread
    // spin waiting for the copying to finish
    while( !is_forwarded(obj) ) pause();
    obj = forwarding_pointer(obj);
    return obj;
}

bool is_forwarded(Object* obj)
{
    Obj_header header = obj_header(obj);
    return (header & FORWARDED_BIT);
}
```

```
Object* forwarding_pointer(Object* obj)
{
    Obj_header header = obj_header(obj);
    return (Object*)(header & ~FORWARD_BITS);
}


bool is_under_forwarding(Object* obj)
{
    Obj_header header = obj_header(obj);
    return (header & FORWARDING_BIT);
}


bool lock_forwarding(Object* obj)
{
    Object_header* p_header = obj_header_addr(obj);
    // set FORWARDING_BIT bit to 1, and return !original_value
    return atomic_testset(p_header, FORWARDING_BIT)
}


void unlock_forwarding(Object* obj)
{
    Obj_header header = obj_header(obj);
    obj_set_header(obj, header & ~FORWARDING_BIT);

}
```

17.1.4 Object-Based "To-Space Invariant"

In the slot-based read-barrier above, it checks if the loaded reference is in from-space, while it does not check if the object containing the reference is already scanned. If it has been scanned, all its reference fields have been forwarded, hence no need to further check any of its contained references. This requires GC to mark the scanned objects. The code of read-barrier with the additional check (in bold face) is as follows.

```
// read-barrier on loading ref in "slot" of object "src"
Object* read_barrier_slot(Object* src, Object** slot)
{
    if( is_marked(src) ){
        return *slot;
    }
    Object* obj = *slot;
    if( in_from_space(obj) ){
        if( !is_forwarded(obj) ){
            obj_forward(obj);
        }
        obj = forwarding_pointer(obj);
        *slot = obj;
    }
```

```
    if( !is_marked(obj) ){
        remember(obj);
    }
    return obj;
}
```

With this read-barrier, if the collectors run faster and mark most of the objects before mutators accesses them, most read-barrier executions will be much light weighted. However, if
the collectors run slower, the additional checking become mostly redundant since is_
marked(src) often returns FALSE. The root cause is slot-based read-barrier updates at
most one slot every time. It does not mark an object as scanned, because it does not know
when an object has all its reference slots updated. In other words, slot-based read-barrier
may only change an object's color from white to gray but never from gray to black.

To facilitate the design, read-barrier can be revised to scan an object and forward all its
contained references, not only the loaded reference. In this way, a mutator can turn an object
from white to black directly, thus marks it. Then even if the collectors run slower, there are
still chances for is_marked(src) to return TRUE, resulting with the light-weighted read-
barrier execution. The pseudocode for object-based read-barrier is the following:

```
// read-barrier on loading ref in "slot" of object "src"
Object* read_barrier_object(Object* src, Object** slot)
{
    if( is_marked(src) ){
        return *slot;
    }
    // turns object "src" from gray to black
    for(each reference field p_ref of src){
        Object* ref = *p_ref;
        *p_ref = obj_forward(ref);
    }
    mark(src);
    return *slot;
}
```

With the object-based read-barrier above, when a mutator accesses an object src, it
ensures all the referenced objects by object src are turned to gray and then marks object
src black. Different from slot-based read-barrier that checks status of the referenced
object, object-based read-barrier checks status of the accessed object that contains the
reference.

As we have seen, for "to-space invariant" concurrent copying collection, there are
two variant designs, one with slot-based read-barrier and the other with object-based
read-barrier. We also saw the similar relation in SATB concurrent marking (slot-based
vs. object-based write-barrier), in INC concurrent marking (remember-reference vs.
remember-root write-barrier), in generational GC (card-table vs. remember-set). Again as
before, there is no essential difference between the two variants. They are different ways to

distribute the tasks among all the mutators and collectors, having different implications on the response time of mutators, collection throughput, and heap size consumption.

When multiple mutators and collectors access same object simultaneously, it is possible for all of them to execute the read-barrier code, but every referenced object can only be forwarded once and by one thread. It is guaranteed by the implementation of obj_forward(). The function mark(src) may be executed multiple times by different threads. It has to be an idempotent operation as the obj_forward().

17.1.5 Virtual Memory-Based "To-Space Invariant"

Object-based read-barrier is triggered on every heap slot access, but only has actual effect when the accessed object is not scanned. It is natural, as always, to extend the object-level granularity to page level, so as to leverage operating system's virtual memory support to implement read-barrier. Before a gray object is scanned, the page where it locates is memory protected to be inaccessible. Any access to the page can trigger a page fault, whose handler executes the read-barrier code and scans the object.

Since read-barrier only has effect on gray objects, it is desirable to memory protect the pages that hold only gray objects. In this way, no compiler instrumentation for read-barrier is needed. Appel et al. proposed the first design. The conceptual code is like below.

```
// read-barrier on loading ref in "slot" of object "src"
Object* read_barrier_page(Object* src, Object** slot)
{
    Page* page = page_of_addr(src);
    if( !is_protected(page) ){
        return *slot;
    }
    lock_page_scan(page);
    scan_page(page);
    unlock_page_scan(page);
    return *slot;
}

void scan_page(Page* page)
{
    if( !is_protected(page) ) return;
    // turns page from gray to black
    Object* obj = first_obj_in_page(page);
    while( obj ){
        scan_obj(obj);
        obj = next_obj_in_page(page, obj);
    }
    unprotect(page);
}
```

```
void scan_obj(Object* obj)
{
   if( is_marked(obj) ) return;
   for(each reference field p_ref of obj){
      Object* ref = *p_ref;
      *p_ref = obj_forward(ref);
   }
   mark(obj);
}
```

This barrier is called by page fault handler. The GC function scan_page() is used by both the page fault handler and collectors. Concurrent collectors can scan the gray pages in parallel.

Before a page is scanned, it is locked so that other threads cannot access it. The code scans the protected pages one by one to unprotect them, turning all the objects in them from gray to black. When a page is scanned, all the referenced white objects by the page are forwarded. Function obj_forward() has to be revised to make sure that they are copied into memory-protected pages (becoming gray objects), so that mutators' access to them will trigger page fault.

The code does not show when the pages are protected. When a new page is allocated for object forwarding, it is immediately *protected* and locked before any object is copied into it. The new page is unlocked when the page scanning (that caused the new page allocation) finishes or when the new page is fully used, either coming earlier. The page protection is still on, until itself is scanned.

The copying page is locked because, when a white object is forwarded to the page, a second thread may finish scanning a page that contains a reference to the forwarded object. The second thread then may access the forwarded object, which should trigger a page fault and the fault handler waits on the lock for the first thread to finish the page copying. To summarize it, page locking is for object forwarding, and page protection is for object forwarding and page scanning.

New objects are allocated black in "to-space invariant" collection, so they do not need to be protected. Any reference installed into new objects must point to a to-space object.

Virtual memory-based solution has a benefit that it can provide dynamic call-back opportunities without requiring compiler instrumentation. Nonetheless, there is technical challenge to resolve for the design above. When a mutator accesses a memory-protected page and triggers page fault handler, the GC functions executed in fault handler and/or the collectors should be able to access the same page for page scanning and object forwarding. This can be achieved by either running the GC functions in kernel mode or mapping the same page to different virtual addresses that have different protection privileges. Since memory protection on a page is enforced on virtual address through memory management unit of the processor, same physical page can have different access permissions when it is accessed through different virtual addresses or from different processes. For example, in Linux, one can use shm_open() to create a shared memory object and then maps it twice with different protection privileges.

17.2 CONCURRENT COPYING: "CURRENT-COPY INVARIANT"

In "to-space invariant," read-barrier requires that when a referenced object is in from-space, the mutator has to copy the object to to-space before it continues or blocks waiting for other thread to finish the object copying. This effectively moves the collectors work to mutators. The upside of this design is the neat property that reachability analysis and object graph mutation are inherently the same procedure. But it also has downside by putting the collection's work into mutator's execution.

17.2.1 Object-Moving Storm

The read-barrier of "to-space invariant" has an effect that, when mutators are resumed after the flipping phase of the collection, most of the objects are in from-space and have to be forwarded to the to-space in the initial short execution period. The intensive objects forwarding is called "object-moving storm." The intensive forwarding, considered as part of collection work, may largely reduce the mutators' execution throughput at the beginning. Then the situation gets better when many of the mutator-accessed references are forwarded.

Mutator's execution throughput can be measured by its allocation rate, or other metrics that can indicate how active in average a mutator is. If we use allocate rate to indicate mutator's execution throughput, we may find the rate is very low right after the flipping phase for some applications. The effect of object-moving storm can be so serious that it almost throttles the mutators' execution in a way similar to STW collection, because every mutator access is piggybacked with or blocked by an object forwarding (marking it gray in slot-based design), or an object scanning (marking it black in object-based design), or a page scanning (marking it black in page-based design).

As we mentioned, read-barrier and write-barrier can be regarded as part of collection work that is conducted by mutator. When the work is trivial, like the one for generational GC to collect remember-set, people would consider it as part of mutator activity. When the work is nontrivial, like the one in "to-space invariant" design, it is more considered as part of "incremental collection," rather than just a barrier. When the work becomes significant that almost starves the mutators for a moment, it is likely to be called an STW phase.

For a concurrent GC design, the expectation is to not disturb the mutators' execution as much as possible, leaving collection work to the collectors as much as possible.

17.2.2 "Current-Copy Invariant" Design

To alleviate object-moving storm, a solution is to allow the mutators to access objects in from-space if they are not forwarded and let the collectors to scan and forward objects whenever possible. In this way, read-barrier does not forward the object but load the forwarding pointer if the referenced object is forwarded.

```
Object* read_barrier_current(Object* obj)
{
    if( is_forwarded(obj) )
        obj = forwarding_pointer(obj);

    return obj;
}
```

With this read-barrier instrumented for every object access, the mutators see only the current copy of any object. We call this design "current-copy invariant."

Brooks suggested to always include a forwarding pointer in an object. When the object is forwarded, its forwarding pointer points to the new copy; otherwise, points to the object itself. Then read-barrier does not need to check if the object is forwarded or not but dereference the reference.

With "current-copy invariant," it is the collector's responsibility to forward the objects. Mutators only ensure to access the right copies. Object forwarding is executed in parallel with mutator execution. There can be two copies of the same object in the system at the same time. Before the object is forwarded, the from-space copy is the current copy. After it is forwarded, the to-space copy is current. The read-barrier for "current-copy invariant" ensures that only the current copy is accessed by mutators. Therefore, whenever a mutator accesses an object's data, it has to check if the object is forwarded before the access. For example, when a mutator accesses a field of an object twice successively, the two accesses may conduct on different copies: the first access is on from-space copy and the second access is on to-space copy.

This means read-barrier is needed not only for loading a reference from an object but also for accessing any data of the object. As a comparison, in "to-space invariant" design, once a reference is in mutator's execution context, this reference is known pointing to to-space. When the mutator uses the reference to access the object data, it does not need to check again since the reference is surely in to-space. In "current-copy invariant" design, a reference in mutator's execution context can point to either from-space or to-space.

In "to-space invariant," read-barrier is executed when mutators load a reference R from an object A. The read-barrier does not check if the object A is forwarded but checks the object pointed by reference R. As a comparison, in "current-copy invariant," the read-barrier does exactly the opposite. It checks if the object A is still in from-space or not, but it does not check the loaded reference R. "Current-copy invariant" only ensures the accessed object is current copy, then the object data (here the value R) is current for sure. It does not matter if the reference R points to from-space, since the read-barrier will be able to find the right copy if the R-referenced object is copied.

Based on the discussion, the read-barrier for "current-copy invariant" actually should be an "access-barrier" for both object read and write. Whenever the mutators need to access an object (for read or write), they should only access the current copy. So read_barrier_current() should be access_barrier_current() that is called for object read and write. The conceptual code to use it is given below.

```
Value object_read_current(Object* obj, int field)
{
    obj = access_barrier_current(obj);
    object_read(obj, field);
}

void object_write_current(Object* obj, int field, Value val)
{
    obj = access_barrier_current(obj);
    object_write(obj, field, val);
}
```

The code above is intuitive, but it is problematic with multiple threads, since the object that was in from-space might be copied after the invocation of access_barrier_current(); then the following actual access is on the stale copy. The code only works if object accesses like forwarding, reading, and writing are atomic to each other.

The following code can work in a multithreaded environment.

```
Value read_barrier_current(Object* obj, int field)
{
    Value val = object_read(obj, field);
    if( in_from_space(obj) && is_forwarded(obj) ){
        obj = forwarding_pointer(obj);
        val = object_read(obj, field);
    }
    return val;
}

void write_barrier_current(Object* obj, int field, Value val)
{
    bool fld_is_ref = field_is_ref(field);
    // write current copy's address to field. This is not optional
    if(fld_is_ref && in_from_space(val) && is_forwarded(val))
        val = forwarding_pointer(val)

    if( !in_from_space(obj) ){
        object_write(obj, field, val);
    }else{ //object in from space
        if( !is_forwarded(obj) ){
            bool success = lock_forwarding(obj);
            if( success ){
```

```
            object_write(obj, field, val);
            unlock_forwarding(obj);
            return;
        }else{
            while( !is_forwarded(obj) );
        }
    }
    //object is forwarded
    obj = forwarding_pointer(obj);
    object_write(obj, field, val);
    }
}
```

The read-barrier reads the field first and then checks if the object is forwarded; if it is forwarded, the mutators read the field again from the forwarded copy. The write-barrier is expensive if the current copy is in from-space, since it needs to lock the object preventing the collectors from copying it. Except that, all other cases of both write and read-barrier are cheap. Depending on the application's behavior, this tradeoff probably is worth compared to the object-moving storm.

The locking operation in write-barrier can be avoided by using similar technique as the read-barrier. That is, if the object is not under forwarding or forwarded (i.e., before it is touched by the collector), the mutator writes the field. Then it checks again if the object is under forwarding or forwarded. If yes, the copying may happen before the writing. The mutator will wait for the object to be forwarded and then write again in the forwarded copy. Without locking, the correctness of the operation depends on the memory consistency model. The sequence described above is correct in processor consistency or stronger ones (such as total store order). Huelsbergen and Larus used this technique. We call this solution "lock-free" copying write-barrier and the solution above "lock-based" copying write-barrier.

17.2.3 Concurrent Copying versus Concurrent Heap Tracing
Assuming the object forwarding work is completely invisible to the mutators, a concurrent copying algorithm can be similar to a concurrent nonmoving design. In tricolor terminology, we only need to redefine the meaning of white, gray, and black colors. For example,

1. Live objects in from-space are white.

2. To mark an object gray here means to forward the object.

3. To mark it black means all the reference fields in the new object have been forwarded.

The following Figure 17.3 is an illustration of the idea.

In the figure, both copies of the forwarded objects are shown, with the original copies in semitransparent color at the corresponding locations of from-space.

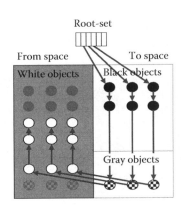

FIGURE 17.3   Similarity between concurrent moving and nonmoving garbage collections (GCs).

17.2.3.1 Concurrent Copying Based on Concurrent Tracing Algorithm

Based on the observation above, it is possible to design concurrent copying algorithm by applying concurrent tracing algorithm, such as the ideas of SATB or INC. This makes sense for "current-copy invariant" concurrent copying. The reason is "current-copy invariant" does not require the mutators to do collection work as "to-space invariant" does. In other words, the mutators in "current-copy invariant" are not involved in reachability analysis (looking for live objects) but only mutating the object connection graph. The collectors conduct the reachability analysis by copying the live objects in background, while the concurrent tracing algorithm works in the same setting and hence applicable.

INC concurrent copying: With the idea of INC algorithm, a write-barrier is needed to catch the reference write in black object that points to white object. It can be remember-reference or remember-root variant.

When it is remember-reference, the write-barrier can directly forward the referenced object so that the object is grayed. When it is remember-root, the black object where the reference is written should be remembered for rescanning.

As in INC concurrent tracing, "INC concurrent copying" has to have a second round of correct copying that rescans root-set and remember-set. If an object is found in from-space in the second round, it will be forwarded and scanned. There can be multiple intermediate rounds of rescanning to reduce the collection time of the final round of correct copying, which can be useful when the round of correct copying is STW.

In this design, new objects can be allocated in from-space as white objects.

STAB concurrent copying: With SATB idea, a write-barrier is needed to catch the overwritten reference in nonblack object that points to white object. It can be slot-based or object-based variant.

If it is slot-based, the write-barrier can directly forward the object pointed by the overwritten reference so that it is grayed. If it is object-based, the nonblack object can be scanned so that all of its referenced objects are grayed. The nonblack object itself is forwarded if not yet and turned black.

Since the total number of white objects (or the snapshot) in from-space is fixed, together with collectors, "STAB concurrent copying" can converge in one pass.

In this design, new objects are allocated in to-space as scanned objects.

17.2.3.2 Correct Design of "Current-Copy Invariant"

From the discussion above, we know there are a few revisions needed to complete the design of "current-copy invariant" GC.

First, the write-barrier `write_barrier_current()` above does not include the code for SATB or INC write-barrier. They can be separately implemented or merged into one write-barrier.

Second, since the mutators can see objects from both spaces, the design should make sure all of the reference values in to-space are updated (to point to to-space) by the end of collection.

"Current-copy invariant" only ensures mutators read and write the data of current copy, which does not require every reference point to the current copy. For example, a reference R to a white object can be written into a black object A. Later, when the white object is forwarded, another reference R' to the new copy (which is now the current copy) may be written into another black object B. Then the black objects (A and B) hold references (R and R') to different copies of same object. Reference R in object A is stale and should be fixed.

In INC design, since the write-barrier ensures all the white references (i.e., references pointing to from-space) written in black objects be caught and the referenced objects are forwarded, the only remaining place that may hold white references is mutators' execution context. The second round of correct tracing will rescan root-set and remember-set to forward and fix all the remaining white references. It is not a problem.

In SATB design, its write-barrier does not catch the white reference writes in black objects as the write-barrier in INC design does. When we say it converges in one pass, we mean that all the white objects in from-space have been forwarded to to-space in one pass. It does not guarantee all the references in mutators' execution context and heap have been fixed. Some of them may point to from-space.

Since "current-copy invariant" write-barrier guarantees to write only the reference of current copy, when the current copies of all the objects are in to-space, the installation of white reference in black object will not happen. These installations can only happen before all the white objects are copied. Since SATB forwards all the white objects in finite time, during this period, the number of those installations is also finite, and hence can be remembered with a revised write-barrier. After SATB converges, those remembered white references can be fixed by the collectors.

But still, as with INC design, there can be white references in mutators' execution context. To complete the design, a round of root-set enumeration is needed to fix those references, which does not need to be STW, because the white reference in a mutator's context cannot escape to other mutators or heap, which is guarded by write-barrier.

The discussion reveals that "current-copy invariant" SATB design needs to remember the white references installed in black objects and needs to rescan root-set, which makes it similar to INC design. In other words, the SATB design probably is not a good choice for "current-copy invariant."

The final revision needed for a correct design is for reference equality check. To compare the equality of two references, a mutator has to check if the referenced object is forwarded. It is possible that the two references point to the different copies of same object. In this case, Brooks' suggestion to always include a forwarding pointer in an object can be useful.

17.3 CONCURRENT COPYING: "FROM-SPACE INVARIANT"

Now we have discussed "to-space invariant" and "current-copy invariant" concurrent copying algorithms. It is natural to consider if it is possible to design a "from-space invariant" concurrent copying-GC. The mutators operate only on from-space objects when the collectors are forwarding the live objects. When all the live objects are forwarded, the roles of from-space and to-space can flip.

This design requires to keep both spaces up to date: one for mutators' current operation and the other for their operation after space flipping. A straightforward idea is to use write-barrier to update both copies of live objects. This idea has an obvious shortcoming compared to the other two copying designs, which only update the current copy. Both of them, the "to-space invariant" and the "current-copy invariant," consider the to-space copy as the current copy. For them, the from-space copy is considered current only if the object is not forwarded.

17.3.1 "From-Space Invariant" Design

In "to-space invariant," the mutators have to be deeply coupled with collection. Every reference loaded into execution context has to be forwarded before the reference becomes visible to the mutator.

In "current-copy invariant," the mutators are less coupled with collection. The object forwarding work can be separated from the mutators' execution path. The mutators just follow the forwarding pointer to access the current copy while synchronization is needed to avoid the race condition between mutators' write and collectors' copy.

"From-space invariant" can further decouple the interaction between mutators and collectors, where mutators never operate on to-space. Starting from root-set, the collectors concurrently trace the heap for live objects and copy them to to-space. A mapping table is setup to map the object addresses from from-space to to-space, which can be a target-table or through forwarding pointers. After the concurrent copying is done, the mutators are suspended again to update the root-set references to point to to-space by following the mapping table. At this moment, the spaces are flipped, and the mutators can be resumed.

17.3.1.1 Write-Barrier for "From-Space Invariant"

When the mutators make changes on any object (i.e., make a mutation) that has been forwarded, write-barrier updates both copies or updates only the original copy while remembering the changes in mutation log so that the collectors can apply the changes to the new copy.

There are potential race conditions in the design. One is when an object is written by mutators while a collector is copying it. The write-barrier should make sure no mutation can be lost by the collector. A simple solution is to always remember all the mutations before the copying starts.

The other potential race condition is that, when multiple mutators write on same data field, the order of the writes appearing in the original copy may not be consistently maintained in the new copy, because the two writes by a mutator to the original copy and new copy (or mutation log) are not a single atomic operation to other mutator's two writes. The possible result is one mutator wins in original copy, while the other wins in the new copy. The problem can be avoided by only remembering the original field address where the write happens. The collector when applying the log will dereference the address to get the current value in original copy. The lock-free version of pseudocode looks like below.

```
Value write_barrier_from(Object* obj, int field, Value val)
{
   object_write(obj, field, val);
   // FORWARDING_BIT is set before collector starts to copying,
   // The bit is never cleared
   if( is_under_forwarding(obj) ){
      remember(obj, field);
   }
}
```

The write-barrier can also be designed in another way that it marks the written object dirty and then the collectors recopy the dirty object. In an extreme case, all of the objects are marked dirty, which means all of them have to be recopied. Once a dirtied object is copied, it is cleaned, and any further write on it will dirty it again. The recopying, just like the rescanning in an INC heap tracing process, can be done for multiple rounds. In the final flipping stage (which is usually an STW stage), the remaining logs or dirtied objects will be processed to keep both spaces consistent.

To avoid too much redundant data copying, the concurrent copying can decouple the heap tracing and object copying in a way that the collectors first only trace the heap to find the live objects and compute their new addresses in to-space, without really copying the live objects. Then the collectors copy the live objects to their precomputed addresses and update the references in to-space. This virtualy turns the concurrent copying collection into concurrent compaction that we will discuss later. In any case, when the collectors start copying objects, write-barrier and the final flipping phase ensures the data consistence.

Note read-barrier is not needed for "from-space invariant." This is an advantage.

17.3.1.2 Heap Tracing for "From-Space Invariant"
The tracing algorithm can be similar to SATB or INC concurrent tracing. The write-barrier can merge the code for heap tracing and write logging. INC algorithm is easier to work with "from-space invariant" write-barrier because both needs to remember writes: INC

algorithm remembers only reference writes, while "from-space invariant" remembers all writes. However, it is also fine to use SATB tracing algorithm.

A choice to make is which space for the collectors to trace: from-space or to-space.

Tracing in from-space: If it is to trace the from-space, when an object is copied, the references contained in the object all are pointing to from-space.

We want the to-space to maintain a characteristic that all the references in it point to to-space. In other words, there is no cross-space reference. This is different from the other two concurrent copying algorithms.

The tricolor terms are defined in the following way.

1. By default, all objects in from-space are white.

2. When an object's new address is computed (i.e., repointed), it is marked gray.

3. When an object is copied, it is marked black.

When a gray object is scanned, all its referenced objects are grayed, that is, repointed. An object is copied only after it is scanned.

When an object reference is pushed on mark-stack, it becomes gray and the collector repoints it. When a reference is popped off mark-stack after the referenced object is scanned, the object becomes black and is copied. When the object is copied, the new copy should update all its contained references to point to their respective new values, by following the mapping table.

When collectors apply the mutation log to copied objects, if the mutation is a reference write, the collector should repoint it (i.e., marking it gray) before applying the mutation, so as to make sure no white reference is written to black object.

Tracing in to-space: If the design traces to-space, the first step is to copy all the root-set referenced objects to to-space, and then the tracing starts from scanning the new copies.

When a reference pointing to from-space is met, the collector copies the referenced object to to-space and then updates the reference to point to new copy. In this design, the tricolor terms are defined as follows.

1. All live objects in from-space are white. There is no white object in to-space.

2. To copy an object is to mark the new copy gray;

3. To scan a new copy is to mark it black.

This is similar to the "to-space invariant" design, except that, now the copying and scanning is done by collectors, rather than by mutators in read-barrier. The fundamental difference is the aliveness of an object is now decided by INC or SATB heap tracing reachability, rather than the "to-space invariant" rule: accessed object is live object.

To-space maintains a characteristic that all black objects have only references pointing to to-space. When applying the mutation log to to-space, if it is a reference write to a scanned object, the referenced object should be copied to maintain the to-space characteristic. The first "from-space invariant" concurrent copying design proposed by Nettles and O'Toole's uses INC tracing in to-space, which they called "replication-based" collection.

The process above for tracing in from-space has single pass that includes all the operations such as marking, new address computing, object copying, and reference updating. They actually can be easily decoupled into two or more separate phases. This property provides many design flexibilities. Tracing in to-space does not have this property, because it has to copy referenced objects to to-space to continue the tracing.

A note on "from-space invariant" design is, if the forwarding pointer is installed in the from-space object header, it may impact the mutator execution that need access object header information. In this case, all the mutator operations on object header should be instrumented to follow the forwarding pointer and retrieve the original object header information from the to-space copy. To avoid this problem, a target-table out of the heap can be used.

17.3.2 Partial-Forward "From-Space Invariant"

New objects, according to the rule of "from-space invariant," should be allocated in from-space. If SATB tracing algorithm is used, all of the new objects are known to be live and are supposed to be copied to to-space with all mutations on them remembered. This can be expensive if not redundant. They should better just stay in to-space so as to avoid the copying and mutation log application.

A solution is to allocate new objects in a special space where objects are not copied. It is similar to the "partial-forward" collection we discussed before, where recently allocated objects after last collection are not forwarded in this collection but forwarded in the next collection when they are 1-year old.

Figure 17.4 below illustrates the idea of separate new space.

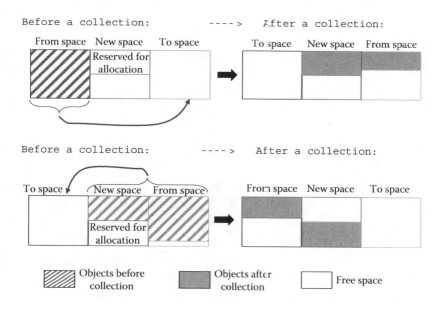

FIGURE 17.4 Partial-forward from-space collection.

After a collection, the reserved free space for allocation holds new objects that were allocated during the concurrent collection. They will be collected together with the from-space in the next collection.

A generational design is another solution, where generation one is the new space, and generation two includes both from-space and to-space.

17.4 FULLY CONCURRENT MOVING WITHOUT STW

The concurrent copying algorithms usually take an STW phase for root-set enumeration or space flipping. This is not always necessary. The initial phase of root-set enumeration can be replaced with concurrent root-set enumeration. The final phase of space flipping does not need STW either, if the following conditions can be met:

1. All the live objects have been scanned.

2. New objects are allocated in to-space.

3. Installation of a reference to white object into the scanned object can be caught.

There is no white object at all in the heap. The remaining white references in mutator contexts can be fixed without STW.

That means a concurrent moving collection without STW can be designed by putting them together.

17.5 CONCURRENT COMPACTING COLLECTION

Compacting here refers to in-place collection. Copying collection is a special form of compacting but with half heap reserved, hence not in-place. It is possible to design concurrent in-place compacting GC, but we will start from partial-copying collection.

17.5.1 Concurrent Regional-Copying Collection

When collecting garbage by copying, the collectors can choose to copy part of the heap, as in partial-forward or regional GC. This is useful when some regions in the heap have low survival rate, hence high collection throughput. This is also useful when the heap does not reserve large enough free space for copying collection of all the objects.

17.5.1.1 Single-Pass Regional Copying

The collectors can copy the survivors from first evacuation area to the reserved free area, leaving the first evacuation area empty. Then the collectors can continue to copy the survivors from the second evacuation area to the remaining free space of the reserved free area. When the free area is full, the copying can use the first evacuation area that is free now. The collectors can effectively recycle the whole heap one area after another, which we call a full round of collection. When the free reserve size is small enough compared to the heap size, the effect of a full-round collection can be similar to an in-place compaction. The free reserve is also used for new object allocation during the collection period.

To enable regional copying, first task is to find all the live objects in the targeted evacuation areas. If the target evacuation area (from-region) and free reserve area (to-region) are known before a collection starts, the heap tracing pass can be merged with the object copying pass as in normal concurrent copying collection. We can apply any of the concurrent copying algorithms discussed previously with minor tweak that does not forward the objects in nonevacuation areas.

For example, the read-barrier for "to-space invariant" in concurrent regional copying can look like below. The collectors, at the same time, scan the entire heap from root-set to forward and update all the references pointing to the from-region.

```
Object* read_barrier_slot(Object* src, Object** slot)
{
    Object* obj = *slot;
    if( in_from_region(obj) ){
        if( !is_forwarded(obj) ){
            obj_forward(obj);
        }
        obj = forwarding_pointer(obj);
        *slot = obj;
    }
    return obj;
}
```

The single-pass regional copying has a problem. For every collection on a region, a full pass of heap tracing is needed to copy objects while tracing. This is a big overhead.

17.5.1.2 Separate Pass for Heap Tracing

One solution is to have a separate pass of heap tracing, then every region's collection only copies the live objects in the region, without tracing the heap again. This saves lots of the tracing time. Another benefit with separate tracing pass is that after tracing, the survival rate of every region is known. Then the collectors can select to first collect the region(s) that can bring highest collection throughput. This design does not preserve the sliding property of compaction.

Since all the live objects in a region are already known, it is possible to compute their new locations (i.e., repointing the objects) in to-region before copying. Then the copying of from-region live objects and the reference-fixing of the objects in whole heap can be done in parallel, since reference-fixing does not need to wait for the object copying to finish.

We use "to-space invariant" to discuss the copying phase. It starts after the heap-tracing pass and all the live objects in from-region have been repointed. Here the tricolor terms are defined as follows:

1. All live objects in from-region are white by default.

2. An object is gray if it is copied to to-region, or if it contains references pointing to from-region.

3. An object is black if it is scanned so that all its contained references are fixed.

As the first step, a flipping phase is needed to repoint root-set references from from-region to to-region, and a read-barrier is turned on to forward all loaded references before they are visible to mutators. Then all the mutators are resumed to continue execution.

At the same time, the collectors conduct two tasks in parallel:

Object copying: Copy the from-region objects to to-region. Since all the new addresses have been computed, the copying just iterates and forwards the live objects one by one in the region.

The copying can start either in from-region or to-region. If it starts in from-region, the collectors can partition the region into blocks. Every collector grabs and processes a block dynamically from from-region.

It is more balanced if the copying starts in to-region. The collectors partition to-region into blocks, that is, target blocks. This is similar to the processing in parallel compaction that we have discussed. Every collector grabs and processes a target block dynamically from to-region. For each target block, the collector finds the first source object in from-region that maps into it and then proceeds to copy the objects linearly in from-region. This requires each target block to remember where to find the first source object. It can be done when the collectors compute new addresses of live objects. This is similar to the dependence tree we built in parallel compaction.

As we have discussed, "to-space invariant" can be slot based or object based. Slot-based design forwards an object from from-region when mutator accesses a reference pointing to it. Object-based forwards not only the object but also all its referenced objects. In tricolor terminology, slot-based design turns an object from white to gray, while object-based design turns a white object to be black. For concurrent regional copying, either design can be used.

Reference-fixing: Scan the heap (except from-region) to update all the references that point to from-region. These are cross-region references pointing to from-region. Since all the new addresses have been computed, reference-fixing does not need to wait for the referenced object to be copied.

If the forwarding pointers are stored in a target-table off the heap, when all the live objects in one region are copied, this region can be reused immediately. The remaining references to it can still be updated by following the target-table.

With "to-space invariant," it is impossible to install a reference into the heap if it points to from-region, so the total number of those white references are limited and can be fixed in one pass.

There might be a data-race between mutator and collector when both update the same object field that holds a reference to from-region. For example, the collector wants to fix the reference value to point to to-region, while the mutator wants to update the reference to point to another object. To avoid the problem, atomic instruction is needed for the collector to do the reference-fixing. That is it fixes the reference with atomic CompareExchange that succeeds only when the old value points to from-region. Otherwise, if the atomic operation fails, the collector just gives up and moves on, since either the slot has been changed by a mutator or fixed by another collector.

17.5.1.3 The Pass for Reference-Fixing

In STW regional copy, the cross-region references can be fixed with prebuilt remember-set instead of through heap scanning. To prepare for a full collection round, all the cross-region references between every pair of regions should be remembered, so that every region can be collected. The cross-region references can be either remembered with write-barrier during mutators' execution, or enumerated during collector full-heap tracing. When moving the objects in a region, all the references pointing to the region are updated to their new locations. Oracle G1 collector in OpenJDK is STW regional copying-GC, using this approach. It employs a separate pass for full-heap concurrent tracing that builds the remember-set for all the cross-region references. Then G1 uses STW regional copy to recycle the target regions.

The cross-region remember-sets can be a big memory overhead. Heap scanning can trade the memory overhead with time overhead by enumerating the heap for reference slots.

With concurrent regional copying, G1's approach is inconvenient, not because of the memory overhead, but because the references are constantly changed by mutators. There is no stable remember-set. A separate pass of heap scanning for reference-fixing can be more straightforward.

Based on the discussion, regional copying basically has following passes.

1. Full-heap tracing to find live objects

2. Select the regions to recycle and repoint the live objects in them

3. Regional collection to move the live objects in the selected regions

4. Full-heap scanning to fix references

Note the passes can be all separate, or some of them can be merged into one pass or conducted in parallel. For example, pass 1 and 2 can be merged if the from-region and to-region are selected before they start. Pass 3 and 4 can be conducted in parallel.

Another note is, every pass here can be concurrent or STW. When they are all STW, the algorithm degenerates to LISP2 compaction, where the selected regions actually cover the whole heap.

However, to scan the entire heap for reference-fixing, the collectors can either iterate the live objects one by one in every region, or it can trace the heap as the live object marking does. Azul's C4 algorithm proposes to fuse the reference-fixing pass of this collection with the live object marking pass of the next collection, which it calls "continuous collector."

1. Full-heap tracing to find live objects and fix the references that point to stale values

2. Select the regions to recycle and repoint the live objects in them

3. Regional collection to move the live objects in the selected regions

4. Go to 1

The collection then becomes endless and pauseless, with one collection recycles one or more regions. To use the whole heap as selected region is impossible in concurrent moving collection, where a free reserve is necessary to hold the new copies, so that the mutators and collectors can work in parallel on different copies.

17.5.2 Virtual Memory-Based Concurrent Compacting

As usual, virtual memory support in operating system (OS) can be used to help object copying in concurrent compaction.

17.5.2.1 Fault Handler with Read-Barrier

Here is a design that uses "to-space invariant." Before the concurrent copying starts, all the live objects in from-region have been repointed, that is, their new addresses in to-space have been computed.

The to-region is memory protected, and its physical pages are double mapped. One virtual address mapping triggers page fault upon access, the other mapping allows the fault handler to access the protected pages.

As the first step of concurrent copying, a flipping phase fixes root-set references to point to to-region for those who point to from-region. A read-barrier is turned on to prevent mutators from seeing references pointing to from-space. Then all the mutators are resumed to continue execution. This is the same as before. The difference is in the read-barrier. Previously, read-barrier forwards an object if it is not yet. Now the read-barrier does not forward it but returns its new address in to-region.

When mutator accesses the object in to-region, a page fault is triggered. The handler copies the repointed objects into the faulting page. The handler has to be able to find the first source object that is mapped into the fault page and then linearly gets other source objects that are mapped to the fault page. Once all the objects to the page have been copied, the protection can be lifted.

In this design, the tricolor terms are defined in the following way:

1. The live objects in from-region are white by default.

2. An object is gray if it contains a reference pointing to from-region.

3. An object in to-region is black.

Read-barrier is needed that prevents the mutators from accessing objects in from-region but allows the access to other regions. Memory protection is to prevent the mutators from accessing the noncopied objects in to-space. The pseudocode below gives the read-barrier and fault handler implementation.

```
Object* read_barrier_slot(Object* src, Object** slot)
{
   Object* obj = *slot;
   if( in_from_region(obj) ){
      obj = forwarding_pointer(obj);
      *slot = obj;
   }
   return obj;
}

void fault_handler_copy_region(void* addr)
{
   Page* fault_page = page_of_addr(addr);
   lock_page_copy(fault_page);
   if( !is_protected(fault_page) ) return;
   // turns page from gray to black.
   // find the obj in from-region that maps to
   // the first obj in fault page.
   Object* src = first_source_obj_to_page(fault_page);
   Object* dst = forwarding_pointer(src);
   Page* dst_page = page_of_addr(dst);
   while( dst_page == fault_page ){
      reference_fix(src);
      obj_copy(src);
      src = next_obj_in_region(src);
      dst = forwarding_pointer(src);
      dst_page = page_of_addr(dst);
   }
   unprotect(fault_page);
   unlock_page_copy(fault_page);

}
```

A page is processed only once by the fault handler that copies all the objects to it. During the page copying, the page is locked, so that only one thread can copy objects to it. Other mutators that fault on the same page will wait on the lock till the copying finishes.

Note when an object is copied, all its contained references are fixed at the same time without copying the referenced objects. This is possible because all the new addresses are known before copying starts. There is no extra step to scan the objects in to-region for reference-fixing. However, collectors should work at the same time to fix the references in other areas than from- and to-region.

17.5.2.2 Fault Handler without Read-Barrier

The design above has to use compiler-instrumented read-barrier to prevent the mutators from accessing objects in from-region. Read-barrier is used because the mutators are allowed to access other regions than from-region. Other regions (except to-region) may have gray objects that contain references pointing to from-region (i.e., white references). When mutators access gray objects, read-barrier is needed to prevent them from seeing the white references.

However, if the mutators can only see black objects, there is no chance for them to see a white reference, thus the read-barrier can be omitted.

To allow the mutators to see only black objects, we can apply the original idea of Appel et al.'s VM-based concurrent copying, where the heap is partitioned into from-region and to-region. There are no other regions in heap. The mutators can only access the to-region.

The design here still uses semi-space, one half for from-space and the other for to-space. The difference from original design is, for concurrent compaction purpose, they are virtual address spaces. The from-space is fully mapped to physical address space, while the to-space does not. Only the reserved free region in to-space is mapped to physical pages. Other regions in to-space are only mapped on demand when a mutator copies objects to them. We call it "virtual semi-space."

Figure 17.5 illustrates the difference between three concurrent moving algorithms: semi-space, regional-copying, and this virtual semi-space.

In virtual semi-space, when all the objects in a region of from-space have been copied, the physical pages for the region can be released. They can be reused by the to-space to copy more objects. Throughout a collection, the physical pages of from-space are released region by region while they are mapped to to-space region by region. In this way, we can achieve the effect of semi-space copying collection with only a relatively small reserved free region, hence the similar result of compacting collection. An intuitive implementation may look like the following.

After flipping the spaces, all mutators' references point to to-space, whose whole virtual space is memory protected and has only one region physically mapped as the seed free region. Accesses to pages in to-space trigger fault handler that forwards the referenced objects and hence maps physical pages.

When an object is copied to to-space, all its contained references are fixed together, since the new addresses for all the white objects have been computed ahead of time. So the objects in to-space have only references to to-space. When a mutator accesses a referenced object that has not been copied, fault handler will be triggered again. This has two implications:

1. The mutators never access the from-space, and hence no read-barrier is needed.

2. Mutators' accesses in to-space may trigger lots of page faults till all the white objects are copied.

Collectors at the same scan the pages in to-space to forward white objects. This can accelerate the collection and alleviate mutators' burden of object copying.

Semi-space:

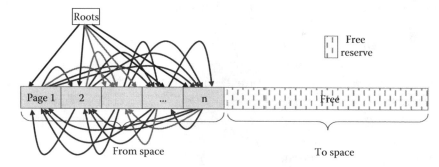

Regional copying:

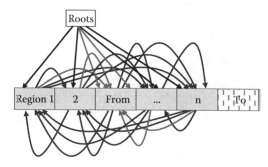

Virtual semi-space:

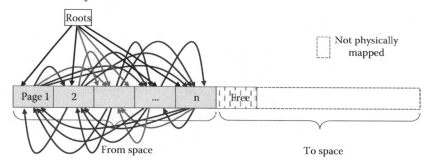

FIGURE 17.5   Differences in concurrent moving algorithms.

This design can allocate pages in to-space on demand, but it cannot release pages in from-space as expected because the objects to copy are decided by reachability path from root sets and mutators access pattern. The original copies of the forwarded objects in from-space do not necessarily stay together on same page or in same region. They can spread across the from-space. It is possible that no page be released in from-space after many pages have been allocated in to-space. This increases the demands on mapped physical pages. In the worst case, it may require the total size of needed physical pages to be almost double of the from-space size, which essentially turns the "virtual semi-space" algorithm into a real semi-space one.

To release from-space pages, the objects in a page should be forwarded together. That requires to treat page as the basic copying unit. That is when a mutator copies an accessed object in to-space, it finds the page in from-space from where the original white object stays and then copies all the live objects in that page to to-space.

17.5.2.3 Virtual Semi-Space Implementation

Based on the considerations above, a complete design for virtual semi-space is like the following. GC traces the entire heap first and then iterates the heap in linear order to compute all the live objects' new addresses in to-space as a sliding-compact algorithm does, but without really copying them. The to-space is protected and only virtually mapped except the reserved pages. Then a flipping is conducted to repoint all the root-set references to to-space and then resume the mutators.

The mutators see only references pointing to to-space. When a mutator dereferences a reference whose address is not yet mapped physically, a page fault is triggered, and the fault handler copies all the live objects that are targeted to the faulting page. Since the new addresses are computed for the live objects in linear order, the original copies of the forwarded objects stay together in one or more pages. When the copying is done, the faulting page is unprotected, and the source page(s) can be released, since the live objects on them have been forwarded. In this way, the expected result of in-place compaction is achieved.

The pseudocode is given below for the fault handler. It is very similar to that of concurrent code given above, but the virtual semi-space does not need read-barrier.

```
void fault_handler_copy_to(void* addr)
{
    Page* fault_page = page_of_addr(addr);
    lock_page_scan(fault_page);
    if( !is_protected(fault_page) ) return;
    // turns page from copy-gray to copy-black
    // find the range of source objects forwarded to fault_page
    Page* next_page = next_page_after(fault_page);
    Object* src_obj_start = first_source_obj_to_page(fault_page);
    Object* src_obj_end = first_source_obj_to_page(next_page);

    Object* src = src_obj_start;
    while( src < src_obj_end ){
        reference_fix(src);
        obj_copy(src);
        src = next_obj_after(src);
    }
    unprotect(fault_page);
    unlock_page_scan(fault_page);
    release_pages_between(src_obj_start, src_obj_end);


}
```

In this design, the target page in to-space needs to know its first object's original copy's address in from-space. This information is bookkept by GC during the object repointing pass, when the collectors compute target addresses for live objects. When mutators are resumed after the flipping phase, the collectors start to copy the objects by iterating the to-space virtual pages one by one. Kermany and Petrank proposed the original design that they called Compressor.

The conceptual passes of this design are given as follows:

1. Trace the whole heap to find live objects

2. Repoint all the live objects

3. Flip the spaces, copy live objects to to-space and fix the references

New objects allocated after the heap tracing pass cannot be traced and should be allocated as live objects in to-space. They may contain references to from-space if they are allocated before the flipping phase. So those new objects should be memory protected as well to prevent their references from escaping. When mutators access them, the fault handler fixes their references then lifts the protection.

The design maintains the sliding property of compaction. But it has the same problem of "object-moving storm" as other "to-space invariant" designs. When the mutators are resumed, it is possible that they can hardly move forward, being overwhelmed by intensive page faults and object copying. In the extreme case, the copying phase may look like STW for a short while. With more and more objects copied, the mutators can move forward, and the collection then is more like incremental. Overall, the felt pause time with virtual semispace can be obviously shorter than an actual STW compaction.

17.5.2.4 Concurrent In-Place Compaction

Apparently, the compaction collection can use other concurrent copying techniques such as "current-copy invariant" or "from-space invariant." We do not discuss them here.

The compaction algorithms above are not exactly in-place. They all need a reserved free region to recycle the first used region, which in turn can be used as the to-region for the second used region, and so on. The reason is simple. All the algorithms are actually copying collection, which need a to-space to hold the moved objects before the from-space can be freed.

The root cause is, as concurrent moving collection, it should ensure the mutators always access valid data while the objects are under moving. It is easy to have a reserved free space so that the object moving does not have to worry about overwriting valid data.

The free reserve size can be as big as half heap such as in semi-space or virtual semi-space. It can be small enough to be a single page or even smaller as long as it can accommodate the biggest object in the recycled heap. In reality, the reserve size should be big enough to achieve reasonable collection throughput.

No matter how small the free reserve size is, it is not strict in-place compaction. Strict in-place compaction allows to slide an object in the heap a little bit that is less than the object size. Strictly in-place concurrent compaction is still possible.

For example, GC can concurrently sliding-move the live objects one after another to one end of the heap. The operations of moving one object are atomic to mutators operations, so that the mutators only access it before or after the movement. When a mutator tries to access an object, an access-barrier intercepts the access and checks if the object is moved or under moving.

1. If it is before moving, return the original address of the object

2. If it is under moving, block the mutator waiting for the moving finish

3. If it is moved, return the new address of the object

The mutators do not move objects. The reason is mutators do not know the order of object compacting (or do not want to be involved in the complications). Collectors move objects in sliding way. They have to precisely control the order so that no valid data is overwritten. The algorithms we developed for parallel compaction can be applied here but with a lock on the object under moving.

This design has to use a target-table to indicate the object moving status, because the original copy of a moved object may have been overwritten, who cannot keep the forwarding pointer in its header. Then a question is how the access-barrier knows if the reference is intended for the original object that has been moved out, or for the current object that was just moved in, in case the moved-out original object and the moved-in new object happen to locate at the same address. A solution is to use different virtual address spaces distinguish them. That is the heap is mapped to two disjoint virtual address ranges, say, from-range and to-range. A reference in from-range is intended to access the original object, and a reference in to-range is intended to access the object in its new location.

The pseudocode for the read and write-barriers is given below.

```
Value read_barrier_current(Object* obj, int field)
{
    return access_barrier(obj, field, 0, IS_READ);
}

void write_barrier_current(Object* obj, int field, Value val)
{
    bool fld_is_ref = field_is_ref(field);
    // write new address to field. This is not optional
    if(fld_is_ref && in_from_range(val) && is_forwarded(val))
        val = forwarding_pointer(val)

    access_barrier(obj, field, val, IS_WRITE);
}

Value access_barrier(Object* obj, int field, Value val, int
acc_type)
```

```
{
    if( in_from_range(obj) ){
        if( !is_forwarded(obj) ){
            bool success = lock_forwarding(obj);
            if( success ){
                Value ret = object_access(obj, field, val, acc_type);
                unlock_forwarding(obj);
                return ret;
            }else{
                while( !is_forwarded(obj) );
            }
        }
        //object is forwarded
        obj = forwarding_pointer(obj);
    }
    return object_access(obj, field, val, acc_type);
}
```

The write-barrier code is the same as "current-copy invariant" write-barrier. This is reasonable because the mutators do not want to move the objects by themselves. To avoid moving objects, the mutators should just access the original copy of an object if it is not moved, or access the new copy when it is moved or under moving. The references to both original and new locations may appear in mutators' contexts.

A mutator can wait for an object's moving to finish when it is under moving, but the mutator cannot wait for an object's moving if the object is not moved yet, since it does not know when the moving will start. Otherwise, the effect would degenerate into STW. If the object is not moved, the mutator should just access its original copy.

The read-barrier code above has a difference from the "current-copy invariant" read-barrier. The "current-copy invariant" read-barrier is much simpler than write-barrier, while here the read-barrier is almost the same as the write-barrier. In the read-barrier of "current-copy invariant," the mutator reads either the old copy or the new copy, depending on if the object is moved. It does not lock the object forwarding, nor wait for the object forwarding to finish. This is the key difference between a GC that has free reserve and a GC that does not.

When the GC uses a free reserve, the old copy and the new copy can coexist during its moving process. The old copy is only marked "forwarded" when the moving is done. Before that the old copy data are valid, since no write can happen on the object when it is under moving. That means it is safe for a mutator to access the old copy when the object is under moving. It does not need to wait for the moving to finish. Moreover, since the mutator's reading and the collector' moving can be conducted in parallel, no mutual exclusion is needed between them. The mutator does not need to lock the object to read it. This is different from in-place compaction.

Here, the in-place compaction does not have free reserve, so the moving of an object may just slide the object a little bit, and then the new copy overwrites the original copy.

That means, when an object starts moving, the data of its original copy may no longer valid. A mutator has to lock the object to prevent its moving in order to access correct data.

Note when the object is moved, it is references are not all fixed to point to the new addresses in to-range, although all the new addresses are available after the pass of object repointing. It only fixes the references whose referenced objects are moved. Otherwise, if an object is not yet moved, the mutators will not be able to get its data in its new location.

For the reason, a pass of reference-fixing is needed after all the objects are moved. Before that the mutators may have to go through the pointer indirection to access the current copy and update the loaded reference fields that contain stale references. Another solution is to build a remember-set for every object during heap tracing pass. Then the collectors can update the slots in the remember-set whenever an object is moved. This incurs big memory overhead, and the remember-set of an object is variable since mutators may write its reference to more places. We will discuss this solution in the chapter on transactional memory.

The conceptual passes of this design are as follows:

1. Trace the whole heap to find live objects

2. Repoint all the live objects

3. Slide-copy live objects to new locations

4. Fix the references

So far, we have developed a concurrent in-place compaction algorithm, but it is hardly to be useful. One reason is that to eliminate the free reserve does not bring obvious benefit. Concurrent collection has to allow new object allocations, while new objects allocation requires free space. The longer time the collection takes, the bigger size free space should be reserved for new objects. The strict concurrent in-place compaction runs much longer than a non-strict one. Although it eliminates the free space reserved for surviving objects, it needs a larger free space reserved for new objects. This only makes sense when the application has very high survival rate and very low allocation rate.

V

Optimizations of Thread Interactions

CHAPTER 18

Optimizing Monitor Performance

BESIDES GARBAGE COLLECTION, THREAD synchronization is another core component that impacts virtual machine (VM) performance significantly.

Java uses monitor and atomics for thread synchronization. Monitor's implementation has big impact on the applications performance if they use synchronizations heavily. Some applications may use synchronizations implicitly through libraries.

We have discussed a simplest form of monitor implementation to explain how it works. In this chapter, we discuss more practical implementations that can largely reduce monitor execution overhead. In the following text, we use lock and monitor interchangeably unless stated otherwise.

18.1 LAZY LOCK

Lock is only meaningful for multithreaded computation. If it is known that the system has a single active thread or a lock is accessed by a single thread, there is no need to actually execute the locking operations.

To detect if the system is single threaded can be simple. In thread manager, there is a counter to track the number of created threads. This approach does not work for lock optimization purpose, because current Java virtual machine (JVM) implementations usually have multiple threads spawned by the VM, such as threads for just-in-time compilation, garbage collection, and finalization.

A better design is not to detect the number of threads created, but the number of threads that access locks. Before a second thread accesses locks, application does not need to execute locking operations. To ensure the correctness, all the locking operations are recorded. When a second thread is going to use a lock, the recorded lock operations are actually conducted. The idea is called "lazy lock."

To implement lazy lock, a "lazy lock list" can be used to record the lock operations, as illustrated in Figure 18.1.

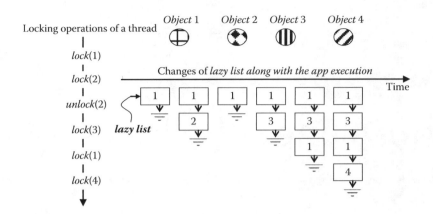

FIGURE 18.1   Lazy list that records the objects that should be locked.

The pesudo-code to implement lazy lock is given below, where an object array is used for lazy lock list.

```
/* lazy list */
Object* lazy_list[];
/* records how many objects are recorded */
int lazy_lock_num = 0;

/* locking for single thread */
void lazy_lock ( Object* obj )
{
    lazy_list[lazy_lock_num++] = obj;
}

/* unlocking for single thread */
void lazy_unlock( Object* obj )
{
    lazy_lock_num--;
    if( lazy_list[lazy_lock_num] != obj ){
        vm_throw_exception("IllegalMonitorState");
    }
}
/* lazily lock the recorded objects right before
    second thread locking any object*/
void lock_lazily()
{   //restore the normal lock implementation code
    retore_normal_lock_code();
    //vm_object_lock() is the API for locking.
    //It now calls the normal implementation code.
    for(int i=0; i<lazy_lock_num; i++ ){
        vm_object_lock( lazy_list[i] );
    }
}
```

When a second thread tries to lock, or when the system has invocation to `Object.wait()`, `lock_lazily()` is invoked to restore lock states.

When recording objects in lazy list, GC module should enumerate the list as part of global root-set.

18.2 THIN-LOCK

Lazy lock can only help single thread performance. For multithreaded locking, we use other optimizations.

For example, in our first implementation of monitor in the chapter on thread design, we use a thread-local `locked_object_list` data structure to track the monitors locked by a thread. It requires every locking and unlocking (i.e., `monitorenter` and `monitorexit`) operation to search the list, which is expensive. When the locking/unlocking operations are very intensive in the application, the cost can be high.

In this section, we analyze the execution paths of locking/unlocking and then come up with optimization on the hot paths.

18.2.1 Locking Path of Thin-Lock

For a monitor locking process, it mainly has the following operations:

- Step 1. Check if the monitor is locked.

- Step 2. If the monitor is not locked, lock it and return.

- Step 3. If the monitor is locked, check if it is locked by self. If yes, increment the recursion number and return.

- Step 4. If the monitor is locked by other thread, wait to lock it again later.

The execution flow of locking is illustrated in Figure 18.2.

In the first implementation, except step 1, all the rest steps need list operation to manage the monitor status. Step 4 by nature is a slow path since it has to deal with

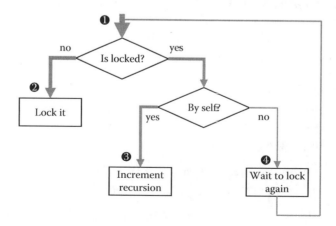

FIGURE 18.2 Operation flow of locking a monitor.

multithreaded locking contention, which usually involves OS calls for thread scheduling and communication.

In reality, most multithreaded applications do not really have lock contentions. Even if multiple threads access the same lock object, their lock periods may not overlap. That means, when a thread tries to lock a monitor, the monitor is often in the unlocked state. Based on this observation, the optimization idea is to make the common path fast, which is mostly the path to step 2 and sometimes includes the path to step 3, as shown as the thickness of the arrows in the operation flowchart of Figure 18.2. We examine the steps one by one.

Step 1. Check if the monitor is locked.

This step in initial implementation is fast enough by checking a bit in the object header. It can be sped up even more by checking a bit in the object reference (i.e., pointer), which does not require to load the object header.

Since step 1 is always followed by step 2 or step 3, the reference bit pattern should be able to encode some information for step 2 or step 3 as well.

To put a bit in reference is not always convenient, because it is unlikely to modify all the references in heap that point to an object. We do not discuss the reference bit pattern optimization here.

Step 2. If the monitor is not locked, lock it and return.

To lock a monitor usually involves atomic instruction to test and set bits in object header. It also needs to remember the owner of the lock, so that a later locking on the same object knows whether it is locked by the same thread. The information of lock owner (i.e., thread ID) has to be associated with the object (i.e., object ID).

In the initial monitor implementation, we use a thread-local `locked_object_list` that remembers the locked objects. This stores the object ID in thread data structure, so as to be associated with thread ID.

The other direction of association is to remember the thread ID in the locked object; then the locking thread can check the current owner by reading the object data, rather than searching the `locked_object_list`. Since every lock can have no more than one owner, this approach is feasible by leaving certain space in object header for thread ID.

This design makes the common path to lock a free monitor fast. By putting thread ID in an object, the VM virtually does not know what locks a thread currently holds, because it is too expensive to examine every object for the lock owner information. Fortunately, this support is usually not needed.

Step 3. If the monitor is locked, check if it is locked by self. If yes, increment the recursion number and return.

In the initial implementation, to check if self is the lock owner, the thread looks up the object in the `locked_object_list`. If the lock owner's thread ID is stored in the object header, the check can be much faster. But if the recursion number is stored elsewhere, for example, in the `locked_object_list`, fast checking of owner does not help much, because then the thread still needs to access the list if the object is locked by self. If we want to make this path (up to returning from the locking operation) fast too, a recursion number can also be put in object header.

To implement the optimizations, the object header now should have at least two words, one is the original slot for vtable, and the other is for locking, which is the "lock word." Assuming VM uses two bytes for thread ID, and one byte for recursion number, then the object header layout in a 32-bit system looks like Figure 18.3.

The two-byte thread ID can accommodate up to 64 K threads, which is big enough and sometimes even more than the maximum thread number that a platform can support. One-byte recursion number allows to recursively lock an object 128 times. This is probably enough too. For safety purpose, when the recursion number overflows, a fallback solution is needed.

With the new layout, it does not need LOCK_BIT to lock the object, since the thread ID can be used to indicate the locked state, as given below. The code assumes word small-endian architecture.

```
bool lock_non_blocking(Object* jmon)
{
   uint16* p_threadID = (uint16*)lock_word_addr(jmon)+1;
   uint16 myID = current_thread()->tid;
   //atomically swap the threadID in lock word
   int oldID = CompareExchange(p_threadID, 0, myID);
   return (oldID == 0);
}
```

Since atomic instruction is very expensive, it can be faster if the locking code checks the current lock owner before locking it with the atomic instruction. When the object is locked by itself, only recursion number is incremented. The pseudo-code is given below.

```
bool lock_non_blocking_fast(Object* jmon)
{
   uint16* p_threadID = (uint16*)lock_word_addr(jmon)+1;
   uint16 myID = (uint16)(current_thread()->tid);
   if( *pthreadID == myID){
      //locked by self, increment recursion number
      uint8* p_recursion = (uint8*)lock_word_addr(jmon)+1;
      uint8 num_recursion = *p_recursion;
```

Vtable pointer		
Thread ID	Recursion	

FIGURE 18.3   Object header layout to support fast monitor locking.

```
      // If recursion overflows, return to fallback solution
      if( num_recursion == RECURSION_OVERFLOW )
         *p_recursion = ++num_recursion;
      if ( num_recursion < RECURSION_OVERFLOW )
         return TRUE;
      else
         return FALSE;
   }else if( *pthreadID == 0 ){
      //free monitor, atomically swap threadID in lock word
      int oldID = CompareExchange(p_threadID, 0, newID);
      return (oldID == 0);
   }
   //locked by other thread, go to the slow path
   return FALSE;
}
```

The recursion number may become too big to be held by the single byte in lock word. In this case, fallback solution is needed, which can simply revert back to the original slow solution. Since the overflow case is uncommon, it does not really impact the fast path performance. The pseudo-code for a complete locking process may look like below.

```
void STDCALL vm_object_lock(Object* jmon)
{
   bool success = lock_non_blocking_fast(jmon);
   if( success ) return;
   //object is either locked by other thread or
   // recursion number overflow
   uint16* p_threadID = (uint16*)lock_word_addr(jmon)+1;
   uint16 newID = (uint16)(current_thread()->tid);
   if( *p_threadID == newID){
      //locked by self, meaning recursion overflow
      //revert to locked_object_list solution
      Locked_obj* plock = null;
      Locked_obj* head = thread_get_locked_obj_list();
      plock = lookup_in_locked_obj_list(head, jmon);
      if( plock->jobject == jmon){
         //already in the list, then increment recursion
         plock->recursion++;
      else{
         //first time overflow, create a node in the list
         plock = (Locked_obj*)vm_alloc(sizeof(Locked_obj));
         plock->jobject = jmon;
         plock->recursion = MAX_FAST_RECURSION + 1;
         plock->next = head;
         thread_insert_locked_obj_list(plock);
      }
   }else{
```

```
    //locked by other thread, sleep on the monitor
    lock_blocking(jmon);
    //when it returns from sleep, it holds the lock
    //this is the first time locking jmon, no overflow
  }
  return;
}
```

The VM application programming interface for locking calls the fast path first. When it returns FALSE, the slow path is taken to deal with the recursion overflow or contended lock.

18.2.2 Unlocking Path of Thin-Lock

The steps when a thread unlocks its locked object are the following.

- Step 1. Check if the lock is held by self.

- Step 2. If it is not locked by self, throw an exception for `IllegalMonitorState` and return.

- Step 3. If it is locked by self, check the recursion number. If the recursion number is bigger than zero, decrement it and return.

- Step 4. If recursion is zero, release the lock, and check if there is any thread blocked waiting to lock the object; return if there is no waiting thread.

- Step 5. If there is waiting thread, wake it up and return.

The execution flow of unlocking is illustrated in Figure 18.4. The thickness of an arrow indicates the hotness of the path.

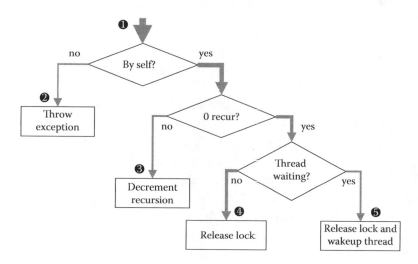

FIGURE 18.4   Operation flow of unlocking a monitor.

The most common path is step 4. It should be optimized to be as fast as possible. Optimizations on other paths such as to step 3 or step 5 are optional. Step 2 is usually the least common path.

In our initial implementation of the unlocking code, step 4 needs to iterate all the mutators in order to know if there is a thread blocked waiting for a released lock. It is obviously slow. From step 1 to step 4, there are three conditions to check: lock owner, recursion number, and waiting thread. The first two are stored in lock word now, and can be checked fast. If the last one (i.e., condition if there is a waiting thread) can be checked in lock word too, the hottest path can be fast.

For this purpose, a flag can be put in lock word to indicate if there is any waiting thread. We call it contention flag. The remaining byte (the lowest byte) of the lock word can be used for it. Then the unlocking code may look like the following.

```
void STDCALL vm_object_unlock(Object* jmon)
{
    uint16* p_threadID = (uint16*)lock_word_addr(jmon)+1;
    uint16 self = current_thread()->tid;
    if( *p_threadID == self){
        //locked by self, check recursion number
        uint8* p_recursion = (uint8*)lock_word_addr(jmon)+1;
        uint8* p_contention = (uint8*)lock_word_addr(jmon);
        if( *p_recursion ){
            recursion_dec(jmon);
        else{
            *p_threadID = 0; //release lock
            if( *p_contention ){
                notify_blocking_threads(jmon);
            }
    }else{
        vm_throw_exception("IllegalMonitorState");
    }
}
```

There is a potential race condition when the unlocking thread checks the contention flag and a contending thread is setting the same flag. In order to make sure the lock owner never misses the contention flag when it unlocks (therefore to wake up the sleeping thread), a protocol is needed between the threads.

A simple protocol is that only the lock owner can set the contention flag. If a locking thread finds the lock is held by another thread and the contention flag is unset, it does not sleep-wait, but spin-waits (or yield-waits), and then retries to lock. It only sleep-waits when it sees the contention flag set. Once it successfully holds the lock, it will set the contention flag. In this protocol, the contention flag can be a single bit, without worrying about the atomicity of its access.

Spin-waiting (or yield-waiting) is undesirable. If the contending thread wants to sleep-wait for a held lock, a little bit more complicated protocol is needed to ensure the memory operations ordering.

First, the contention flag has to stay away from other lock data, so that its setting/checking does not interfere with the operations on other bytes of the lock word. In other words, the contention flag should be able to be set and reset atomically and independently. In this way, the ordering of their accesses can be designed to meet our demand. The lowest byte of the lock word can be used for this purpose, as we do.

Second, in the locking implementation, after the contending thread sets the contention flag, it should try the nonblocking locking path again before it goes to sleep. The retry is critical because of the following:

- If the lock is not yet released in retry, the contending thread will go to sleep-waiting. The lock owner will be able to see the contention flag when it releases the lock, since it checks the contention flag "after" it releases the lock. As a result, it knows there is a sleeping thread and will wake it up.

- If the lock is released in retry, the contending thread will not sleep-wait for the lock, even after it sets the contention flag. So it does not need to be wakened up by anyone.

In a modern microprocessor that uses relaxed memory consistency, the nonblocking locking operation by itself is a memory fence (or memory barrier) for all memory read/write operations, due to the atomic compare-exchange instruction in it. It effectively builds the ordering between contention flag and thread ID accesses. The pseudo-code for locking looks like the following.

```
void STDCALL vm_object_lock(Object* jmon)
{
    bool result = lock_non_blocking_fast(jmon);
    if( result ) return;
    //object is either locked by other thread or
    // recursion number overflow
    uint16* p_threadID = (uint16*)lock_word_addr(jmon)+1;
    uint16 myID = (uint16)(current_thread()->tid);
    if( *p_threadID == myID){
        //locked by self, meaning recursion overflow
        lock_recursion_overflow(jmon);
    }else{
        //locked by other thread, sleep on the monitor
        unit8* p_contention = (uint8*)lock_word_addr(jmon);
        *p_contention = 1;
        result = lock_non_blocking_fast(jmon);
        if( result ) return;
        lock_blocking(jmon);
    }
}
```

In this way, the sleeping thread will never miss wakening up.

18.2.3 Support Contention Flag Resetting

No matter what protocol to use, the contention flag cannot be reset in current design. That means, once the contention flag is set, it stays there forever till the monitor object is recycled. The lock owner then always needs to assume there is contention, and therefore tries to wake up the possibly nonexisting waiting threads. This can be a problem if the application has only sporadic locking contentions throughout its lifetime.

If we want to support contention flag resetting, the accesses to the contention flag by multiple threads should be carefully arranged. To avoid a tricky design, a choice is to use common threading synchronization constructs, such as mutex and conditional variable, to control the contention flag. When a contending thread is blocked, it can set the contention flag, and wait on the conditional variable. When the lock owner releases the lock, it resets the flag and notifies all the waiting threads. The conditional variable and its guarding mutex are put in a control data structure. An instance of the control data structure is created for a contented lock, at the first time when it is needed. Then the new pseudo-code looks like the following.

```
struct Control{
    Mutex* mutex;
    Condvar* condvar;
}

void STDCALL vm_object_lock(Object* jmon)
{
    bool result = lock_non_blocking_fast(jmon);
    if( result ) return;
    //object is either locked by other thread or
    // recursion number overflow
    uint16* p_threadID = (uint16*)lock_word_addr(jmon)+1;
    VM_Thread* self = current_thread();
    uint16 myID = (uint16)self->tid;
    if( *p_threadID == myID){
        //locked by self, meaning recursion overflow
        recursion_overflow(jmon);
    }else{
        //locked by other thread, sleep on the monitor
        unit8* p_contention = (uint8*)lock_word_addr(jmon);
        Control* control = lookup_control(jmon);
        //use the mutex to guard the conditional variable
        lock(control->mutex);
        while(true){
            *p_contention = 1;
            result = lock_non_blocking_fast(jmon);
            if( result ) break;
            self->status = THREAD_STATE_MONITOR;
            wait(control->condvar, control->mutex);
```

```
        self->status = THREAD_STATE_RUNNING;
      }
      unlock(control->mutex);
   }
}


void STDCALL vm_object_unlock(Object* jmon)
{
   uint16* p_threadID = (uint16*)lock_word_addr(jmon)+1;
   uint16 self = (uint16)(current_thread()->tid);
   if( *p_threadID == self){
      //locked by self, check recursion number
      uint8* p_recursion = (uint8*)lock_word_addr(jmon)+1;
      uint8* p_contention = (uint16*)lock_word_addr(jmon);
      if( *p_recursion ){
         recursion_dec(jmon);
      else{
         *p_threadID = 0; //release lock
         if( *p_contention ){
            Control* control = lookup_control(jmon);
            lock(control->mutex);
            cond_notify_all(control->condvar);
            *p_contention = 0;
            unlock(control->mutex);
         }
      }
   }else{
      vm_throw_exception("IllegalMonitorState");
   }
}
```

In this design, the contending threads are managed with the conditional variable, so the lock owner does not need to iterate the mutator list to wake up the waiting threads. When there are multiple contending threads, after they are wakened up, one of them will successful lock the object, and the rest will again be blocked. They will set the contention flag again. The contention flag will only be finally reset to 0 by the last contending thread. When it releases the lock, the last contending thread will find the contention flag set by itself and then resets it.

Although only one thread can acquire the lock, the design has to waken up all the waiting threads, because the contention flag is reset. Next time when the lock is released, the lock owner will not try to waken up any waiting threads, unless other contending threads set the flag again. It is sometimes possible to waken up only one thread. That requires to reset the flag only when there is no waiting thread. Unfortunately, the number of waiting threads on a conditional variable is not usually available, so we cannot tell when to reset the flag. Consequently, we have to always reset it, and hence waken up all the waiting threads.

The mutex used here protects the consistence property between the contention flag and thread waiting status. When the flag is unset, there must not be a waiting thread. If there is a waiting thread, the flag must be set. At the same time, this design still keeps the ordering property as before: If a flag is set, it must be seen by the unlocking thread, since the flag is set before it tries the nonblocking lock. With both the properties of state consistence and operation ordering, this design allows to reset the contention flag.

Since the accesses to the contention flag is now protected by mutex, it does not have to be a byte that supports atomic memory access. A bit is fine as long as it does not interfere with other operations.

The optimizations above use a lock word in the object header to implement the common cases of locking and unlocking. It can be called "thin-lock," although it is not completely the same as the original design proposed by Bacon et al. Bacon's thin-lock alone is not a complete solution to monitor, since it cannot support sleep-waiting for contending lock, recursion overflow, and `Object.wait()`.

18.3 FAT-LOCK

The common path optimization is usually good enough, but sometimes the uncommon paths are also important to performance. Some applications may have lots of lock contentions or recursive locking.

When recursion number overflows, for instance, the owner thread needs to iterate its `locked_object_list` to increment/decrement recursion number. When there is lock contention, the unlocking thread needs to iterate global mutator list to waken up the blocked threads, or an additional control data structure is used to support contention resetting.

18.3.1 Consolidated Monitor Data Structure

To simplify the design, it is possible to create a simple monitor data structure that is associated with a lock object and includes all the needed information for its operations. For example, the data structure can include the recursion number and threads blocked for the lock. It may look like below.

```
struct VM_Monitor{
    VM_Thread* owner;
    int recursion;
    //threads blocked on locking this monitor. Replace blocked_lock
    Thread_List* blocked_list;
    //threads waiting on this monitor. Replace waited_condition
    Thread_List* waited_list;
}
```

This data structure consolidates all the monitor-related information in one place. The initial implementation spreads the information across all the involved threads.

In order to associate such a data structure with the lock object, similar to "forwarding pointer" in GC design, a mapping table is needed. It can use a pointer in the lock word of the object header, or a target-table off the heap.

We first discuss the "pointer" solution, where the lock word in an object's header installs a pointer to its associated monitor data structure. In actual implementation, a monitor ID can be used in lock word as long as it can be used to find the monitor data structure efficiently.

All of the monitor operations can be conducted over the monitor data structure. For example,

```
void STDCALL vm_object_lock(Object* jmon)
{
    VM_Monitor* mon = monitor_pointer(jmon);
    VM_Thread* self = current_thread();

    if( mon->owner == NULL){
        int oldID = CompareExchange(&mon->owner, NULL, self);
        if( oldID == NULL ) return;
    }else if ( mon->owner == self ){
        //locked by self
        mon->recursion++;
        return;
    }
    //locked by other thread
    insert_self_in_list(mon->blocked_list);
    lock_blocking(mon);
    delete_self_in_list(mon->blocked_list);
    mon->owner = current_thread();
}


void STDCALL vm_object_unlock(Object* jmon)
{
    VM_Monitor* mon = monitor_pointer(jmon);

    if( mon->owner == current_thread() ){
        //locked by self
        if( mon->recursion ){
            mon->recursion --;
        }else{
            mon->owner == NULL;
            notify_blocking_threads(mon);
        }
    }else{ //lock held by other thread
        vm_thread_exception("IllegalMonitorState");
    }
}
```

This is much easier to maintain, with the cost of a pointer in the object header.

Note there is no contention flag in this design. The thread that releases the lock will always check the `blocked_list` to waken up any waiting threads.

18.3.2 Offload Supports to OS

As we discussed earlier, monitor's semantics consist of mutext, for lock/unlock, and conditional variable, for wait/notify. (The code above only shows the mutex part.) It is easier to directly use the mutex and conditional variable support of the underlying OS. Some OSes even provide native monitor support. Then VM does not need to maintain the blocked thread list and signaling stuff. It is actually tricky to implement correct and efficient threading synchronization primitives, especially in multicore platforms with relaxed memory consistence.

For a platform that has mutex and conditional variable, VM can define the following monitor data structure.

```
struct VM_Monitor{
    VM_Thread* owner;
    int recursion;
    Mutex* mutex;
    Condvar* condvar;
}
```

The new code for locking can be the following.

```
void STDCALL vm_object_lock(Object* jmon)
{
    VM_Monitor* mon = monitor_pointer(jmon);
    monitor_lock(mon);
}

void STDCALL vm_object_unlock(Object* jmon)
{
    VM_Monitor* mon = monitor_pointer(jmon);
    monitor_unlock(mon);
}

void monitor_lock(VM_Monitor* mon)
{
    if( mon->owner == current_thread() ){
        //locked by self
        mon->recursion++;
    }else{
        mutex_lock(mon->mutex);
        mon->owner = current_thread();
    }
```

```
}

void monitor_unlock(VM_Monitor* mon)
{
   if( mon->owner == current_thread() ){
      //locked by self
      if( mon->recursion ){
         mon->recursion --;
      }else{
         mon->owner == NULL;
         mutex_unlock(mon->mutex);
      }
   }else{ //lock held by other thread
      vm_thread_exception("IllegalMonitorState");
   }
}
```

The Object.wait()/notify() pseudo-code can be the following.

```
void STDCALL vm_object_wait(Object* jmon, unsigned int ms)
{
   VM_Monitor* mon = monitor_pointer(jmon);
   monitor_wait(mon);
}

void STDCALL vm_object_notify(Object* jmon)
{
   VM_Monitor* mon = monitor_pointer(jmon);
   monitor_notify(mon);
}

void monitor_wait(VM_Monitor* mon, unsigned int ms)
{
   VM_Thread* self = current_thread();
   if( mon->owner != self ) {
      vm_throw_exception("IllegalMonitorState");
      return;
   }
   self->status= THREAD_STATE_WAIT;
   //use OS support for conditional timed wait
   int temp_recursion = mon->recursion;
   mon->recursion = 0;
   bool signaled = cond_timed_wait(mon->condvar, mon->mutex, ms);
   //wake up
   self->status= THREAD_STATE_RUNNING;
   mon->recursion = temp_recursion;
```

```
    if(self->interrupted) {
        self->interrupted = false;
        vm_throw_exception("Interrupted");
    }
}

void monitor_notify(VM_Monitor* mon)
{
    if( mon->owner != current_thread() ) {
        vm_throw_exception("IllegalMonitorState");
        return;
    }
    //use OS support for notify
    cond_notify(mon->condvar);
}
```

The implementation with monitor data structure trivially supports all the scenarios including the corner cases like recursion overflow, thread blocking, etc. that are not gracefully supported by thin-lock. It does not use contention flag to tell a lock owner if there are sleep-waiting threads, because the mutex has the support by default. To unlock a mutex automatically wakens up the waiting thread(s) on it.

This implementation has both performance and space overhead. Compared to thin-lock, the performance cost is that this implementation always needs to access the monitor data structure for monitor operations, rather than directly operate on the object header. The spatial cost is the additional data structure for every monitor. For this reason, the design sometimes is called "fat-lock."

18.3.3 Thin-Lock Inflation to Fat-Lock

It is desirable if the implementation can support thin-lock for common cases, and fat-lock for other cases. An object can start from thin-lock and only changes to fat-lock when its operation involves recursion overflow and thread blocking (due to blocked locking or Object.wait()). This process is called "inflation" in the community.

Inflation design can be similar as the contention flag discussed previously, by using an inflation flag. When inflation happens (due to recursion overflow or lock contention), the lock word is changed from thin-lock data to a pointer to a monitor data structure (the fat-lock), together with the inflation flag being set.

The inflation function reproduces the thin-lock state in the fat-lock, by locking the fat-lock the same times as the thin-lock has been locked, as given below.

```
void lock_inflate(Object* jmon)
{
    uint8 recursion = *((uint8*)lock_word_addr(jmon)+1);

    VM_Monitor* mon = vm_alloc(sizeof(VM_Monitor));
    mon->mutex = new_recursive_mutex();
```

```
    mon->condvar = new_condvar();
    //the thin-lock has been locked recursion+1 times
    mon->owner = current_thread();
    mon->recursion = recursion;
    monitor_pointer_set(jmon, mon);
}
```

Since inflation changes the lock word, there may be race conditions between inflation and other locking operations. To avoid race conditions, a protocol is needed between the threads.

A simple protocol allows only the lock owner to inflate a lock, and never deflates an inflated lock, similar to the first design of contention flag that does not support resetting. Here setting contention flag is replaced by inflating thin-lock. That is, the thin-lock owner inflates the lock after it acquires the thin-lock through contending. At the same time, other contending threads spin-wait (or yield-wait) for the lock to transition from thin-lock to fat-lock. Since contending threads rely on the monitor data structure to sleep on, they cannot sleep-wait before inflation is done.

This design does not use contention flag to tell a lock owner if there are sleep-waiting threads. When the thin-lock is contended, the contending threads just spin-wait. When the lock is inflated, the fat-lock will take care of the contention management.

When a lock is being inflated by its owner, another thread may be contending for the lock. The contending thread may have seen a thin-lock before the lock is inflated; then the contending thread still uses thin-lock algorithm to lock it. That is, between the two operations, seeing a thin-lock and locking it, the lock may become fat-lock. The design should ensure that the operation to lock a thin-lock should fail on a fat-lock. A solution is to limit the two-byte thread ID to 15 bits, leaving the top bit to inflation flag. When the inflation flag is set, the two bytes together constitute a number different from any thread ID. The thin-lock algorithm still treats the whole two bytes as thread ID. When a thread tries to lock an inflated lock with thin-lock algorithm, it considers the lock is locked by other thread, hence always fails.

The pseudo-code for lock with inflation support looks like below.

```
void STDCALL vm_object_lock(Object* jmon)
{
    //first try with thin-lock non-blocking locking
    bool success = lock_non_blocking_fast(jmon);
    if( success ) return;
    // object is either 1) locked by other thread, or
    // 2) recursion number overflow, or 3) becomes fat-lock
    uint16* p_threadID = (uint16*)lock_word_addr(jmon)+1;
    uint16 newID = (uint16)(current_thread()->tid);
    if( *p_threadID == newID) // recursion overflow, inflate it
        lock_inflate(jmon);  // not return, lock it below
    // locked by another thread
    while( !lock_is_fat(jmon) ){
        //maybe acquired and inflated by other thread
```

```
        yield();
        success = lock_non_blocking_fast(jmon);
        if( success ){
            lock_inflate(jmon);
            return;
        }
    }
    //fat-lock
    VM_Monitor* mon = monitor_pointer(jmon);
    monitor_lock(mon);
    return;
}

void STDCALL vm_object_unlock(Object* jmon)
{
    if( !lock_is_fat(jmon) ){
        object_unlock_thin(jmon);
    }else{ //fat-lock
        VM_Monitor* mon = monitor_pointer(jmon);
        monitor_unlock(mon);
    }
}

void STDCALL vm_object_wait(Object* jmon, unsigned int ms)
{
    if( !lock_is_fat(jmon) ){
        lock_check_state(jmon);
        lock_inflate(jmon);
    }
    VM_Monitor* mon = monitor_pointer(jmon);
    monitor_wait(mon, ms);
}

void STDCALL vm_object_notify(Object* jmon)
{
    if( !lock_is_fat(jmon) ){ // thin-lock
        lock_check_state(jmon);
        // thin-lock does not have any waiting thread on the lock
        return;
    }
    VM_Monitor* mon = monitor_pointer(jmon);
    monitor_notify(mon);
}
```

Note the monitor data structure is allocated in VM, whose address is fixed as the vtable pointer in object header. Garbage collection does not move it. Otherwise the pointer in object lock word needs to be updated as an object reference.

18.3.4 Sleep-Waiting for the Contended Thin-Lock

It is easy to find that, the design above has two drawbacks. First is that, before the lock is inflated, the contending threads on thin-lock have to yield-wait for the lock rather than sleep-wait. Second drawback is that once a lock is inflated, it cannot be deflated.

The first problem is not necessarily always serious, especially when the lock duration is short. When it becomes serious, the design of contention flag can be reused to attack the problem. The design allows the contending threads to set the contention flag and then go to sleep on a control data structure. The main changes compared to the previous design for contention flag resetting are as follows:

- **When to reset the contention flag:** The contention flag is to indicate there is contention for thin-lock. Once the lock is inflated, the contention flag is no longer useful, since fat-lock does not need that. For this purpose, the contention flag is reset during lock inflation, rather than being reset during unlocking in previous design.

  The unlocking thread of a thin-lock only checks if the contention flag is set so as to waken up the waiting thread on the control data structure.

- **How many threads to waken up:** When the owner of a thin-lock releases the lock, if contention flag is set, it needs to wake up a contending thread that is waiting on the control data structure. This wakened-up thread possibly acquires the lock and inflates it.

  It does not make much sense to waken up all the waiting threads as the previous design, because no more than one wakened-up thread can win the contention. It is even possible that a newly created thread acquires the lock before any of the wakened-up thread.

  The nonwakened-up threads will continue waiting on the control data structure until one contender wins the lock and inflates it to fat-lock; then they will move on to sleep on the flat-lock.

  In previous design, all the waiting threads are wakened up because the contention flag is reset at the same time. In current design, that happens during inflation.

- **Where the contending threads sleep on:** When the contending threads are waiting for a thin-lock, they sleep on the control data structure associated with the contention flag management.

  When the contention flag is reset and the lock is inflated, all the waiting threads on the control data structure are wakened up to reacquire the lock. If any of them fail to acquire the lock, they then will sleep-wait on the fat-lock, instead of the control data structure.

  In previous design, the control data structure is the only place for sleeping since there was no fat-lock.

Now that the lock inflation action includes operations to reset contention flag and notify waiting threads on the conditional variable, it has to be protected by the mutex of the control data structure to keep the consistence property. The inflation algorithm above without contention flag does not need the protection.

Inflation can happen in three places: recursion overflow, a contending thread acquires the lock, and a lock owner calling `Object.wait()` waits on the object. All should be protected with mutex.

The following pseudo-code gives the design of lock inflation without thread spin-waiting.

```
void STDCALL vm_object_lock(Object* jmon)
{
    //first try with thin-lock non-blocking locking
    bool result = lock_non_blocking_fast(jmon);
    if( result ) return;
    // object is either 1) locked by other thread, or
    // 2) recursion number overflow, or 3) becomes fat-lock
    uint16* p_threadID = (uint16*)lock_word_addr(jmon)+1;
    VM_Thread* self = current_thread();
    uint16 newID = (uint16)self->tid;
    if( *p_threadID == newID){ // recursion overflow, inflate it
        Control* control = lookup_control(jmon);
        mutex_lock(control->mutex);
        lock_inflate(jmon);
        mutex_unlock(control->mutex);
    }
    // fat-lock
    if( lock_is_fat(jmon) ){
        VM_Monitor* mon = monitor_pointer(jmon);
        monitor_lock(mon);
        return;
    }
    // thin-lock, but locked by other thread, waiting
    Control* control = lookup_control(jmon);
    mutex_lock(control->mutex);
    while( !lock_is_fat(jmon) ){
        *p_contention = 1;
        result = lock_non_blocking_fast(jmon);
        if( result ){
            lock_inflate(jmon);
            mutex_unlock(control->mutex);
            return;
        }
        self->status = THREAD_STATE_MONITOR;
        cond_wait(control->condvar, control->mutex);
        self->status = THREAD_STATE_RUNNING;
    }
    mutex_unlock(control->mutex);
```

```
    VM_Monitor* mon = monitor_pointer(jmon);
    monitor_lock(mon);
    return;
}


void lock_inflate(Object* jmon)
{
    uint8 recursion = *((uint8*)lock_word_addr(jmon)+1);

    VM_Monitor* mon = vm_alloc(sizeof(VM_Monitor));
    mon->mutex = new_recursive_mutex();
    mon->condvar = new_condvar();
    mon->owner = current_thread();
    mon->recursion = recursion;
    monitor_pointer_set(jmon, mon);
    Control* control = lookup_control(jmon);
    *p_contention = 0;
    cond_notify_all(control->condvar);
}


void STDCALL vm_object_unlock(Object* jmon)
{
    if( !lock_is_fat(jmon) ){ // thin-lock
        lock_check_state(jmon);
        uint16* p_threadID = (uint16*)lock_word_addr(jmon)+1;
        //locked by self, check recursion number
        uint8* p_recursion = (uint8*)lock_word_addr(jmon)+1;
        uint8* p_contention = (uint16*)lock_word_addr(jmon);
        if( *p_recursion ){
            recursion_dec(jmon);
        else{
            *p_threadID = 0; //release lock
            if( *p_contention ){
                Control* control = lookup_control(jmon);
                mutex_lock(control->mutex);
                cond_notify(control->condvar);
                mutex_unlock(control->mutex);
            }
    }else{ //fat-lock
        VM_Monitor* mon = monitor_pointer(jmon);
        monitor_unlock(mon);
    }
}


void STDCALL vm_object_wait(Object* jmon, unsigned int ms)
{
    if( !lock_is_fat(jmon) ){
```

```
        lock_check_state(jmon);
        Control* control = lookup_control(jmon);
        mutex_lock(control->mutex);
        lock_inflate(jmon);
        mutex_unlock(control->mutex);
    }
    VM_Monitor* mon = monitor_pointer(jmon);
    monitor_wait(mon, ms);
}

void STDCALL vm_object_notify(Object* jmon)
{
    if( !lock_is_fat(jmon) ){
        lock_check_state(jmon);
        return;
    }
    VM_Monitor* mon = monitor_pointer(jmon);
    monitor_notify(mon);
}
```

The key in this design is that it uses a control data structure for every lock object to allow the contending threads to sleep on. This data structure ceases to be used when the lock is inflated to fat-lock, and the contending threads move on to be blocked on the fat-lock.

For correctness, this design mainly ensures two things. One is that, when a thread is sleeping on thin-lock, it should not be missed for wakening up; second is that, when the lock becomes fat-lock, all the sleeping threads are moved to fat-lock.

Although in both cases the threads are blocked sleeping, the threads are sleeping at different places in different ways. In thin-lock, they sleep on the control data structure, waiting on the conditional variable, which can be wakened up by another thread notifying the conditional variable. In fat-lock, they sleep on the monitor data structure, blocked on the monitor's mutex, which can be wakened up by another thread unlocking the mutex. This difference has essential impact on the design we will discuss next.

The inflation action is always protected by the mutex, so it is fine to directly put the mutex locking/unlocking operations into the inflation function. But then we need to add a mutex unlocking after a contending thread successfully acquires the thin-lock, before the inflation, as follows.

```
result = lock_non_blocking_fast(jmon);
if( result ){
    mutex_unlock(control->mutex);
    lock_inflate(jmon);
    return;
}
```

The design in this section allows the contending threads on thin-lock to sleep-wait on a control data structure. It does not support deflation. To add deflation support is relatively easy.

What it needs is to check if there is no threads blocked or waiting on the fat-lock, and then turn the lock word back to thin-lock.

18.4 TASUKI LOCK

The design that allows the blocked threads to sleep-wait relies on the control data structure. An observation is that, the control data structure virtually implements a nonrecursive monitor. It is possible to use a monitor data structure to replace the control data structure. We actually can reuse the fat-lock implementation for the control data structure.

One more observation is that the control data structure in the design is only used before a thin-lock is inflated into a fat-lock. In other words, the use of the control data structure and the use of the monitor data structure are not overlapping. If we want to replace the control data structure with a monitor data structure, it is convenient to just use the same monitor data structure of the lock object.

18.4.1 Use Same Fat-Lock Monitor for Contention Control

When using the same monitor data structure for both control and fat-lock, there are a few changes in the design.

18.4.1.1 Access to Monitor

In previous design, the control data structure for contention flag is accessed through a global mapping table that maps an object address to it. The monitor data structure for a fat-lock is accessed through the lock word. Now when we use the same data structure, we should support both paths, so that the monitor data can always be accessed no matter if the lock is thin or fat, as given below.

```
VM_Monitor* lookup_monitor(Object* jmon)
{
   if( lock_is_fat(jmon) )
      return monitor_pointer(jmon);
   else
      return lookup_control(jmon);
}
```

The monitor data structure of an object is created the first time when `lookup_control(jmon)` is invoked for the object. It happens when there is a contention on the thin-lock, or its recursion number overflows, or `Object.wait()` is called on the lock object.

18.4.1.2 Inflation Process

In previous design, the inflation function reproduces the thin-lock state in the monitor, by locking the monitor the same times as the thin-lock has been locked. The inflation operation is protected by a mutex of the control data structure, which is now replaced by the monitor.

That means, in current design, before inflation is invoked, the monitor has been locked once, in order to protect the inflation process. Therefore, when the inflation function reproduces the lock state in the monitor, it does not set the lock owner again, but set the recursion number.

Moreover, in previous design, the monitor data structure is created in inflation. Now that the monitor is used for thin-lock contention management and for inflation protection, the monitor data structure has to exist before inflation. The inflation function does not need to create a data structure; instead, the monitor data structure is passed to it as an argument. The pseudo-code is given below.

```
void lock_inflate(Object* jmon, VM_Monitor* mon)
{
    uint8 recursion = *((uint8*)lock_word_addr(jmon)+1);
    // reproduce the lock state to be recursion + 1 times.
    mon->recursion = recursion;
    monitor_pointer_set(jmon, mon);
    *p_contention = 0;
    monitor_notify_all(mon);
}
```

18.4.1.3 Dual Roles of Monitor during Inflation

Lock inflation can only be conducted by the thread who is holding the lock. The owner switches the thin-lock to fat-lock. In previous design when the inflation is protected by a mutex of the control data structure, the mutex should be unlocked after the inflation process. Now that the control data structure is replaced by the same monitor that the thin-lock inflates into, the owner should continue to own it rather than unlock it after inflation.

That means, for the inflation process, the monitor now has dual roles. One is to protect the inflation process, and the other is to act as the new owned lock. After the inflation, its role of protecting the inflation process is over, but its role as an owned lock continues; hence it does not need to be unlocked after the inflation.

18.4.1.4 Redundant Monitor Locking/Unlocking Pair

In previous design, when there is a contention on locking, the contending thread needs to lock the control data structure, then sets the contention flag, and retries to lock the thin-lock (if it is still a thin-lock). The lock of the control data structure and the thin-lock are different locks.

Now by replacing the control data structure with the monitor, the contending thread needs to lock the monitor first, before it sets the contention flag and retries the thin-lock. This looks problematic by locking both the monitor and thin-lock of the same object at the same time. It actually does not, because the monitor at the moment (when the object is a thin-lock) is only acting as a protective control data structure, instead of the real monitor of the object.

However, it does act as the real monitor if the lock is inflated. The following scenario is possible: A contending thread for thin-lock acquires the monitor (as control data structure) and sleeps on it. When it is wakened up, the monitor it slept on becomes fat-lock monitor (no longer as control data structure). In this case, when it wakes up, the thread does not need to unlock the control data structure and lock the fat-lock monitor, because the waking-up process acquires the fat-lock already. The pair of control unlocking and monitor locking can be removed.

Looked from another angle, if there is no code in between, any pair of fat-lock locking/unlocking can be removed. Pairs of locking/unlocking may exist because, in previous design, locking/unlocking are operating on different data structures, that is, one on the control data structure, and the other on the monitor data structure. Now by using the same data structure for both, they become a pair of redundant operations.

18.4.1.5 Implementation with Merged Monitor and Control
Following is the pseudo-code that uses the same fat-lock monitor for contention control. It is an annotated revision based on the previous design.

```
void STDCALL vm_object_lock(Object* jmon)
{
    //first try with thin-lock non-blocking locking
    bool result = lock_non_blocking_fast(jmon);
    if( result ) return;
    // object is either 1) locked by other thread, or
    // 2) recursion number overflow, or 3) becomes fat-lock
    uint16* p_threadID = (uint16*)lock_word_addr(jmon)+1;
    VM_Thread* self = current_thread();
    if( *p_threadID == newID){ // recursion overflow, inflate it
        VM_Monitor* mon = lookup_monitor(jmon);
        monitor_lock(mon);
        lock_inflate(jmon);
        //removed after inflation
        monitor_unlock(mon);
        return;
    }
    // fat-lock. This logic is merged into code below
    if( lock_is_fat(jmon) ){
        VM_Monitor* mon = monitor_pointer(jmon);
        monitor_lock(mon);
        return;
    }
    // fat-lock or to-be fat-lock
    VM_Monitor* mon = lookup_monitor(jmon);
    monitor_lock(mon);
```

```
    while( !lock_is_fat(jmon) ){
        *p_contention = 1;
        result = lock_non_blocking_fast(jmon);
        if( result ){
            lock_inflate(jmon, mon);
            //removed after inflation
            monitor_unlock(mon);
            return;
        }
        monitor_wait(mon);
    }
    // redundant pair of lock and unlock
    monitor_unlock(mon);
    VM_Monitor* mon = monitor_pointer(jmon);
    monitor_lock(mon);
    return;
}

void STDCALL vm_object_unlock(Object* jmon)
{
    if( !lock_is_fat(jmon) ){ // thin-lock
        lock_check_state(jmon);
        uint16* p_threadID = (uint16*)lock_word_addr(jmon)+1;
        //locked by self, check recursion number
        uint8* p_recursion = (uint8*)lock_word_addr(jmon)+1;
        uint8* p_contention = (uint16*)lock_word_addr(jmon);
        if( *p_recursion ){
            recursion_dec(jmon);
        else{
            *p_threadID = 0; //release lock
            if( *p_contention ){
                VM_Monitor* mon = lookup_monitor(jmon);
                monitor_lock(mon);
                monitor_notify(mon);
                monitor_unlock(mon);
            }
        }
    }else{ //fat-lock
        VM_Monitor* mon = monitor_pointer(jmon);
        monitor_unlock(mon);
    }
}

void STDCALL vm_object_wait(Object* jmon, unsigned int ms)
{
    if( !lock_is_fat(jmon) ){
        lock_check_state(jmon);
        VM_Monitor* mon = lookup_moniter(jmon);
```

```
        monitor_lock(mon);
        lock_inflate(jmon, mon);
        //removed after inflation
        monitor_unlock(mon);
    }
    VM_Monitor* mon = monitor_pointer(jmon);
    monitor_wait(mon, ms);
}

void STDCALL vm_object_notify(Object* jmon)
{
    if( !lock_is_fat(jmon) ){
        lock_check_state(jmon);
        return;
    }
    VM_Monitor* mon = monitor_pointer(jmon);
    monitor_notify(mon);
}
```

The design uses one monitor data structure to support both sleep-waiting contention management and lock inflation.

18.4.2 Fat-Lock Deflation to Thin-Lock

The design above looks elegant, but it does not support deflation. To add deflation support, the lock owner needs to ensure there is no threads blocked (for `monitorenter`) or waiting (for `Object.wait()`) on the fat-lock. Then it can turn the lock word back to thin-lock.

18.4.2.1 Conditions for Lock Deflation

Deflation should be conducted by the lock owner when it unlocks its fat-lock. The unlocking code in the fat-lock path needs to check the following conditions before deflating the lock:

1. No blocked threads on the fat-lock due to calling `monitorenter`, that is, `vm_object_lock()`.

2. No waiting threads on the fat-lock due to calling `Object.wait()` on the lock object, that is, `vm_object_wait()`;

3. The fat-lock's recursion number is no more than the overflow number, that is, `RECURSION_OVERFLOW`.

Only when all of the conditions above are true, can the lock be deflated. It is worth to examine how they can be changed by other threads, so as to avoid race conditions between lock owner's checking and other threads' modification.

- **Blocked threads:** Another thread can call "monitorenter" at any time and be blocked. There is no way to prevent that from happening, unless we use another mutex to protect the monitor, which is obviously contradicting to the design purpose, since that virtually becomes monitor's monitor.

  As a result, even if there is no blocked thread at the moment when the deflating thread checks the condition (num_blocked), some threads may come to be blocked right after the checking. So the purpose of checking the blocked threads is only for heuristic purpose, rather than for correctness. To support deflation, we surely do not want the deflated lock get inflated again immediately, and the lock thrashes between inflation and deflation. But the deflation design has to support the case when there are or there will be sleeping threads.

- **Waiting threads:** Since the deflating thread holds the lock, it is impossible for another thread to call Object.wait() at the same time, because calling of Object.wait() requires to hold the lock.

  In other words, if we instrument a counter in the vm_object_wait() code that increments and decrements before and after the thread waits, then this counter is protected by the lock naturally.

  The deflating thread can check the counter value and action upon the checking result without worrying about the atomicity problem, as long as the "checking and action" happens before it releases the lock.

  Note there can be some threads trying to acquire the lock in order to call Object.wait() at the same time. The situation of these threads is the same as those we discussed above on "blocked threads."

- **Recursion number:** A thread cannot deflate its lock if the recursion overflows. This number is completely under its own control; no race condition can occur.

To summarize, the only situation to consider for lock deflation design is the case of blocked threads on "monitorenter."

18.4.2.2 Design of Lock Deflation

Deflation changes the fat-lock to thin-lock. During this process, it is possible for some threads to be blocked on the fat-lock and some others on the thin-lock. In current design, thin-lock uses fat-lock monitor for its contention management. That means, no matter whether a thread is blocked on fat-lock or thin-lock, it is blocked on the same monitor data structure. In other words, if deflation does not free the lock, then the deflation process is not visible to other threads at all. This is super neat. It is ascribed to the nature of using the same monitor data structure for fat-lock and contention management.

At the same time, when the lock is deflated, the lock owner still holds the lock on the monitor data structure, which is now acting as the control data structure that protects the deflation process' atomicity with respect to other blocking or waiting threads. This is actually the reverse of inflation process. The inflation process is also protected by the control data structure, which is locked before the inflation. Then the inflation process locks the fat-lock monitor one time less than the thin-lock has been locked, because the monitor has been locked once as control data structure before the inflation.

The deflation function is simple, as given below. It reproduces the fat-lock state in the lock word of thin-lock, and makes sure the fat-lock monitor is still locked once.

```
void lock_deflate(Object* jmon)
{
    VM_Monitor* mon = monitor_pointer(jmon);
    uint8* p_threadID = (uint16*)lock_word_addr(jmon)+1;
    uint8* p_recursion = (uint8*)lock_word_addr(jmon)+1;
    *p_recursion = mon->recursion
    // leave fat-lock locked once (no recursion)
    mon->recursion = 0;
    // turn to a thin-lock
    *p_threadID = (uint16)mon->owner->tid;
}
```

As we mentioned, deflation is conducted by the lock owner when it unlocks its fat-lock. When the deflation conditions are met, the lock owner first deflates the lock, then unlock the lock. Since now the lock is thin-lock, the lock owner should unlock the thin-lock. Then, finally it also unlocks the fat-lock monitor, to finish the whole unlocking process. If the lock is deflated, the final step lifts the protection on the deflation (by unlocking the control data structure). If the lock is not deflated, the final step unlocks the fat-lock.

Based on the discussion, the unlocking code becomes the following.

```
void STDCALL vm_object_unlock(Object* jmon)
{
    if( !lock_is_fat(jmon) ){ // thin-lock
        ...// (no change, omitted)
    else{ //fat-lock
        VM_Monitor* mon = monitor_pointer(jmon);
        lock_check_state(mon);
        if(!num_blocked && !num_waiting){
            if( mon->recursion <= RECURSION_OVERFLOW ){
                lock_deflate(jmon);
                object_unlock_thin(jmon);
            }
        }
        monitor_unlock(mon);
    }
}
```

If the lock is not recursive, the unlocking frees the thin-lock, and other threads may immediately operate on the thin-lock, without knowing that there may have been some threads already being blocked on the fat-lock monitor.

Especially, between the lock owner unlocks the thin-lock and unlocks the fat-lock monitor, the lock cannot be inflated by other threads, even if the lock has been freed as a thin-lock.

The existing blocked threads (on the fat-lock monitor) or the new blocked threads (on the thin-lock control data structure) can only restart activities after the deflating thread unlocks the fat-lock.

As just mentioned, the double-unlocking process for deflation is the reverse of the double-locking process for inflation, where the thread acquires the fat-lock (as control data structure) first, and then acquires the thin-lock and inflates it.

18.4.2.3 Supports to Lock Deflation

We should track the number of waiting threads, and desirably also the number of blocked threads. To track the number of blocking and waiting threads, two counters are added in the monitor data structure, and instrumented in the locking and waiting code of fat-lock.

```
struct VM_Monitor{
    VM_Thread* owner;
    int recursion;
    Mutex* mutex;
    Condvar* condvar;
    int num_blocked;
    int num_waiting;
}

void monitor_lock(VM_Monitor* mon)
{
    if( mon->owner == current_thread() ){
        //locked by self
        mon->recursion++;
    }else{
        atomic_inc(mon->num_blocked);
        mutex_lock(mon->mutex);
        atomic_dec(mon->num_blocked);
        mon->owner = current_thread();
    }
}

void monitor_wait(VM_Monitor* mon, unsigned int ms)
{
    VM_Thread* self = current_thread();
    if( mon->owner != self ) {
        vm_throw_exception("IllegalMonitorState");
        return;
    }
    self->status= THREAD_STATE_WAIT;
    //use OS support for conditional timed wait
    int temp_recursion = mon->recursion;
    mon->recursion = 0;
```

```
atomic_inc(mon->num_waiting);
bool signaled = cond_timed_wait(mon->condvar, mon->mutex, ms);
atomic_dec(mon->num_waiting);
//wake up
self->status= THREAD_STATE_RUNNING;
mon->recursion = temp_recursion;

if(self->interrupted) {
    self->interrupted = false;
    vm_throw_exception("Interrupted");
}
}
```

As we discussed, the num_blocked condition is only heuristic. When it is zero, the design cannot guarantee there is no blocking thread when deflation happens. The num_waiting condition is mandatory. When there is a waiting thread on the fat-lock, the lock cannot be deflated, since thin-lock in the design does not support Object.wait().

The original design for this lock was proposed by Onodera and Kawachiya. They called it Tasuki lock. The reasoning process here is different from theirs though. Here the design starts from the contention flag setting problem in thin-lock.

Supporting both inflation and deflation helps the applications that exhibit sporadic lock contentions. In order to avoid the frequent thrashing between inflation and deflation, adaptive deflation based on the dynamic behavior is desirable.

18.5 THREAD-LOCAL LOCK

In the lock implementations discussed so far, a thread always needs to use atomic instruction to acquire ownership, unless it already owns the lock. The assumption is that a free lock may be contended by multiple threads. If the assumption can be proven untrue, the atomic operation can be saved, which is usually expensive. Lazy lock is one of the optimization ideas. It is only applicable when there is only one thread having lock operations.

When there are multiple threads using locks, it is possible that some lock objects are only accessed by a single thread. Techniques are needed to identify those lock objects, so as to optimize their lock operations. Escape analysis and escape detection are often used for the purpose.

Escape analysis uses compiler technique to analyze an object's access flow. It follows an object's access starting from its creation spot till its reference either being accessed by another thread (i.e., escaping) or being useless (or nullified). If an object is identified not escaping, lock operations on it can be optimized.

Escape detection dynamically monitors if an object is accessed by a second thread (i.e., escaping) at runtime. It usually allocates an object in the thread-local state, and then uses access barrier to catch any accesses from another thread and then marks the object as global. As lazy-lock does, VM should track the lock operations so that correct lock state can be restored when the object escapes.

When an object escapes, it does not necessarily mean the lock operations on the object will be conducted by multiple threads. As a monitor, the object may be only locked/unlocked by a single thread. It is not thread-local object, but it is thread-local lock.

Thread-local lock does not need atomic instruction either. Object access-based detection does not work here. It should use lock access-based detection.

18.5.1 Lock Reservation

VM community developed various techniques to identify thread-local lock, such as *Lock Reservation* by Kawachiya et al., *Biased Lock* by Dice et al. and *Lazy Unlocking* by Hirt and Lagergren, and *Private Lock* by the author of the book.

18.5.1.1 Design of Lock Reservation

The ideas for all the designs are similar conceptually. When an object is locked by a thread, this thread becomes the default owner of the object. When it unlocks the object, the ownership remains. We call this thread "lock reserver" of the object. Then later when the same thread (lock reserver) locks the object again, it does not need atomic instruction, assuming this lock is thread-local. The locking/unlocking sequence the lock reserver uses is thread-unsafe.

If a second thread tries to lock an object that is reserved by another thread, no matter if the object is currently free or not, the second thread cannot simply lock the object as with a thin-lock or fat-lock, because that will conflict with the thread-unsafe code the lock reserver uses. VM has to have a way to inform the lock reserver to use thread-safe code sequence for locking/unlocking upon the reserved object, before it allows the second thread to lock it.

There are different ways to inform the lock reserver of its untrue assumption on the lock's thread locality. A commonly used protocol is for the second thread to suspend the lock reserver, restore the lock state to nonreservable mode, and then resume the thread, who is no longer the lock reserver. This process is to "unreserve" a lock.

The thread suspension mechanism has to ensure that the lock reserver is not suspended at a spot within the range of unsafe code for locking/unlocking. GC safe-point mechanism can help here so that the lock reserver is only suspended at a safe-point. The unsafe code is not a safe-point, because it is supposed to be very fast, hence not prepared for safe-point suspension.

If the reservation design keeps the similar lock word as a thin-lock, it can take one bit from the recursion byte as the "reservable bit," indicating if the lock is in reservable mode or not. This design is only valid when the inflation bit is unset.

When the reservable bit is not set, the lock word is used as usual as a thin-lock.

When the reservable bit is set, the two-byte thread ID (minus the inflation bit) is used for the lock reserver's ID. When the ID has a value, it means the lock is reserved by the thread of that ID, rather than being locked as in thin-lock. Reservable mode does not mean the object is already reserved.

Now the recursion number is used to indicate the locking status. When the recursion number is 0, the lock is free. When the object is locked once, the recursion number is 1. When the recursion overflows, the lock has to be inflated.

An object is created with reservable bit set, and the first thread locking it reserves it naturally. It will set the thread ID field with its ID, and set the recursion number to 1.

Fat-lock can also have reservation design. The reservable flag can be in the monitor data structure.

18.5.1.2 Implementation of Lock Reservation

The locking and unlocking code for reservable thin-lock may look like below.

```
void STDCALL vm_object_lock(Object* jmon)
{
    if( is_reservable_mode(jmon) ){
        if( reserved_by_self(jmon) ){
            recursion_inc(jmon);
            return;
        }else if( lock_is_free(jmon) ){
            //compete for lock reserver
            bool result = lock_non_blocking(jmon);
            if( result ){
                //hold the lock as reserver,
                //set recursion to indicate it is locked
                recursion_inc(jmon);
                return;
            }
            //failed locking it, fall through to unreserve it
        }
        //lock is reserved by other thread
        lock_unreserve(jmon);
    }
    //lock is not reserved or just unreserved above
    object_lock_normal(jmon);
}

void STDCALL vm_object_unlock(Object* jmon)
{
    if( lock_is_reserved(jmon) ){
        lock_check_state(jmon);
        recursion_dec(jmon);
        return;
    }
    //lock is not reserved
    object_unlock_normal(jmon);
}
```

It is possible for multiple threads to unreserve the same lock at the same time. So the operation to unreserve a lock has to be thread-safe, such as the pseudo-code below.

```
void lock_unreserve(Object* jmon)
{
    if( !is_reservable_mode(jmon) ) return;
    VM_Thread* reserver = lock_reserver( jmon );
    vm_suspend_thread( reserver );
    // lock reserver is suspended at safe-point
    int* p_lockword = lock_word_addr(jmon);
    int old_word = *p_lockword;
    if ( !reservable_bit_on(old_word) ) return;
    int new_word = normalize_lock_word(old_word);
    CompareExchange(p_lockword, old_word, new_word );
    vm_resume_thread( reserver );
}
```

When a second thread tries to unreserve a lock, the lock can be held or free. Even if the lock is free, the unreserving process still needs to suspend the lock reserver to prevent it from locking (unsafely) again.

The atomic CompareExchange does not need to check if it succeeds or not. Once the lock reserver is suspended, the lock word can only be changed by this line of code. If one thread fails, there must be another thread succeeding.

18.5.1.3 Contention Management on Lock Reservation

It is obvious that, when a reservable lock is locked, its state looks like it is locked one more time than that of a corresponding thin-lock. In other words, in the first-time of the reserver locking the thread-local lock, it actually locks the object twice in terms of thin-lock: once to hold the lock, once to increment the recursion number. Later when the reserver locks/ unlocks the same object, it acts as usual as a thin-lock.

The result is the object always looks like being locked once more than actual times. Even after the object is freed by the reserver, it still looks like being locked once in the eyes of a thin-lock, that is, the thread ID field is set and the recursion number is 0. This additional time of locking facilitates the lock reserver to lock/unlock the object without atomic instruction, while preventing other threads from locking the object. When another thread wants to lock the object, it has to inform the lock reserver to unlock the object one more time. This is to unreserve the lock. In this way, when the lock reserver releases the lock, the lock is "really" free. Apparently, other threads can only acquire a lock when it is "really" free, being not reserved or locked.

In other words, lock unreserving is a process of threads contending to modify the lock word. Locking a thin-lock is also a process of threads contending to modify the lock word. Since they are virtually similar processes, it is possible to use the same contention management for both scenarios.

In our previous design, we use a control data structure to manage the thread contention on thin-lock. The contending threads for thin-lock should first acquire the control data structure associated with the thin-lock. Now that those threads need to contend for lock unreserving (before they contend for the thin-lock), it makes sense to use the same control data structure to manage the thread contention for lock unreserving.

As with Tasuki lock, we can use the fat-lock monitor for this purpose without any problem. The pseudo-code for lock unreserving is given below.

```
void lock_unreserve(Object* jmon)
{
    VM_Monitor* mon = lookup_monitor(jmon);
    monitor_lock( mon );
    if( !is_reservable_mode(jmon) ){
        monitor_unlock( mon );
        return;
    }
    VM_Thread* reserver = lock_reserver( jmon );
    vm_suspend_thread( reserver );
    // lock reserver is suspended at safe-point
    int* p_lockword = lock_word_addr(jmon);
    int old_word = *p_lockword;
    if ( !reservable_bit_on(old_word) ) {
        monitor_unlock( mon );
        return;
    }
    int new_word = normalize_lock_word(old_word);
    *p_lockword = new_word;
    vm_resume_thread( reserver );
    monitor_unlock( mon );
}
```

Using the monitor to manage the contention for lock unreserving has no problem because of the following:

- The fat-lock monitor is purely for control purpose before the thin-lock becomes fat-lock, while lock unreserving normally happens before the reserved lock becomes a normal thin-lock.

- It is possible that the thin-lock inflates to fat-lock before another thread T tries to unreserve it. The inflation happens after thread T finds the lock is reserved, and before thread T starts to unreserve it. Then the control data structure becomes acting as the fat-lock.

    If the fat-lock is held by a thread S, the unreserving thread T will be blocked when it tries to acquire the fat-lock. As we mentioned, lock unreserving is only the prelude of locking operation. Blocking here for lock unreserving has no essential difference from blocking for locking the fat-lock.

If the fat-lock is free, the unreserving thread T then acquires it. It finds the lock is unreserved already, and then releases the lock. After that, thread T will enter the actual locking sequence.

- It is also possible that the thin-lock tries to inflate after the lock unreserving thread T already holds the monitor. In this case, the lock owner S cannot inflate it, because inflation process is protected by the monitor data structure. Thread S has to wait on the monitor until thread T returns from lock unreserving function. This holds back the lock owner for a little while. It happens when the lock reserver tries to inflate the thin-lock due to recursion overflow.

In any case, the processes of lock inflation and lock unreserving are serialized. This is useful if we want to let the fat-lock also support lock reservation. The lock unreserving can happen before or after the lock inflation, but never in parallel with the lock inflation while the lock word is under transformation. The design then is consistent: The monitor data structure is used to manage the thread contention for lock word modification.

Looking from another angle, we conceptually allow only the thread that can acquire the lock to unreserve the lock. This makes sense, because the purpose of unreserving a lock is to lock it finally.

18.5.1.4 Discussion on Lock Reservation

The lock unreserving in both designs above requires to suspend the lock reserver, which is usually more expensive than an atomic instruction by one or more orders of magnitude. As a consequence, neither design encourages to make the same lock reservable again later, due to the potential cost of frequent lock unreserving.

One solution is to use heuristics to decide when to turn an object into reservable mode. Current design sets reservable mode when an object is created, blindly assuming all the objects have thread-local property, and blindly assuming they are thread-local to their respective creating threads. A good heuristic may predict the potentially thread-local duration of a lock, and then only turns on reserve mode when the duration is long enough. That a lock is thread-local "long enough" means the object is locked many times only by one thread before a second thread may lock it. It is possible to restore a normal lock back to reservable mode if it is deemed beneficial.

The other solution is to eliminate the need of lock unreserving. Lock unreserving is needed because the lock reserver modifies the lock word with thread-unsafe code. But the root cause is that all the threads must modify the same lock word data for locking/unlocking. For example, when a free lock is reserved by a lock reserver, it looks like "being locked" in the eyes of other threads. Before another thread can lock it, the lock word must be modified to look like "being free."

18.5.2 Thread-Affined Lock

To eliminate the need of lock unreserving, the "lock reserver" field should not indicate the state of whether the lock is held or not, or locked by who. For this purpose, we use two more fields that indicate the *locking state*: One is "reserver-locked" field (rlocked) indicating the lock is held by the lock reserver, and the other is "other-locked" field (xlocked) indicating the lock is held by other thread. The two fields always operate together with opposite states (mutual exclusion property), that is, when one is set, the other should not be set.

18.5.2.1 Design of Thread-Affined Lock

With the two separate fields, we can use atomic CompareExchange instruction on the word to set the "other-locked" field, which allows all the nonreserver threads to safely compete; and we use nonatomic set-check-reset to set the "reserver-locked" field, which is only accessed by the lock reserver. It is very common to use the access-check-access pattern plus an atomic instruction to maintain the mutual exclusion property of two different fields that may be accessed by multiple threads.

For example, in concurrent GC design for "current-copy invariant" moving algorithm, we use a field for the forwarding bit to indicate if an object is under forwarding, which is competed by all the collector threads with atomic instruction. When a mutator wants to access the object, it can use read-check-reread pattern to ensure it always reads the latest copy of the object, or write-check-rewrite pattern to ensure it always writes to the latest copy, without the need of an atomic instruction.

A little difference from the forwarding bit design is that here the "other-locked" field should only be set when "reserver-locked" field is unset (i.e., value is 0). This can be easily achieved by packing the two fields in the same word for the atomic CompareExchange. The atomic instruction includes "reserver-locked" field in its compared operand.

An object initially is not reserved. The first thread that locks it reserves it. Once an object is reserved, the reserved state never changes, and the reserver never changes.

Based on this idea, the thread-local lock can be supported in the following pseudo-code.

```
// for description simplicity, one byte is used for one field
// lock word layout: xlocked - rlocked - recursion - reserver
#define XLOCKED(a)   ((int8)a<<24)   //"other locked" field
#define RLOCKED(a)   ((int8)a<<16)   //"reserver locked" field
#define RECURSION(a) ((int8)a<<8)    //recursion of lock owner
#define RESERVER(a)  ((int8)a)       //ID of lock reserver

bool lock_non_blocking(Object* jmon)
{
    uint8* p_word = (uint8*)lock_word_addr(jmon);
    uint8* p_xlocked = p_word + 3;
    uint8* p_rlocked = p_word + 2;
    uint8* p_reserver = p_word;
    uint8 myID = (uint8)(current_thread )->tid);
    uint8 reserver = *p_reserver;

    if( reserver == 0){
        //not reserved yet, compete to lock and reserve it
```

```
            int newword = XLOCKED(0) | RLOCKED(myID) | RESERVER(myID);
            int oldword = CompareExchange(p_word, 0, newword);
            if( oldword == 0 ) return TRUE;
            return FALSE;
        }else if( reserver == myID ){
            //lock is reserved by self, check if it is held
            if( *p_rlocked == myID ){
                //lock is held by self
                return recursion_inc(jmon);
            }
            //lock is not held by self, compete it with non-atomic ops
            //in pattern write-check-rewrite
            *p_rlocked = myID;
            if( *p_xlocked ){  //if the lock is held by other thread
                *p_rlocked = 0; //I give up
                return FALSE;
            }
            return TRUE;        //otherwise, I got it.
        }else{  //reserved by other thread, write p_xlocked field
            if( *p_xlocked == myID ){
                //held by self
                return recursion_inc(jmon);
            }
            //not held by self, compete it with atomic ops
            //the atomic instruction will fail if rlocked field is set
            If( *p_rlocked !=0 ) return FALSE;
            int newword = XLOCKED(myID) | RLOCKED(0) | reserver;
            int tmpword = XLOCKED(0) | RLOCKED(0) | reserver;
            int oldword = CompareExchange(p_word, tmpword, newword );
            return ( oldword == tmpword);
        }
    }
}

void lock_release(Object* jmon)
{
    uint8* p_word = (uint8*)lock_word_addr(jmon);
    uint8* p_xlocked = p_word + 3;
    uint8* p_rlocked = p_word + 2;
    uint8* p_recursion = p_word + 1;
    uint8* p_reserver = p_word;
    uint8 myID = (uint8)(current_thread()->tid);

    // find the right lock owner's ID
    uint8* p_lockID;
    if( *p_reserver == myID ){
        p_lockID = p_rlocked;
    else
```

```
    p_lockID = p_xlocked;

if( *p_lockID != myID ){
    vm_throw_exception("IllegalMonitorState");
    return;
}

if( *p_recursion != 0 )
    recursion_dec(jmon);
else //no recursion, free lock
    *p_lockID = 0;
    }
}
```

In this lock, the lock reserver always acquires the lock without atomic instruction. More importantly, the reservation of a lock does not prevent other threads from acquiring the lock. They still can acquire the lock with atomic instruction without the need to unreserve the lock.

Once a lock is reserved by a thread, it is reserved forever. It is good for the applications where the same object is locked by multiple threads, while one of the threads locks it in most times. In other word, the lock is not necessarily local to any thread for a long period, but it is intimate to a specific thread. We call it "thread-affined lock."

The code above only gives the nonblocking path. It is not difficult to add the blocking path, by either using thread-local data structure or inflating to a fat-lock.

Note that when releasing the lock, the current lock owner only needs to check its own locking state field. There can be a short period that both fields of locking state (i.e., the reserver-locked field and other-locked field) may have data. This happens when a nonreserver thread acquires the lock and then quickly releases the lock. At the same time, the reserver tries to acquire the lock by writing its lock state field, and finds nonreserver's field has been written. Both lock state fields have data then. Now when the nonreserver releases the lock, it may see the reserver's lock state field has not been cleared yet. So it only needs to clear its own lock state field. Figure 18.5 shows the status of the lock-word where reserver-locked field is set but the lock is not held by the reserver.

It is possible that, before the lock reserver clears its state field, it is scheduled off the processor. After the nonreserver releases the lock, the nonzero value in the reserver's state field will prevent other threads from acquiring the lock, while the lock reserver is not holding the lock. This leads to a scenario when all the threads are failing to acquire the lock. Depending on the lock design, the failed threads can yield-wait for the lock, or go to sleep-waiting. Fortunately, it is impossible for all the contending threads go to sleep. The lock reserver has to clear its lock state field before it goes to the slow path for blocking locking, where it will check the lock state again before falling sleep. So the progress is guaranteed.

Onodera et al. call the design "asymmetric spin lock" that they developed based on Dekker's mutual exclusion algorithm. They applied the design to replace the thin-lock of Tasuki lock, achieving the benefit of thread-local lock without the need of lock

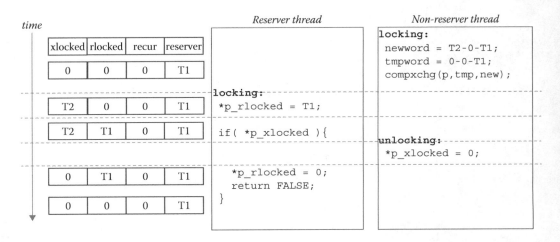

FIGURE 18.5   Lock-word status.

unreserving. We will not describe their implementation but discuss the inflation support next. Interesting readers are encouraged to read their original papers.

18.5.2.2 Inflation Supports to Thread-Affined Lock

To provide inflation/deflation support to thread-affined lock, a few points are worth mentioning.

The first point is about the data fields in lock word. The thread-affined lock above misses two flags that are needed in Tasuki lock. One is the contention flag, and the other is the inflation flag. To achieve high-performance implementation, a design has to find an efficient way to pack all the needed data into the object header. The followings are the data items needed:

1. Lock reserver's ID: This field represents the current lock reserver. It has to stay in the lock word to support the atomic operations. In our code above, this field uses one byte that can support up to 127 threads. (Zero means not reserved.) This field can be expanded to support more threads.

2. Lock reserver's lock state (i.e., the reserver-locked field): This field represents if the lock reserver holds the lock. It has to stay in the lock word for the atomic operations. In our code above, it encodes the same information as the lock reserver's ID. It actually needs only one bit to indicate if the lock is held or not, to avoid the information redundancy.

3. Other thread's lock state (i.e., the other-locked field): This field represents the nonreserver lock owner, so it needs to encode a thread ID. It has to be in the lock word to support the atomic operations.

4. Inflation flag: This field can be a single bit to indicate if the lock word is a monitor ID or not. It has to be in the lock word to prevent the atomic operations on a fat-lock

from succeeding. It ensures a monitor ID plus the inflation flag never coincidentally have the same bit pattern as a legitimate thread-affined lock word.

5. Contention flag: The field can be a single bit to indicate if the thread-affined lock is contended and expected to be inflated. It is not used by the atomic operations. Actually it has to stay away from the previous four fields, because setting contention flag by contending thread should not interfere with the atomic operations. The atomic operations are for contending, while the contention flag is for the loser(s) in the contending.

6. Recursion number: This field is only for performance optimization to avoid inflating the thread-affined lock early or frequently. It is not mandatory, and the number of its bits is purely opportunistic. It does not have to stay in the lock word, because it is only accessed when the lock is held, hence not involved in any contending.

The second point is to add a lock reserver's ID in the monitor data structure, so as to hold the value when the thread-affined lock is inflated, and restore the value in lock deflation.

The final point is that, during lock inflation and deflation, if the lock is held by the lock reserver, the process is the same as before, that is, set a monitor ID in the lock word together with the inflation flag.

If the lock is held by a nonreserver thread during inflation/deflation, the process has to take care of the reserver-locked state. As we mentioned above, it is possible for the reserver-locked field to have a value when a nonreserver holds the lock, because the lock reserver always unconditionally sets the field when it tries to acquire the lock.

The nonreserver may acquire the lock before the reserver sets the reserver-locked field. Then the nonreserver may inflate, deflate, and even free the lock before the reserver executes its next step: checking the other-locked field. When it comes to the checking operation, the reserver may find the other-locked field is empty, and then return with the lock acquired. So the whole process of the inflation, deflation, and release by the nonreserver thread can be conducted with the reserver-locked field is set. The value in the reserver-locked field should be preserved in the process as is, no matter it is set or not. There is no such problem with the lock reserver inflation/deflation, because then the reserver-locked field is under its control.

In order to support the unconditional setting of reserver-locked field by the reserver, this field has to be put in the lock word even when the lock is inflated. It has to stay with the monitor ID and the inflation flag. If we use the last byte in the lock word for the reserver-locked field, the monitor ID will be reduced to have three bytes minus one top bit for the inflation flag.

Based on this discussion, when a nonreserver thread inflates/deflates the lock, it cannot do as the lock reserver. It has to use atomic instruction to ensure the reserver-locked field is not changed by it. Following is the pseudo-code for lock inflation and deflation, with the new monitor data structure definition.

```
struct VM_Monitor{
   VM_Thread* owner;
   int recursion;
```

```
   Mutex* mutex;
   Condvar* condvar;
   int num_blocked;
   int num_waiting;
   VM_Thread* reserver;
}

void lock_inflate(Object* jmon, VM_Monitor* mon)
{
   uint8* p_word = (uint8*)lock_word_addr(jmon);
   uint8 recursion = lock_recursion(jmon);
   uint8 myID = (uint8)(current_thread()->tid);
   // reproduce the lock state
   mon->recursion = recursion;
   mon->reserver = lock_reserver(jmon);
   if( myID == mon->reserver ){ //reserved by self
      // atomic operation is not needed for lock reserver.
      *p_word = (mon | INFLATION_FLAG);
   }else{ //lock owner is not the reserver
      do{  //preserve the reserver-locked state
         int tmpword = *p_word;
         int rlocked_state = tmpword & RLOCKED_MASK;
         int newword = (mon | INFLATION_FLAG | rlocked_state)
         int oldword = CompareExchange(p_word, tmpword, newworld);
      }while( oldword != tmpword );
   }
   //reset contention flag to FALSE
   lock_set_contention(jmon, FALSE);
   monitor_notify_all(mon);
}

void lock_deflate(Object* jmon)
{
   VM_Monitor* mon = monitor_pointer(jmon);
   // leave fat-lock locked once (i.e., no recursion)
   uint8 recursion = mon->recursion;
   mon->recursion = 0;

   //turn to thread-affined lock
   uint8 myID = (uint8)(current_thread()->tid);
   uint8 reserver = (uint8)(mon->reserver->tid);
   uint rlocked_state;  //reserver-locked state
   uint xlocked_state;  //other-locked state
   if( myID == reserver ){ //lock owner is the reserver
      rlocked_state = myID;
      xlocked_state = 0;
```

```
        *p_word = lockword_pack(xlocked_state, rlocked_state,
                                recursion, reserver);
    }else{ //lock owner is not the reserver
        do{  //preserve the reserver-locked state
            int tmpword = *p_word;
            rlocked_state = tmpword & RLOCKED_MASK;
            xlocked_state = myID;
            int newword = lockword_pack(xlocked_state, rlocked_state,
                                        recursion, reserver);
            int oldword = CompareExchange(p_word, tmpword, newworld);
        }while( oldword != tmpword );
    }
}
```

The code above uses thread ID as before for the reserver-locked state, while a single bit is fine too.

There are still rooms to improve lock implementation. Like garbage collection, it is hard to design one algorithm that meets all applications' behavior. Heuristics-based adaption is needed, or the users have to specify the desirable options in command line when running their applications.

CHAPTER 19

Hardware Transactional Memory (HTM)-Based Design

S O FAR OUR DISCUSSIONS have been focused on the virtual machine (VM) design for traditional microprocessors. New development in microarchitecture enables us to design the software in a different way. Hardware transactional memory (HTM) is one of the recent microarchitecture innovations. It is interesting to VM design because it changes the way of thread interactions, which is the core of monitor design and also critical to garbage collector design. Since HTM is new to the community as of the year 2014 when the book was written, the discussions in this chapter are only for brainstorming purpose.

19.1 HARDWARE TRANSACTIONAL MEMORY

Transaction processing is common in software design to maintain data integrity. The operations in a transaction are considered as an atomic unit, in the sense that all the results of a transaction are committed either completely or not at all. The intermediate results are not visible to external of the transaction. (Strictly speaking, a transaction is not necessarily an atomic unit. We do not dive into details here, since it does not impact our discussions.)

19.1.1 From Transactional Database to Transactional Memory

The concept of transaction can be applied to multithread programming when dealing with data sharing among the threads. For example, execution instances of critical sections protected by the same lock can be regarded atomic to each other. The behavior is similar to transactions. If the system can provide transaction support to general-purpose multithread programming, there are chances to avoid writing the lock-based delicate logics, or to improve the lock-based code performance.

Based on this observation, the community has developed various models of or solutions to transactional programming. The goal is to enable the programmers to focus on a high-performance design, leaving the tricky correctness logics to transaction, thus to achieve both (1) better performance and (2) better programmability, simultaneously.

Unlike database transaction, the majority of a general-purpose application's execution states are maintained in memory that is visible to all threads. To commit execution states then means to write data into the memory hierarchy, including cache whose data are consistent with memory. Therefore, to provide transaction support to applications here means to provide *transactional memory* support. That is, all that the memory writes in a transaction are either completely committed to memory hierarchy, or nothing at all.

This kind of transactional memory can be implemented in software or hardware or hybrid. Software transactional memory (STM) provides transactional programming API on top of traditional processors. HTM provides the support at processor level, with the expectation of much higher performance than STM.

As to the two goals (i.e., performance and programmability), transactional memory is unlikely to achieve better programmability as a general programming model. One reason is transactional memory is too low level for a programmer to reason about. This problem is similar to the weak-order memory consistence model, which is always a challenge for multithread programmers to handle.

The other reason is the single-thread operational semantics of a code region wrapped in a transaction may be inconsistent with the same code without the transaction construct. For example, when there is an exception in the code region, then the results of its single-thread execution with or without transaction construct can be different. As a contrast, a single-thread program on different weak-order memory models always achieves the same result, with and without the lock construct or memory fences (barriers) that are purely intended for multithread execution.

As a result of the problems, it makes more sense to use transactional memory as the underlying mechanism by system software, rather than a general-purpose programming model.

By hiding transactional memory from common application developers, its remaining goal is to achieve better performance than lock-based synchronizations. It is natural to investigate how to apply transactional memory to VM design, keeping the original language APIs intact. Since STM has much lower performance than HTM, STM is not interesting to us.

19.1.2 Intel's HTM Implementation

In this chapter we will use Intel's HTM implementation to show how it can be used to design thread interactions in a VM for monitor support and garbage collector. All of the usages are hidden from Java developers.

Intel HTM ABI: Intel processor HTM implementation is called transactional synchronization extensions (TSX). It includes restricted transactional memory (RTM) programming interface, which provides a few new instructions that can be used to program transactions. Specifically, XBEGIN and XEND instructions denote the start and end of a transactional region. XBEGIN instruction also specifies a fallback handler. The code structure in assembly is like below.

```
XBEGIN _fallback_handler
... //transactional region
XEND

_fallback_handler:
... // fallback processing
```

Intel processor flattens nested transactions. No matter which level of the nested transaction aborts, the architectural state rolls back the outmost level.

Fallback handler: When a transaction aborts due to data conflict, exception, I/O, or other reasons, the processor state rolls back to what it was before the transaction starts, and the control flow goes to a fallback handler, whose address is given by the XBEGIN instruction. The fallback handler can decide to go back to retry the transaction or proceed to the normal nontransactional path. It cannot only retry the transaction, since RTM does not guarantee that a transactional execution will ever commit. It is the fallback handler's responsibility to ensure the eventual forward progress.

Data conflict: To support transactional execution, the processor keeps a read-set and a write-set during the transaction execution that track all the memory locations accessed in the transaction. The sets are empty before the transaction started and after its results committed. Traditionally when multiple threads access to the same memory location, and one of the accesses is write, a data race happens. Now with transaction, when an access involved in data racing is from a transaction, a *data conflict* happens.

More accurately, when a transaction is executed in a processor, a data conflict occurs if another processor reads a memory location that is in the transaction's write-set, or another processor writes a memory location that is in the read- or write-set of the transaction. All the conflicting transactions abort. Data conflict can happen between transaction and non-transaction executions. When two transactions do not have data conflict, they can execute in parallel.

Transaction aborts: Besides data conflict, a transaction may abort for various microarchitectural reasons. The following examples are probably most relevant to our discussions.

One microarchitectural reason is that the buffered memory accesses in the transaction exceed the capacity of the buffer of a logical processor. That means the transactional region cannot be too large in terms of memory access set.

The second reason to abort a transaction is that the transaction executes an operation that cannot be buffered locally, that is, cannot be executed transactionally such as I/O operation, exception, and system call.

The third reason is to directly call XABORT instruction in a transaction. This instruction is necessary when threads interact between transaction and non-transaction. We will see its use soon.

19.2 MONITOR IMPLEMENTATION WITH HTM

An intuitive idea to implement monitor with HTM is to treat the whole synchronized region (method or block) as a transaction. Bytecode `monitorenter` is treated as XBEGIN, and `monitorexit` as XEND.

For instance, when JIT compiler generates the code for `monitorenter`, it simply generates the XBEGIN instruction. The pseudo-code may look like the following.

```
void STDCALL vm_object_lock(Object* jmon)
{
  _fallback_handler:
   XBEGIN _fallback_handler;
}

void STDCALL vm_object_unlock(Object* jmon)
{
   XEND;
}
```

Note we still use the same function names with suffixes of `_lock` and `_unlock` as before to keep the naming convention consistence, although the transaction may have nothing to do with actual locking.

When two threads execute transactions at the same time, if they do not have data conflict or other abort conditions, both threads can finish the transactions successfully. That means, even if the two synchronized regions are supposed to lock the same object, they may execute in parallel if they are wrapped in transactions. In other words, whether synchronized regions need to be serialized is not decided by whether they use the same lock; instead, it is decided at runtime by the actual correctness requirement, that is, whether there is data conflict. This is the major motivation of using transaction.

Unfortunately, the code above does not really work for either correctness or performance reasons.

19.2.1 Correctness Issues in HTM-Based Monitor

In regard to correctness, Intel's HTM implementation does not guarantee the forward progress. A transaction may always abort no matter how many times it retries.

For example, when two transactions have data conflict in their simultaneous executions, both may roll back and retry, and then conflict and abort again. The situation is not uncommon in Java applications.

19.2.1.1 Problem without Fallback Handler

The fallback handler should decide how to deal with the abort properly to ensure the forward progress rather than just retry the transaction. A revision of the pseudo-code above becomes the following.

```
void STDCALL vm_object_lock(Object* jmon)
{
   XBEGIN _fallback_handler;
   return;

   _fallback_handler:
   object_lock_normal(jmon);
}

void STDCALL vm_object_unlock(Object* jmon)
{
   if( object_is_locked(jmon) ){
      lock_check_state(jmon);   //exception if locked by others
      object_unlock_normal(jmon);
      return;
   }
   XEND:
}
```

Since XBEGIN/XEND does not touch the object header for lock word manipuation, when the application is executing a transaction, the object header looks like the lock is free.

The code above puts the normal locking process in the fallback path, so that when a transaction aborts, the synchronization region can restart with the lock-based monitor implementation.

Accordingly, the unlocking function uses normal unlocking code when the lock is held (by itself). If the lock is free in the unlocking function, it means this is a transactional execution, and hence only needs the XEND instruction. Instruction XTEST can be used to test if the processor is currently in transactional execution mode.

19.2.1.2 Problem with Nontransactional Execution

The code is still problematic. Now that there are two kinds of synchronized region executions: one transaction-based, the other lock-based. It is possible that the first thread enters its region with lock-based monitor (after transaction abort), and then the second thread enters its region with transaction-based monitor.

The problem is data races of the synchronized regions in this situation may not be caught as data conflict, since the first thread may access shared memory locations before or after the second thread transaction's execution. Then the second thread thinks there is no data conflict, and successfully commits its results.

The erroneous condition is illustrated in Figure 19.1. It gives two cases as a comparison. In case 1 both threads execute transactions. In case 2 one thread uses lock-based monitor, and the other uses transaction.

In the figure, when both threads execute the synchronized regions as transaction (case 1), there is a data conflict. If the first thread uses lock-based monitor, it does not

Case 1: Both threads execute transactions

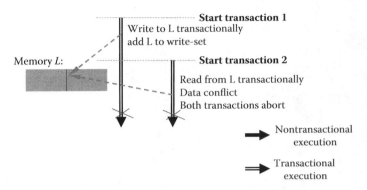

Case 2: One thread executes transaction, the other nontransaction

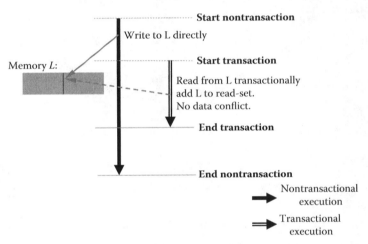

FIGURE 19.1 Synchronized regions are executed with and without transaction.

maintain the read-/write-set. When it accesses the shared memory location before or after the transactional execution, the transaction can not detect the conflicting access (case 2).

19.2.1.3 Conflict Detection in Transaction
In order to catch the data conflict between the transaction-based and lock-based synchronized regions, we have to ensure the transaction could detect if the lock variable (i.e., lock word in object header) has been locked by another thread. It means to do the following two cases.

Case 1. Although the transaction code does not modify the lock variable, it should add the lock variable into the transaction's read-set, so that any modification to it by another processor can be detected and will abort the transaction.

This ensures that any lock acquisition *during* the transaction period can be detected, as Figure 19.2 shows.

Case 2. The transaction should check if the monitor has been locked when the transaction starts. If yes, the transaction should be serialized, hence aborts.

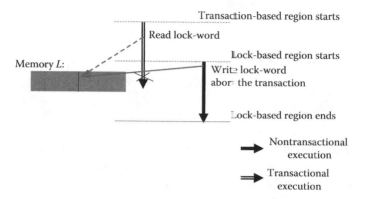

FIGURE 19.2   Add lock word into read-set of transaction.

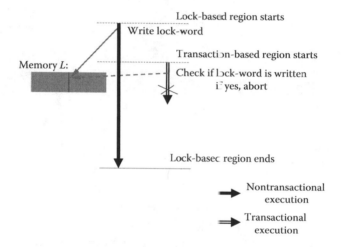

FIGURE 19.3   Check if lock word is written in transaction.

This ensures that any lock acquired *before* the transaction starts can be detected, as shown in Figure 19.3.

The lock checking operation in case 2 automatically adds the lock variable into read-set, so this operation naturally covers the requirement of case 1.

We do not need to worry about the lock acquired *after* the transaction finishes.

With the lock checking operation added, the pseudo-code becomes the following. It solves the correctness issue.

```
void STDCALL vm_object_lock(Object* jmon)
{
   XBEGIN _fallback_handler;
   if( object_is_locked(jmon) ){
      XABORT;
   }
```

```
    return;

  _fallback_handler:
    object_lock_normal(jmon);
}
```

```
// unlock function keeps unchanged.
```

The design does not mention the requirements to support the object's wait() and notify(). It is fine to use the traditional nontransactional implementation with Intel HTM. Java requires the thread to hold the monitor before calling wait() and notify(). If the monitor is entered transactionally, the traditional code in wait() and notify() will cause the transaction to abort due to either system call or exception, so there is no correctness issue to use the traditional implementation.

19.2.2 Performance Issues in HTM-Based Monitor

As to performance, there are more to discuss. Current HTM implementation on Intel processor has significant cost. In order to support the atomicity of transactional execution, the cost of a transaction can be one or a few times as much as an atomic instruction.

19.2.2.1 Introduce Thin-Lock to Transaction

Using the pair of XBEGIN/XEND to replace monitorenter/monitorexit seemingly eliminates the need to execute monitor code; it can be slower than a thin-lock implementation, which usually involves only a little bit more than an atomic instruction.

Even if the cost of XBEGIN/XEND is no more than an atomic instruction, potential transaction abort incurs additional overhead compared to lock-based solution. Transaction abort requires to restore the architectural state of the processor, which can be much more expensive than an atomic instruction, not to mention the completely wasted transaction operation.

If the thin-lock supports thread-local lock such as lock reservation or thread-affined lock, the locking overhead is even smaller. Due to this fact, the transaction-based monitor may want to use thin-lock as is, and only uses transaction to replace fat-lock implementation. The pseudo-code may look like below.

For the purpose of brevity, the code significantly simplifies the logic compared to the implementation we gave in the previous chapter on monitor optimization design.

```
void STDCALL vm_object_lock(Object* jmon)
{
    // thin lock
    bool success = object_lock_thin(jmon);
    if( success ) return;

    // fat lock
    XBEGIN _fallback_handler;
```

```
   if( object_is_locked_fat(jmon) ){
      XABORT;
   }
   return;

  _fallback_handler:
   object_lock_fat(jmon);
}

// unlock function
void STDCALL vm_object_unlock(Object* jmon)
{
   // thin lock
   if( object_is_locked_thin(jmon) ){
      lock_check_state(jmon);  //exception if locked by others
      object_unlock_thin(jmon);
      return;
   }

   // fat lock
   if( object_is_locked_fat(jmon) ){
      lock_check_state(jmon);  //exception if locked by others
      object_unlock_fat(jmon);
      return;
   }

   XEND;
}
```

The implementation above does not use transaction when it is a thin-lock. In other words, thin-lock always serializes the execution of synchronized region. This is fine since the pre-assumption of thin-lock is that the lock is not contended. Otherwise, thin-lock will inflate to fat-lock. Contention means that, when one thread holds the lock, another thread tries to acquire the same lock. When there is no contention, thin-lock execution is already serialized by nature, so there is no benefit to use transaction-based solution.

However, when the lock is contended, transaction-based solution may exhibit its performance advantage. When multiple threads execute in parallel trying to acquire the same lock, lock-based solution serializes their executions of the synchronized regions. If the synchronized regions of the threads do not have any conflicting data accesses, they can be executed as transactions in parallel and successfully. That is why we choose to use transaction for fat-lock, which is intended for contended lock.

19.2.2.2 Retry Transaction to Alleviate Lemming Effect

When the transactions really conflict, they abort and fall back to the fat-lock path. The problem is, once one synchronized region goes to the fat-lock path, all the concurrent transactions have to abort and be serialized for correctness, no matter if other transactions have data conflict or not, as we have discussed.

Furthermore, when all the synchronized regions are serialized, they will cause new coming transactions to abort as well, until there is no lock-based synchronized region under execution. This is called *lemming effect* by the community. It degrades the performance of transaction-based solution seriously. To alleviate the problem, a common practice is to retry the aborted transaction before going to the fat-lock path. The pseudo-code is given below.

```
void STDCALL vm_object_lock(Object* jmon)
{
    // thin lock
    bool success = object_lock_thin(jmon);
    if( success ) return;

    // fat lock
    int retry_count = 0;
_RETRY:
    XBEGIN _fallback_handler;
    if( object_is_locked_fat(jmon) ){
        XABORT;
    }
    return;

_fallback_handler:
    retry_count += + 1;
    if( retry_count < MAX_RETRIES ){
        goto _RETRY
    }else{
        object_lock_fat(jmon);
    }
}
```

```
// unlock function keeps unchanged.
```

The times to retry a transaction is an experience value depending on the application behavior. If a lock-based synchronized region does not finish quickly, retrying the transaction cannot solve the problem, because the retry threshold can easily be exceeded; then the transaction falls back to fat-lock, hence the lemming effect. To retry the transaction before the lock is released is doomed to abort. An improvement is to delay the retrying till the lock is released, as shown in the pseudo-code below.

```
void STDCALL vm_object_lock(Object* jmon)
{
    // thin lock
    bool success = object_lock_thin(jmon);
```

```
    if( success ) return;

    // fat lock
    int retry_count = 0;
_RETRY:
    XBEGIN _fallback_handler;
    if( object_is_locked_fat(jmon) ){
        XABORT;
    }
    return;

_fallback_handler:
    retry_count += + 1;
    if( retry_count < RETRY_THRESHOLD ){
        //wait till lock is released before retry
        while( object_is_locked_fat(jmon) ) pause();
        goto _RETRY
    }else{
        object_lock_fat(jmon);
    }
}

// unlock function keeps unchanged.
```

To wait before retry can improve the chances of successful transaction. In any case, it is no worse than continued failed transaction if without the waiting, and no worse than sleeping on the monitor if without the retry.

Transaction-based solution does not always bring benefit, even compared to fat-lock. For some applications that are highly contending on shared data, transaction almost never succeeds; then using transaction can be a pure loss. For some other applications that are not sensitive to monitor performance, using transaction may not show any visible differences either.

The design so far only applies the transaction concept to the entire synchronized region. There can be other designs to leverage the transactional support. For example, transaction makes multiple-word atomic operation simple, which enables more delicate thread-local lock design such as to switch the reserver of a thread-affined lock.

19.3 CONCURRENT GARBAGE COLLECTION (GC) WITH HTM

One of the major tasks in GC design is to deal with the interference among mutators and collectors. When there are thread synchronizations, HTM may have a chance to play a role.

19.3.1 Opportunities for HTM in GC

In order for HTM to benefit a synchronized region, the region has to have the following properties:

1. **High contention ratio**: The synchronized region causes lots of execution serialization among multiple threads, and it is difficult to alleviate the serialization problem with finer-grained lock. When it is implemented with transaction, multiple threads may execute the same region in parallel, hence benefited from HTM.

2. **Low data-race ratio**: The synchronized region should have low chances of data races when executed in parallel. When it is implemented in HTM, the transaction abort ratio due to data conflict should be low.

3. **Long-enough execution time**: Transaction itself has overhead. The overhead can only be amortized when the synchronized region is big enough. Otherwise, lock-based synchronized region can be more efficient than transaction.

4. **Small memory footprint**: The transaction abort ratio due to capacity overflow should be low.

5. **Having nontransactional solution**: In theory, a nontransactional path is always necessary for the fallback handler, unless the developer is absolutely sure that the transaction would commit finally so as to make eventual progress.

6. **Low abort ratio** due to other factors like I/O, system call, and exception.

Based on these conditions, next we go through the possible thread interactions in GC design one by one. The first is object allocation.

19.3.1.1 Object Allocation

When a mutator needs to allocate an object, it traps to GC module for the service. Almost all VM designs simply let the mutator to invoke a function in GC module, without interaction with collectors. Actually, collectors also need to allocate objects if the design is a moving-GC. Therefore, allocator does not need to be a dedicate thread. Instead, allocator is only a hat that both mutator and collector put on when they are allocating objects.

However, allocators may compete for heap memory when they allocate new objects, where the memory is shared among threads. The common solution is to use thread-local allocation block for each allocator, so that the allocators only need to compete to grab a memory block from the heap, and then the allocation in the block is thread-local.

When allocating objects that are too big, a global space is used that is shared among all allocators. Thread synchronization is needed to access the global space.

The competition between allocators upon shared space can be implemented in HTM. The process to lock the space, allocate a block (or a large object), and unlock the space is a synchronized region. The same HTM design in the previous section is applicable here. But it does not necessarily bring any benefit though, since the transaction may be too short.

Next we have a look at garbage collection. A pure reference-counting GC can recycle an object in real time when the object is no longer referenced by the system. There is no collector involved, same as the allocation operation. Updating reference counters has to be synchronized between mutators, but the synchronized region is too small. When it is a tracing GC, the situation is different, which entails the following tasks.

19.3.1.2 Root-Set Enumeration

The root-set of a mutator can be enumerated by itself or by other thread. If it is enumerated by other threads, there is a potential race condition between the mutator that actively manipulates its execution context and the enumerating thread that needs to read the context. If the mutator suspends for root-set enumeration, the race condition can be avoided. Otherwise, synchronization is needed to coordinate the interaction. HTM can be used to protect the stack frames so that the enumeration on those frames aborts if the mutator manipulates them.

When it is a regional or generational GC, write-barrier is usually used to track the cross-region or cross-generation references, that is, remember-set, as a complement to root-set. The operation does not involve collectors. The possible thread synchronization is when the root-sets and/or remember-sets of all mutators are maintained in a global pool. But the synchronization region is too small to benefit from HTM.

19.3.1.3 Live-Object Marking

If it is stop-the-world (STW) parallel marking, the collectors collaborate on marking tasks for load balance and scalability. With task-pool sharing, all the marking tasks are put in a global task-pool. A collector locks the pool to deposit or to pick up a task or a group of tasks. Similar to root-set and remember-set management, the synchronization region is too small. Moreover, task-pushing technique allows parallel live-object marking without synchronization.

During parallel marking, multiple collectors may reach the same object and try to mark it at the same time. This is usually fine without synchronization, because object marking can be designed to be idempotent so that the lost update does not cause any problem.

When the tracing process is concurrent, traditional solution is to use write-barrier that either remembers the object graph's snapshot-at-the-beginning (SATB) or incrementally update (INC) the object graph to match the current state. It does not require any explicit thread synchronization. Implicitly the write-barrier actually tries to resolve the competition between mutators and collectors, where the former actively modifies the object graph and the latter actively reads it.

There is a potential to leverage HTM to resolve the competition as well as the write-barrier does. The problem is the object graph is variable and hard to be pre-partitioned. That means, no matter which part of the object graph is traced by the collectors in a transaction, the chances for the mutators to write the same part of the graph can be high. In other words, there is no confidence on the success ratio of the transaction.

Read-barrier can be used for concurrent live-object marking as well. That is, whenever a mutator accesses an object, the mutator marks the object (if it is not yet marked), and pushes the object reference to mark-stack for scanning. The scanning can be done incrementally by mutators or concurrently by collectors. In this design, the collectors only trace the part of object graph that has not yet been accessed by mutators. Their works are complementary rather than competitive; hence there is no significant synchronization incurred here.

19.3.1.4 Dead Object Reclamation

In a mark-sweep collection, the sweeping phase is simple that it does not involve much thread interaction, no matter if it is STW, concurrent or deferred.

In a STW moving collection, the object moving process involves object allocation that has been discussed above. Other parallel operations among collectors can also be easily coordinated.

In a concurrent moving collection, there are data races mainly in following two cases:

- A thread copies an object while other threads access the same object;

- A thread updates the heap references to an object while other threads change the heap slots.

Next we will discuss if HTM can help concurrent moving collection.

19.3.2 Copying Collection

During concurrent copying collection, there is competition between the threads when an object is being copied.

19.3.2.1 To-Space Invariant

If GC uses "to-space invariant" concurrent copying, for one object, its forwarding is only allowed to one thread, either mutator or collector, by locking the object in the object forwarding duration. No other thread can access the object before the copying is finished, because any access to the object either can only happen in the to-space after the object is copied or just triggers the object copying.

The object forwarding process is a synchronized region that is highly possible to be data-race-free, since intuitively the chance for more than one threads to access the same object at the same time is not very high. Therefore, it is possible to use HTM for the object forwarding routine.

However, the object forwarding code we developed previously for "to-space invariant" uses per-object lock for the synchronized region. This is the finest lock possible to object-based copying. That means, although the data-race ratio is low, the serialization ratio is low too. The lock-based solution is good enough to achieve high parallelism.

19.3.2.2 Current-Copy Invariant with Mutator Transaction

If GC uses "current-copy invariant" concurrent copying, there is data racing between the mutator's access and the collector's copying, when the current copy is in from-space.

Traditional design is to make the operations of object forwarding, reading, and writing atomic to each other. For example, when a copying is started by a collector, the mutator who wants to write to the same object has to wait till the copying finishes, and then writes to the new copy. Or in the other way around, a collector has to give up the copying when a mutator is accessing it; and then either the collector retires the copying or the mutator has the obligation to forward the object. HTM can be used to implement the atomicity.

If mutator's object access is transactional, the pseudo-code may look as follows, using object write as an example. The modified part is shown in bold face, compared to the original code we developed for "current-copy invariant" GC.

```
void write_barrier_current(Object* obj, int field, Value val)
{
    bool fld_is_ref = field_is_ref(field ;
    //only write current copy address to field
    if(fld_is_ref && in_from_space(val) && is_forwarded(val))
        val = forwarding_pointer(val)

    if( !in_from_space(obj) ){
        object_write(obj, field, val);
    }else{ //object in from space
      _RETRY:
        if( !is_forwarded(obj) ){
            XBEGIN _RETRY
            if( under_forwarding(obj))
                XABORT;
            object_write(obj, field, val);
            XEND
        }
        //cbject is forwarded
        obj = forwarding_pointer(obj);
        object_write(obj, field, val);
    }
}
```

The code above follows the HTM programming principles we developed with monitor implementation in the last section.

It does not assume the collector's object copying is transactional, but assumes that collector uses the object header to indicate the object forwarding status. The transaction starts when the object is not forwarded yet. The code checks if the object is under forwarding at the beginning of the transaction, which essentially puts the object header into the read-set of the transaction. When a collector tries to copy the object by setting the object header, the mutator's transaction will abort.

The control flow from an aborted transaction goes to retry path. The abort and retry together virtually form a spin-waiting loop if the object is under forwarding. Since the object copying by a collector will surely finish, the retry will make eventual progress.

In this design, the transaction is only for object access in from-space, because only the write in from-space has data-racing problem with object copying.

19.3.2.3 Current-Copy Invariant with Collector Transaction
If collector's object copying is transactional, the pseudo-code may look like the function `obj_forward_transactional()` below. The original function `obj_forward()` we developed for concurrent copying-GC is called in the fallback path.

```
Object* obj_forward_transactional(Object* obj)
{
  _RETRY:
  // start copying transaction
  XBEGIN _fallback_handler
  if( under_forwarding(obj) )
     XABORT
  //copy the object to new addr
  Object* new = obj_copy(obj);
  //install forwarding pointer
  Obj_header header = obj_header(obj);
  header = new | FORWARD_BITS;
  obj_set_header(obj, header);
  XEND
  return new;

  _fallback_handler:
  retry_count += 1;
  if( retry_count < RETRY_THRESHOLD ){
     goto _RETRY

  return object_forward(obj);
}
```

The code above also uses FORWARDING_BIT at the beginning of the transaction. But this is not for the interaction between mutator's object access and collector's object copying transaction, since both only read this FORWARDING_BIT bit, hence no data conflict on it. Their interaction correctness is ensured by the fact that collector's object copying puts the whole object into read-set, so mutator's write to any of the object fields is a data conflict, and will abort the collector's object copying.

The FORWARDING_BIT is to guarantee the correct interaction between collectors' transactional copying and nontransactional copying in the fallback path. The nontransactional copying locks the FORWARDING_BIT during object copying.

19.3.2.4 Discussion on the Transaction Designs
Due to the high overhead of transaction, it is not a good idea to implement all the synchronized operations as transactions. Instead, we can use transaction when we can afford for abort and times of retries; and we use lock-based (or atomic instruction-based) operation we care more about latency. When the lock-based operation is executed,

the concurrent transaction-based operation aborts. It virtually gives the lock-based operation higher priority.

For example, in the concurrent copying design, it is considered better to use transaction for the collector's copying operation, but give the mutator's access higher priority with lock-based solution, so as to achieve better mutator responsiveness, that is, better minimum mutator utilization (MMU).

Since the chances for a collector and a mutator to access the same object is usually low in common applications, the transaction success ratio can be high. However, since the traditional design uses fine-grained per-object lock for the synchronization, the execution serialization ratio between the mutator access and the collector copying is not very high. The benefit of HTM solution can be limited. One way to reduce the transaction overhead here is to copy multiple objects in one transaction.

19.3.3 Compacting Collection

As we have discussed in the chapter on concurrent compacting GC, copying collection can use single heap pass for both live-object marking and copying, while the downside is low utilization of heap space and probably also low data locality. To support sliding and seemingly "in-place" compacting collection, it makes sense to mark live objects in a separate pass, so that GC can collect the heap region by region to achieve the compaction effect. A by-product is that GC can select to compact only the regions that can bring maximum collection throughput.

19.3.3.1 Idea of Utilizing HTM

Once the live objects are marked, the two remaining tasks for concurrent collectors are the following:

1. **Object-moving**: Forward the live objects in the select from-region to to-region;

2. **Reference-fixing**: Update all the stale references in the heap to the new addresses of their referenced objects.

Both of the tasks have potential data races between collectors and mutators. In the object-moving task, a mutator may access the same object that a collector is forwarding. In the reference-fixing task, a mutator may write to the same reference field where a collector tries to update. Concurrent compacting GC has solutions to both of the problems with either lock or atomic instruction. Now with HTM, it is possible to use transaction to deal with the potential data races.

One idea is to put the two tasks for one object into a transaction, that is, to forward an object and to update all the heap slots holding the object's stale reference. One transaction is for one live object. Conceptually, if all the transactions finish successfully for all live objects, the compaction collection ends.

When there is a data conflict with mutator, the transaction aborts. Data conflict happens if there is a mutator writing to the same object in from-region, or if there is a mutator accessing a heap slot that holds a reference to the object in from-region. Iyengar et al. proposed the design they called Collie based on Azul's C4 algorithm.

To design a transaction, the first thing is to know the memory locations that a transaction is going to touch, that is, the read-set and write-set. For object-moving and reference-fixing, the collector reads the object in from-region, writes the object in to-region, and writes its new address to all the heap slots holding its old address. The initial pseudo-code of the transaction may look like the following.

```
_XBEGIN
Object* new = obj_copy( obj );
Object** slot;
for( each slot in remember-set(obj) ){
    *slot = new;
}
_XEND
```

19.3.3.2 Find all Heap Slots Pointing to an Object

To find all the heap slots to update, the collectors should remember the heap slots for every live object during the live-object marking phase. That is, every live object has an associated per-object remember-set that includes the heap slots that hold references to it. (The total size of all the remember-sets for all live objects is the same as the number of all heap reference slots, so the average size of the per-object remember-set is the average number of reference fields per object, which is usually only a few.)

The problem is the per-object remember-set is not fixed at runtime. The following kinds of changes happen during mutators' execution.

Kind 1: Slot content changes: After the live-object marking phase, and before the transaction for object S is executed, some of its remember-set slots may be overwritten with other reference values.

This is not a big problem. The transaction can check the value in every remember-set slot before updating it. If it is not the old reference to the object of the transaction, the collector simply skips that slot as given below.

```
_XBEGIN
Object* new = obj_copy( obj );
Object** slot;
for( each slot in remember-set(obj) ){
    if( *slot != obj ) continue;
    *slot = new;
}
_XEND
```

Kind 2: New slots out of the remember-set: There can be additional heap slots holding references to object S, beyond the remember-set. The mutators may overwrite some other heap reference slots with references to S, or create new objects holding references to S.

This is problematic because the additional reference slots are not recorded in the remember-set of object *S*. The transaction for object *S* either has to use the latest updated remember-set or has to give up since it will not accomplish its mission.

If we do not want to pause the mutators, it is virtually impossible to have a stable updated remember-set per object for its transaction. A straightforward solution is to take the give-up path, that is, to use a write-barrier to catch the case and then inform the transaction to give up.

When the write-barrier detects that a reference to an object is written to the heap, it flags the case by setting the object header with a bit, NO_TRANSACTION. The transaction for the object will read the bit, and aborts if the bit is set. The revised transaction code is given below.

```
_XBEGIN
if( is_no_transaction(obj) )
    XABORT
Object* new = obj_copy( obj );
Object** slot;
for( each slot in remember-set(obj) ){
    if( *slot != obj ) continue;
    *slot = new;
}
_XEND
```

Kind 3: Transaction-caused remember-set changes: If the forwarded object contains references to other objects, the moving of the object essentially changes the remember-sets of those objects, because the original slots in the old copy now should be replaced by the slots in the new copy. This makes the per-object remember-set unstable due to transaction itself.

Fortunately, the collectors' behavior can be well designed, unlike the mutators' behavior that is beyond the VM's control. For example, the simplistic design is to use only one collector, so that all the transactions are serialized and there is no data conflict caused by the collector's update of remember-sets.

Kind 4: Slots in mutators' execution contexts: To correctly forward an object, not only the remember-set but also the references in mutators' execution contexts should be updated.

In traditional concurrent moving-GC design, a flipping phase is needed to update those references in execution contexts. If we want a transaction to accomplish the complete moving of an object without the flipping phase, we have to give up transaction for objects that are pointed to by references in execution contexts.

To identify those objects pointed from execution contexts, the mutators have to be paused one by one to enumerate the root-set on-the-fly. The objects pointed by root references are tagged as NO_TRANSACTION. This process is called a check-point.

After the check-point, any reference value read by the mutators, that is, loaded into the execution context, should be caught by a read-barrier. What the read-barrier does is to tag the referenced object as NO_TRANSACTION.

With the check-point and read-barrier, all the objects directly accessible to the mutators are surely tagged as NO_TRANSACTION. In this way, the write-barrier above actually is not strictly needed, since the reference being written either comes from the execution context or is loaded from the heap. The former case is caught by the check-point, and the latter by the read-barrier. The read-barrier should be turned on at the check-point before any mutator is resumed, so that it does not miss any loaded reference.

19.3.3.3 Deal with Potential Data Conflicts

Besides the remember-set stability problem, there are three kinds of potential data-conflicts.

Kind 1: Mutator accesses (read or write) a remember-set slot: Data conflict happens when a mutator accesses a heap slot that holds a reference to from-region. Since a transaction writes to every slot of the remember-set to fix the reference, any mutator access to a remember-set slot aborts the transaction.

The problem is the mutator access may happen after the live-object marking phase and before the transaction, which does not conflict with the transaction execution. They should be caught by read-/write-barrier.

If the access is a mutator write that overwrites reference T with reference S, it produces an additional heap slot pointing to object S, and a useless slot in object T's remember-set. As mentioned above, the write will be caught by write-barrier, which tags object S with NO_TRANSACTION, and does nothing on object T.

If the access is a mutator read on a remember-set slot, it loads the reference S into the mutator's execution context, which is impossible for the transaction to update. Therefore, the read-barrier mentioned above needs to catch the read and tags object S as NO_TRANSACTION.

Kind 2: Mutator writes the object: A data conflict happens when a mutator writes to the object. If the write happens before the transaction, there should be no problem from the viewpoint of the transaction execution. But in order for mutator to write to the object, the mutator has to hold the reference to the object, which, as mentioned above, has already excluded the object from transactional moving, either by the check-point or by the read-barrier.

If an object has a field holding a reference to itself, the slot, as an element of the remember-set, should be updated within the transaction by the collector. This is not a data conflict.

The pseudo-code below allocates a new address for the object first, updates the remember-set, and finally copies the object to its new address. It ensures the self-pointing reference in the object is correctly fixed.

```
_XBEGIN
if( is_no_transaction(obj) )
   XABORT
Object* new = obj_new_address( obj );
Object** slot;
for( each slot in remember-set(obj) ){
   if( *slot != obj ) continue;
   *slot = new;
}
mem_copy(obj, new);
_XEND
```

When a transaction finishes successfully, the system will see only the single new copy. There is no forwarding pointer needed in the old copy, because there is no remaining reference in the heap pointing to the old copy. When a transaction aborts, there is only the old copy in the system.

The objects that cannot be moved transactionally are those tagged as NO_ TRANSACTION by check-point or read-/write-barrier. They should be moved with nontransactional solution. The design can choose to use traditional concurrent compaction algorithm to move the objects tagged NO_TRANSACTION. To avoid complexity, the nontransactional moving can be conducted after the transactional moving phase. We will not discuss the details here.

The study here is for brainstorming purpose. It does not mean the transaction-based design brings any actual benefit.

Bibliography

A.-R. Adl-Tabatabai, M. Cierniak, G. Lueh, V. M. Parikh, and J. Stichnoth. Fast, Effective Code Generation in a Just-In-Time Java Compiler. In Proceedings of the SIGPLAN '98 Conference on Programming Language Design and Implementation (PLDI), Montreal, Canada, June 1998.

O. Agesen, D. Detlefs, A. Garthwaite, R. Knippel, Y. S. Ramakrishna, and D. White. An efficient meta-lock for implementing ubiquitous synchronization. In OOPSLA 1999, pages 207–222, October 1999. doi: 10.1145/320384.320402.

A. W. Appel, J. R. Ellis, and K. Li. Real-time concurrent collection on stock multiprocessors. In ACM SIGPLAN Notices, volume 23, pages 11–20. ACM, 1988.

D. F. Bacon, P. Cheng, and V. Rajan. The Metronome: A simpler approach to garbage collection in real-time systems. In On the Move to Meaningful Internet Systems 2003: OTM 2003 Workshops, pages 466–478. Springer, 2003.

D. F. Bacon, R. B. Konuru, C. Murthy, and M. J. Serrano. Thin locks: Featherweight synchronization for Java. In ACM SIGPLAN Conference on Programming Language Design and Implementation, pages 258–268, Montréal, Quebec, June 1998. doi: 10.1145/989393.989452.

H. G. Baker Jr. List processing in real time on a serial computer. Communications of the ACM, 21(4):280–294, 1978.

M. Ben-Ari. On-the-fly garbage collection: New algorithms inspired by program proofs. In Automata, Languages and Programming, pages 14–22. Springer, 1982.

M. Ben-Ari. Algorithms for on-the-fly garbage collection. ACM Transactions on Programming Languages and Systems (TOPLAS), 6(3):333–344, 1984.

A. Bendersky and E. Petrank. Space overhead bounds for dynamic memory management with partial compaction. ACM Transactions on Programming Languages and Systems (TOPLAS), 34(3):13, 2012.

G. E. Blelloch and P. Cheng. On bounding time and space for multiprocessor garbage collection. ACM SIGPLAN Notices, 34(5):104–117, 1999.

M. D. Bond and K. S. McKinley. Bell: Bit-encoding online memory leak detection. In International Conference on Architectural Support for Programming Languages and Operating Systems, pages 61–72, San Jose, CA, October 2006. doi: 10.1145/1168857.1168866.

R. A. Brooks. Trading data space for reduced time and code space in real-time garbage collection on stock hardware. In Proceedings of the 1984 ACM Symposium on LISP and Functional Programming, pages 256–262. ACM, 1984.

M. Cierniak, B. Lewis, and J. Stichnoth. The Open Runtime Platform: Flexibility with Performance Using Interfaces. In Proceedings of Joint ACM Java Grande - ISCOPE 2002 Conference, Seattle, November 2002.

M. Cierniak, G. Lueh, and J. Stichnoth. Practicing JUDO: Java Under Dynamic Optimizations. In Proceedings of the SIGPLAN '00 Conference on Programming Language Design and Implementation (PLDI), Vancouver B.C., Canada, June 2000.

P. Cheng and G. E. Blelloch. A parallel, real-time garbage collector. In ACM SIGPLAN Notices, volume 36, pages 125–136. ACM, 2001.

P. Cheng, R. Harper, and P. Lee. Generational stack collection and profile-driven pretenuring. ACM SIGPLAN Notices, 33(5):162–173, 1998.

C. Click, G. Tene, and M. Wolf. The pauseless GC algorithm. In Proceedings of the 1st ACM/ USENIX International Conference on Virtual Execution Environments, pages 46–56. ACM, 2005.

A. Demers, M. Weiser, B. Hayes, H. Boehm, D. Bobrow, and S. Shenker. Combining generational and conservative garbage collection: Framework and implementations. In Proceedings of the 17th ACM SIGPLAN-SIGACT Symposium on Principles of Programming Languages, pages 261–269. ACM, 1989.

D. Detlefs, C. Flood, S. Heller, and T. Printezis. Garbage-First garbage collection. In Proceedings of the 4th International Symposium on Memory Management, pages 37–48. ACM, 2004.

D. Dice. Biased locking in HotSpot. http://blogs.oracle.com/dave/entry/biased_locking_in_hotspot.

D. Dice. Implementing fast Java monitors with relaxed-locks. In Java Virtual Machine Research and Technology Symposium (JVM), pages 79–90, Monterey, CA, April 2001.

D. Dice, H. Huang, and M. Yang. Asymmetric Dekker synchronization. Technical report, Sun Microsystems, 2001.

E. W. Dijkstra, L. Lamport, A. J. Martin, C. S. Scholten, and E. F. Steffens. On-the-fly garbage collection: An exercise in cooperation. Communications of the ACM, 21(11):966–975, 1978.

D. Doligez and G. Gonthier. Portable, unobtrusive garbage collection for multiprocessor systems. In Proceedings of the 21st ACM SIGPLAN-SIGACT Symposium on Principles of Programming Languages, pages 70–83. ACM, 1994.

D. Doligez and X. Leroy. A concurrent, generational garbage collector for a multithreaded implementation of ML. In Proceedings of the 20th ACM SIGPLAN-SIGACT Symposium on Principles of Programming Languages, pages 113–123. ACM, 1993.

T. Domani, E. K. Kolodner, and E. Petrank. A generational on-the-fly garbage collector for Java. In ACM SIGPLAN Notices, volume 35, pages 274–284. ACM, 2000.

H. Franke and R. Russell. Fuss, futexes and furwocks: Fast userlevel locking in Linux. In Ottawa Linux Symposium, pages 479–495, Ottawa, Ontario, June 2002. http://www.kernel.org/doc/ols/2002/ols2002-pages-479-495.pdf.

N. Glew, S. Triantafyllis, M. Cierniak, M. Eng, B. Lewis, and J. Stichnoth. *LIL: An Architecture-Neutral Language for Virtual-Machine Stubs*. In Proceedings of Third Virtual Machine Research and Technology Symposium (VM '04), San Jose, CA, May 2004.

M. P. Herlihy and J. M. Wing. Linearizability: A correctness condition for concurrent objects. ACM Transactions on Programming Languages and Systems (TOPLAS), 12(3):463–492, 1990.

R. L. Hudson and J. E. B. Moss. Sapphire: Copying GC without stopping the world. In Proceedings of the 2001 Joint ACM-ISCOPE Conference on Java Grande, pages 48–57. ACM, 2001.

B. Iyengar, G. Tene, M. Wolf, and E. Gehringer. The Collie: A wait-free compacting collector. In ACM SIGPLAN Notices, volume 47, pages 85–96. ACM, 2012.

K. Kawachiya, A. Koseki, and T. Onodera. Lock reservation: Java locks can mostly do without atomic operations. In ACM SIGPLAN Conference on Object-Oriented Programming, Systems, Languages, and Applications, pages 130–141, Seattle, WA, November 2002. doi: 10.1145/582419.582433.

G. Kliot, E. Petrank, and B. Steensgaard. A lock-free, concurrent, and incremental stack scanning for garbage collectors. In Proceedings of the 2009 ACM SIGPLAN/SIGOPS International Conference on Virtual Execution Environments, pages 11–20. ACM, 2009.

C. Lai, V. Ivan, and X.-F. Li. Behavior characterization and performance study on compacting garbage collectors with Apache Harmony. In The 10th Workshop on Computer Architecture Evaluation using Commercial Workloads (CAECW-10) Held with HPCA-13, Phoenix, AZ, February 2007. https://home.apache.org/~xli/papers/caecw07-compacting-GCs.pdf.

X.-F. Li. Quick hacking guide on Apache Harmony GC, 2008-04-09. https://home.apache.org/~xli/presentations/harmony_gc_source.pdf.

X.-F. Li. Quick guide on Tick design, the Apache Harmony concurrent GC, 2009-04-12. https://home.apache.org/~xli/presentations/harmony_tick_concurrent_gc.pdf.

X.-F. Li. Managed Runtime Technology: General Introduction, 2012-10-11. https://home.apache.org/~xli/presentations/managed-runtime-introduction.pdf.

X.-F. Li, L. Wang, and C. Yang. A Fully Parallel LISP2 Compactor with Preservation of the Sliding Properties, Languages and Compilers for Parallel Computing (LCPC) 21st Annual Workshop, Edmonton, Alberta, July 31–August 2, 2008.

T. F. Lim, P. Pardyak, and B. N. Bershad. A memory-efficient real-time non-copying garbage collector. ACM SIGPLAN Notices, 34(3):118–129, 1999.

S. Liu, J. Tang, L. Wang, X.-F. Li, and J.-L. Gaudiot. Packer: Parallel Garbage Collection Based on Virtual Spaces. IEEE Transactions on Computers, 61(11):1611–1623, November 2012.

S. Liu, L. Wang, X.-F. Li, and J.-L. Gaudiot. Space-and-time efficient Garbage collectors for parallel systems. In ACM International Conference on Computing Frontiers (CF 2009), Ischia, Italy, May 18–20, 2009.

M. M. Michael. Hazard pointers: Safe memory reclamation for lock-free objects. IEEE Transactions on Parallel and Distributed Systems, 15(6):491–504, 2004.

S. Nettles and J. O'Toole. Real-time replication garbage collection. In ACM SIGPLAN Notices, volume 28, pages 217–226. ACM, 1993.

T. Onodera and K. Kawachiya. A study of locking objects with bimodal fields. In OOPSLA 1999 [14], pages 223–237, October 1999. doi: 10.1145/320384.320405.

T. Onodera, K. Kawachiya, and A. Koseki. Lock reservation for Java reconsidered. In M. Odersky, editor, European Conference on Object Oriented Programming (ECOOP), volume 3086 of Lecture Notes in Computer Science, pages 559–583, Oslo, Norway, June 2004, Springer. doi: 10.1007/b98195.

OOPSLA 1999. ACM SIGPLAN Conference on Object-Oriented Programming, Systems, Languages, and Applications, Denver, CO, October 1999. doi: 10.1145/320384.

OOPSLA 2006. ACM SIGPLAN Conference on Object-Oriented Programming, Systems, Languages, and Applications, Portland, OR, October 2006. doi: 10.1145/1167473.

E. Osterlund and W. Lowe. Concurrent compaction using a Field Pinning Protocol. In Proceedings of the 2015 ACM SIGPLAN International Symposium on Memory Management, ISMM 2015, New York, pages 56–69. ACM, 2015.

J. O'Toole and S. Nettles. Concurrent replicating garbage collection. In ACM SIGPLAN Lisp Pointers, volume 7, pages 34–42. ACM, 1994.

F. Pizlo, E. Blanton, A. Hosking, P. Maj, J. Vitek, and L. Ziarek. Schism: Fragmentation-tolerant real-time garbage collection. In ACM SIGPLAN Conference on Programming Language Design and Implementation, pages 146–159, Toronto, Ontario, June 2010. doi: 10.1145/1806596.1806615.

F. Pizlo, D. Frampton, and the Jikes RVM Team. Configurable lock framework. http://jikesrvm.svn.sourceforge.net/viewvc/jikesrvm/rvmroot/branches/RVM-791/working-15440/.

F. Pizlo, D. Frampton, E. Petrank, and B. Steensgaard. Stopless: A real-time garbage collector for multiprocessors. In Proceedings of the 6th International Symposium on Memory Management, pages 159–172. ACM, 2007.

F. Pizlo, E. Petrank, and B. Steensgaard. A study of concurrent real-time garbage collectors. ACM SIGPLAN Notices, 43(6):33–44, 2008.

F. Pizlo, L. Ziarek, P. Maj, A. L. Hosking, E. Blanton, and J. Vitek. Schism: Fragmentation-tolerant real-time garbage collection. In ACM SIGPLAN Notices, volume 45, pages 146–159. ACM, 2010.

F. Pizlo, L. Ziarek, and J. Vitek. Real time Java on resource constrained platforms with Fiji VM. In M. T. Higuera-Toledano and M. Schoeberl, editors, International Workshop on Java Technologies for Real-Time and Embedded Systems (JTRES), pages 110–119, Madrid, Spain, September 2009. doi: 10.1145/1620405.1620421.

C. G. Ritson, T. Ugawa, and R. E. Jones. Exploring garbage collection with haswell hardware transactional memory. In Proceedings of the 2014 International Symposium on Memory Management, pages 105–115. ACM, 2014.

J. M. Robson. An estimate of the store size necessary for dynamic storage allocation. Journal of the ACM (JACM), 18(3):416–423, 1971.

J. M. Robson. Bounds for some functions concerning dynamic storage allocation. Journal of the ACM (JACM), 21(3):491–499, 1974.

K. Russell and D. Detlefs. Eliminating synchronization-related atomic operations with biased locking and bulk rebiasing. In OOPSLA 2006 [15], pages 263–272, October 2006. doi: 10.1145/1167473.1167496.

F. Siebert. Realtime garbage collection in the Jamaica VM 3.0. In Proceedings of the 5th International Workshop on Java Technologies for Real-Time and Embedded Systems, pages 94–103. ACM, 2007.

D. Spoonhower, J. Auerbach, D. F. Bacon, P. Cheng, and D. Grove. Eventrons: A safe programming construct for high-frequency hard real-time applications. In Proceedings of the 2006 ACM SIGPLAN Conference on Programming Language Design and Implementation, PLDI, New York, pages 283–294. ACM, 2006.

G. L. Steele Jr. Multiprocessing compactifying garbage collection. Communications of the ACM, 18(9):495–508, 1975.

G. Tene, B. Iyengar, and M. Wolf. C4: The continuously concurrent compacting collector. In Proceedings of the International Symposium on Memory Management, ISMM'11, New York, pages 79–88. ACM, 2011.

The Java Language Specification, Java SE 8 Edition, http://docs.oracle.com/javase/specs/jls/se8/jls8.pdf.

The Java Virtual Machine Specification, Java SE 8 Edition, http://docs.oracle.com/javase/specs/jvms/se8/jvms8.pdf.

M. Wu and X.-F. Li. Task-pushing: A Scalable Parallel GC Marking Algorithm without Synchronization Operations. In IEEE International Parallel and Distribution Processing Symposium (IPDPS) 2007, Long Beach, CA, March 2007.

L. Xiao and X.-F. Li. Cycler: Improve heap management for allocation-intensive applications with on-the-fly object reuse. In Parallel and Distributed Computing and Systems (PDCS 2011), Dallas, TX, December 14–16, 2011.

T. Yuasa. Real-time garbage collection on general-purpose machines. Journal of Systems and Software, 11(3):181–198, 1990.

Index

Note: Page numbers followed by f and t refer to figures and tables, respectively.